The Capital and the Colonies

Between 1660 and 1700 London established itself as the capital and commercial hub of a thriving Atlantic empire, accounting for three-quarters of the nation's colonial trade, and playing a vital coordinating role in an increasingly coherent Atlantic system. Nuala Zahedieh's unique study provides the first detailed picture of how that mercantile system was made to work. By identifying the leading colonial merchants, she shows through their collective experiences how London developed the capabilities to compete with its continental rivals and ensure compliance with the Navigation Acts. Zahedieh shows that in making mercantilism work Londoners helped to create the conditions which underpinned the long period of structural change and economic growth which culminated in the Industrial Revolution.

NUALA ZAHEDIEH is a senior lecturer in economic and social history at the University of Edinburgh. She has previously contributed to various journals and edited books of essays including *The Oxford History of the British Empire,* volume I (1998).

T0367789

The Capital and the Colonies

London and the Atlantic Economy, 1660–1700

Nuala Zahedieh

CAMBRIDGE
UNIVERSITY PRESS

CAMBRIDGE UNIVERSITY PRESS
Cambridge, New York, Melbourne, Madrid, Cape Town,
Singapore, São Paulo, Delhi, Tokyo, Mexico City

Cambridge University Press
The Edinburgh Building, Cambridge CB2 8RU, UK

Published in the United States of America by Cambridge University Press, New York

www.cambridge.org
Information on this title: www.cambridge.org/9780521514231

First published 2010

A catalogue record for this publication is available from the British Library

Library of Congress Cataloguing in Publication Data
Zahedieh, Nuala.
  The capital and the colonies : London and the Atlantic economy,
  1660–1700 / Nuala Zahedieh.
     p.   cm.
  ISBN 978-0-521-51423-1 (Hardback)
  1. Great Britain–Colonies–Commerce–History–17th century.   2. London (Eng.)–
  Commerce–History–17th century.   3. Mercantile system–Great Britain–History–17th
  century.   I. Title.
  HF3093.Z35 2010
  330.9171′24105–dc22   2009053749

ISBN 978-0-521-51423-1 Hardback

To Sophie, Miranda, and Thomas

Contents

Illustrations

Tables

Figures and Maps

Acknowledgements

My greatest debt is to Peter Earle who supported the portbook project which underpins this book and the Leverhulme Trust which provided the necessary funding. I am also grateful to the London School of Economics for housing the project, their computer support department for helping with the design of the database, and Dwyryd Jones for invaluable advice and price data from his own earlier work on commercial life in seventeenth-century London. Thanks go to Tim Wales, Duncan Ross, and Kelly Boyd for assistance with entering the data and Sophie Zahedieh for help with the tedious task of cleaning it up.

The subsequent work of filling out the bare picture provided by the portbooks was greatly assisted by funding from the British Academy, the University of Edinburgh, Harvard University, the John Carter Brown Library, the Massachusetts Historical Society, and the Pasold Fund, which allowed me to tap rich sources in North American and Caribbean archives. All was much appreciated as was the help of staff at the many archives and libraries cited in the book.

I have been greatly helped in processing the research findings by the opportunities offered for discussion in a large number of seminars and conferences and, above all, extended stays at Harvard, Lagos, Madrid, Milan, Prato, and at Oxford in preparation of the *Oxford History of the British Empire*. I am very grateful to the organizers of all these events for my inclusion. Larry Epstein (who sadly died in 2007), Negley Harte, David Ormrod, Patrick Wallis, Paul Warde, and other regular participants in the Premodern World seminar at the Institute of Historical Research have provided repeated inspiration, insight, and steady support. Guillaume Daudin, Perry Gauci, Regina Grafe, David Hancock, David Mitchell, and Jack Price have offered valuable advice from the perspective of their own work on commerce. I thank them all. I am especially grateful to Peter Earle and Norris Nash for their kind and careful reading of earlier entire drafts and the anonymous referees for Cambridge University Press for their constructive comments. Finally, I want to thank Paul Laxton for producing the high-quality maps; Andrew Buurman and Serge Krouglikoff for valuable assistance with the pictures; and Hilary Scannell for help with editing, Michael Watson, and other staff at Cambridge University Press for their help and support in the production of the book.

Abbreviations

APS	American Philosophical Society, Philadelphia
BA	Archives of Barbados, Cave Hill
BEA	Bank of England Archive
BHR	*Business History Review*
BL	British Library, London
BLO	Bodleian Library, Oxford
CMH	Centre for Metropolitan History
CSPC	*Calendar of State Papers, Colonial, America and West Indies*
CSB	*Common Serjeants' Book*
CTB	*Calendar of Treasury Books*
CLRO	Corporation of London Records Office
CUL	Cambridge University Library
EcHR	*Economic History Review*
EHR	*English Historical Review*
GL	Guildhall Library, London
HJ	*Historical Journal*
HMC	Historical Manuscripts Commission
HSP	Historical Society of Pennsylvania, Philadelphia
JA	Jamaica Archives, Spanish Town, Jamaica
JBMHS	*Journal of the Barbados Museum and Historical Society*
JEH	*Journal of Economic History*
JEEH	*Journal of European Economic History*
JIH	*Journal of Interdisciplinary History*
JICH	*Journal of Imperial and Commonwealth History*
JHR	*Jamaican Historical Review*
JHSET	*Jewish Historical Society of England Transactions*
MCD	Mayor's Court Depositions, Corporation of London Records Office
MHS	Massachusetts Historical Society, Boston

NLJ	National Library of Jamaica, Kingston, Jamaica
NMM	National Maritime Museum, Greenwich
NYHS	New York Historical Society, New York
ODNB	*Oxford Dictionary of National Biography* (Oxford, 2004)
PCC	Prerogative Court of Canterbury
PCSM	*Publications of the Colonial Society of Massachusetts*
PRO	Public Record Office, London
SRO	Somerset Record Office, Taunton
TRHS	*Transactions of the Royal Historical Society*
VCH	*Victoria County History*
VMHB	*Virginia Magazine of History and Biography*
WAM	Westminster Abbey Muniments
WMQ	*William and Mary Quarterly*

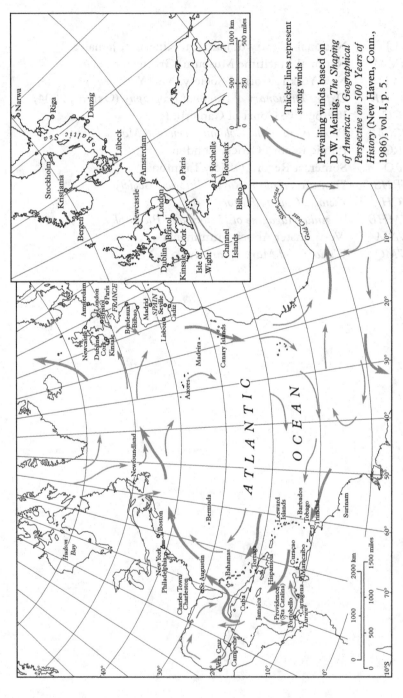

Map 1. The North Atlantic world in the late seventeenth century

Prevailing winds based on
D.W. Meinig, *The Shaping
of America: a Geographical
Perspective on 500 Years of
History* (New Haven, Conn.,
1986), vol. I, p. 5.

Thicker lines represent
strong winds

1   Introduction

On the eve of Britain's Industrial Revolution, Adam Smith looked back at the long period of slow, but persistent, structural change and economic development upon which the later technological thrust was built.[1] In seeking to explain a century or more of growth he saw the 'Discovery of America' as one of the 'two greatest and most important events recorded in the history of mankind' along with the finding of the passage to the East Indies by the Cape of Good Hope.[2] Modern historians might raise an eyebrow at the eurocentricity of Smith's version of the 'history of mankind' but, none the less, even one-time sceptics see much validity in his view that Britain's large investment in empire had paid dividends through an addition of resources, and an extension of markets, which had carried the economy to a 'plateau of possibilities' from which still higher growth based upon accelerated technical change 'appeared and became irreversible'.[3]

---

[1] On the nature of this long period of growth see Jan de Vries, 'Economic growth before and after the Industrial Revolution: a modest proposal', in Maarten Prak (ed.), *Early Modern Capitalism. Economic and Social Change in Europe, 1400–1800* (London, 2001), pp. 177–94. On the importance of technology in the Industrial Revolution see David S. Landes, *The Unbound Prometheus* (Cambridge, 1969); Joel Mokyr, *The Gifts of Athena: Historical Origins of the Knowledge Economy* (Princeton, 2002).

[2] Adam Smith, *An Inquiry into the Nature and Causes of the Wealth of Nations* (London, 1776), 1812 edn, p. 557. Similar sentiments have remained powerful in subsequent historiography: see Fernand Braudel, *The Wheels of Commerce* (London, 1982); Immanuel Wallerstein, *The Modern World System*, 2 vols. (New York, 1974, 1980); Andre Gunder Frank, *ReOrient: Global Economy in the Asian Age* (Berkeley and Los Angeles, 1998); Kenneth Pomeranz, *The Great Divergence: China, Europe, and the Making of the Modern World Economy* (Princeton, 2000).

[3] Patrick K. O'Brien, 'The reconstruction, rehabilitation, and reconfiguration of the British Industrial Revolution as a conjuncture in global history', *Itinerario*, 24 (2000), 126. For evidence of a shifting consensus on the importance of trade and empire see Patrick K. O'Brien, 'European economic development: the contribution of the periphery', *EcHR*, 35 (1982), 1–18; Patrick K. O'Brien, 'European industrialization: from the voyages of discovery to the Industrial Revolution', in Hans Pohl (ed.), *The European Discovery of the World and its Economic Effects on Pre-Industrial Society, 1500–1800* (Stuttgart, 1990), pp. 154–77; Stanley L. Engerman and Patrick K. O'Brien, 'The industrial revolution in global perspective', in Roderick Floud and Paul Johnson (eds.), *The Cambridge Economic*

After years of neglect by economic historians looking at industrialization, overseas expansion has returned to centre stage in explanations of economic development; but the links remain poorly specified.[4] As Smith, and the original projectors of colonial expansion, comprehended and, as Pomeranz has recently restated, the acquisition of new lands in America dramatically raised Britain's productive capacity: it unleashed new potential for extensive growth.[5] However, as mercantilist writers such as Davenant also understood, land and resources are not the whole 'wealth' of a nation: maritime knowledge, technical and military skills, appropriate institutions, and strategic political alliances are 'more truly riches of a nation than (gold and silver)' and needed 'to be put into the scale when we weigh the strength and value of a nation' and its capacity to achieve economic growth.[6] Comparisons of sectoral growth rates establish the importance of England's Atlantic commerce which, in the decades after 1660, grew far more rapidly than other branches of overseas trade, agriculture, or manufacturing industry.[7] However, they do not capture the full influence of overseas expansion on Davenant's conception of the wealth of the nation, or what North has called 'adaptive efficiency': the willingness and

History of Modern Britain, 3 vols. (Cambridge, 2004), vol. I, pp. 451–64; Robert C. Allen, 'Progress and poverty in early modern Europe', EcHR, 56 (2003), 403–43. Sceptics remain; see for example S. R. Epstein, Freedom and Growth: the Rise of States and Markets in Europe, 1300–1750 (London, 2000), p. 3.

[4] For a recent discussion of the historical treatment of international trade, above all Atlantic trade, in England's industrialization see Joseph E. Inikori, Africans and the Industrial Revolution in England: a Study in International Trade and Development (Cambridge, 2002).

[5] Pomeranz, Great Divergence, p. 113. A statement of Elizabethan colonial policy is found in Richard Hakluyt's 'A particular discourse concerning the great necessitie and manifold comodyties that are like to grow to this realme of England by the western discoveries lately attempted' (1584), reprinted in Maine Historical Society Collections, vol. II (1877). By 1700 England's New World holding of over 100,000 square miles was greater than the 58,410 square miles contained in England and Wales. Not all historians agree that extensive growth in the New World was important; see E. A. Wrigley, 'The divergence of England: the growth of the English economy in the seventeenth and eighteenth centuries', TRHS (2000), 117–41; E. A. Wrigley, 'The transition to an advanced organic economy: half a millennium of English agriculture', EcHR, 59 (2006), 435–80.

[6] Charles Whitworth (ed.), The Political and Commercial Works of the Celebrated Writer Charles D'Avenant, 5 vols. (London, 1771), vol. I, pp. 381–2. Davenant's conception is akin to the modern economist's idea of 'useful knowledge' used by Simon Kuznets as the source of modern economic growth. The distinction between 'useful' and 'useless' knowledge is slippery, as discussed by Machlup, who suggests that 'useful' can be aligned with practical, or capable of making contributions to material welfare: Simon Kuznets, Economic Growth and Structure (New York, 1965); Fritz Machlup, Knowledge: its Creation, Distribution, and Economic Significance, 3 vols. (Princeton, 1980–4), vol. II, p. 10.

[7] W. E. Minchinton (ed.), The Growth of English Overseas Trade in the Seventeenth and Eighteenth Century (London, 1969), pp. 11–13; William R. Scott, The Constitution and Finance of English, Scottish and Irish Joint-Stock Companies to 1720, 3 vols. (Cambridge, 1910–12), vol. I, pp. 311–19; Phyllis Deane and W. A. Cole, British Economic Growth, 1688–1959, 2nd edn (Cambridge, 1967), p. 28.

capacity to acquire knowledge and understanding; to take risks; to resolve problems and bottlenecks; and to introduce innovation.[8] This study looks at how late-seventeenth-century Londoners, who heavily dominated England's colonial trade, responded to the opportunities and challenges posed by the infant imperial project and set in place a durable mercantile system which underpinned both extensive and intensive growth and made the Industrial Revolution more likely.[9]

Economic historians working on English overseas trade and colonial expansion have focused on three big themes: the aspirations of early empire builders; the success of their project as measured in the commercial revolution; and the links between the growth of Britain's Atlantic economy and the Industrial Revolution. In the early twentieth century writers such as Andrews, Beer, Harper, and Newton drew a full, and convincing, picture of what Englishmen hoped to gain from westward expansion and how they designed the institutional framework of an Atlantic system which would reserve these benefits for Englishmen.[10] This work was later filled out by Kenneth Andrews and others while a second body of scholarship, dominated by Ralph Davis's work on trade and shipping, provided measurements of the project's success in what was, long ago, dubbed a 'commercial revolution'.[11] Detailed empirical work showed that, in the century after the Restoration, there was a major redirection

[8] Douglas North provides an elaborate discussion of the ways in which economics, politics, and culture interact in the long-term process of development to determine the way particular economies perform: Douglas C. North, *Institutions, Institutional Change and Economic Performance* (Cambridge, 1990).

[9] Rachel Laudan has argued that one way to think of the cognitive activity that generates technical knowledge is to see it as problem solving; the choice of problems which are solved will be based in part on signals sent to the potential inventor by the market, or another device, about the private and social benefits: Rachel Laudan, 'Cognitive change in technology and science', in Rachel Laudan (ed.), *The Nature of Knowledge: Are Models of Social Science Relevant?* (Dordrecht, 1984), pp. 83–104.

[10] Charles M. Andrews, *The Colonial Period of American History*, 4 vols. (New Haven, Conn., 1934–8); G. L. Beer, *The Origins of the British Colonial System, 1578–1660* (New York, 1908); Lawrence A. Harper, *The English Navigation Laws: a Seventeenth Century Experiment in Social Engineering* (New York, 1939); J. Holland Rose, A. P. Newton, and E. P. Benians (eds.), *The Cambridge History of the British Empire* (Cambridge, 1929), vol. I; Kenneth R. Andrews, *Trade, Plunder and Settlement: Maritime Enterprise and the Genesis of the British Empire, 1480–1630* (Cambridge, 1984); Carole Shammas, 'English commercial development and American colonization, 1560–1620', in K. R. Andrews, N. P. Canny, and P. E. H. Hair (eds.), *The Westward Enterprise: English Activities in Ireland and America, 1480–1650* (Liverpool, 1978), pp. 151–74.

[11] Bolingbroke used the phrase in the 1730s: J. H. Plumb, *The Growth of Political Stability in England, 1675–1725* (London, 1967), p. 3. For a survey of the discussion of the 'commercial revolution' see editor's introduction and essays by Ralph Davis in Minchinton (ed.), *The Growth of English Overseas Trade*, pp. 1–58, 78–120; Ralph Davis, *A Commercial Revolution: English Overseas Trade in the Seventeenth and Eighteenth Centuries* (London, 1967).

of England's overseas trade to areas beyond Europe; an expansion in the shipping and ship-building industries; a dynamic growth in new import and re-export trades; a diversification of manufacturing exports away from traditional woollen cloths; and the development of expertise in a range of commercial services. All combined to ensure that overseas commerce, which was heavily concentrated in the capital, played an unusually important role in the nation's economic life, the nation's financial liquidity, and the national consciousness.[12]

The third area of discussion has attracted the most controversy and is dominated by the arguments presented in Eric Williams's influential text, *Capitalism and Slavery*, published in 1944, which suggests that the accumulation of financial capital arising from the success of Britain's Atlantic system (underpinned by slavery) caused, or at least contributed greatly to, the Industrial Revolution.[13] Similar sentiments underpin the world-systems interpretation of the causes of development and underdevelopment which emerged in the writings of Frank, Wallerstein, and others in the 1970s.[14] In very general terms, these writers perceived that the post-1800 divergence between 'the West and the rest' had its origins in the period between 1450 and 1750, when Europeans deployed military power, and superior state organization, to exploit the opportunities opened up by long-distance commerce and turn the terms of trade heavily in their favour. The mineral wealth and raw materials produced on the periphery were exchanged for the manufactures and high-quality farm produce of the core on highly unequal terms. 'Over time such patterns of specialization pushed the economies of Western Europe towards industrialization and higher standards of living and the economies of the periphery towards primary production, monoculture, and far lower levels of per capita income.'[15]

Both the Williams thesis and the world-systems analysis have been strongly criticized for their lack of a systematic statistical underpinning. Attempts to remedy the defect have come up with 'small numbers' for any measure of the importance of the Atlantic economy, even in Britain, and led to O'Brien's famous conclusion that 'the periphery was peripheral'.[16]

[12] Ralph Davis, 'English foreign trade, 1660–1700', *EcHR*, 7 (1954), 150–66; Ralph Davis, 'English foreign trade, 1700–1774', *EcHR*, 15 (1962), 285–303; Ralph Davis, *The Rise of the English Shipping Industry in the Seventeenth and Eighteenth Centuries* (Newton Abbot, 1962); David Ormrod, *The Rise of Commercial Empires: England and the Netherlands in the Age of Mercantilism, 1650–1770* (Cambridge, 2003).
[13] Eric Williams, *Capitalism and Slavery* (Chapel Hill, N.C., 1944); Inikori, *Africans and the Industrial Revolution*.
[14] Andre Gunder Frank, *World Accumulation, 1492–1789* (New York, 1978); Andre Gunder Frank, *Dependent Accumulation and Underdevelopment* (New York, 1979); Wallerstein, *The Modern World System*.
[15] O'Brien, 'European economic development', p. 2.
[16] *Ibid.*, p. 18.

However, the small ratios argument has itself been questioned on the grounds that it fails to recognize the strategic significance of the imperial project in encouraging economic development and ignores the innumerable feedback effects and linkages generated by overseas expansion, which are seen particularly well in the work of Jacob Price.[17] Peter Mathias claimed that the small numbers approach 'is rather like trying to measure the importance of ball bearings to the dynamic performance of a motor car by measuring their cost as a percentage of the capital cost of the vehicle'.[18] The narrow version of the Williams thesis which asserts that the profits generated by the slave trade were the main source of finance for the Industrial Revolution has little purchase, but the work of Solow, Engerman and O'Brien, Inikori, Pomeranz, and others has refined, and reinforced, the more general notion that the rise of Britain's Atlantic trading system did much to stimulate, and shape, the long period of slow structural change and economic development that culminated in the Industrial Revolution.[19] Many former sceptics have amended their views, as illustrated by O'Brien's recent conclusion that 'for the British Industrial Revolution the significance of foreign commerce should not be denied, denigrated nor exaggerated. It was obviously important.'[20]

In concentrating on these major themes, historians have paid scant attention to the 'nuts and bolts' of the processes by which the early aspirations outlined by Harper and others were translated into the concrete reality of the 'commercial revolution' and the nature of its much debated links with the Industrial Revolution. Yet early-seventeenth-century Englishmen could not have predicted with confidence that by 1713 colonial trade would have 'conformed in almost every particular to the Navigation system' designed by Restoration legislators; a system intended to create a sealed, self-contained, English Atlantic world which would allow Englishmen rather than the Dutch middlemen to benefit from their large investment in empire.[21] When claiming that this ideal was

---

[17] Jacob M. Price, 'Colonial trade and British economic development, 1660–1775', *Lex et Scientia: The International Journal of Law and Science*, 14 (1978), 101–26; Jacob M. Price, 'What did merchants do? Reflections on British overseas trade, 1660–1790', *JEH*, 49 (1989), 267–84.

[18] Quoted in Kenneth Morgan, *Slavery, Atlantic Trade and the British Economy, 1660–1800* (Cambridge, 2000), p. 48.

[19] Barbara L. Solow and Stanley L. Engerman (eds.), *British Capitalism and Caribbean Slavery: the Legacy of Eric Williams* (London, 1987); Engerman and O'Brien in Floud and Johnson (eds.), *Economic History of Britain*; Inikori, *Africans and the Industrial Revolution*; Pomeranz, *Great Divergence*.

[20] O'Brien in Pohl (ed.), *European Discovery*, p. 177.

[21] John J. McCusker and Russell R. Menard, *The Economy of British America, 1607–1789* (Chapel Hill, N.C., 1985), p. 49. Also see John J. McCusker, 'British mercantilist policies and the American colonies', in Stanley L. Engerman and Robert E. Gallman (eds.),

realized, McCusker and Menard accept Harper's notion that the legislation itself had been responsible for England's commercial success and yet,
on even brief examination, this is not plausible. The seventeenth-century
state did not have the resources to enforce commercial legislation, which
seriously raised private costs. The risks of evasion were low and, if the
costs of English services had remained 20 or 30 per cent above those of
the Dutch (as they were claimed to be in the 1650s) then the Acts would
have been largely ignored and trade would have flowed through illegal
channels.[22] Furthermore, if a strong state had been able to enforce legislation that imposed high private costs by diverting Englishmen from low-
price services to more expensive providers (as McCusker and Menard,
like Adam Smith and Harper, implicitly suggest) then the plantation
economy and trade would have been unable to compete with continental
rivals and would have suffered stagnation and decline. In fact, the reverse
was true and, in the decades after the Restoration, there was unprece-
dented growth in colonial trade and shipping. The Navigation legislation
might have helped but cannot entirely explain how, between the 1650s
and 1700, England developed the commercial capabilities which allowed
it to improve efficiency, close a substantial cost gap with its Dutch rivals,
and make mercantilism work.[23]

In this study the evidence of general compliance with the Navigation
Acts by the 1680s, despite weak enforcement capacity, is taken as a measure of increasing convergence between English and Dutch commercial

The Cambridge History of the United States, 3 vols. (Cambridge, 1996), vol. I, pp. 337–62.
Analysis of the impact of the Navigation Acts has focused on the damage caused to
the colonial economy and their role in causing the American Revolution: Lawrence A.
Harper, 'The effects of the Navigation Acts on the thirteen colonies', in R. B. Morris
(ed.), *The Era of the American Revolution* (New York, 1939), pp. 3–39; Robert P. Thomas,
'A quantitative approach to the study of the effects of British imperial policy upon
colonial welfare: some preliminary findings', *JEH*, 25 (1965), 615–38; Gary Walton,
'The new economic history and the burden of the Navigation Acts', *EcHR*, 24 (1971),
533–42.

[22] Worsley suggested that the Dutch undercut English freight charges by 20 per cent in the
1650s: Benjamin Worsley, *The Advocate: or, a Narrative of the State and Condition of Things
between the English and Dutch Nation in relation to Trade* (London, 1651), p. 4; Harper
used contemporary pamphlets to suggest that, in the 1650s, the gap was around 30 per
cent. Harper, *Navigation Laws*, p. 312; Beeston to Lords of Trade, 5 April 1694, PRO
CO 138/7, fo. 191; Beeston to Lords of Trade, 9 December 1697, PRO CO 138/9, fo.
184.

[23] As English efficiency improved in the late seventeenth century, the Dutch economy went
into a period of stagnation, or even decline, in the 1670s: Jan de Vries and Ad van der
Woude, *The First Modern Economy: Success, Failure, and Perseverance of the Dutch Economy*
(Cambridge, 1997), p. 673; J. C. Riley, 'The Dutch economy after 1650: decline or
growth?', *JEEH*, 13 (1984), 521–69; M. Aymard (ed.), *Dutch Capitalism and World
Capitalism* (Cambridge, 1982), pp. 1–10; Ormrod, *Rise of Commercial Empires*, pp.
31–59.

capabilities and costs rather than as a forced shift towards inefficient providers. The study seeks to explain the sources of this catch-up, and the likely consequences, by providing a detailed picture of the routines and ramifications of England's late-seventeenth-century colonial trade from the vantage point of the capital, which accounted for over three-quarters of the country's plantation trade, and acted as the hub, or clearing house, of its Atlantic system.[24] In these years England established a larger stake in the Atlantic than any other country in northern Europe and, as the imperial project moved out of its early experimental stage, it firmly fixed its claim to attention as a major source of national wealth and strength.[25] A regulatory framework designed to create a sealed self-contained commercial system was set in place and the mechanisms for distributing the spoils of empire were resolved. In this period the rules of the game were established and the incentive structure that shaped investment and the accumulation of financial and human capital took lasting form. A detailed account of the workings of the capital's colonial trade in this crucial period highlights where, how, and why efficiency gains could be obtained. It brings into focus the causes of both the take-up of best practice and the innovations, which improved commercial capabilities and stimulated further economic growth.

London's hub position in Restoration England's expanding network of Atlantic exchange is well attested in contemporary commentaries and more recent overviews of the Atlantic economy.[26] But, although provincial ports which were important in the Atlantic economy have received attention, the capital's much larger colonial commerce has not been given the same comprehensive treatment.[27] Work has been done on major sectors of colonial commerce with strong bases in London such as the shipping industry and the slave trade.[28] Peter Earle and Richard Grassby have undertaken extensive work on the middling sorts and the business

---

[24] Taking an annual average for the three year period between 1699 and 1701, London accounted for 80 per cent of the nation's colonial imports, 65 per cent of exports to the colonies, and 85 per cent of all re-exports among which colonial commodities were important: PRO CUST. 3/3–5.

[25] K. G. Davies, *The North Atlantic World in the Seventeenth Century* (Oxford, 1974), pp. 313–14; Ralph Davis, *The Rise of the Atlantic Economies* (London, 1973); G. V. Scammell, *The First Imperial Age: European Overseas Expansion, c. 1400–1715* (London, 1989).

[26] N. H. *The Compleat Tradesman* (London, 1684), p. 5; Davies, *North Atlantic World*; Davis, *Rise of the Atlantic Economies*; Scammell, *First Imperial Age*.

[27] David Harris Sacks, *The Widening Gate: Bristol and the Atlantic Economy, 1450–1700* (Berkeley, Calif., 1991); K. R. Morgan, *Bristol and the Atlantic Trade in the Eighteenth Century* (Cambridge, 1993); P. G. E. Clemens, 'The rise of Liverpool, 1665–1750', *EcHR*, 29 (1976), 211–25; T. M. Devine, *Tobacco Lords: a Study of the Tobacco Merchants of Glasgow and their Trading Activities c. 1740–90* (Edinburgh, 1975).

[28] Davis, *The Rise of the English Shipping Industry*; K. G. Davies, *The Royal African Company* (London, 1957).

world of Restoration London, highlighting the risks and rewards of a life in commerce which Natasha Glaisyer has placed in a cultural context.[29] Individual colonial merchants and joint-stock companies have received attention.[30] Robert Brenner has highlighted the distinctive character of the 'new merchants' who pioneered London's colonial trade in the early seventeenth century – returned planters, domestic tradesmen, sea captains, and shopkeepers. He also identified the colonial entrepreneurial leadership that had emerged from among the 'new merchants' by the eve of the Civil War: a coherent social group linked by a multiplicity of family and business ties who had benefited from early involvement in the imperial project and links with colonial governments to form a 'merchant-councillor' interest, and remained aloof from the old chartered companies. Typically republican in politics, independent in religion, and militarily expansionist in their commercial programmes, these merchants played a prominent part in the politics of opposition, and ultimately revolution.[31] Although colonial trade remained largely open, or 'free', after the Restoration, and men in the mould of Brenner's 'new merchants' could still gain access, their numbers dwindled, merchant-councillor interests became increasingly entrenched and, as Price and Clemens have shown for the Chesapeake trade, colonial commerce in general became concentrated in fewer hands.[32] Colonial merchants feature as a group in Gary De Krey's analysis of the fracturing of London's political life after the Restoration, Perry Gauci's survey of the politics of trade, and Dwyryd Jones's analysis of mercantile involvement in war finance, but the membership of the group, and the nature of the material interests at stake in the Atlantic, lack clear definition and highlight the need for a detailed study of this important commercial sector.[33]

[29] Peter Earle, *The Making of the English Middle Class: Business, Society, and Family Life in London, 1660–1730* (London, 1989); Richard Grassby, *The Business Community in Seventeenth Century England* (Cambridge, 1995); Natasha Glaisyer, *The Culture of Commerce in England, 1660–1720* (Woodbridge, Suffolk, 2006).
[30] Jacob M. Price, *Perry of London: a Family and a Firm on the Seaborne Frontier, 1615–1753* (Cambridge, Mass., 1992); David Hancock ' "A world of business to do": William Freeman and the foundations of England's commercial empire, 1645–1707', *WMQ*, 57 (2000), 3–34; Davies, *African Company*; E. E. Rich, *The History of the Hudson's Bay Company, 1670–1870* (London, 1958–9). Ann Carlos and others have produced a clutch of articles about the workings of the colonial joint-stock companies: for example, Ann Carlos and Stephen Nicholas, 'Giants of an earlier capitalism: the early chartered companies as modern multi-nationals', *BHR* (1988), 398–419.
[31] Robert Brenner, *Merchants and Revolution: Commercial Change, Political Conflict, and London's Overseas Traders, 1550–1653* (Cambridge, 1993).
[32] Jacob M. Price and P. G. E. Clemens, 'A revolution of scale in overseas trade: British firms in the Chesapeake trade, 1675–1775', *JEH*, 47 (1987), 1–43.
[33] Gary Stuart De Krey, *A Fractured Society: the Politics of London in the First Age of Party, 1688–1715* (Oxford, 1985); Gary Stuart De Krey, *London and the Restoration, 1659–83*

No doubt the lack of a study of London's colonial commerce reflects the fact that, unlike the East India trade (the other major pillar of the commercial revolution), the sector lacked centralized direction or single corporate control. As a result, both quantitative and qualitative source material is fragmentary and dispersed. Any study of commercial change and development requires a statistical framework but, despite the rise of a new spirit of scientific enquiry which applied the same empirical observation to the study of society as it did to that of the natural world, and the accompanying interest in political arithmetic, the late seventeenth century is renowned as an age of statistical darkness.[34] There is no continuous series of commercial statistics until 1696 when, anxious to improve the management of the tax revenues needed to finance the massive wartime expenditures, the king appointed an Inspector General of the customs and initiated a permanent series of customs ledgers detailing annual trade by country, and commodity, for London and the outports.[35] After this date the discussion of trade moves on to more solid foundations, and the figures do, at least, provide some cross-sectional data for the end of the century.

However, discussion of commercial trends over the Restoration period relies on scrappy information. Ralph Davis combined the customs ledgers of 1699–1701 with surviving figures for London trade in 1663 and 1669 to outline the main contours of what he described as a 'revolution in trade'.[36] The exercise presented a range of problems. The earlier figures have limited detail: they group all the plantations together; and they list only English-produced exports and not re-exports. Both sets of figures leave out the important trades in ships and bullion. However, the most serious difficulty arose from the valuations as, although the Inspector General provided a clear statement that, in the 1690s, export values were based on the 'current price here at home', and import values on the 'current price abroad', the basis for the values used in the 1660s is unclear.[37] Davis suggested that the prices used to value imports were

(Cambridge, 2005); Perry Gauci, *The Politics of Trade: the Overseas Merchant in State and Society, 1660–1720* (Oxford, 2001); D. W. Jones, *War and Economy in the Age of William III and Marlborough* (Oxford, 1988).

[34] F. J. Fisher, 'London's export trade in the early seventeenth century', *EcHR*, 3 (1950), 151–61; Davis, 'English foreign trade, 1660–1700', 155.

[35] The ledgers are found in the PRO CUST. 1–3. For a detailed description see G. N. Clark, *Guide to English Commercial Statistics, 1696–1782* (London, 1938); T. S. Ashton, Introduction in E. B. Schumpeter (ed.), *English Overseas Trade Statistics, 1697–1818* (Oxford, 1960), pp. 1–14.

[36] Davis, 'English foreign trade: 1660–1700', 162. The figures for 1663 and 1668 are found in BL Add. MS 36,785.

[37] For discussion of valuations see Clark, *Commercial Statistics*, pp. 37–8; John J. McCusker, 'The current value of English exports, 1697–1800', *WMQ*, 28 (1971), 607–28; S. D.

probably the selling prices in England (including freight, insurance, and duty) and, on this best-guess basis, he adjusted the values of some highly taxed goods (wine, brandy, and tobacco) to make their valuations more comparable with the later figures. Although Davis's figures lack precision, his broad conclusions about commercial trends, and the rise of long-distance trade, seem secure and provide the figures in Table 1.1. The value of London's total overseas trade grew slowly between the Restoration and the end of the century, with imports increasing by about a quarter, and exports by a third, although re-exports (dominated by linens, Indian textiles, sugar, and tobacco) probably more than doubled. However, along with the 'dynamic', and closely linked, re-export trades the transoceanic trades grew much more rapidly and, within this sector, colonial commerce performed best of all, rising at around four times the rate of total trade and, by 1700, accounting for nearly 20 per cent of the capital's imports and 15 per cent of exports. Davis's valuable statistical sketch of London's overseas trade in the late seventeenth century provides a broad framework for discussion and has been supplemented by Robert Nash in his unpublished thesis, which used the Inspector General's ledgers to provide important additional detail about the multilateral trades, and invisible earnings, which is drawn on in this study.[38]

Davis suggested that his general picture would be improved by work on the portbooks. It is true that, if the portbooks had been kept with a reasonable degree of accuracy, and if they survived in complete series from their inception in the sixteenth century, they would certainly provide materials for a useful import and export series, although there would be major omissions as, like the figures used in Table 1.1, they do not include ship sales or bullion.[39] Unfortunately, even in the eighteenth century a committee of the House of Commons found the books in the 'greatest disorder and confusion' with many gaps.[40] Subsequent loss, damage, and the destruction of the London portbooks from 1696 have further reduced their potential. However, even with gaps, the task of processing the surviving data in a systematic way is huge. A report of 1696 suggested that it would require the full-time work of four men to deal

Smith, 'Prices and the value of English exports in the eighteenth century: evidence from the North American colonial trade', *EcHR*, 48 (1995), 575–90.

[38] Robert C. Nash, 'English transatlantic trade, 1660–1730: a quantitative study', unpublished doctoral thesis, University of Cambridge (1982).

[39] For discussion of the portbooks see Clark, *Commercial Statistics*, pp. 52–6; Neville Williams, 'The London port books', *Transactions of the London and Middlesex Archaeological Society*, 18 (1955), 13–26.

[40] *Journals of the House of Lords*, 19, 586, 606–7, 612; *Manuscripts of the House of Lords*, 8, 29–30.

Table 1.1 *London's trade in the late seventeenth century (£000)*

	North-west Europe[a]	North[b]	South[c]	British islands[d]	Colonies[e]	East Indies	Total
Imports							
1663/9	1,281	272	1,085	27	421	409	3,495
1699–1701	1,195	414	1,384	55	863	756	4,667
Exports							
1663/9	746	89	974	37	163	30	2,039
1699–1701	763	151	1,284	43	410	122	2,773
Re-exports							
1663/9	–	–	–	–	–	–	c. 700
1699–1701	1,101	73	195	40	254	14	1,677

Source: Ralph Davis, 'English foreign trade, 1660–1700', *EcHR*, 7 (1954), 163–6.
[a] North-west Europe = Germany, Holland, Flanders, France.
[b] North = Norway, Denmark, the Baltic.
[c] South = Spain, Portugal, their islands, the Mediterranean.
[d] British islands = Scotland, Ireland, Channel Isles.
[e] Colonies = English colonies in North America and the West Indies.

with the London books alone for each year and experience suggests that, even with modern technology, productivity is little improved.[41] Although it was not possible to complete a detailed analysis of the portbooks over the whole period of this study, a comprehensive survey of colonial commerce in the London portbooks for 1686 (a year for which the books survive in full) and limited samples of data for other years, provide a more detailed picture of London's Atlantic trade than it is possible to draw from the broad statistical outlines.[42]

By 1686, the year chosen for the detailed portbook analysis, the mercantile system framed after the Restoration had been in place for a generation and had assumed an air of permanence. The year came towards the end of a long period of commercial expansion which was brought to a sharp halt by the outbreak of war with France in 1689 and the onset of a period of much slower growth lasting until the 1740s.[43] After

[41] Davis, 'English foreign trade, 1660–1700', 155.
[42] The database was compiled from the following volumes: imports from PRO E 190 143/1, 137/2, exports from E 190 137/8, 139/1, 141/5, 136/4, 136/6 (hereafter portbook database).
[43] Whitworth (ed.), *Works of D'Avenant*, vol. I, pp. 374–7; Minchinton (ed.), *Growth of English Overseas Trade*, pp. 11–16.

suffering the setbacks of plague, fire, and two Dutch wars, the English had, after 1675, the advantage of a period of peace (only mildly disrupted by internal rebellion led by Monmouth in 1685) and including three years of valuable neutrality while their main commercial rivals, the Dutch Republic and France, remained embroiled in an intensely damaging war. While, in the 1680s, England's agriculture suffered from low prices, and woollen cloth producers faced stagnation in traditional export trades, there was a boom in long-distance commerce including, above all, the plantation trade, reflected in soaring customs receipts which allowed the late Stuarts to almost dispense with Parliament.[44] However, colonial merchants did face political and commercial problems. The Crown had mounted a determined effort to undermine merchant-councillor elites and tighten its own grip over colonial administration culminating in the establishment of the Dominion of New England in 1685, heightened efforts to enforce prerogative monopolies and charters, and very heavy taxes on tobacco and sugar.[45] At the same time, both sugar and tobacco planters produced bumper crops in 1686 – in fact, the governor of Barbados reckoned that it was the greatest crop the island had yet produced – and with abundant supplies, prices fell to their lowest level in the century.[46] No doubt tough trading conditions encouraged further consolidation among merchant firms in what was to become an increasingly concentrated trade.[47]

Using the portbooks to compile a statistical database presented a range of problems. It is difficult to assess the level of care with which the records were collected, although it is reassuring to find almost total agreement between books kept by different officers. However, there is less complete correspondence between surviving ships' accounts and the portbooks.[48] Valuations also create difficulty. Most goods were taxed at the official valuations given in the book of rates (last updated in 1660 and bearing an unknown relationship to market prices) and thus no value was recorded

---

[44] C. D. Chandaman, *The English Public Revenue, 1660–1688* (Oxford, 1975), pp. 35–6.

[45] I. K. Steele, 'The empire and the provincial elites: an interpretation of some writings on the English Atlantic, 1675–1696', in Peter Marshall and Glyn Williams (eds.), *The British Atlantic Empire before the American Revolution* (London, 1980), pp. 2–32; Richard S. Dunn, 'The Glorious Revolution and America', in Nicholas Canny (ed.), *The Oxford History of the British Empire*, 5 vols. (Oxford, 1998), vol. I; *The Origins of Empire: British Overseas Enterprise to the Close of the Seventeenth Century*, pp. 445–66; Nuala Zahedieh, 'Regulation, rent-seeking and the Glorious Revolution in the English Atlantic economy', *EcHR* (2009).

[46] Stede to Lords of Trade, 27 April 1686, PRO CO 1/49, fo. 227; Russell R. Menard, 'The tobacco industry in the Chesapeake colonies, 1617–1730: an interpretation', *Research in Economic History*, 5 (1980), 139, 159.

[47] Price and Clemens, 'A revolution of scale in overseas trade', 1–43.

[48] 'Account Book of the *Cadiz Merchant*', PRO HCA 30/664.

in the portbooks. The valuations used in the analysis presented here are official values taken from the Inspector General's ledgers of 1697 which no doubt provide a better fit than those in the earlier book of rates but do not represent the market values current in 1686.[49] The difficulties are exacerbated by the wide range of goods listed 'at value', as they cannot be incorporated into the figures, other than at the price sworn by the trading merchant, and bear an unknown relationship to the official values. Identification of merchants and captains also posed problems as there is duplication of common names such as John Hill, Thomas Lane, or John Taylor. Furthermore, many merchants designated in the portbooks were acting partly or entirely on another person's behalf, and the portbooks do not reveal this detail. Overall, the portbook database should not be treated as having great precision, but it does give a more detailed insight than hitherto available into the structure and organization of London's colonial trade in the late seventeenth century.

The portbook database lists over 1,500 individuals, exporting or importing almost 28,000 consignments of goods to, and from, the colonies, in over three hundred ships, and displays new detail about the connections between people, places, and commodity flows around the Atlantic in 1686. Detailed analysis of only one year – one slice in time – might have given the study a static quality but the focus on the careers of the 170 merchants who dominated the year's trading activity (accounting for almost 70 per cent of its value) and above all, the 59 with the largest turnover in 1686, provides a broader frame of analysis.[50] These 59 merchants did not constitute a dominant group in a long-term sense. Turnover in the trade was high, and each year new merchants would enter or leave the ranks of the leading merchants. However, the combined careers of these 'big colonial merchants' spanned a century from the 1630s to the 1730s and this collective experience illuminates change and development in colonial trade. The book has drawn on a broad range of sources to uncover information about the merchants and ships listed in the portbooks of 1686: records of the Admiralty, Chancery, Exchequer, and Mayor's Courts; wills and probate inventories; business records and merchant correspondence; state papers; the colonial Naval Officers' returns; and the burgeoning print culture of the period provide materials with which to piece together a detailed picture of

---

[49] I am very grateful to D. W. Jones for providing these valuations at the start of the project. According to Menard farm prices of tobacco were similar in 1686 and 1697 but according to Davies sugar prices had risen sharply: Russell R. Menard, 'The tobacco industry in the Chesapeake colonies, 1617–1730: an interpretation', *Research in Economic History*, 5 (1980), 109–77; Davies, *African Company*.

[50] For a time-slice approach to Atlantic migration see Alison Games, *Migration and the Origins of the English Atlantic World* (Cambridge, Mass., 1999).

14   The Capital and the Colonies

how colonial commerce worked in the first phase of the 'commercial revolution' and how Londoners, at the hub of the system, developed the capabilities needed to secure the Navigation Acts.

After first placing Restoration London in its national, and Atlantic context, and examining the institutional framework within which colonial commerce operated, the book projects a picture of growing commercial capabilities through chapters on merchants, shipping, imports, and exports. The chapter on merchants describes the competitive structure of colonial commerce within the supposedly sealed Navigation system and looks at how, while retaining low entry barriers, the participants fashioned the day-to-day workings of this atomistic world, and devised strategies designed to reduce risk, promote profit, and reserve the benefits of New World settlement for Englishmen. These included the modernization of education and training; the take-up, and development, of increasingly sophisticated and specialized commercial services; and investment in associational activities which promoted trust. Intensely competitive conditions also encouraged efforts to engage in rent-seeking activities – 'rents' being the difference between the prices paid in a perfectly competitive market and the prices paid to suppliers (often monopolists or near monopolists) in a regulated market. However, the contested control of the institutions used to enforce regulation made it difficult for any interest group to capture the profits of empire until the Glorious Revolution created a consolidated state with improved opportunities for rent-seeking activities and ushered in a period of slower growth.[51]

The next chapter on shipping provides a rough measure of the expanding freight needs of London's plantation trade and how, on account of the long distances involved, these were far greater than suggested by the value of the trade alone. It considers how the commercial community was able to provide the capital, labour, and skills needed to supply its own shipping services at a competitive cost: an achievement which underpinned increasing adherence to the Navigation Acts without damaging

[51] Rent-seeking is the socially costly pursuit of wealth transfers: the social cost arises because the resources used for transfer seeking have a positive opportunity cost elsewhere in the economy. Normally the concept of rent-seeking is applied to cases where government intervention in the economy leads to the creation of artificial or contrived rents, e.g. through a monopoly or licences. Seeking such returns leads to social costs because output is fixed by definition in for example a government regulation. But it can take place in other settings for example families with an inheritance at stake, or a crime mob: J. M. Buchanan, R. D. Tollinson, and G. Tullock (eds.), *Toward a Theory of a Rent-Seeking Society* (College Station, Tex., 1980); R. B. Ekulund and R. D. Tollinson, *Mercantilism as a Rent-Seeking Society: Economic Regulation in Historical Perspective* (College Station, Tex., 1981); R. B. Ekulund and R. D. Tollinson, *Politicized Economies. Monopoly, Monarchy, and Mercantilism* (College Station, Tex., 1997); Zahedieh, 'Regulation, rent-seeking, and the Glorious Revolution'.

the growth and prosperity of England's plantation system in the decades after the Restoration. It also looks at how the expansion of port activity shaped the economy of London, reinforced its pivotal position in the national distribution network, and strengthened the capital's external economies.

Chapter 5 considers how England benefited from the exploitation of American resources. Although its New World territories did not produce gold and silver they did offer abundant supplies of fish, furs, and forest products and the lands could be improved to offer a range of other desirable commodities – above all tobacco and sugar – which enhanced national self-sufficiency both by substituting for foreign imports and providing goods for re-export. As merchants accumulated capital and commercial expertise they succeeded in making improvements in the sorting, processing, marketing, and distribution of colonial commodities in ways that lowered costs and encouraged increased consumption, strengthened London's industrial and commercial base, consolidated the city's position as hub of an increasingly integrated national economy, and established its role as a leading emporium to rival Amsterdam in Europe.

Chapter 6 looks at the capital's export trade to the colonies, which has been neglected in studies of the early phases of English expansion. Despite recent emphasis on import-led growth, contemporaries valued the colonies at least as much as markets for English manufactured goods as sources of supply, and in fact the export sector both grew as fast as the much vaunted re-export sector and proved to be the most profitable branch of trade.[52] Merchants who supplied colonial markets were encouraged to invest in a broad range of industries, old and new, that had been previously confined to the domestic market and this had a qualitative impact on development. The emphasis on bulk production of standard-quality goods, at low unit cost, channelled innovation and enterprise in directions that were important for the long-term development of Britain's manufacturing industry.

The detailed picture of London's colonial commerce in the late seventeenth century throws into relief the way in which extensive growth in the New World not only expanded the nation's resource base, and relieved Malthusian pressures, as highlighted in recent literature, but also encouraged investment in new skills and industry, useful knowledge, or 'adaptive efficiency', with important consequences for development.[53]

---

[52] On contemporary understanding of the importance and value of adding labour to raw materials see William Petyt, *Britannia Languens or a Discourse of Trade* (London, 1680), pp. 23–4.

[53] Pomeranz, *Great Divergence*; Whitworth (ed.), *Works of D'Avenant*, vol. I, pp. 381–2; Mokyr, *Gifts of Athena*; North, *Institutions*.

The acquisition of new lands in America was not alone sufficient to set any nation on an inevitable route to commercial, financial, scientific, or industrial revolution and, as shown by Spain and Portugal, a large part of the gains of imperial expansion could be captured by enterprising foreigners. However, after the Restoration, England's colonial merchants operated in a relatively competitive environment which encouraged efforts to improve efficiency in trade and shipping which, in turn, under-pinned the catch-up with their Dutch rivals which was measured in the growing adherence to the Navigation Acts. The institutional changes brought about by the Glorious Revolution enhanced the value of rent-seeking activities and served to direct capital and entrepreneurial effort away from productive activities. Growth slowed but the gains to national efficiency made in the earlier period were not entirely lost. By this time England had set in place a Navigation system and developed the com-mercial capabilities which underpinned the long period of Smithian growth, helping eighteenth-century Britain to move more rapidly than other regions of Europe and east Asia up to that 'plateau from where technical progress and an Industrial Revolution became potentially likely (and with hindsight) all too probable'.[54]

[54] O'Brien, 'Reconstruction, rehabilitation, and reconfiguration of the Industrial Revolution', 126.

2   London and the Atlantic economy

This chapter puts London in its national and Atlantic context and discusses the institutional framework within which overseas expansion took place and the Navigation system was made to work. London's pivotal place in seventeenth-century England's expanding network of imperial exchange arose naturally from the city's long-established command over the nation's economy and polity. London had exploited its favourable location at the mouth of the River Thames to become the country's premier port and was also the centre of government, professional services, industry, and all sorts of useful knowledge (Illustration 1). Colonial projectors and Atlantic traders were attracted by the capital's large concentration of people, wealth, political patronage, commercial expertise, and information, as well as good supply chains linking it to the remotest reaches of the home market and overseas.[1]

London's combination of functions was unique among European cities and gave its citizens a competitive advantage when embarking on the extension and consolidation of empire that took place in the late seventeenth century.[2] Londoners played a prominent role in promoting overseas expansion and a central part in the design of a regulatory framework which aimed to ensure that the fruits of empire would not be appropriated by foreigners at the expense of England, or by the Crown at the expense of citizens.[3]

---

[1] N. H. *The Compleat Tradesman* (London, 1684), p. 5. On the business world of London see Peter Earle, *The Making of the English Middle Class: Business, Society, and Family Life in London, 1660–1730* (London, 1989); Richard Grassby, *The Business Community in Seventeenth Century England* (Cambridge,1995); Jacob M. Price, *Perry of London: a Family and a Firm on the Seaborne Frontier, 1615–1753* (Cambridge, Mass., 1992); Peter Earle, 'The economy of London, 1660–1730', in Patrick O'Brien (ed.), *Urban Achievements in Early Modern Europe: Golden Ages in Antwerp, Amsterdam, and London* (Cambridge, 2001), pp. 81–96.

[2] Ralph Davis, *The Rise of the Atlantic Economies* (London,1973); K. G. Davies, *The North Atlantic World in the Seventeenth Century* (Oxford, 1974); G.V. Scammell, *The First Imperial Age: European Overseas Expansion, c. 1400–1715* (London, 1989).

[3] Robert Brenner, *Merchants and Revolution: Commercial Change, Political Conflict, and London's Overseas Traders, 1550–1653* (Cambridge, 1993).

Illustration 1 Panoramic view of the City of London, c. 1690 showing Southwark and the River Thames in the foreground. By Johannes de Ram, Guildhall Library.

London in the late seventeenth century

As London acquired its hub role in an expanding network of imperial exchange, it also strengthened its position in the national economy and it seems plausible that the two developments were linked.[4] After a long period of growth, England's total population stabilized, and even fell a little, in the late seventeenth century. However, London's numbers continued to expand from around 400,000 in 1650 to 575,000 in 1700 and the capital increased its share of national population from around 7 to 11 per cent.[5] Although growth began to accelerate in certain second-rank towns after 1670, London far outstripped all English rivals, and in 1700 accounted for 70 per cent of the urban population; Norwich, the second city, had a population of 30,000 in 1700 and Bristol, the third city and second port, had 20,000. Only in Holland, another trading nation, does one city appear to have approached London's level of dominance. In 1650 Amsterdam had a population of about 150,000 people, and contained 8 per cent of the Dutch total, but it then ceased to grow. Meanwhile, London had outstripped all continental rivals to become, by 1700, the largest city in western Europe.[6]

London's growth depended on immigration as, in the seventeenth century, its death rates consistently exceeded birth rates.[7] Movement to London partly reflected difficulties in making a living in the countryside as both agriculture, and the woollen industry, underwent substantial structural change in the late seventeenth century. However, the level of arrivals also reflected the attractions of life in the capital which not only housed a high proportion of England's population but also accounted for an even greater share of its wealth. According to estimates made in the 1690s, houses within the area covered by the London bills of mortality numbered 8 per cent of the national stock but accounted for 46 per cent of the rental value of all houses in the realm. Overall, in the late 1680s London contributed more than 40 per cent of the ordinary revenue of the state and, as noted by Craig Spence, it was self-evidently the 'vitals of the Commonwealth'.[8]

---

[4] Robert C. Allen, 'Progress and poverty in early modern Europe', *EcHR*, 56 (2003), 403–43.

[5] E. A. Wrigley, 'A simple model of London's importance in changing English society and economy, 1650–1750', *Past and Present*, 37 (1967), 44–70.

[6] E. A. Wrigley, 'Urban growth and agricultural change: England and the continent in the early modern period', *JIH*, 15 (1985), 683–728.

[7] William Petty, *Essays on Political Arithmetic* (London, 1699), pp. 121–2. On national population trends see E. A. Wrigley and R. S. Schofield, *The Population History of England, 1541–1871: a Reconstruction* (Cambridge, 1981).

[8] Craig Spence, *London in the 1690s: a Social Atlas* (London, 2000), p. 1.

London's wealth was broadly based. By the late seventeenth century the king, Parliament, and central law courts were all permanently resident in the capital. London was also the country's biggest manufacturing centre, catering for a wide range of local, provincial, and foreign markets.[9] However, above all, the city owed 'its glory and riches and many other blessings to the excellent river of Thames'.[10] The river gave the city access deep into England's interior, in addition to its good coastal links with provincial ports, and a short sea crossing to continental markets (Illustration 2). Favourable location combined with political patronage to make London the country's pre-eminent seaport, possessing about three-quarters of the nation's merchant fleet, and accounting for a similar proportion of the value of the nation's overseas trade, being well placed to assemble goods for export, and to distribute imported goods to the remotest corners of the realm.[11] Commerce was generally agreed to be the most important staple of the capital's prosperity and, in a period when national population stagnated, overseas trade continued to expand.

As indicated in Chapter 1, it was long-distance and, above all, Atlantic trade which was driving expansion in this period. Although the commercial statistics produced by Ralph Davis suggest that the overall value of London's trade increased slowly, the value of plantation imports rose by around 100 per cent, and exports by around 150 per cent, between 1663/9 and 1699/1701 (Table 1.1) and, on account of the long distances and bulky commodities involved in colonial commerce, it accounted for a higher proportion of the growth in demand for the capital's shipping and other commercial services than suggested by value alone.[12] Furthermore, plantation trade had a qualitative significance in that it encouraged a diversification in manufacturing industry, both to supply a wide range of wants beyond woollen cloths, and to process novel imports. Finally, the colonies provided a high proportion of the commodities traded in the new re-export sector that allowed London to challenge Amsterdam's position as Europe's main redistribution centre.[13]

---

[9] A. L. Beier and Roger Finlay (eds.), *The Making of the Metropolis: London 1500–1700* (London, 1986), p. 4.

[10] Richard Burton, *Historical Remarques and Observations of the Ancient and Present State of London and Westminster* (London, 1684), p. 71; Rupert C. Jarvis, 'The metamorphosis of the port of London', *The London Journal*, 3 (1977), 55–72.

[11] Ralph Davis, *The Rise of the English Shipping Industry in the Seventeenth and Eighteenth Centuries* (Newton Abbot, 1962); Ralph Davis, 'English foreign trade, 1660–1700', *EcHR*, 7 (1954), 150–66; T. S. Willan, *The Inland Trade: Studies in English Trade in the Sixteenth and Seventeenth Centuries* (Manchester, 1976).

[12] Davis, *Shipping Industry*, pp. 15, 17, 398–9.

[13] For a contemporary appreciation of the importance of Atlantic trade see Davenant's works, Charles Whitworth (ed.), *The Political and Commercial Works of the Celebrated Writer Charles D'Avenant*, 5 vols. (London, 1771), vol. II, pp. 13–22; John Cary, *An Essay on the*

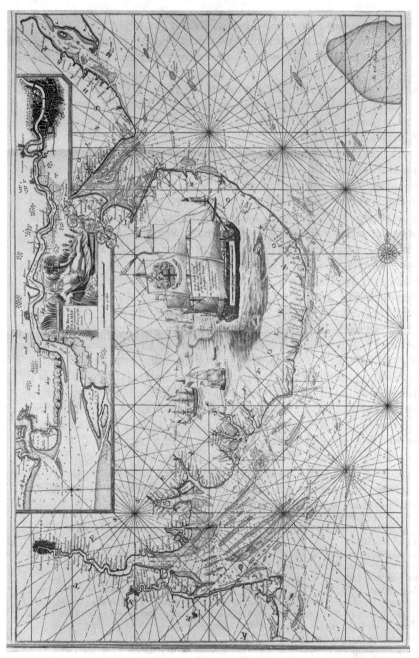

Illustration 2 Chart of the east coast of England and the Thames estuary showing the shoals and sands of the Thames estuary taken from Greenvile Collins's *Great Britain's Coasting Pilot* of 1693. Most Englishmen were using Dutch charts until the end of the seventeenth century and Collins's project, initiated by Charles II in 1681, was based on original surveys and marked a major step in improving English map-making.

Early modern London is usually portrayed as three spatially distinct worlds – City, west end, and suburbs – each with its own institutions and occupational structure (Map 2). Overseas trade, and within it colonial commerce, was most strongly connected to the ancient City which, at the Restoration, housed around a quarter of London's population and had little room for further growth in the seventeenth century. Perhaps 10 per cent of the City's 20,000 or so householders were merchants, and it contained 93 per cent of the 1,829 active overseas merchants listed in Lee's *London Directory* of 1677, many of whom had at least a flutter in the open colonial trades.[14] Most merchants lived in the eastern parishes within easy distance of the Royal Exchange in Cornhill, the Custom House, and the twenty-one Legal Quays (where overseas traders loaded and unloaded) crowded along a short stretch of the river between London Bridge and the Tower of London.[15]

Ostentatious display of wealth and power provided by the livery companies, City government, and individual merchants, advertised the rich fruits of commerce.[16] However, perhaps the greatest testament to the wealth of the City was the speed and efficiency of the rebuilding after the total destruction of the Great Fire of 1666.[17] A strikingly modern city was created at a cost of over £10 million. By the 1670s most private housing had been rebuilt to new uniform standards using brick or stone, while streets were widened, and gradients reduced, to improve traffic circulation (Illustration 3). Ambitious schemes drawn up by such as John Evelyn were passed over and the new city had 'none of the absolute monarch's inclination towards the grandiose'.[18] It was a citizens' city, but it did have a sober splendour and, by the 1690s, there were a

State of England in Relation to its Trade (Bristol, 1695); Josiah Child, *A New Discourse of Trade* (London, 1692); Thomas Leng, *Benjamin Worsley (1618–1677): Trade, Interest and the Spirit in Revolutionary England* (Woodbridge, Suffolk, 2008), pp. 138–62.

[14] J. C. Hotten (ed.), *The Little London Directory of 1677: the Old Printed List of the Merchants and Bankers of London* (London, 1863).

[15] Perry Gauci, *The Politics of Trade: the Overseas Merchant in State and Society, 1660–1720* (Oxford, 2001), pp. 24–7; Gary Stuart De Krey, *A Fractured Society: the Politics of London in the First Age of Party, 1688–1715* (Oxford, 1985).

[16] N. H. *Compleat Tradesman.* John Verney described how people pressed around the Guildhall in 1679 to see the 'rich clothes and jewels worn by the Lady Mayoress' who had a famous collar of pearls 'each as big as the top of ones finger': Margaret M. Verney, *Memoirs of the Verney Family from the Restoration to the Revolution, 1660–1696*, 4 vols. (London, 1899), vol. IV, p. 258.

[17] The fire started on Sunday 2 September 1666 and died down the following Wednesday evening. It laid waste an area extending from the Tower to Fetter Lane and from the Thames to Cripplegate.

[18] T. F. Reddaway, *The Rebuilding of London after the Great Fire* (London, 1940); E. S. de Beer (ed.), *John Evelyn. London Revived. Consideration for its Rebuilding in 1666* (*Londinium Redivivum, or London Restored not to its Pristine, but to far greater Beauty, Commodiousness and Magnificence*)(Oxford, 1938).

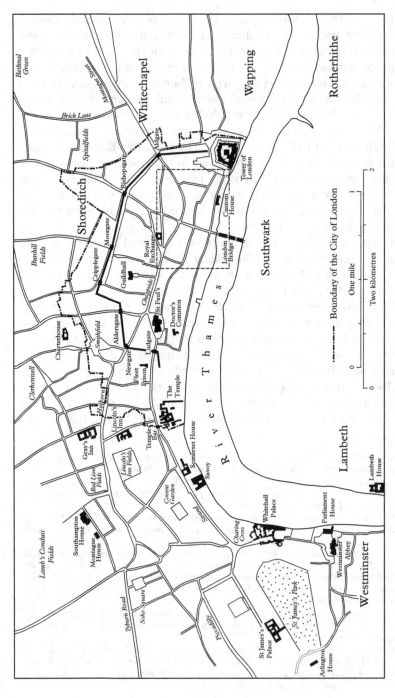

Map 2 London *c.* 1680. Based on a draft by Paul Laxton. The area in the box is shown in more detail in Map 4.

Bethnal
Green

Montague Street

Brick Lane

Whitechapel

Spitalfields

Aldgate

Bishopsgate

Wapping

Shoreditch

Moorgate

Tower of
London

Bunhill
Fields

Cripplegate

Custom
House

Rotherhithe

Guildhall

Royal
Exchange

Charterhouse

Clerkenwell

Cheapside

St Paul's

London
Bridge

Southwark

Smithfield

Aldersgate

Newgate

Doctor's
Common

Holborn

Fleet
Prison

Ludgate

Boundary of the City of London

Lincoln's
Inn

The Temple

River Thames

One mile

Gray's
Inn

Red Lion
Fields

Lincoln's
Inn Fields

Temple
Bar

Somerset House

Two kilometres

Southampton
House

Savoy

Lamb's Conduit
Fields

Montague
House

Strand

Covent
Garden

Lambeth

Charing
Cross

Whitehall
Palace

Tyburn Road

Soho
Square

Lambeth
House

Parliament
House

Piccadilly

Westminster

St James's
Palace

St James's Park

Westminster
Abbey

Arlington
House

Illustration 3 The London which burned down in 1666 was crowded, irregular, and dangerously combustible. Although ambitious schemes for a completely new lay-out were rejected in favour of more selective improvements the rebuilding did create a thoroughly modern city. By 1672, 7,700 houses had been rebuilt on their old sites and often on their old foundations; but all were subject to strict regulations as to the manner of construction. As seen in this detail of Cheapside, taken from William Morgan's *London &c Actually Survey'd* (1682), the City was ordered and regular and above all a commercial city. The houses of merchants were not just houses but shops, warehouses, and workshops.

number of new, and some grand, public buildings: parish churches, livery company halls, the Royal Exchange, and slowly rising above it all, St Paul's cathedral, which was begun in 1675 and completed in 1710. All reflected the prosperity of the City, the strength of its increasingly global commerce, and the independence of its governing institutions. Citizens jealously guarded against outside encroachments which might sap their wealth and stem their influence in the national decision-making arena, protecting the 'rights' and 'freedoms' of the Corporation, alongside those of Parliament, as a counterweight against an assertive, or absolute, Crown.[19]

However, the interest in commerce that dominated life in the City was by no means confined within its walls. According to Gregory King, overseas commerce accounted for around 20 per cent of national income in 1688 but, mainly on account of the long-distance sector, it was growing fast and it generated a much larger share of liquid funds which – at a time of falling

[19] De Krey, *Fractured Society*; Gary Stuart De Krey, *London and the Restoration, 1659–83* (Cambridge, 2005).

agricultural prices and rents – other sectors were anxious to tap.[20] King, courtiers, gentry, members of the professions, and others living in the west end, displayed their interest in commerce through their intellectual endeavours – participating in 'informal colleges', the Royal Society (founded in 1662), and coffee-house culture – in support of a Baconian programme that attempted to harness natural philosophy to the pursuit of improvements in manufacturing and the extension of trade.[21] However, they also sought more direct links with commerce through loans, investments, and family connections.[22] Landed families, such as the Verneys and Norths, obtained a maintenance (and more) for younger sons through apprenticeships to merchants, and an older son's marriage to a City heiress could restore a family fortune.[23] 'Trade, in a word', declared Daniel Defoe 'raises ancient families when sunk and decayed: And plants new families where the

[20] Gregory King's figures suggest that in 1688 the nation's overseas trade was worth around £9 million (exports at £2.46 million, re-exports at £600,000, and imports at £6 million) which was equal to about 20 per cent of a national income of £43 million: 'Seventeenth century manuscript book of Gregory King', in P. Laslett (ed.), *The Earliest Classics: John Graunt and Gregory King* (Farnborough, 1973), p. 207; Phyllis Deane and W. A. Cole, *British Economic Growth, 1688–1959*, 2nd edn (Cambridge, 1967), p. 28.

[21] The drive to catalogue, collect, and disseminate information in the interest of 'improvement' is reflected in the material in Houghton's weekly,

on the vast number of inventions and great advantages that accrue to a trading nation. Nothing can be in any country but one or another is apt to bring some account home; and especially here in England since the Royal Society was founded who are always enquiring what is done abroad, and telling all the travellers they meet with what they should enquire after.

John Houghton, *A Collection for Improvement of Husbandry and Trade,* 12 vols. (London, 1692–8), 17 November 1699; C. Webster, *The Great Instauration: Science, Medicine, and Reform, 1626–60* (London, 1975); M. Hunter, *Establishing the New Science: the Experience of the Early Royal Society* (Woodbridge, Suffolk, 1989); Leng, *Benjamin Worsley*; Margaret Jacob, *Scientific Culture and the Making of the Industrial West* (New York, 1997); Larry Stewart, *The Rise of Public Science* (Cambridge, 1992); Margaret C. Jacob and Larry Stewart, *Practical Matter: Newton's Science in the Service of Industry and Empire, 1687–1851* (Cambridge, Mass., 2004); Joel Mokyr, *The Gifts of Athena: Historical Origins of the Knowledge Economy* (Princeton, 2002), pp. 34–40, 43.

[22] Sir John Oglander remarked that

it is impossible for a mere gentleman ever to grow rich or raise his house. He must have some other vocation with his inheritance. if he hath no other vocation, let him get a ship and judiciously manage her ... by only following the plough he may keep his word and be upright, but will never increase his fortune.

Quoted in H. R. Roper, *Men and Events: Historical Essays* (New York, 1957), pp. 199–200. 'By... small threads [new outlets for economic enterprise] the landed gentleman was being stitched into the new economic fabric of society; trade, speculation, and venture ceased at least, to be alien to them': J. H. Plumb, *The Growth of Political Stability in England, 1675–1725* (London, 1967), p. 8.

[23] On the overlapping of gentry and City circles see Susan E. Whyman, *Sociability and Power in Late-Stuart England: The Cultural Worlds of the Verneys, 1660–1720* (Oxford, 1999); Richard Grassby, *The English Gentleman in Trade: the Life and Works of Sir Dudley North, 1641–1691* (Oxford, 1994).

old ones are lost and extinct' and the colonial trades which he marked the 'most profitable we drive' were by this time a byword for wealth.[24]

Commerce also influenced the rhythm of life in the sprawling suburbs as the rapidly growing merchant fleet, with its substantial Atlantic tonnage, provided employment for the mariners and port-related tradesmen who moved into the housing strung out alongside the river to the south and east.[25] New World imports stimulated a range of processing industries such as tobacco manufacture, sugar refining, and dyeing, as well as new export opportunities for industries such as hat-making and silk-weaving which, with the help of merchant capital and immigrant skills, flourished in the low-rent suburban parishes away from City guild restrictions.[26] Londoners, from any walk of life, participated in colonial commerce through their growing consumption of New World goods, and being seldom far from the river, the sight of the floating forest of masts from Blackwall to London Bridge was a perpetual reminder of whence these new goods came and the 'great traffick and commerce whereby this city doth flourish'.[27] Each of the capital's separate worlds intersected with the others in multiple ways, and all were firmly connected to the wide world overseas and, above all, the new lands in America.

The extension and consolidation of England's New World colonies

The colonial project that provides the context of this study was first articulated during the population surge of Elizabeth's reign and took lasting shape after a permanent settlement was established at Virginia after 1607.[28] At the Restoration, empire building was still in its early stages but the lines of future development were clearly mapped.[29] By 1660 England had a

---

[24] Daniel Defoe, *A Plan of the English Commerce* (London, 1728), pp. 61–2.

[25] Roger Finlay and Beatrice Shearer, 'Population growth and suburban expansion', in Beier and Finlay (eds.), *London 1500–1700*, pp. 37–59.

[26] A. L. Beier, 'Engine of manufacture: the trades of London', in Beier and Finlay, (eds.), *London 1500–1700*, pp. 115–40.

[27] Burton, *Historical Remarques*, p. 74; Natasha Glaisyer, *The Culture of Commerce in England, 1660–1720* (Woodbridge, Suffolk, 2006).

[28] Robert Gray expressed current concerns about overcrowding:

Our multitudes like too much blood in the body do infect our country with plague and poverty. Our land hath brought forth but it hath not milk sufficient in the breast thereof to nourish all those children which it hath brought forth. It affordeth neither employment nor preferment to those that depend upon it.

Robert Gray, *A Good Speed to Virginia* (London, 1609). M. Campbell, 'Of people either too few or too many', in W. A. Aitken and B. O. Henning (eds.), *Conflict in Stuart England: Essays in Honour of Wallace Notestein* (London, 1960), pp. 169–201.

[29] Kenneth R. Andrews, *Trade, Plunder, and Settlement: Maritime Enterprise and the Genesis of the British Empire, 1480–1630* (Cambridge, 1984); Scammell, *First Imperial Age*; William

well-established migratory fishery in Newfoundland, and around 140,000 subjects settled in three regions: almost 25,000 people in the Chesapeake; over 80,000 in the six islands in the Caribbean; and over 35,000 in New England.[30]

All the colonial projects (apart from Jamaica, the prize of Cromwell's ambitious Western Design of 1655) were promoted by private individuals. Londoners, with their easy access to capital, commercial expertise, shipping, supplies, and political influence, were prominent from the start.[31] Mainly driven by material (but some spiritual) ambitions, promoters used different methods, but all envisaged a similar strategy for survival and growth, drawing on the ideas of empire expressed by Hakluyt and others in the late sixteenth century – and foreshadowing those recently expressed by Kenneth Pomeranz – which highlighted the possibilities of extensive growth being used to relieve Malthusian pressures at home. However, new lands also encouraged intensive growth by allowing Europeans to allocate capital and labour in ways conducive to long-run development and to escape the labour-intensive path followed in east Asia.[32] Through the institutions of indentured servitude and slavery, surplus labour from the mother country and coerced African workers were combined with abundant territory in America (with scant regard for the rights of indigenous peoples) to produce valuable land-intensive commodities. These exports could be exchanged for English manufactured goods (capital and labour intensive) in a trade that was intended to employ English ships and seamen, and generate a spiralling improvement in national wealth, strength, and security.[33]

R. Scott, *The Constitution and Finance of English, Scottish, and Irish Joint-Stock Companies to 1720*, 3 vols. (Cambridge, 1910–12).

[30] Scotland was (with minor exceptions) excluded from the English Atlantic system by the Navigation Acts until the Union of the English and Scottish Parliaments in 1707: John J. McCusker and Russell R. Menard, *The Economy of British America, 1607–1789* (Chapel Hill, N.C., 1985), pp. 103, 136, 154, 172, 203.

[31] Brenner, *Merchants and Revolution*; Theodore K. Rabb, *Enterprise and Empire: Merchant and Gentry Investment in the Expansion of England, 1575–1630* (Cambridge, Mass., 1967).

[32] In 1668 Benjamin Worsley elaborated in detail on how the 'increaseth [to] the limits of our dwelling' in different climatic zones could, with the application of sufficient labour, greatly expand both the quantity and range of English output: 'The peculiar advantages which this nation has by the trading of our plantations', BLO, MS Rawl. A 478, fos. 65–72. A statement of Elizabethan colonial policy is found in Richard Hakluyt's 'A particular discourse concerning the great necessitie and manifold comodyties that are like to grow to this realme of England by the western discoveries lately attempted' (1584), reprinted in *Maine Historical Society Collections*, vol. II (1877); Kenneth Pomeranz, *The Great Divergence: China, Europe, and the Making of the Modern World Economy* (Princeton, 2000), p. 113.

[33] Abbot E. Smith, *Colonists in Bondage: White Servitude and Convict Labour in America, 1607–1776* (Chapel Hill, N.C., 1947); David W. Galenson, *White Servitude in Colonial America: an Economic Analysis* (Cambridge, 1981); K. G. Davies, *The Royal African Company* (London, 1957).

Once Virginia's tobacco trade was put on a firm footing in the 1610s, the feasibility of plantation projects was proven, labour was imported on a large scale and the settlers made rapid progress in clearing and planting the land.[34] The introduction of sugar into Barbados in the 1640s, and the phenomenally high profits earned in the early days of the trade, caused the island to be compared with a 'silver mine', and generated great wealth for those who could command a sufficient labour supply.[35] White servants were supplemented by black slaves, and English merchants responded to the new market by expanding their activities on the African coast in competition with the Dutch, who had established a strong presence earlier in the century. Planters in the other English islands took steps to emulate Barbados's successful sugar and slave model, although those in Jamaica were, as yet, too uncertain of their future to make such a large investment.[36] In 1660 the island was a garrison colony rather than a plantation, and on the return of the king it was widely expected that it would be restored to Spain.[37] Meanwhile, the third area of settlement, New England, had proved something of a disappointment to those with an imperial vision as it did not produce a staple crop with a market in England. However, the settlers were able to secure the future of their economy by providing fish, horses, lumber, and provisions to other colonial regions, Spain, Portugal, and the wine islands with which they earned credits in England.[38] All regions used a substantial part of their earnings to purchase manufactured goods in England. By 1660, although colonial commodity trade accounted for as little as 4 per cent of England's overseas commerce, the main directions of what Davis dubbed 'a revolution in trade' were signposted: a surge of raw material imports; a surplus for

[34] Edmund S. Morgan, *American Slavery, American Freedom: the Ordeal of Colonial Virginia* (New York, 1975); Russell R. Menard, 'The tobacco industry in the Chesapeake colonies, 1617–1730: an interpretation', *Research in Economic History*, 5 (1980), 109–77.

[35] Russell R. Menard, *Sweet Negotiations: Sugar, Slavery, and Plantation Agriculture in Early Barbados* (Charlottesville, Va., 2006); Barry W. Higman, 'The sugar revolution', *EcHR*, 53 (2000), 213–36.

[36] Richard S. Dunn, *Sugar and Slaves: the Rise of the Planter Class in the English West Indies, 1624–1713* (Chapel Hill, N.C., 1972); Richard B. Sheridan, *Sugar and Slavery: an Economic History of the British West Indies, 1623–1775* (Barbados, 1974); Carl Bridenbaugh and Roberta Bridenbaugh, *No Peace Beyond the Line: the English in the Caribbean, 1624–1690* (New York, 1972).

[37] Nuala Zahedieh, 'Trade, plunder, and economic development in early English Jamaica, 1655–89', *EcHR*, 39 (1986), 205–22.

[38] The papers of the Salem merchant, Philip English, provide a vivid picture of the workings of this trade: Essex Institute, Salem, Massachusetts, English Papers; Cary, *Essay on the State of Trade*, pp. 204–5; Child, *Discourse of Trade*, pp. 204–5; Bernard Bailyn, *The New England Merchants in the Seventeenth Century* (Cambridge, Mass., 1955); Richard Pares, *Yankees and Creoles: the Trade Between North America and the West Indies before the American Revolution* (London, 1956).

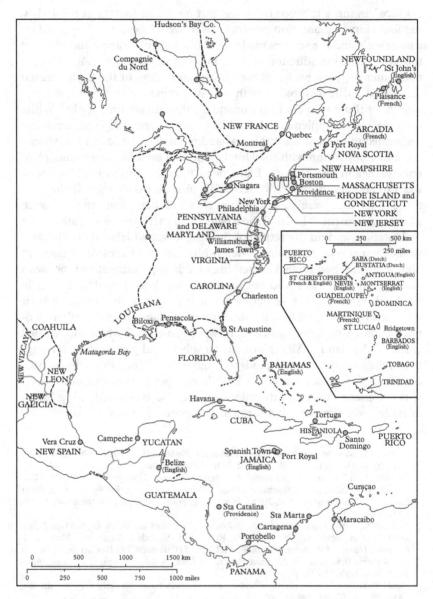

Map 3 English America in the late seventeenth century

re-export; a diversification of manufactured exports away from woollen cloths; and the development of a complex network of multilateral trades in which London merchants played a central coordinating role.[39]

Over the four decades after the Restoration, empire was extended and consolidated, colonial imports and exports expanded to account for almost 20 per cent of overseas commerce, and the 'revolution in trade' took strong root.[40] In the north Atlantic Nova Scotia was surrendered to the French in 1667, but the Newfoundland fishery continued to flourish – although there was rising tension between the migratory fishermen and permanent residents – and steps were taken to put the fur trade on a sound footing in Hudson's Bay with the formation of a chartered company in 1670.[41] On the east coast, New Netherland was seized from the Dutch in 1665, and – largely on account of its strategic importance in sealing the Navigation system – it was retained, presented to the Duke of York, and renamed in his honour.[42] In 1664 a group of courtiers were granted a charter for land in Carolina, and serious settlement began in the 1670s, although it was not until the 1690s, with the introduction of rice, that the region established profitable cash-crop agriculture.[43] Companies were set up to develop the Jerseys and, in 1681, the king settled a debt by granting a large tract of land to the Quaker, William Penn, who lost little time in planting a new colony, Pennsylvania, in which the settlers established a diverse and balanced economy, similar in many ways to that of New England.[44] By 1700 the English had established a strategic advantage over their rivals in the north Atlantic with a narrow strip of continuous settlement along the coast of North America from Maine to South Carolina, which allowed all the colonies easy, and secure, access to cheap sea transport, and encouraged the growth of a buoyant intra-colonial trade as well as providing strategic bases for commerce raiding (Map 3).

In the Caribbean extension was more piecemeal. The proximity to Spanish centres of wealth, and major trade routes, made the stakes higher

---

[39] Davis, 'English foreign trade', 162.
[40] For a survey of regional developments see Nicholas Canny (ed.), *The Oxford History of the British Empire* (Oxford, 1998) 5 vols., vol. I, *The Origins of Empire: British Overseas Enterprise to the Close of the Seventeenth Century*.
[41] Peter E. Pope, *Fish into Wine: the Newfoundland Plantation in the Seventeenth Century* (Chapel Hill, N.C., 2004); E. E. Rich, *The History of the Hudson's Bay Company, 1670–1870* (London, 1958–9).
[42] Cathy Matson, *Merchants and Empire: Trading in Colonial New York* (Baltimore, Md., 1998).
[43] Converse D. Clowse, *Economic Beginnings in Colonial South Carolina, 1670–1730* (Columbia, S.C., 1971); R. C. Nash, 'South Carolina and the Atlantic Economy in the late seventeenth and eighteenth centuries', *EcHR*, 45 (1992), 677–702.
[44] Gary B. Nash, *Quakers and Politics: Pennsylvania, 1681–1726* (Princeton, N.J., 1968); Frederick B. Tolles, *Meeting House and Counting House: the Quaker Merchants of Colonial Philadelphia, 1682–1763* (Chapel Hill, N.C., 1948).

than on the mainland and sugar raised them further.[45] Land was heavily
contested and islands often changed hands. In 1667 England abandoned
its settlement in Surinam to the Dutch (in exchange for New York) and it
was obliged to give way to the French in Tortuga, west of Hispaniola, a loss
lamented as national humiliation and presaging the rise of Santo Domingo
and French competition at the end of the century.[46] English attempts to
settle other small islands, such as Tobago and St Lucia, were rebuffed by
the Dutch, or the French, who were increasingly seen as the main enemy
to English interests.[47] St Christopher was not firmly secured for the
English until 1713 after decades of uneasy coexistence with the French.[48]
Furthermore, the native Americans maintained a continuous campaign of
violence in the eastern Caribbean.[49] However, Cromwell's prize, Jamaica
(which contained ten times the acreage of the other English islands put
together), was retained, despite widespread fears that Charles would return
it to Spain, and gave England a foothold in the heart of the Spanish Indies
which was well positioned for contraband trade and plunder. The island's
security was enhanced by the Treaty of Madrid in 1670, which promised
peace and friendship between England and Spain in America, as well as
allowing that England could retain territory which was already settled.[50]

By 1700 England had planted seventeen colonies in America, alongside
France's eight, and the Dutch Republic's three (Illustration 4). England's
New World lands contained over 100,000 square miles and exceeded its

[45] C. H. Haring, *Trade and Navigation between Spain and the Indies in the Time of the
Hapsburgs* (Cambridge, Mass., 1918); Violet Barbour, 'Privateers and pirates in the
West Indies', *American Historical Review*, 16 (1911), 529–66; Kenneth R. Andrews, *The
Spanish Caribbean: Trade and Plunder, 1530–1630* (New Haven, Conn., 1978); Nuala
Zahedieh, ' "A frugal, hopeful and prudential trade": privateering in Jamaica, 1655–89',
JICH, 18 (1990), 145–68; Letter to Nottingham, March 1689, NLJ, MS 390. Ward
shows plantation profits of 40–50 per cent in the 1650s: J. R. Ward, 'The profitability of
sugar planting in the British West Indies, 1650–1834', *EcHR*, 31 (1978), 197–213.
[46] R. C. Latham and W. Matthews (eds.), *The Diary of Samuel Pepys*, 11 vols. (1970–83),
vol. IX, p. 556. In 1655 Cromwell's expeditionary force (the Western Design) had experienced humiliating defeat at Hispaniola.
[47] By the 1660s, Barbados planters had become heavily reliant on timber supplies from
St Lucia: *CSPC, 1661–8*, no. 1898. By the 1680s they were being dispossessed by the
French: *CSPC, 1685–8*, nos. 540, 541, 603, 871, 923, 1032, 1441, 1516, 1718, 1736,
1830, 1876, 1898; *CSPC, 1699*, nos. 775, 970, 1037, 1087; Paul Butel, 'France, the
Antilles, and Europe in the seventeenth and eighteenth centuries: renewals of foreign
trade', in James D. Tracy (ed.), *The Rise of Merchant Empires: Long Distance Trade in the
Early Modern World*, 1350–1750 (Cambridge, 1990), pp.153–73. On the shift in sentiment see S. Pincus, 'From butterboxes to wooden boxes: the shift in English popular
sentiment from anti-Dutch to anti-French in the 1670s', *HJ*, 28 (1995), 333–61.
[48] Charles S. Higham, *The Development of the Leeward Islands under the Restoration, 1660–
1688: a Study of the Foundations of the Old Colonial System* (Cambridge, 1921).
[49] Hilary McD. Beckles, 'The "Hub of empire": the Caribbean and Britain in the seventeenth century', in Canny (ed.), *Origins of Empire*, pp. 233–4.
[50] A. P. Thornton, *West India Policy under the Restoration* (Oxford, 1956), pp. 39–123.

Table 2.1 *The population of England and English plantations, 1660 and 1700 (thousands)*

		England	Chesapeake	New England	Middle colonies	Lower south	West Indies	Total colonies
1660	white	na	24.0	32.6	4.8	1	47	109.4
	black	na	0.9	0.6	0.6	–	34	36.1
	total	5,141	24.9	33.2	5.4	1	81	145.5
1700	white	na	85.2	90.7	49.9	13.6	33	272.4
	black	na	12.9	1.7	3.7	2.9	115	136.2
	total	5,058	98.1	92.4	53.6	16.5	148	408.5

Sources: Wrigley and Schofield, *The Population History of England, 1541–1871*, pp.528–9; McCusker and Menard, *The Economy of British America, 1607–1789*, pp. 103, 136, 154, 172, 203.

acreage in the Old World (less than 60,000 square miles).[51] Furthermore, although domestic population was falling after 1650, the English used the institutions of indentured servitude and slavery to expand colonial population to reach around 400,000 by 1700 (see Table 2.1), a valuable addition to the domestic market of 5 million or so consumers.[52] Meanwhile, France, with a population approaching 20 million in 1700, and a European land area of 210,000 square miles, had a mere 70,000 colonial subjects, and the tiny Dutch Republic – heavily dependent on immigration to maintain its own population – had fewer than 20,000 settlers in its American plantations.[53] England, and above all London, had made a major, and exceptional, investment in planting New World lands which shaped economic, social, and political developments leading from commercial to industrial revolution.[54]

[51] In 1700 England, Wales and the Channel Islands contained 58,410 square miles; Ireland contained 32,055 square miles; Bermuda and the English West Indies contained 4,909 square miles; and the narrow strip settled by the English along the east coast of North America contained around 95,000 square miles (below a quarter of the current area of the thirteen colonies).

[52] The outflow of young men in the early seventeenth century had left women with reduced opportunities for marriage and contributed to lower fertility rates: Wrigley and Schofield, *Population History of England*, pp. 201, 227–32, 469.

[53] Davies, *North Atlantic World*, p. 85. England's success in peopling its colonies can be partly attributed to its fuller use of indentured servitude. The Dutch were hampered by a small population and their eschewal of the use of bound white labour: Ernst van den Boogaart, 'The servant migration to New Netherland, 1624–64', in P. C. Emmer (ed.), *Colonialism and Migration: Indentured Labour Before and After Slavery* (Dordrecht, 1986), pp. 55–81; Jan de Vries, 'The Dutch Atlantic economies', in Peter A. Coclanis (ed.), *The Atlantic Economy during the Seventeenth and Eighteenth Centuries* (Columbia, S.C., 2005), pp. 1–29.

[54] Davies, *North Atlantic World*, pp. 313–15. Defoe discusses England's head start in colonial expansion and France and Holland's backwardness in settlement: Defoe, *Plan of Commerce*, pp. 105–7.

Illustration 4 Map of North America, *c.* 1712. Herman Moll, NMM.

The institutional framework of England's
Atlantic system

By the mid-seventeenth century it was apparent that empire would deliver both profit and power. England's political classes united to assert that it 'was a matter of exact justice' that any benefits to shipping, trade, and entrepot activity should be reserved for the mother country which had provided the initial start-up labour and capital needed for colonization and continued to supply defence. England should stand like the 'sun in the midst of its plantations' and needed strict laws to prevent the benefits being syphoned off by foreigners, above all the Dutch.[55] The Republic's success in obtaining wealth and independence from Spain had shown how trade and shipping could allow even a small territory to achieve power, and it provoked fear, envy, and emulation.[56] Dutch designs 'to lay a foundation to themselves for engrossing the Universal trade, not only of Christendom, but indeed of the greater part of the known world' became a central theme of seventeenth-century commercial discourse.[57] By the mid-seventeenth century, the Republic's combined merchant, fishing, and naval tonnage was more than double that of England and Dutch commercial domination was seen to depend on 'the great number of shipping they have constantly built'.[58] Furthermore, they had exploited their large carrying capacity to take advantage of England's troubles during the Civil War and established a strong foothold in the Chesapeake tobacco

[55] Cary, *State of Trade*, p. 70; Child, *Discourse of Trade*, pp. 6, 164; Whitworth (ed.), *Works of D'Avenant*, vol. II, pp. 24, 397; Clarendon quoted in G. L. Beer, *The Old Colonial System, 1660–1754*, 2 vols. (New York, 1912), vol. I, p. 8.

[56] Benjamin Worsley, *The Advocate: or, a Narrative of the State and Condition of Things between the English and Dutch Nation, in Relation to Trade* (London, 1651). For an account of Anglo-Dutch rivalry see Charles Wilson, *Profit and Power* (London, 1957); David Ormrod, *The Rise of Commercial Empires: England and the Netherlands in the Age of Mercantilism, 1650–1770* (Cambridge, 2003). For a recent survey of the social, economic, and cultural history of the Dutch Golden Age see Maarten Prak, *The Dutch Republic in the Seventeenth Century* (Cambridge, 2005).

[57] Worsley, *The Advocate*, p. 76. Violet L. Barbour, 'Dutch and English merchant shipping in the seventeenth century', *EcHR*, 2 (1930), 261–90.

[58] *The Advocate*, p. 77. Davis, estimated that England's combined overseas and coastal tonnage was 150,000 tons in 1640, 200,000 tons in 1660, and 340,000 tons in 1686. Estimates of Dutch tonnage suggest figures between 450,000 and 550,000 tons in the mid-century with later decline: Davis, *Shipping Industry*, pp. 1–21; Richard W. Unger, 'The tonnage of Europe's merchant fleets', *The American Neptune*, 52 (1992), 247–61; Jan de Vries and Ad van der Woude, *The First Modern Economy: Success, Failure, and Perseverance of the Dutch Economy, 1500–1815* (Cambridge, 1997), pp. 296–300. According to Jan Luyten van Zanden the gap was even wider but his figure for England excludes coastal shipping: 'Early modern economic growth: a survey of the European economy, 1500–1800', in Maarten Prak (ed.), *Early Modern Capitalism: Economic and Social Change in Europe, 1400–1800* (London, 2001), p. 82.

trade.[59] They also played a role in Barbados's conversion to sugar cultivation, and large-scale use of slave labour, although, as Russell Menard
has recently emphasized, their contribution was less important than
is often claimed.[60] The Dutch were seen to be 'masters of the field in
trade' and it was generally believed that unless they were excluded
'they will carry away the greatest of advantage by the plantations of all
the princes in Christendom, leaving us and others only the trouble of
breeding men and sending them abroad to cultivate the ground and
have bread for their industry'.[61]

The Commonwealth responded to the Dutch threat with the Navigation
Act of 1651.[62] However, in attempting to exclude all Dutch shipping from
all English foreign trade, the ordinance was 'staggeringly ambitious' and
proved impossible to enforce.[63] Any opportunity to make improvements
was delayed as the Act helped to precipitate war with the Dutch between
1652 and 1654, and was followed by war with Spain between 1655 and
1660, during which time the legislation was suspended.[64] Real refine-
ment was made at the Restoration when the king and Parliament combined to take measures to ensure that the plantations profited the mother
country rather than foreigners by re-enacting Cromwell's regulation.

The Act of 1660 required that all goods taken to, and from, the colonies should be carried in English or colonial ships; masters and three-
quarters of the crew were to be English or colonial subjects. A list of

[59] John R. Pagan, 'Dutch maritime and commercial activity in mid-seventeenth century
Virginia', *VMHB*, 90 (1982), 485–501; Brenner, *Merchants and Revolution*, pp. 586–98;
Leng, *Benjamin Worsley*, pp. 55–60; Claudia Schnurmann, 'Atlantic trade and American
identities: the correlations of supranational commerce, political opposition, and colonial
regionalism', in Coclanis (ed.), *The Atlantic Economy*, pp. 186–204.

[60] Brenner, *Merchants and Revolution*, pp. 586–98; P. C. Emmer, ' "Jesus Christ was good,
but trade was better": an overview of the transit trade of the Dutch Antilles, 1634–1795',
in Robert L. Paquette and Stanley L. Engerman (eds.), *The Lesser Antilles in the Age of
European Expansion* (Gainesville, Fla., 1996), pp. 206–22; J. M. Postma, *The Dutch in
the Atlantic Slave Trade, 1600–1815* (Cambridge, 1990); de Vries, 'Dutch Atlantic economies'; Menard, *Sweet Negotiations*, pp. 49–66; John J. McCusker and Russell R. Menard,
'The sugar industry in the seventeenth century: a new perspective on the Barbadian
"Sugar Revolution"', in Stuart B. Schwartz (ed.), *Tropical Babylons: Sugar and the
Making of the Atlantic World, 1450–1680* (Chapel Hill, N.C., 2004), pp. 289–330.

[61] Child, *A New Discourse of Trade*, p. 94.

[62] For an account of the political circumstances surrounding the 1651 Act see J. E. Farnell,
'The Navigation Act of 1651, the first Dutch war, and the London merchant commu-
nity', *EcHR*, 16 (1961–2), 439–54; Brenner, *Merchants and Revolution*, pp. 577–632;
Leng, *Benjamin Worsley*, pp. 73–9.

[63] Ormrod, *Commercial Empires*, p. 32.

[64] The first Dutch war did allow England to capture between 1,000 and 1,700 Dutch ships
although many were lost in the war with Spain: Davis, *Shipping Industry*, pp. 12–13,
50–2; R. Baetens, 'The organization and effects of Flemish privateering in the seventeenth century', *Acta Historiae Neerlandicae*, 9 (1976), 561–96.

colonial-produced commodities including cotton, dye-woods, ginger, indigo, sugar, and tobacco, were 'enumerated' and were to be exported to no place other than England, or an English possession. In so far as the Act could be enforced, it eliminated the Dutch, and other foreigners (including the Irish and Scots) from England's colonial trade. Fiscal policy was used to strengthen the programme. Colonists were compensated for the trade restrictions by being given very substantial preference in the domestic market with heavy duties on foreign tobacco and sugar. Differential duties were further used to encourage planters to export semi-processed muscovado, which had much greater bulk than refined sugar, and maximized demand for shipping as well as encouraging a new industry at home. Finally, a provision that duties should be almost entirely refunded on re-exported goods, so that they would not be placed at a competitive disadvantage in European markets, reflects the scale of the legislators' ambitions. The programme for national enrichment went well beyond mere revenue-raising considerations and aspired to make London, rather than Amsterdam, the leading emporium in Europe.

The Staple Act of 1663 further bolstered England's entrepot function. All European goods intended for sale in English colonies were to be laden in England or Wales and carried directly to the colonies, with some strategic exceptions: salt for the Newfoundland fisheries; wine from Madeira and the Azores; and servants, horses, and provisions from Scotland and Ireland. An Act of 1673 placed duties on goods sent from one colony to another to prevent colonists (and New Englanders, in particular) being able to undercut English merchants if they engaged in illicit trade and took enumerated goods direct to Europe. It also provided for the appointment of Naval Officers in colonial ports to improve enforcement procedures. After widespread, and openly acknowledged, evasion during the 1690s, when merchant shipping was diverted into wartime uses, an Act of 1696 confirmed and codified the legislation which remained intact until 1849.[65]

Contemporaries widely claimed that the Acts were responsible for the rapid increase in colonial trade and the merchant fleet after the Restoration. 'In relation to trade, shipping, profit, and power it [the Navigation Act] is one of the choicest and most prudent acts that ever was made in England, and without it we had not now been owners of

---

[65] Lawrence A. Harper, *The English Navigation Laws: a Seventeenth Century Experiment in Social Engineering* (New York, 1939); G. L. Beer, *The Origins of the British Colonial System, 1578–1660* (New York, 1908); Beer, *Old Colonial System*; Davis, *Shipping Industry*, pp. 305–14. On evasion during the war see Davenant, *Discourse of Plantations*, in Whitworth (ed.), *Works of D'Avenant*, pp. 396–9; Beeston to Lords of Trade, 5 April 1694, PRO CO 138/7, fo. 191.

half of the shipping, nor trade, nor employed half of the seamen which we do at present'.[66] No doubt the legislation did help to divert colonial commerce into new channels, but it cannot alone explain the increased use of English services, as the state had limited capacity to enforce the laws. Shipmasters were required to give substantial bonds (£1,000 or £2,000 depending on the tonnage of the ship) that they would carry any enumerated commodities to a legal destination and they were not formally released until they produced a certificate of compliance; but even in London which, as headquarters of the customs service, was more closely monitored than other places, merchants made frequent reference to 'feeing' the officers and it was a simple matter to make a false entry, as shown in William Freeman's detailed accounts of illegal trading in the late 1670s.[67]

In the colonies scrutiny was more lax than in England. At first the task of enforcing the Navigation Acts was left to colonial governors, who were drawn from the local elites, and had neither capacity nor desire to police legislation which raised their own costs. In an attempt to improve enforcement, Naval Officers were appointed after 1673 to monitor entries and clearances in colonial ports, and check the bonds designed to ensure compliance with the Acts; but these officers were not sufficiently well paid to be independent of local interests, and their presence was not strongly felt. In 1699 Bellomont, the governor of New York, complained that the 'business of a Naval Officer employs a man's whole time and 'tis somewhat difficult and intricate to perform it well. [but the fees] will amount to £40 per annum'. At this rate, he claimed that he could not find anyone willing to fill the place who was both honest and able to provide security but nor could he raise the remuneration because 'the people here are all envious of such an officer whose business is to watch the trade and curtail the fees to discourage them'.[68] Of course, New York posed particular enforcement difficulties as the strong Dutch community which survived even after final cession of the colony in 1673 maintained active trading links with Amsterdam and Curaçao; but the system of bonds, central to enforcement of the Acts, was weakly administered throughout the empire.[69] In 1681 Dutton, the governor of

---

[66] Child, *A New Discourse of Trade*, p. 91.
[67] David Hancock (ed.), *The Letters of William Freeman, London Merchant, 1678–1685* (London, 2002), pp. 168–9, 111–13; Marion Balderston (ed.), *James Claypoole's Letterbook, London and Philadelphia, 1681–84* (San Marino, Calif., 1967), p. 212.
[68] Bellomont to Lords of Trade and Plantations, 24 October 1699, *CSPC, 1699*, no. 890.
[69] Court records provide evidence; for example, a mariner described a voyage of 1683 in a New York-owned ship from Amsterdam to Guinea and then to Barbados with gold and slaves and back to New York: 'Deposition of William Baker', 1686, CLRO, MCD, box 40;

Barbados, reported that no ship had entered the required bonds since 1666, 'to Your Majestie's great prejudice and encouragement of fraud' and in 1683 the governor was admonished for the disarray of the system in this valuable island. 'It appears that there are upwards of 2,000 bonds delivered to you and your predecessors in Barbados by masters of vessels and that on these bonds there is a sum of over £200,000 uncertified for'.[70] When goods were scarce, or freight was dear, the islanders and their mainland counterparts could turn to foreigners with little risk of punishment from colonial governments. When outsiders attempted to tighten procedures, they were easily thwarted by entrenched local interests.

Land-based enforcement officers were supplemented by the Royal Navy which was charged with policing the seas; but in the seventeenth century it managed only scant service in the Atlantic. In 1655 the leaders of the large expeditionary force involved in Cromwell's Western Design seized sixteen Dutch vessels at Barbados, but such a squadron was exceptional.[71] There was no regular presence in North America and a patchy peacetime presence in the Caribbean.[72] Naval captains who did serve in colonial waters had a strong incentive to police the legislation as they were allowed half the proceeds of ships seized on the open sea, and a third of those taken in port, but, as with other officers of empire, they experienced difficulties in face of local opposition. Captain George St Loe, stationed at the Leeward Islands in the 1680s, described how colonists used St Eustatia, the nearby Dutch island, as a warehouse for well-organized illicit commerce with Europe.[73] However, St Loe was under command of the local governor, Sir James Russell, who was clearly colluding with illegal traders and thwarted St Loe's efforts at suppression at every turn.[74]

There were numerous channels for illicit commerce. There was no register of ships and it was easy to disguise a vessel's provenance, especially

Matson, *Merchants and Empire*, pp. 13–91; Schnurmann, 'Atlantic trade and American identities', in Coclanis (ed.), *Atlantic Economy*, pp. 186–204; April Lee Hatfield, 'Dutch and New Netherland merchants in the seventeenth-century English Chesapeake', in Coclanis (ed.), *Atlantic Economy*, pp. 205–28.

[70] Dutton to king, 7 September 1681, PRO CO1/47, fo.133; Lords of Trade to Governor of Barbados, 21 November 1683, PRO CO 1/53, fo. 176

[71] 'Whistler's Voyage to the West Indies', BL Sl. MS 3,926, fo. 8.

[72] I. R. Matthew, 'The role of the Royal Navy in the English Atlantic empire, 1660–1720', unpublished doctoral thesis, University of Oxford (1995).

[73] 'Letter from Mr Guy to Mr Blathwayt with a report upon the Dutch trading at the Leeward Islands', 7 June 1687, PRO CO 153/3, fo. 263.

[74] 'Petition of Capt St Loe touching ship *Good Intention* and petition of John Kirwan', PRO CO 153/3, fo. 266. For an account of the seizure of the *Good Intention*, see PRO HCA 13/27 24/122; *CSPC, 1685–8*, nos. 1,111, 1,136, 1,232, 1,281, 1,288, 1,293, 1,303, 1,312, 1,313, 1,350, 1,356.

in the colonies where foreign ships were routinely made 'free' to trade within the English system.[75] Goods could be picked up on the continent and taken direct to the plantations – as in a private design organized by William Baxter and William Freeman – without expensive precautions or much risk of seizure.[76] Larger ships stood outside port to unload and smaller vessels could put into a quiet creek or harbour.[77] It was notoriously easy to transport enumerated goods direct to foreign markets using the 'very fine expedient' of covering them with legal cargoes of fish or flour which were not enumerated.[78] Finally, if English shipping was scarce or expensive in the colonies, it was not difficult to trade with foreign captains outside the main harbours, or through one of the empire's many 'back doors' such as Curaçao, St Eustatia, Newfoundland, or New York.[79] Although only fragmentary records survive from the early colonial admiralty courts official correspondence does mention a small number of seizures; but most were motivated by an official's desire to make a profit or used to constrain commercial competition between Englishmen rather than against foreigners.[80] Surviving records of illegal ventures, such as those relating to Baxter and Freeman's design, show that captains, crews, planters, colonial officials, and a number of reputable merchants were all linked in webs of complicity; there was widespread toleration of illegal activity (even among Londoners who had most to gain from the system) and evasion of the Acts carried low risks and costs.

The evidence of widespread compliance with the Acts displayed in the recorded increase in England's Atlantic trade and shipping in the Restoration period, despite the undoubted weakness of the enforcement machinery, suggests that adherence was not as burdensome as many

---

[75] Molesworth reported that the *Swallow* 'was a ship had past the ceremonys of being made free according to the practice of the place ever since my remembrance' and subsequent discussion by the Lords of Trade revealed sloppy procedures and corruption on the part of governors: Molesworth to Blathwayt, 17 December 1686, PRO CO 138/5, fo. 328; Lords of Trade, 6 May 1687, PRO CO 138/6, fos. 4, 9; Molesworth to Lords of Trade, 17 April 1687, *ibid.*, fos. 31–2.

[76] William Freeman to Robert Helmes, 19 September 1678, 'Letterbook of William Freeman', NLJ, MS 134.

[77] Halls to Brailsford, 13, 14 March, 21 May 1689, PRO C 110/152; Hancock (ed.), *Letters of William Freeman*, pp. 111, 169–70.

[78] See for example the 'Case of the *Olive Branch*', BL Add. MS 29,800, fo. 758; 'Case of ships loading the enumerated commodityes in the colonies without giving bond', 5 January 1688, PRO CO 138/6, fos. 12–20.

[79] 'Letter from Mr Guy to Mr Blathwayt with a report upon the Dutch trading at the Leeward islands', 7 June 1687, PRO CO 153/3, fo. 263; Wim Klooster, *Illicit Riches: Dutch Trade in the Caribbean, 1648–1795* (Leiden, 1998), pp. 89–91; Matson, *Merchants and Empire*, pp. 13–91; Pope, *Fish into Wine*, pp. 360–81.

[80] H. J. Crump, *Colonial Admiralty Jurisdiction in the Seventeenth Century* (London, 1931); Mathew Meverill to Lords of Trade, 9 May 1681, PRO CO 138/4, fos. 262–3.

contemporaries, and later historians, came to suggest. If the price of English goods and services had been substantially higher than that of their foreign rivals, then the cost of compliance would have been heavy, and the legislation would have been largely ignored – as it certainly was during the 1690s when large numbers of English ships and seamen were diverted away from trade into wartime uses.[81] Despite initial warnings of dire disaster if the colonies were denied the 'liberty' to trade with whom they pleased, colonial complaints about the Acts faded away as English merchants and shippers responded well to the challenge provided by the legislation of the 1660s and were, at least in peacetime, increasingly able to offer services at a price which matched that of their competitors.[82] It was as a result of improved performance, as much as protectionist policies, that England – and above all London – fulfilled national hopes and came to stand 'like the sun in the midst of its plantations'.[83]

Within the walls of the national monopoly provided by the Navigation Acts, England's colonial trade was largely open, or 'free', to all subjects as traditional measures to restrict competition did not take hold.[84] Merchants had long used corporate organization to raise large capital sums, share sunk costs such as forts and garrisons, and obtain privileges which allowed them to restrict entry and maintain large profits with which they could furnish their patron with loans and gifts; Crown and merchants colluded to secure monopoly rents.[85] In this tradition, between 1607 and 1689, London merchants set up at least fifteen companies to engage in Atlantic trade and colonization, and as late as 1687, a group was lobbying for a West India Company with a monopoly of the sugar trade while another sought monopoly privileges in exploiting the timber and mineral resources in the northern colonies.[86] However, company organization did not flourish in colonial trade.

---

[81] Beeston to Lords of Trade, 5 April 1694, PRO CO 138/7, fo. 191; 9 December 1687, CO 138/9, fo. 184; de Vries, 'Dutch Atlantic economies', pp. 6–10.

[82] Sir William Berkeley, 'A discourse and view of Virginia', 1662, BL Egerton MS 2,395, fo. 354; Schnurmann, 'Atlantic trade and American identities', p. 190.

[83] Cary, An Essay on Trade, p. 70.

[84] For a contemporary discussion of this 'free trade' see 'Advantages of trading with our plantations', BLO, MS Rawl. A 478, fo. 67–67b.

[85] 'Companies of merchants', BLO, MS Locke c30, fo. 109.

[86] Scott's enquiry revealed that thirty-one important companies were formed in England before 1680: ten for long-distance trade; nine for colonization; three for fisheries; three for the introduction of new metallurgical industries; two for mining; four for water supply; two for drainage; two for colonization in Ulster; one for insurance, Scott, Joint-Stock Companies; 'Address to the king as to the West India Company', Minutes of Council of Nevis, 28 August 1688, PRO CO 155/1, fos. 172–83; Dalby Thomas, An Historical Account of the Rise and Growth of the West India Colonies and the Great Advantage they are to England in Respect of Trade (1690), Dedication and pp. 48–9; BL Sl. MS 3,984, fo. 210; Bernard Bailyn, The New England Merchants in the Seventeenth Century (Cambridge,

Colonial commerce depended on financing, and settling, permanent export producing plantations as well as carrying commodities and, as stressed by Brenner, 'old [corporate] forms [of organization] were inappropriate'.[87] The London merchants who financed the Virginia Company on traditional lines proved unwilling to risk the very large sums needed to furnish long-term investment in production and were also unable to monitor their agents. The success of England's colonial project largely rested on individuals who risked their lives in crossing the Atlantic in response to the opportunities offered by American land abundance and, once they were established, it was impossible to force them to buy and sell to a monopoly company.[88] Corporate organization survived longer in sectors of Atlantic commerce concerned with trade alone – notably the fur and slave trades; however, large, cumbersome companies found it difficult to compete with small, flexible, more closely managed operations and, in all spheres of colonial commerce, the independent traders (legal or illegal) outperformed the giants.[89]

Far from degenerating into anarchy, and withering away, as predicted by advocates of corporate trading, the open colonial trades flourished and, along with the successful Spanish and Portuguese trades, established the viability of what contemporaries labelled 'free trade'. As Josiah Child, Tory director of the East India Company, was forced to admit 'we have declined more, or at least have increased less, in those trades limited to companies than in others where all His Majesty's subjects have had equal freedom to trade'.[90] Where for diplomatic or defence reasons company organization might be justified – as in the African trade – there was a growing consensus that access should be open to all Englishmen who would contribute to costs by payment of a small fine or purchase of shares.[91] A pamphleteer of 1645 used simple metaphors: 'Nothing [is] more pernicious and destructive to any kingdom or commonwealth than monopolies.

Mass., 1955), p. 133; Viola F. Barnes, 'Richard Wharton, a seventeenth century New England colonial', *PCSM*, 26 (1924–6), 258–70.

[87] Brenner, *Merchants and Revolution*, pp. 93–4; Davies, *North Atlantic World*, pp. 314–15.

[88] For a summary of the difficulties of establishing a new settlement see David W. Galenson, 'The settlement and growth of colonies: population, labour, and economic development', in Stanley L. Engerman and Robert E. Gallman (eds.), *The Cambridge Economic History of the USA*, vol. I, *The Colonial Era* (Cambridge, 1996), pp. 135–41; Wesley Frank Craven, *Dissolution of the Virginia Company: the Failure of a Colonial Experiment* (New York, 1932); Morgan, *American Slavery, American Freedom*.

[89] For recent discussion of this issue see S. R. H. Jones, 'Efficient transactors or rent seeking monopolists? The rationale for early chartered trading companies', *JEH*, 56 (1996), 898–915; Ann Carlos and Stephen Nicholas, 'Joint stock chartered trading companies', *JEH*, 56 (1996) 916–25.

[90] Child, *A New Discourse of Trade*, p. 8.

[91] 'Companies of Merchants', BLO MS Locke c30, fo. 109.

Trade ... is like dung which being kept close in a heap or two stinks, but being spread abroad it doth fertilize the earth and make it fructible.'[92]

Much of the writing on trade had a political edge as corporate organization and monopoly were linked, in opposition minds, with Crown corruption. However, an increasingly subtle and sophisticated consensus was being forged and found eloquent expression after the Restoration.[93] A rich cross-fertilization of ideas drawn from simultaneous developments in the understanding of mathematics, the mechanical workings of the universe, and the functioning of the human body (most notably the discovery of the circulation of blood) is apparent in the language, metaphor, and method used by leading writers such as Mun, Petty, Child, Barbon, North, Martyn, and Davenant to create models of the economy which, as Joyce Appleby has shown, have proved decisive for all subsequent thinking about economic relations.[94] The world of trade was invested with its own self-sustaining mechanism: a complex mechanical system with springs, balances, and interchangeable parts. It was, in some sense natural, and operated without political direction, but could be manipulated to some extent if care was taken to understand the structure, and measure the parts, and this need underpinned contemporary interest in political arithmetic.[95] However, even with careful empirical observation and measurement, the scope for intervention was limited as the sensitive system could easily be destroyed. Davenant warned that 'all new fancies and advises pretending to limit or direct [trade's] course prove generally pernicious to it. One branch may seem prejudicial but to lop it off may kill another which by secret fibres had relation to it.' Too much interference in the laws of supply and demand could be damaging for he added 'trade is in its nature free ... [it] finds its own channels, and best directs its own course and all laws to give it rules and directives ... may serve

[92] T. Johnson, *A Discourse Consisting of Motives for the Enlargement and Freedome of Trade* (London, 1645), pp. 4, 25.
[93] Hutchison suggests that 'it might indeed reasonably be held that at no other period have English writers been so outstandingly in the lead on the subject of trade, political economy and economics as between 1662 and 1700': Terence Hutchison, *Before Adam Smith: the Emergence of Political Economy, 1662–1776* (Cambridge, 1988), pp. 6–7, 12–13, 27–86.
[94] The three great collections of seventeenth-century English economic publications are at the British Library, the Goldsmith's Library in London, and the Kress Library of Business and Economics at the Harvard Business School. For discussion of the literature see Joyce Oldham Appleby, *Economic Thought and Ideology in Seventeenth Century England* (Princeton, 1978); Lars Magnusson, *Mercantilism: the Shaping of an Economic Language* (London, 1994); Hutchinson, *Before Adam Smith*; Thomas Leng, 'Commercial conflict and regulation in the discourse of trade in seventeenth century England', *HJ*, 48 (2005), 933–54.
[95] Magnusson, *Mercantilism*, pp. 116–46.

the particular ends of private men but are seldom advantageous to the public'.[96] Although light regulation of trade might be necessary to constrain private greed it was increasingly seen as best left to an overarching central authority rather than companies of interested merchants.[97]

As both practical and ideological conditions undermined company organization in colonial trade it remained largely open, or 'free', to all citizens of empire and participants were exposed to heavy competition which not only promoted efforts to reap efficiency gains, but also encouraged interested parties to vie for control of the institutions which could be used to manage economic activity, secure access to the most profitable opportunities, and reduce risk. Crown, Parliament, and colonial governments all laid claim to rights to control regulation, and direct income streams but, in the Restoration period, their respective legitimacy was still contested and rent-seeking enterprises were of uncertain title until the political settlement which followed the Glorious Revolution consolidated power in the hands of Parliament and the transatlantic trading elite – Brenner's merchant-councillor interest.[98]

Although the early Stuarts had shown little interest in overseas expansion, the restored king pursued the same 'attentive, aggressive approach to commercial policy' that has been widely identified as the 'most characteristic feature of Cromwell's rule'.[99] Parliament voted the customs to Charles for life, and the revenues (of which colonial trade made up a larger proportion than suggested by its share of the total value of trade) were to account for between 30 and 40 per cent of his income; but the king clearly hoped that the new lands in America would offer more than tariffs alone to compensate for the substantial loss of Crown estates in England and reduce his dependence on Parliament.[100] After years of exile, and an uncertain future, Charles and his followers shared an opportunism and adventurous spirit that attracted them

[96] Charles D'Avenant, 'An essay on the East India trade', in Whitworth (ed.), *Works of D'Avenant*, vol. I, p. 98.
[97] 'Advantages of dealing with our plantations', BLO, MS Rawl. A 478, fos. 68–71b.
[98] Economic rent is defined as a surplus earned by any factor of production over and above the minimum price at which that factor would be supplied: see above, p. 14. The concept of rent-seeking was introduced to economics by Tullock: see G. Tullock, 'The welfare costs of tariffs, monopolies, and theft', *Western Economic Journal* (1967), 224–32. For discussion of institutional change and control of the supply of regulation in early modern England in a rent-seeking framework see Robert B. Ekulund and Robert D. Tollinson, *Mercantilism as a Rent-Seeking Society: Economic Regulation in Historical Perspective* (College Station, Tex., 1981); Robert B. Ekulund and Robert D. Tollinson, *Politicized Economies: Monopoly, Monarchy, and Mercantilism* (College Station, Tex., 1997).
[99] Brenner, *Merchants and Revolution*, p. 542.
[100] A major weakness of the Restoration settlement was in the financial detail that left the Crown short of money: J. R. Jones, *Country and Court: England 1658–1714* (London,

to the imperial project: the king, James, Duke of York, Prince Rupert, and Edward Hyde, Lord Clarendon, joined Ashley Cooper (later Lord Shaftsbury), George Monck, the Duke of Albemarle, and other survivors from the Interregnum in enthusiastic support of expansion.[101] They helped to extend England's frontier (Jamaica was retained and Carolina was chartered in the first years of the Restoration), acquired colonial land, invested in privateering, the slave trade, and colonial joint-stock companies and, in all cases, hoped to use the political levers of power to extract a profit.

The Crown's main instrument of power was the royal prerogative which it claimed, as late as 1685, gave it the 'undoubted' right to 'license, limit, and regulate foreign trade'.[102] However, its value had been reduced by the behaviour of the early Stuarts and their willingness to renege on promises, which had eroded trust in the Crown. Charles I's brazen use of monopoly patents and charters to finance his personal rule and dispense with Parliament played a major part in the constitutional and legal arguments which, alongside religion, led to civil war. The struggle between Crown and Parliament was presented in terms of a contest between the royal prerogative backed by the king's courts and statute backed by the common law; between the Crown's right to regulate trade and manufacture and the common law doctrine that every man should have liberty to practise his own trade without restraint; between the Crown's undoubted need for revenue to pursue national aims and Parliament's claim to the sole right to levy taxation and render every man's property secure from Crown encroachment. In this political context the common law courts evolved a doctrine that held that royal monopoly and prerogative were illegal while the special interests sanctioned by Parliament were legitimate. The king's courts naturally disagreed and under these conditions there was, in effect, no legal basis for enforcing a universally valid monopoly right.[103]

1978), pp. 44–70; C. D. Chandaman, *The English Public Revenue, 1660–1688* (Oxford, 1975), pp. 9–36. Pepys observed that the king and his brother were concerned to 'lay up a hidden treasure of money … against a bad day' and clearly perceived empire as a promising source of funds: Latham and Matthews (eds.), *Diary of Samuel Pepys*, vol. V, p. 21.

[101] BLO, MS Clarendon 71, 72; PRO, Shaftsbury Papers, 30/24/49; John Callow, *The Making of James II: the Formative Years of a Fallen King* (Stroud, Gloucs., 2000); Charles M. Andrews, *British Committees, Commissions and Councils of Trade and Plantations 1622–75* (Baltimore, Md., 1908), p. 65; Thornton, *West India Policy*.

[102] *A Proclamation to Prohibit His Majesty's Subjects to Trade within the Limits Assigned to the Royal African Company of England except those of the Company* (London, 1685); Gauci, *Politics of Trade*, p. 180.

[103] Jennifer Carter, 'Law, Courts and Constitution', in J. R. Jones (ed.), *The Restored Monarchy* (London, 1979), pp. 71–93.

The issues were far from resolved at the Restoration, and although the prerogative rights were reduced, and the Star Chamber was abolished, Charles II did all he could to exploit his remaining powers and use them to promote his colonial revenues. Alongside his support for the Navigation Acts – which were expected to provide improved customs receipts – he issued a number of licences and patents designed to allow the Crown to profit from expanding colonial trade, including the grant of a Crown chartered monopoly to the Royal African Company, set up under his brother's leadership in 1660, with substantial backing from the king, other members of the royal family, and the court.[104]

As no regulations could be enforced without support in the colonies the king took steps to tighten his control over imperial government at the expense of vested interests. Early English settlers had been able to design political institutions with little outside interference and, by the Restoration, a template was in place in the Crown colonies which, with minor variations, became the norm in English America.[105] A governor, usually chosen from the local elite, with a council filled with his own appointees or 'creatures', exerted executive authority and also controlled the judiciary.[106] The power was balanced by an assembly elected on a narrow franchise which, in the style of the House of Commons, controlled money bills, including payment of the governor's salary. Ownership of these institutions was closely confined to a small group of substantial property holders who saw their constitutions 'as much [their] property as was the soil' and their value was enhanced by strong personal connections, and effective lobby groups, in the metropolis.[107] A transatlantic merchant-planter elite – or merchant-councillor interest – could enforce

---

[104] G. F. Zook, *The Company of Royal Adventurers Trading into Africa* (Lancaster, Penn., 1919); Davies, *Royal African Company*, pp. 41–3.

[105] Jack P. Greene, *Peripheries and Centre: Constitutional Development in the Extended Polities of the British Empire and the United States, 1607–1780* (Athens, Ga., 1986), pp. 7–42.

[106] The governors filled 'all places of trust and profit' with their own 'creatures' which was the 'infallible way of binding [them] to good behaviour': 'The Present State of Virginia', October 1697, PRO CO 5/1,309, fos. 94–98b. On the value of the governor's patronage see Cary Helyar to brother, 10 September 1671, Walker SRO, Heneage MSS DD/WHh 1089.

[107] *The Case of William Penn Esq. As to the Proprietary Government of Pennsylvania* (London, 1701). Dunn's analysis of the census of Barbados taken in 1680 shows that 175 big planters with over sixty slaves constituted 7 per cent of property owners but owned 54 per cent of the land and maintained an even tighter grip on high office accounting for ten out of twelve councillors, twenty out of twenty-two assemblymen, and nineteen out of twenty-three judges: Dunn, *Sugar and Slaves*, pp. 96–103. A similar situation was found in Virginia; see Bernard Bailyn, 'Politics and social structure in Virginia', in James Morton Smith (ed.), *Seventeenth-Century America: Essays in Colonial History* (Chapel Hill, N.C., 1959), pp. 90–115; Antony S. Parent, *Foul Means: the Formation of a Slave Society in Virginia, 1660–1740* (Chapel Hill, N.C., 2003). As Henry Morgan complained, without the 'care and watchfulness' of friends at home, colonial officials

regulation, distribute land, timber, and other resources, and allocate commercial opportunities and so capture a large share of the profits of colonial commerce at the expense of both Crown and smaller planters and merchants.[108] In an attempt to undermine merchant-councillor power, Charles set up councils for trade and plantations – on a continental model used by the Commonwealth in 1650 – and also moved to reduce and regulate the colonial proprietors; in 1663, he brought Barbados and the Leeward Islands under Crown control, alongside Virginia and Jamaica, so that all the most valuable parts of the empire were now under direct state supervision.[109] However, in a decade of war (in which the Dutch destroyed the Royal African Company's forts), plague, fire, and financial crisis, the Crown was unable to pose a real threat to the colonial elites and their grip on plantation government.

Signs of true trouble for colonial vested interests became increasingly apparent after 1670 with the formation of the monopoly Hudson's Bay Company; an abortive Crown attempt to persuade Parliament to impose punishing duties on sugar and tobacco in 1671; a new Committee of Trade and Plantations in 1672; a new Royal African Company chartered in 1672; and a new tougher Navigation Act in 1673 which aimed to improve enforcement procedures with the appointment of Naval Officers in the colonies. However, colonists remained neglectful of imperial regulations and Randolph, sent to New England as collector, surveyor, and searcher of the customs, claimed that pervasive flouting of the Navigation Acts allowed the region to cheat the Crown of £100,000 per year – enough to finance the peacetime navy.[110] After the third Dutch war ended in 1675, the king, with a new committee of the Privy Council, with executive, as well as advisory powers, spearheaded what Steele has

in remote places could find themselves 'falsely scandalized' by a 'malicious confederacy': Henry Morgan to Jenkins, 9 April 1681, 13 June 1681, PRO CO 138/3, fo. 480; Lillian M. Penson, *The Colonial Agents of the British West Indies* (London, 1924); Alison G. Olson, *Making the Empire Work: London and American Interest Groups, 1690–1790* (Cambridge, Mass., 1992).

[108] J. M. Sosin, *English America and the Restoration Monarchy of Charles II: Transatlantic Politics, Commerce and Kinship* (Lincoln, Nebr., 1980), pp. 31, 79, 151, 157; Zahedieh, 'Regulation, rent-seeking and the Glorious Revolution'. The letterbook of William Freeman, merchant, absentee planter, agent for the Leeward Islands and partner of William Baxter (one of the big colonial merchants of 1686) reveals how metropolitan, and colonial, governing elites colluded in manipulating regulation in the Atlantic economy in their mutual interests. For example see the details of a contraband venture in 1678: William Freeman to Robert Helmes, 19 September 1678, NLJ MS 134.

[109] Andrews, *British Committees*; Thornton, *West India Policy*, pp. 1–21, 22–66, 68–123; Sosin, *English America and the Restoration Monarchy*, pp. 40–1.

[110] On Randolph's attempts to prosecute abuses of the Acts see PRO CO 1/46, fos. 1, 3, 60, 142, 243, 250, 258; M. G. Hall, *Edward Randolph and the American Colonies, 1676–1703* (Chapel Hill, N.C., 1960), p. 35; W. A. Speck, 'The international and imperial context',

described as a 'unique and formative' monarchical drive to obtain 'order and control' that was designed to improve the enforcement of regulation and raise the extraction rate.[111] This brought the Crown into headlong conflict with the colonial elites and their metropolitan associates.

The office of governor, previously left to local magnates such as Willoughby in Barbados, Modyford and Lynch in Jamaica, and Berkeley in Virginia, was seen as the key tool in promoting central control and undermining colonial elites. A number of outsiders, with supposed imperial loyalties, but more limited powers, and patronage, than their predecessors were appointed to the Crown colonies (Atkins in Barbados, Vaughan, and then Carlisle in Jamaica) and despatched with instructions to tame the councils, disable the assemblies, and harness the constitutions to the Crown by obtaining permanent revenue bills.[112] None was given sufficient resources to fulfil the Crown's ambitions but, having agreed to risk their lives in distant lands, these new governors did hope to make their fortunes and invariably upset entrenched interests; they installed their own 'creatures' in office, disrupted well-established restrictive practices, and used regulation (above all the Navigation Acts) to promote their own interests and extract large fees and fines.[113]

Consternation mounted among the colonial elites, and their metropolitan associates, as they saw the security and value of their established rent-seeking enterprises eroded by what they denounced as 'arbitrary power' backed by the Crown prerogative and they organized increasingly vocal opposition. In 1671, as Charles's centralization drive sharpened its bite, a group of 'Gentlemen Planters of Barbados' began to meet weekly at the

in Jack P. Greene and J. R. Pole (eds.), *Colonial British America: Essays in the New History of the Early Modern Era* (Baltimore, Md., 1984), p. 393.

[111] 'State of the business of the plantations as it is depending before the king', BLO, MS Rawl. A 478, fos. 148–53; I. K. Steele, 'The empire and the provincial elites: an interpretation of some recent writings on the English Atlantic, 1675–1740', in Peter Marshall and Glyn Williams (eds.), *The British Atlantic Empire before the American Revolution* (London, 1980), pp. 2–32; R. P. Bieber, *The Lords of Trade and Plantations, 1675–1696* (Allentown, Penn., 1919); Thornton, *West India Policy*, pp. 161–213; Richard S. Dunn, 'The Glorious Revolution and America', in Canny (ed.), *Origins of Empire*, pp. 445–66.

[112] Coventry to Vaughan, 30 July 1675, BL Add. MS 25,120; L. W. Labaree, *Royal Government in America* (New Haven, Conn., 1930); Thornton, *West India Policy*; Sosin, *English America and the Restoration Monarchy*; Dunn, 'Glorious Revolution', pp. 449–52.

[113] For example, in Jamaica Carlisle aligned with Morgan, the famous privateer and deputy governor in promoting privateering, and used the Navigation legislation to undermine elite control of the lucrative Spanish slave trade: Zahedieh, 'Regulation, rent-seeking and the Glorious Revolution'. In five years as governor of Barbados, Dutton extracted nearly £18,000 in salaries, perks, bribes, and so-called presents from the Assembly: PRO CO 29/3, fos. 248–9, 295–7; Dunn, *Sugar and Slaves*, p. 100.

Cardinal's Cap tavern in Cornhill, near the Exchange, and organized representations on behalf of the island elite to the Lords of Trade.[114] Other
groups were formed in imitation, and in 1679 a group of West India
merchants successfully defended Jamaica's 'ancient constitution' against
Crown encroachments.[115] In the same year Parliament prepared to take
on Crown chartered monopolies and established an investigative committee to examine allegations of the African Company's 'unjust' practices
in seizing private traders.[116] William Freeman informed his Nevis correspondent that 'its much to be doubted the Royal Company's charter will
fall... And generally believed the trade will be layd open.'[117]

In fact, the Company was saved by Charles's decision to prorogue
Parliament and, as the Exclusion Crisis mounted, an accompanying
trade boom, and high customs revenues, allowed him to more or less
dispense with the Commons until his death in 1685.[118] Furthermore,
he moved to strengthen his power base and guarantee a loyal elector-
ate by undermining those institutions which provided vehicles for Whig
opposition. Town corporations were remodelled, including the City of
London – a power base for the Whigs – which lost its charter in 1683
after a two-year legal battle. The City was governed by royal officials until
1688 and, during these years, no elections were held and no Common
Council sat. The livery companies also lost their charters and freedom to
elect aldermen or Members of Parliament of their choosing. Whig control of the City was thoroughly smashed and its place usurped by loyal
opponents.[119] In parallel with the attack on parliamentary power, and the
chartered town corporations in England, the king took on the chartered

[114] 'Minutes of Meetings of the Committee for the Concern of Barbados', PRO CO 31/2,
    fos. 37–9, 104–5; Penson, Colonial Agents; Olson, Making the Empire Work, pp. 51–75.
[115] 'A journal kept by Coll. Wm Beeston from his first coming to Jamaica', BL Add. MS
    12,430, fos. 71–4.
[116] Davies, African Company, pp. 106–9. Two interlopers off the coast of Africa were
    reported to have made 'great bragge of an assistance they expect from Parliament',
    PRO T 70/1, fo. 42b.
[117] Hancock (ed.), Letters of William Freeman, pp. 121, 132, 134, 150.
[118] Chandaman, English Public Revenue, pp. 35–6.
[119] In December 1681 a writ of quo warranto was issued to determine whether or not
    London had abided by the terms of its charter. A breach was ascertained, the charter
    was revoked, and the privilege to form a corporation was forfeited to the king. Charles
    now had the power to appoint a royal commission to govern the City and, by virtue
    of this power, he could appoint the Lord Mayor, sheriffs, and aldermen. The motive
    behind Charles's actions was clearly political rather than judicial. Charles was not only
    using the Crown's legitimate powers but abusing them and fuelled the redefinition of
    rights and liberties. After the Revolution they became natural or civil rights rather than
    privileges granted by the monarch: W. A. Speck, 'Some consequences of the Glorious
    Revolution', in Dale Hoak and Mordechai Feingold (eds.), The World of William and
    Mary: Anglo-Dutch Perspectives on the Revolution (Stanford, Calif., 1996), pp. 33–5; De
    Krey, Fractured Society; De Krey, London and the Restoration; Gauci, Politics of Trade.

proprietary colonies, which were notorious for their neglect of imperial regulation and even went so far as to deny its legal authority.[120] The chief target was the Massachussetts colony where the church members who governed – confident that God would protect their charter – refused to reach a compromise with the Crown over the company's 'liberties' so that, in 1684, it was liquidated and the colony was taken under direct – and secular – royal rule with Joseph Dudley in temporary charge.[121]

After Charles died in 1685, James, as intent on the pursuit of absolutism as his brother and with an exceptional interest in America, continued the imperial centralizing policies and endeavoured to further raise the extraction rate.[122] The Loyal Parliament of 1685 not only conferred the customs on James for life, but also agreed to punishing impositions on sugar and tobacco, despite howls of protest from planters and merchants.[123] With buoyant trade receipts, James was able to maintain the Crown's independence from Parliament – between 1679 and 1688 it met five times for a total of only 171 days – and the existing Crown chartered monopolies were preserved from attack.[124] Furthermore, in 1687, there was news that a small group of Tory merchants had advanced plans to set up a Crown chartered monopoly of the whole sugar trade, and another Tory group, led by Richard Wharton (a New England merchant) and Sir John Shorter (mayor of London), was attempting to engross the naval stores trade in New England.[125]

Meanwhile, in America all the remaining charter colonies came under assault and accepted royal take-over. It appeared that the king wished to consolidate his American territories into large vice-royalties on the Spanish model but only one was actually established: the Dominion of New England of 1685 which united eight previously separate colonies in a vast province that extended from the Delaware River to the Canadian border. The governor-general, Sir Edmund Andros, ruled without a legislative assembly, reduced local government powers, remodelled the law courts, levied new taxes without consent, and jailed those who protested.

---

[120] Philip S. Haffenden, 'The crown and the imperial charters, 1675–1688: Part 1', *WMQ*, 15 (1958), 297–311.

[121] Sosin, *English America and the Restoration Monarchy*, pp. 253–301.

[122] 'James II was, in his heavy handed way, more aware of America, and indeed of the Atlantic, than any other European king in the seventeenth century': Davies, *North Atlantic World*, p. 60.

[123] 'The bill to impose additional impositions was much opposed by members of the House who had either themselves or their friends an interest in the plantations', 1 June 1685, L. F. Stock, *Proceedings, and Debates of the British Parliament Respecting North America*, 5 vols. (Washington, D.C., 1924–41), vol. I, p. 425.

[124] Julian Hoppit, *A Land of Liberty? England 1689–1727* (Oxford, 2000), pp. 7, 26.

[125] Thomas, *Historical Account*, Dedication and pp. 48–9; BL Sl. MS 3,984, fo. 210; Bailyn, *New England Merchants*, p. 133; Barnes, 'Richard Wharton'.

At first many of New England's commercial elite had welcomed the overthrow of the Massachusetts charter, and Church control and, under Dudley from 1685 to 1686, they benefited from new access to a secular government; but they were soon alienated by what they portrayed as Andros's 'arbitrary' rule and exhorted their London associates to organize effective opposition in the metropolis.[126] The merchant-councillor interests were equally unhappy in the Crown colonies where a further round of outsider, 'loyal', governors (Stede in Barbados, Albemarle in Jamaica, Johnson in the Leewards, and Effingham in Virginia) did little to enhance royal control but did play to populist concerns, exploit regulation in their own interests, and levy heavy duties.[127] The damage to the rent-seeking enterprises of the established elites was exacerbated by appointments of further outsiders to patent offices, and efforts to tighten the regulation of privateering, treasure hunting, naval stores supply, and other lucrative business.[128] As the transatlantic trading elites became increasingly vocal in protest against their 'slavery' and the 'arbitrary' behaviour of Crown appointees, the news that William of Orange had overthrown James triggered a series of rebellions in English America in 1689.[129] The merchant-councillor interests were able to exploit events to restore the balance of power that had prevailed before the centralization drive of the late Stuarts.

After thirty years of contested power, the Revolution settlement did much to align the interests of Crown, Parliament, City, and colonial elites, and encouraged them to unite behind the imperial project. The king lost all vestiges of financial independence and any hope that colonial revenues might help him to 'live off his own'; he was required to rule and spend through Parliament and as a result the Commons was in regular session.[130] The competition to supply regulation was resolved in favour of Parliament and, as it obtained increased control over commercial

---

[126] Under Dudley, the merchants were able to grant each other title to large stretches of unoccupied land, award each other offices, and grant exemptions to taxation: Haffenden, 'Crown and colonial charters'; J. M. Sosin, *English America and the Revolution of 1688: Royal Administration and the Structure of Provincial Government* (Lincoln, Nebr. 1982), pp. 64–78; Bailyn, *New England Merchants*; Theodore B. Lewis, 'Land speculation and the Dudley Council of 1686', *WMQ*, 31 (1974), 255–72.

[127] Thornton, *West India Policy*; Sosin, *English America and the Restoration Monarchy*; Zahedieh, 'Regulation, rent-seeking and the Glorious Revolution'.

[128] PRO CO 138/6, fos. 44–7, 63–5, 118, 134, 129–32, 316–17; 'Minutes of Council of Jamaica', PRO CO 140/4, fos. 225–30.

[129] 'Humble petition of the planters and merchants trading to Jamaica', November 1688, PRO CO 1/65, fo. 373; Sosin, *English America and the Revolution of 1688*; Steele, 'Provincial elites'; Dunn, 'Glorious Revolution'.

[130] Between 1689 and 1698 there were eleven Parliaments which met for 1,300 days: Hoppit, *Land of Liberty*, pp. 7, 26.

patronage, it was able to secure the property rights that colonial merchants cared about: power to charter companies; to define monopolies; to appoint to colonial offices; and to oversee government contracts. Although the Crown retained its prerogative, it had much diminished power and needed to be used with care; Crown chartered monopolies lost any real value.[131] The Hudson's Bay Company did obtain a short-term statute charter in 1690, but the Royal African Company's efforts to obtain similar privileges were thwarted by well-organized Whig opposition and, as a result, private traders were able to continue operating without making any contribution to the costs of the company's African establishment or facing any risk of seizure.[132] Only in 1698, in a reaction against Whig corruption, was the African trade formally opened to all on payment of a levy to the company. Neither side was pleased: the company lost all claim to monopoly and the private traders lost their free-riding benefits.[133] The Crown did retain overall responsibility for colonial trade, and the king thwarted efforts to establish a parliamentary committee of trade with the foundation of the Board of Trade in 1696, but this did not have the executive powers of the earlier Committee of the Privy Council, and further limited the Crown's scope for tightening its independent control over imperial administration.[134] Meanwhile, in the colonies, constitutions and charters were restored, assemblies were strengthened to guard against future Crown encroachments, and governors were chosen from among the ranks of merchant-councillor interests: Kendall and Russell in Barbados; Molesworth and Beeston in Jamaica; Phips in Massachusetts; a new-style Andros in Virginia.[135] The Crown continued to hope it would make a profit from empire but effectively subcontracted its management to the merchant-planter elites.

---

[131] Organizations seeking trading privileges, such as a New England Company proposed in the 1690s, resorted to Parliament rather than the Crown and eschewed outright monopoly grants: 'Memorial of the subscribers to an undertaking for working copper-mines and producing naval stores in New England to the Council of Trade and Plantations', 5 July 1697, *CSPC, 1697*, no. 1,150.

[132] For an extended attack on the Royal African Company see William Wilkinson, *Systema Africanum or a Treatise Discovering the Intrigues and Arbitrary Proceedings of the Guinea Company* (London, 1690); K. G. Davies, Introduction, in E. E. Rich (ed.), *Hudson's Bay Copybooks of Letters, Commissions, Instructions Outward, 1688–96* (London, 1957).

[133] BL Add. MS 14,034, fo. 93; 'Entry Book on outgoing exports and 10 per cent duty', PRO T 70/1198–9; Tim Keirn, 'Monopoly, economic thought and the Royal African Company', in John Brewer and Susan Staves (eds.), *Early Modern Conceptions of Property* (London, 1996), pp. 427–66; William A. Pettigrew, 'Free to enslave: politics and the escalation of Britain's transatlantic slave trade, 1688–1714', *WMQ*, 64 (2007), 3–38.

[134] I. K. Steele, *Politics of Colonial Policy: the Board of Trade in Colonial Administration, 1696–1770* (Oxford, 1968), pp. 3–41.

[135] Dunn, 'Glorious Revolution', pp. 461–5.

Renewed control over the levers of political power allowed the colonial elites, and their metropolitan partners, to regulate the Atlantic economy in their own interests and capture an increased share of imperial revenues and their strength was further enhanced by an expensive war. William's dynastic ambitions in Europe chimed with colonial merchant concern to curb French commercial competition and, above all, prevent France securing succession to the Spanish crown and, with it, control of the valuable Spanish American trade.[136] The war also offered well-placed individuals opportunities to profit from government contracts and credit. In the 1680s peace had prevailed as the last Stuarts could not afford an expensive foreign policy while attempting to 'live off their own'; but the advent of Parliament's tighter control over state finances allowed it to use taxes to secure government loans – provided by its own stake-holders – and encouraged an expansion of debt.[137] A series of institutional innovations, such as the creation of the national debt, and the Bank of England – collectively known as the Financial Revolution – further reduced the risks of government lending.[138] The transatlantic trading elites exhorted government to become involved in large-scale American campaigns at massive cost and massive profit to themselves and, although the war seriously disrupted colonial commodity trade in the Atlantic to the detriment of lesser planters and merchants, it both heightened the Crown's need to preserve a good relationship with colonial governments and also allowed the merchant-councillor interests to consolidate their economic, social, and political pre-eminence.[139]

A recent 'new Whig' interpretation of the Glorious Revolution has portrayed the ensuing settlement as a model of an economically optimal political arrangement that created a 'balanced constitution' in which

[136] 'A brief view of the weight and conveyance of the general trade and of some considerable places in the Indies', BLO, MS Rawl. C 840; 'Essay on the nature and methods of carrying on a trade to the South Sea', BL Add. MS 28,140, fos. 20–8; G. H. Guttridge, *The Colonial Policy of William III in America and the West Indies* (Cambridge, 1922).

[137] It can be argued that the desire to place public credit on a sound footing was a major cause as well as a consequence of the Glorious Revolution. Government expenditures increased from £1.7 million in the 1680s to £4.9 million in the Nine Years War: Roseveare, *Financial Revolution*, pp. 2, 33–8; Hoppit, *Land of Liberty*, pp. 124–7.

[138] P. G. M. Dickson, *The Financial Revolution in England: a Study in the Development of Public Credit, 1688–1756* (London, 1967); Douglas C. North and Barry R. Weingast, 'Constitutions and commitment: the evolution of institutions governing public choice in seventeenth century England', *JEH*, 49 (1989), 803–32; S. R. Epstein, *Freedom and Growth: the Rise of States and Markets in Europe, 1300–1750* (London, 2000).

[139] The impact of war on colonial commodity trade was reflected in the proceeds of the 4.5 per cent duty on exports from Barbados and the Leewards. A report to the Treasury in 1701 concluded that in times of peace the medium of the 4.5 per cent was £7,000 and in times of war £5,000: CUL, CH (H) Papers 84/1; Dunn, 'Glorious Revolution'; Steele, 'Provincial elites'.

Parliament was able to constrain the 'absolutist' ambitions of the Crown and limit the state's ability to manipulate the economy to its own advantage. It is argued that the settlement strengthened private property rights, reduced transaction costs, deterred rent-seeking behaviour, and allowed free markets to flourish.[140] However, this Whig story of steady 'progress' towards optimal institutional arrangements does not fit developments in England's Atlantic world. In the three decades before the Glorious Revolution, the contest between Crown and Parliament for control of the supply and enforcement of regulation had made it difficult for either side to secure rent-seeking enterprises or pursue a bellicose foreign policy detrimental to trade. Within the walls of the Navigation Acts colonial trade operated in unusually peaceful and competitive conditions which encouraged efforts to obtain the efficiency gains which underpinned the growing capacity to comply with the legislation without suffering financial penalties. However, after 1689, as the interests of Crown, Parliament, and the transatlantic trading elite became increasingly aligned, they cooperated in using political institutions to protect vested interests and support a major war at vast public expense, and great private profit; in consolidating imperial authority, they pursued policies which increased transaction costs, raised the security and value of rent-seeking enterprises, and limited competition. Perhaps the outcome of the contest between Crown and Parliament was the best that could be expected in the Europe of 1689 but it was not the optimal economic solution of Whig mythology. In allowing the political classes to capture a larger share of the profits of empire, it halted the rapid rise in colonial trade and shipping which had characterized the Restoration decades, and ushered in a period of slower growth which lasted until the 1740s.[141] None the less, as Defoe asserted, England was like 'a strong horse in the race, who having shot ahead of the rest at their first setting out … holds it all the way'.[142] Conditions in the earlier period had allowed England to consolidate the territory, trade networks, and operating rules needed to construct an Atlantic system which proved sufficiently resilient to allow colonial trade to continue to grow faster than other sections of the economy and encouraged investment in developments which made industrial revolution more likely.

---

[140] Douglas C. North, *Institutions, Institutional Change and Economic Performance* (Cambridge, 1990); North and Weingast, 'Constitutions and commitment'; Ekulund and Tollinson, *Politicized Economies*; Bruce C. Carruthers, *City of Capital: Politics and Markets in the English Financial Revolution* (Princeton, 1999).

[141] W. E. Minchinton (ed.), *The Growth of English Overseas Trade in the Seventeenth and Eighteenth Centuries* (London, 1969), pp. 11–16.

[142] Defoe, *Plan of Commerce*, pp. 105–7.

3   Merchants

The material ambitions, and entrepreneurial skill, of London merchants played a crucial role in shaping England's westward expansion and in making mercantilism work. The merchant's ability to organize the 'punctual rotation of credit and change of commodities from one place to another' drove the wheels of commerce and without it, proclaimed Dalby Thomas, 'the whole produce of agriculture and industry would be but dead matter'.[1] The task of organizing this 'punctual rotation' was especially challenging in the case of colonial commerce as it involved a complex web of multilateral exchanges which were conducted without the comfort of collective control. Unlike most other long-distance trades, colonial commerce was largely open and unregulated, a field of individual, rather than corporate, endeavour.

This chapter describes the competitive structure of colonial commerce and looks at how participants fashioned the day-to-day workings of their atomistic business world and dealt with the perils, and pitfalls, that faced traders at every turn. The tempting opportunities and high risks in the growing Atlantic trade raised the incentives to develop a wide range of increasingly sophisticated and specialized commercial services in the City (Map 4). It stimulated modernization of education and training methods, and it encouraged the fashioning of associational activities which promoted trust. All served to raise efficiency in London's colonial commodity trade, and underpinned a convergence with Dutch commercial costs, which was reflected in the evidence of substantial compliance with the Navigation legislation; merchants would have ignored the legislation if English services had been substantially more costly than those of their rivals.

Although competitive conditions did provide a strong incentive to seek efficiency gains they also encouraged merchants to look for ways to use institutions to limit entry, reduce risk, and raise profits. Merchants

---

[1] Dalby Thomas, *An Historical Account of the Rise and Growth of the West India Colonies and the Great Advantage they are to England in Respect of Trade* (London, 1690), p. 7.

Map 4 The commercial City: The Royal Exchange (1) stood at the heart of the commercial City. Space was confined and business spilt into the profusion of taverns and coffee houses in Change Alley (2) and surrounding streets. Grocers Hall (3) which housed the original Bank of England, Africa House in Leadenhall Street, and the Custom House (4) were all in easy walking distance. William Morgan, *London & Actually Survey'd* (1682).

were deeply embedded in political networks which were used to promote their material interests but scope was limited in the three decades
after the Restoration, as the contest between Crown and Parliament for
control over the political institutions which could be used to regulate
the economy served to undermine the value of rent-seeking enterprises.
However, after the Glorious Revolution the interests of Crown and City
became increasingly aligned, and they combined to constrain competition, and engross profits, in ways that allowed leading players in the
Atlantic trade to amass vast fortunes at the expense of smaller players,
consumers, and overall efficiency.

The structure of London's colonial commodity trade and merchant careers

London's largely open, and unregulated, plantation trades attracted
crowds of investors throughout the late seventeenth century but, alongside a massive increase in the volume and value of colonial commerce,
they became increasingly concentrated in specialist hands. Price and
Clemens have shown that, while London's annual imports of tobacco
increased from under £2 million in the late 1630s to £11 million in
1676, the number of traders grew much more slowly, and the 600 or so
importers operating between 1672 and 1676 entered roughly ten times
as much tobacco as those handling the trade in the earlier period. By
1686 London's tobacco imports had further increased to over £14 million, but the number of importers had halved and, by 1719, London's
tobacco imports of £22.5 million were handled by 111 firms.[2]

Concentration also took place in the more recently established sugar
trade, which displayed very rapid growth in the Restoration period, and
while the volume of London's sugar imports trebled between the 1660s and
1680s, the number of importers increased more slowly from around 400 in
1672 to around 600 in 1686. A long period of stagnation in the volume of
sugar imports after 1689 was accompanied by a substantial decline in the
number of importers and by 1719 the number had fallen below 400.[3]

[2] J. M. Price and P. G. E. Clemens, 'A revolution of scale in overseas trade: British firms in the Chesapeake trade, 1675–1775', *JEH*, 47 (1987), 1–43. This figure leaves out sub-stantial imports via Cowes – £3 million in 1686.
[3] Imports increased from 163,348 hundredweight in 1663/9 to 435,622 hundredweight in 1686 and were around 425,000 hundredweight in 1719: BL Add. MS 36,785; 'Imports by denizens, Xmas 1671–Xmas 1672', PRO E 190/56/1; PRO CUST. 3/21; London portbook (Xmas 1718–Xmas 1719), Leeds City Library, Sheepscar Branch, Archives Department, Newby Hall MS 2,440. In 1696 the London portbooks list 460 individuals importing sugar but only eighty-five firms were of any importance: D. W. Jones, 'London overseas merchant groups at the end of the seventeenth century and the moves against the East India Company', unpublished doctoral thesis, University of Oxford (1970), p. 205.

Table 3.1 *Merchants exporting English goods from London, 1686*

	Value of trade (£ sterling)				
	0–99	100–999	1,000–4,999	5,000–9,999	Total
West Indies					
No. merchants	521	166	20	2	709
Value of trade, (£ sterling)	14,355	54,393	31,303	11,341	111,392
% total	13	49	28	10	100
North America					
No. merchants	476	176	18	1	671
Value of trade, (£ sterling)	13,379	51,500	29,780	5,881	100,540
% total	13	51	30	6	100

Source: Portbook database, 1686.

Table 3.2 *Merchants importing colonial goods into London, 1686*

	Value of trade (£ sterling)					
	0–99	100–999	1000–4,999	5,000–9,999	10,000 and over	Total
West Indies						
No. of merchants	742	427	86	15	13	1,283
Value of trade (£ sterling)	25,845	101,847	187,533	118,104	217,186	650,515
% of total	4	16	29	18	33	100
North America						
No. of merchants	339	172	38	5	2	556
Value of trade (£ sterling)	10,972	57,923	77,078	32,992	28,166	207,131
% of total	5	28	37	16	14	100

Source: Portbook database, 1686.

The figures in Tables 3.1 and 3.2, taken from the 1686 portbooks, high-light the unusual structure of London's colonial commerce even after a period of some consolidation. Large numbers continued to take part: the records listed around 1,500 individuals with a colonial venture although a London directory of 1677 listed only 1,829 full-time merchants in the capital. In contrast to Atlantic commerce, the city's Baltic import trade (worth around the same as imports from North America) was in the hands of 122 men, and the regulated Levant trade was in the hands of a mere 50 active participants.[4] Furthermore, as it was common to trade in partnership, and usual to enter only one name in the portbooks, the figures in Tables 3.1 and 3.2 leave out a number of individuals concerned in colonial commerce including some important players such as John Bawden (in partnership with John Gardner) although, as many partnerships were short-term, overlapping affairs, some unlisted in one partnership appear elsewhere in the books.[5]

Even in the late seventeenth century low barriers to entry and expectations of high returns combined to tempt a wide range of investors into colonial commerce. Retailers, wholesalers, wharfingers, mariners, gentry, and others with spare cash saw it as an attractive way to diversify their business interests. Writing from Philadelphia in 1684, the merchant James Claypoole reported that a London ironmonger would 'fain have sent a ton of assorted pots and have trusted me for the returns'.[6] However, most of the adventures were small, with 72 per cent of the exporters, and 60 per cent of the importers, in the portbook database trading in goods valued at below £100 in either direction. Women trading on their own account were concentrated in the very smallest ventures. They accounted for over 11 per cent of those importing goods worth less than £10, and below 3 per cent of those importing goods worth between £10 and £99 (although other evidence shows that married women did, at times, trade under their husbands' names).[7] The lesser traders accounted for a tiny share of total value: 13 per cent of English exports and 4 per cent of imports. They also experienced low survival rates, with ease of entry joined with frequent failure, especially

---

[4]   Samuel Lee, *The Little London Directory of 1677* (London, 1878). Gregory King estimated that England had a total of 2,000 merchants and traders by sea in 1688: 'A scheme for the income and expense of the several families of England calculated for the year 1688', in Peter Laslett (ed.), *The Earliest Classics: John Graunt and Gregory King* (Farnborough, 1973); Richard Grassby, *The English Gentleman in Trade: the Life and Works of Sir Dudley North, 1641–1691* (Oxford, 1994), p. 22; Perry Gauci, *The Politics of Trade: the Overseas Merchant in State and Society, 1660–1720* (Oxford, 2001), pp. 19–24; Sven-Erik Astrom, *From Cloth to Iron: the Anglo-Baltic Trade in the Late Seventeenth Century* (Helsingfors, 1963), p. 158.

[5]   For example, both the partners Perry and Lane appear separately, as well as together, as do John and Francis Eyles.

[6]   Marion Balderston (ed.), *James Claypoole's Letterbook, London and Philadelphia, 1681–84* (San Marino, Calif., 1967), p. 242.

[7]   'Deposition of John Barefoot' 1662, master of the *Paragon*, a slave trader captured by the Dutch in Guinea, mentions 'private adventures of … merchants' wives': PRO CO 388/1, part 1, fo. 17. In 1686 Samuel Hassell, citizen and salter, described how he 'did send goods [to Barbados] as an adventure for his wife': CLRO MCD, box 40.

as falling commodity prices (reaching a low point in 1686), and heavy increases in taxation after 1685, eroded profit margins and made it more and more difficult for small, inexperienced, opportunistic traders to make a good return. Taking a sample of the small traders of 1686, only five out of thirty were listed in the portbooks of 1679, 1681, or 1685. None the less, the large (if dwindling) fringe of small adventurers (72 per cent of exporters and 62 per cent of importers) played an important role in shaping colonial commerce by maintaining intense competition and making it difficult for large merchants to collude to rig markets.[8]

Whereas trade was a sideline for many small investors in colonial commerce, a high proportion of the 342 middling traders (concerned with importing or exporting goods valued between £100 and £999) are likely to have been merchants or mariners, although many were not colonial specialists but were seeking to diversify their core business. Many were just starting out in trade, such as Daniel Foe (later known as Defoe) who exported a miscellany of English goods valued at £100.07 to New England.[9] As with the smallest traders, disappointment and failure were clearly commonplace – Foe was bankrupted in 1691. However, this group does display a higher survival rate than that of the smallest traders: eleven from a sample of thirty of the middling traders of 1686 appeared in the portbooks of 1679, 1681, or 1685. Some went on to become substantial merchants.

In 1686 a group of 170 traders was importing or exporting English goods over the value of £1,000 in London's colonial commerce, and this group accounted for almost 70 per cent of the turnover in these branches. The traders included the Royal African Company, the Hudson's Bay Company, and John Thrale (the king's agent for receiving goods on account of the 4.5 per cent duty on exports from Barbados and the Leewards), a number of large wholesalers, a wharfinger (Mark Mortimer), six ship's captains, and a sugar refiner (George White).[10] However, most of the group were merchants acting in small, flexible partnerships. They included William Baxter (who had earlier

[8] The difficulties of thwarting 'litle traders' are described by the African Company's factors: PRO T 70/10, fo. 28; T 70/12, fos. 63, 71, 75.
[9] Foe (Defoe) operated as a merchant in London throughout the 1680s, his main business being shipment of hosiery to Spain in exchange for wine and brandy, and general cargoes to the American plantations in exchange for tobacco. A wide knowledge of business is apparent in his works and this was acquired in the 1680s: Peter Earle, *The World of Defoe* (Newton Abbot, 1976), pp. 8–9.
[10] John Thrale received a warrant on 16 February 1686 for payment of his salary of £100 per year 'for receiving and taking up into the king's custody all goods consigned from His Majesty's plantations in America for the 4.5 per cent duty and for delivering said goods after sale thereof and for paying the proceeds to the customs cashier, he having officiated in that capacity since 1684': *CTB, 1685–89*, vol. VIII, no. 600.

Table 3.3 *London's thirty largest importers of colonial commodities, value of imports (£ sterling)*[a] *1686.*

	West Indies	North America	Total
Gardner, John	28,394	–	28,394
Eyles, Bros.	26,200	–	26,200
Jeffreys, John	1,433	20,301	21,734
Lane, Thomas	145	18,704	18,849
Harwood, John	15,174	–	15,174
Tryon, Thomas	14,360	–	14,360
Clarke, Thomas	13,240	1,799	15,039
Allestree, Paul	13,523	–	13,523
Perkins, Joseph	13,255	216	13,471
Hunt, Thomas	12,321	55	12,376
Fowler, Christopher	11,812	–	11,812
Gracedieu, Bart.	11,800	–	11,800
Hill, John	10,544	918	11,462
Skinner, Stephen	10,460	91	10,551
Tilden, Richard	10,260	–	10,260
Elliot, Thomas	9,856	44	9,900
Wrayford, Wm.	9,621	–	9,621
Cary, Richard	9,005	–	9,005
Barnes, Wm.	9,003	–	9,003
Martin, Joseph	8,367	70	8,437
Starke, Thomas	–	8,350	8,350
Hale, Henry	8,299	36	8,335
Thomas, Dalby	7,864	86	7,950
Skutt, Benjamin	7,522	–	7,522
Crow, John	1,372	5,774	7,146
Baxter, Wm.	6,701	–	6,701
Carleton, Edward	217	6,586	6,803
Richards, George	6,606	26	6,632
Thornburgh, Wm.	5,970	–	5,970
Duck, Thomas	5,870	–	5,870

Source: Portbook database, 1686
[a] The Royal African Company and John Thrale (agent for 4.5 per cent duty) are not included.

been in partnership with William Freeman), William Beeston, Thomas Brailsford, and John Ive whose correspondence and diaries have been used extensively in this book; Edward Haistwell, who had been apprenticed to William Claypoole, another valuable source, who had emigrated to Philadelphia in 1683; and fourteen of the twenty large commission agents identified by Davies.[11]

[11] Davies examined around 1,500 bills recorded in the Royal African Company's books for 1672–94 and found that twenty merchants engrossed two-thirds of the business: K. G. Davies, 'The origins of the commission system in the West India trade', *TRHS* (1951), 89–107.

The 170 big colonial merchants displayed a high level of regional specialization around the Atlantic, reflecting the settled nature of colonial trade by the Restoration, in contrast to the more opportunistic enterprise of the early seventeenth century undertaken by Brenner's 'new merchants'.[12] Two-thirds of the group had substantial trade in the Caribbean, one-third concentrated on North American trade, and only around a fifth had dealings in both regions. Twenty-three of the thirty top importers (see Table 3.3) had more than 80 per cent of their trade concentrated on one destination in a region: twelve with Barbados; five with the Leewards; three with Jamaica; two with the Chesapeake; and one with New England. However, a sample of thirty men in the group of 170 bigger traders suggests that many of them had interests in regions other than the Atlantic, especially Spain (35 per cent), and the Baltic (16 per cent) which were both closely linked to colonial commerce. Baltic iron and German linens were exported to Africa, and the plantations, and paid for with American sugar, tobacco, and bullion. Spanish wine was sold in the colonies, and paid for with Newfoundland fish.[13] Some, such as the great Hamburg merchant, William Gore, or the naval stores importer, John Taylor, were, in fact, primarily concerned in other trades and colonial commerce was a lesser sideline.[14] Merchants such as Brailsford, Gore, Heathcote, and Taylor, who could integrate these related trades, were able to reduce transaction costs but needed substantial capital, and this kind of diversification was most common among the largest traders.[15] The lesser traders importing sugar and tobacco might have correspondents in Europe but, none the less, sold colonial commodities to specialist re-exporters such as Fleet and Gore.[16] Over half the sample of thirty big merchants concentrated the bulk of their commercial activity on colonial

---

[12] Brenner characterized the 'new merchants' who invested in early colonial commerce as being very different from the company merchants, coming largely from outside London and having begun their careers as domestic shopkeepers, ships' captains, or colonial settlers: Robert Brenner, *Merchants and Revolution: Commercial Change, Political Conflict, and London's Overseas Traders, 1550–1653* (Cambridge, 1993), p. 685.

[13] On specialization and diversification in London trade see Astrom, *From Cloth to Iron*, pp. 167–78; Robert C. Nash, 'English transatlantic trade 1660–1730: a quantitative study', unpublished doctoral thesis (University of Cambridge, 1982), ch. 4; D. W. Jones, *War and Economy in the Age of William III and Marlborough* (Oxford, 1988), pp. 260–73.

[14] Gore and Taylor were among the eight most prominent naval contractors in the 1690s: John Ehrman, *The Navy in the War of William III, 1689–1697* (Cambridge, 1953), pp. 59–66, 474.

[15] Balderston (ed.), *Claypoole's Letterbook*, pp. 124, 146–7.

[16] In 1686 Fleet did import sugar to the value of £1,287 on his own account but he relied mainly on purchases in London for his large re-export trade. Both Claypoole and Freeman record frequent sales to Fleet and Gore: Balderston (ed.), *Claypoole's Letterbook*, pp. 124, 146–7; David Hancock (ed.), *The Letters of William Freeman, London Merchant, 1678–1685* (London, 2002), pp. 2, 3, 86, 129, 384.

business, with around three-quarters of their recorded trade with the colonies and Africa (including the wine islands). Most of the sample also had a sustained interest in colonial commerce, with twenty-five of the thirty big merchants having trade recorded with the plantations in the portbooks of 1679, 1681, or 1685. The group of 170 big merchants, and, above all, a sub-group of the 59 traders handling the largest volumes of imports and English exports (hereafter the big colonial merchants), provide the focus of attention in the following account.[17]

Although colonial commerce became increasingly concentrated in the seventeenth century, the barriers to entry remained low, and it was able to draw on a wide pool of talent. Information available about the fifty-nine big colonial traders of 1686 suggests that (like Gauci's sample from a wider merchant community) around a third were drawn from the capital's own ranks (including sons of foreign immigrants such as Jacob Lucy), almost half were born in the provinces, and the rest were born overseas.[18] The demands of commerce necessitated a solid education and ensured that although recruits were attracted from a wide geographical area they were drawn from the classes that could afford this investment in training. Information about the father's occupation suggests that 51 per cent of the group of big colonial merchants were sons of merchants,

[17] The group excludes the Royal African Company, which was the largest single importer from the West Indies with imports of over £32,000, and the king, who received the 4.5 per cent duty from Barbados and the Leewards in kind and was the fourth largest importer from the West Indies in 1686 (with imports valued at £17,658). The fifty-nine merchants in this sub-group are Paul Allestree, William Barnes, Moses Barrow (otherwise known as Anthony Lauzado), William Baxter, Joseph Bueno, Edward Carleton, Richard Cary, Thomas Clarke, William Coward, William Crouch, John Crow, Robert Curtis, John Daveson, Thomas Duck, Thomas Elliot, John Eston, Francis Eyles, John Eyles, Christopher Fowler, Paul Freeman, John Gardner, Anthony Gomezsera, William Gore, Bartholomew Gracedieu, Samuel Groome, Henry Hale, John Harwood, Gilbert Heathcote, Peter and Pierre Henriques, John Hill, Thomas Hunt, John Jackson, John Jeffreys, Jeremy Johnson, Thomas Lane, Sir Thomas Lane, John Lovero, Jacob Lucy, Joseph Martin, Manuel Mendez, Richard Merriweather, Arthur North, William Paggen, Emanuel Perara, Micajah Perry, Joseph Perkins, John Pitt, George Richards, Stephen Skinner, Benjamin Skutt, Thomas Starke, John Taylor, Dalby Thomas, William Thornburgh, Richard Tilden, Thomas Tryon, William Walker, and William Wrayford. The biographical information available in wills, inventories, court records and business papers is uneven.
[18] Birthplace was found for thirty-three of the fifty-nine. Lucy's father was born in Antwerp and was an elder of the Dutch church. Those born overseas include Paggen (a Huguenot born in the Low Countries); Perry was born in New England, Baxter was born in the Leewards, and a number of Jews were born in France, Spain, and Portugal: J. R. Woodhead, *The Rulers of London, 1660–85* (London, 1965), p. 110; Jacob. M. Price, *Perry of London: a Family and a Firm on the Seaborne Frontier, 1615–1753* (Cambridge, Mass., 1992); David Hancock, ' "A world of business to do": William Freeman and the foundations of England's commercial empire, 1645–1707', *WMQ*, 57 (2000), 3–34; on the Jews see 'Deposition of Antony Gomezsera', 25 September 1672, PRO HCA 13/77.

26 per cent of artisans, 15 per cent of gentlemen, and 7 per cent of yeomen or husbandmen.

The scale of trade was, of course, partly a lifecycle phenomenon. Among the 170 larger traders, many were in their twenties – like the Quaker, Edward Haistwell, who had recently completed his apprenticeship to co-religionist William Claypoole – and in the early stages of a highly successful independent career.[19] However, among the smaller group of fifty-nine big merchants, none of the thirty-eight for whom information could be obtained was below thirty, and the mean age was forty-four.[20]

The senior member of the smaller group was John Jeffreys, aged seventy-two, younger son of a Welsh gentleman, who was apprenticed to a London grocer in 1632, when the tobacco trade was in its early stages. After completing his training, Jeffreys went into partnership with Thomas Colclough and built up a firm which specialized in the Virginia trade and, by the 1650s, had become the dominant tobacco importer while also becoming heavily involved in the African slave trade.[21] After the Restoration, Jeffreys's tobacco business continued to flourish (he was reputed to have lost £20,000 worth of leaf in the Great Fire of 1666) and his firm (in which his nephews replaced Colclough on his death in 1680) remained the leading importer of tobacco into London until his death in 1688 (see Table 3.3).[22] Only one other merchant in the group of fifty-nine big colonial merchants of 1686 is known to have been aged over sixty, Richard Tilden (aged sixty-three), and under a fifth were in their fifties.[23]

Most of the fifty-nine big colonial merchants of 1686 were still fairly young men, with around a quarter in their forties and around half in their thirties.[24] The three youngest were already established as major commission agents: John Gardner (in partnership with his older kinsman,

[19] Balderston (ed.), *Claypoole's Letterbook*, pp. 183, 119–20, 127.
[20] The best sources of data on age are court depositions. Age data were obtained for 115 men, including 38 in the group of 59 big merchants: PRO HCA 13/77–80; HCA 14/55–7; C 24/1129–35; CLRO, MCD, boxes 40–42.
[21] 'Meeting of committee appointed to consider how the trade of the nation may be inspected and advanced': PRO CO 388/1, part 2, fos. 309–12.
[22] Theophilus Jones, *A History of the County of Brecknock*, 4 vols. (Brecknock, 1909–30); PRO CO 388/1, fos. 389, 48, 18.
[23] Paul Allestree, William Crouch, Jacob Lucy, Thomas Tryon, and two Jews, Emanuel Perara and Anthony Gomezsera were in their fifties.
[24] In their forties were William Barnes, Thomas Duck, William Gore, Thomas Hunt, John Jackson, Thomas Lane, Micajah Perry, George Richards, Benjamin Skutt, and William Wrayford. In their thirties were Edward Carlton, Richard Cary, Thomas Clarke, John and Francis Eyles, Christopher Fowler, John Gardner, Bartholomew Gracedieu, John Harwood, Gilbert Heathcote, John Hill, Thomas Lane, Joseph Martin, Richard Merriweather, Arthur North, Thomas Starke, Dalby Thomas, John Taylor, and William Thornburgh.

John Bawden, who was reputed to be London's greatest dealer to the West Indies), Francis Eyles (in partnership with his brother, John), and Bartholomew Gracedieu.[25] These men had entered colonial commerce after the Restoration and, in 1686, most were near the beginning of careers that extended well beyond the Glorious Revolution into the eighteenth century, and a handful such as Gilbert Heathcote survived into the 1730s. Thus, the combined careers of the fifty-nine big colonial merchants of 1686 spanned a century from 1632.

The mean age of death among the big colonial merchants of 1686 was sixty-six. Gilbert Heathcote, Joseph Martin, and Micajah Perry survived into their eighties. This high life expectancy suggests that, unless the previous cohort of traders had experienced a very different pattern of mortality, the scarcity of older men among the leading merchants of 1686 was caused largely by early retirement from active trade rather than forced exit. Although at least three of the group (Carleton, Gracedieu, and Hunt) went bankrupt, and others (such as Jacob Lucy) died in substantial debt, it seems that most of the big colonial merchants were able to accumulate sufficient capital to diversify investment around their core business into ship-owning, joint-stocks, insurance, wharf-leases, and industry which all provided scope for either active, or passive, involvement.[26] Most also ventured into property, loans, and public credit.[27] As shown in the remainder of this chapter, a career in colonial commerce required intensely hard work, and involved large risks, and while merchants operating in this relatively open and unregulated sector did what they could to reduce transaction costs and improve efficiency, a preference for a rentier lifestyle was unsurprising. Trade was a stepping stone to a broadly based fortune.

The day-to-day workings of London's colonial trade

London's colonial commerce was not directed from a central headquarters like other long-distance trades but from many individual houses which served as homes as well as workplaces for participating merchants (Illustrations 3 and 5). None the less, merchant advice books, letterbooks, commercial correspondence, and court records provide a detailed insight into the time-consuming, often tedious, routines of London's late-seventeenth-

[25] Balderston, (ed.), *Claypoole's Letterbook*, p. 173.
[26] 'Sir B– Grace–, a great merchant of this city has stopped payments', Newsletter, 19 January. 1710, BL Add. MS 70,421. On Carleton see Price and Clemens, 'Firm scale in colonial trade', p. 18. On Hunt see *London Gazette*, 5–9 August 1697. On Lucy's financial position see *St John* v. *Blackman*, 1691, PRO C 24/1139, 1142.
[27] Wills were found for eighteen of the fifty-nine big merchants of 1686. Evidence about wealth is also found in probate inventories and court cases; see Table 3.6.

Illustration 5 No. 34 Great Tower Street was a large brick merchant's house incorporating a warehouse in its basement; it stood in Beckford Court, set back from the street on its south side. It was built around 1670 and by the early twentieth century it was the best preserved late seventeenth-century merchant's house remaining in the City, retaining its original panelling and staircases. It was destroyed by bombing in the Second World War. Photo in Guildhall Library.

century colonial commerce and the risks that faced participants in this rapidly expanding, but largely unregulated, trade. Anyone embarking on an export adventure had first to assemble a suitable cargo either on his own

Table 3.4 *Consignments of plantation exports and imports into London, 1686*

	Total no. of consignments	Total no. of merchants	Mean no. of consignments	No. of merchants exporting/ importing over £1000 value (a)	Mean no. of consignments among (a)
Exports of English goods					
North America	7,461	671	11	19	83
West Indies	6,509	709	9	22	65
Imports					
North America	4,502	556	8	45	38
West Indies	9,411	1,283	7	114	50

Source: Portbook database, 1686.

independent account, in partnership with others, or on behalf of a colonial principal (either planter or merchant). The small adventurers, such as the ironmonger mentioned by Claypoole, might send only one consignment of goods, but in 1686, those traders exporting English goods over the value of £1,000 sent, on average, eighty-three separate consignments spread between different ships (Table 3.4). Those involved in West Indian trade on a similar scale sent an average of sixty-five consignments. In 1686 almost 14,000 consignments, of about 600 different English commodities (valued at £212,000), were exported from London to the colonies and each consignment required some individual attention. The customs returns for the period between 1696 and 1700 suggest that the value of exports of foreign commodities was similar to those of English goods sent to the plantations, although re-exports were not analysed for 1686.[28] In addition, between 1674 and 1688 the Royal African Company shipped cargoes to Africa with a mean annual value of £52,292, and similar quantities may well have been despatched by private traders (Table 6.2).[29]

Traders needed to pay careful attention to the quantity, quality, and price of the wares exported. Merchants were eager to obtain information about purchasing power, climate, seasonality, and taste in colonial markets, which would allow them to match cargoes with consumer demand, but advice was typically fairly general. At the end of the century, Edward Higginson, of New England, advised a novice trader that 'everything (that is not the produce of this country) that is fit for the use of mankind for use and delight' would do.

[28] PRO CUST. 2/4, 6, 8.
[29] K. G. Davies, *The Royal African Company* (London, 1957), pp. 351–7.

However, he cautioned against sending expensive things as 'the meaner sort' were 'most vendible'.[30] Even in the Caribbean, where the spread of sugar and slavery was making some white men rich, the bulk of demand was still from 'middle and common planters'. In 1674 Henry Blake of Montserrat warned John Bawden (an experienced Barbados merchant) against supplying too many 'fine goods' to his poorer island, still dominated by tobacco and indigo makers, although he reckoned a 'small parcel would not be amiss'.[31] On occasion merchants sent over detailed lists of requirements, but assembling these cargoes was especially troublesome, and the effort miscarried if market conditions changed. [32] In July 1684 James Claypoole warned his London agent, Edward Haistwell, against sending stockings to him in Philadelphia, although only four months earlier he had described them as a 'good commodity'.[33] Meanwhile, prices also fluctuated in the London market.[34] In such an environment instructions were frequently ignored, despite loud protests from correspondents.[35] Advice was weighed, and considered, but the London trader relied above all on his own skill and judgement, and those with good information and experience were at an advantage.

The merchant made use of London's position at the hub of national transport networks to draw commodities from suppliers all over the country and overseas. Richard Ligon's account of the history of Barbados reveals that, as early as the 1640s, Monmouth caps were made to order in Wales, Irish rugs and stockings were purchased in St James's fair in Bristol, boots and shoes were bought in Northampton, gloves in Somerset, and iron pots in Sussex. Imported linen was bought in London and the merchant had it made up into shirts, drawers, petticoats, and smocks for export.[36] Woollen cloths were ordered from West Country or Norwich clothiers and collected from Blackwell Hall.[37] Some commodities were

---

[30] Edward to Nathaniel Higginson, 29 August 1700, MHS, Higginson Family Papers box 2.

[31] Letter from Henry Blake to John Bawden, 4 November 1674, PRO HCA 15/10.

[32] In 1699 a New England merchant sent detailed directions on how to dispose of £100: Edward Higginson to Mathew Collet, 3 September 1699, MHS, Higginson Family Papers, box 2.

[33] Balderston (ed.), *Claypoole's Letterbook*, p. 242.

[34] In 1680 a London merchant informed his Boston correspondent that he had sent speckled calicoes in place of narrow coloured calicoes or Bengalls, as ordered because the situation in the London market made them more attractive and 'I am informed will double my money': Walter Mico to Isaac Waldron, August 1680, MHS, Jeffries Family Papers, vol. VII, fo.12.

[35] Letters from Halls to Brailsford, 10 September 1688, 11 March, 22 April 1689, *Brailsford and Taylor v. Peers and Tooke* (hereafter Brailsford Papers), PRO C 110/152.

[36] Richard Ligon, *A True and Exact History of the Island of Barbadoes* (London, 1657), pp. 109–10.

[37] For details of buying woollens for shipment to New England see 'Day book of Charles Peers', 1689–95, GL, MS 10, 187, fos. 17, 19, 21.

ordered and despatched direct from the provinces to the colonies, saving on transport costs. In 1679 Freeman informed his correspondent in the Leewards that good 'hoes, bills, and axes' could not be obtained in London and ordered a parcel of tools to be sent from Bristol.[38] Provisions, servants, and horses were picked up in Ireland, and wine was loaded in Madeira or the Canaries.[39] It was impossible to view all the commodities, even if sent from London, and the merchant had to trust his supplier to provide goods of the contracted quantity and quality. Not surprisingly, tales of short measure and shoddy standards abounded.[40]

Once purchased, and assembled, goods needed to be packed with great care if they were to survive the long Atlantic voyage in good condition. Linens and woollens were packed in multiple layers of strong paper. Hats and books were packed in casks or boxes. Cheshire cheeses were sown in canvas and tarred to protect them from rats.[41] An awkward shaped item, such as a coach despatched to New England in 1683, had to be wrapped in large quantities of flannel and haircloth, and needed particular packing expertise.[42] However, despite all the attention, damage in transit remained one of the merchants' most persistent sources of loss.

While assembling his cargo the trader arranged transport to the colonial market. Some used their own ships and some, like the Royal African Company, chartered whole vessels. However, most preferred to despatch goods at the first available opportunity to spread risks and minimize warehousing times. Bulky, odd-shaped items were often difficult to accommodate, and John Ive, the agent handling the coach mentioned above, waited some time before a sufficiently large ship was available.[43] Merchants relied on information in the Exchange, Custom House, and specialist coffee houses to find a sea-worthy vessel with a reputable master. An increasing number of ships and cargoes were insured, but pay-outs did not cover total losses, and it remained important to find a captain who could be trusted to make the crossing with maximum

---

[38] Hancock (ed.), *Letters of William Freeman*, p. 101.

[39] David Hancock, 'A revolution in trade: wine distribution and the development of the Atlantic market economy, 1703–1807', in John J. McCusker and Kenneth Morgan (eds.), *The Early Modern Atlantic Economy* (Cambridge, 2000), pp. 105–53.

[40] Byrd's letters to leading merchants such as Perry and Lane and Arthur North reveal a very high level of complaints about quality and it was difficult then, as now, to judge their validity: Marion Tinling (ed.), *The Correspondence of the Three William Byrds of Westover, Virginia, 1684–1776* (Charlottesville, Va., 1977), vol. I, pp. 14, 26–7, 29,30, 41.

[41] Balderston (ed.), *Claypoole's Letterbook*, p. 210.

[42] Account, 8 August 1698, MHS, Jeffries Family Papers, vol. VII, fo. 124.

[43] Richard Chiswell to John Usher, 11 May 1678, MHS, Jeffries Family Papers, vol. II, fo. 107.

Illustration 6 The first Custom House was built on Wool Wharf
in the early fourteenth century for the collection of custom duties
on imports and exports. Rebuilt twice in the later middle ages,
it was destroyed in the Great Fire and rebuilt between 1669 and
1671 to Wren's design. The tall windows on the upper storey of
the main block lit the Long Room where merchants paid duty and
obtained passes to clear their goods. The west end was destroyed
by a gunpowder explosion in 1714 and the whole was rebuilt to a
similar design provided by Thomas Ripley between 1717 and 1725.
Engraving by Jonas Dunstall, Guildhall Library.

speed, and minimum damage, or embezzlement.[44] Unfortunately, many
apparently 'honest fellows' proved to be 'knaves'.[45]

When the goods were packed, and freight secured, the merchant took
the required papers to the Custom House, and after paying all appropriate duties, used a lighter to transfer the goods to the intended ship
(Illustration 6).[46] The author of the handbook *The Compleat Merchant*,

[44] In 1666 artificers were invited to repair to 'Mr Mathew Wilkinson, ironmonger, at the
Sign of the Three Feathers in Bishopsgate Street where they may be informed what ships
will be ready [for Carolina] and what they must carry with them': *A Brief Description
of the Province of Carolina* (London, 1666); in 1682 Wilson reported that 'some of the
Lords Proprietors [of Carolina] or myself will be every Thursday at 11 o'clock at the
Coffee House in Burching Lane to inform all people what ships are going or anything
whatsoever': Samuel Wilson, *An Account of the Province of Carolina* (London, 1682).

[45] Balderston (ed.), *Claypoole's Letterbook*, p. 241; Hancock (ed.), *Letters of William Freeman*,
p. 29.

[46] The importance of ensuring that paperwork was in good order is shown in court cases.
For example, see 'Deposition of Benjamin Scott', 1687, CLRO, MCD, box 41.

published in 1684, claimed that these formalities were conducted with 'all order imaginable', but merchants were vociferous in their complaints about time-wasting and venal officers.[47] John Ive, who exported twenty consignments in 1686, complained that the Custom House was so troublesome that the usual 2.5 per cent commission was 'dearly' earned. 'A porter in London is paid better for his time.'[48]

Small, opportunistic adventurers often consigned their export cargoes to travellers, captains, or mariners, relying on them to sell their goods as best they could on arrival in the colonies.[49] Larger operators consigned their cargoes to regular correspondents who might be acting as principals, partners, or agents – often all three. The consignee was trusted to deal with legal formalities, settle with the ship's master for freight and damage, and take steps to restore spoiled goods to merchantable condition. In 1674 two women were paid £5 to wash and dry John Bawden's goods after they were swept overboard in Antigua.[50] Goods were warehoused and sold, with the London merchant having to trust his correspondent to judge the market, and obtain the best price possible, from the most reliable paymasters.[51]

Despite rapid growth after the Restoration, colonial markets remained easily glutted so that prices could halve overnight if ships arrived together with similar goods.[52] Holding commodities in expectation of a better market was costly, as fashions changed and goods decayed – even items such as hats and shoes might be spoiled by moths or damp – but, above all, because the longer goods lay on hand unsold, the longer the time the merchant had to 'put in the forbearance of money'.[53] However, while taking care to

---

[47] N. H. *The Compleat Tradesman* (London, 1684), pp. 147–9; Balderston (ed.), *Claypoole's Letterbook*, pp. 59–60.

[48] John Ive to John Usher, 1 March 1683, MHS, Jeffries Family Papers, vol. II, fo. 109.

[49] Court cases provide details of such transactions. For example, Charles Redford of Salem in New England gave bond for £550 to sell a parcel of goods valued at £207 4s 2d, on behalf of Edward Ellis of London, silkman. 'Deposition of John Ellinger', 10 July, 1986, CLRO MCD, box 40.

[50] 'Deposition of Robert Shelton', 19 April 1675, PRO HCA 15/10.

[51] The goods being stored in a warehouse ... your correspondent must reserve a handsome room for a shop, where his servants must attend; for then his customers will come about him and he must be careful whom he trusts; for there are some good, so there are many bad pay-masters; for which reason, he must provide himself of a horse, and ride into the country to get acquaintance; and half a dozen good acquaintance, will be able to inform him, how the pulse beats of all the rest. (Ligon, *History of Barbadoes*, p. 111)

[52] Halls to John Aylward, 21 November 1688, Brailsford Papers, PRO C 110/152.

[53] Samuel Wickins to Isaac Waldron, 12 March 1680, MHS, Jeffries Family Papers, vol. VII, fo. 10; William and Francis Hall to Thomas Brailsford, 10 September 1688, 11 March 1689, 21 May 1689, Brailsford Papers, PRO C 110/152. For repeated examples of hats valued at very low prices (8–10 shillings) because 'damnified with moth' or 'out of fashion', see 'Boston Merchant's Account Book', 1688–94, MHS, fos. 2, 4.

sell goods as quickly as possible, it was important to avoid extending long credits. As Freeman warned in 1681, 'be sure to trust none but such whose payment will be good and speedy [in three or six months after sale] though you sell them cheaper. For a quick return is the life of trade.'[54]

Throughout the late seventeenth century merchants contemplating a colonial adventure were advised that they could 'double their money' on outward cargoes, and this was regarded as the most profitable leg of the trade.[55] Scrutiny of transactions in merchant records suggests that the reality often fell far short of rosy expectations. A Boston account book, listing several hundred sales between 1686 and 1694, records sale prices between 0 and 150 per cent above invoice price, and a sample of thirty transactions from 1688 indicates that the mean rate was 42.5 per cent.[56] After making deductions for customs, freight, storage, and commission, there would have been a book profit of around 10 per cent. A sample of thirty merchant invoices from the Caribbean in the 1680s indicates slightly higher advances, with a mean rate of 50 per cent, but also higher costs, as agents usually charged 10 per cent commission on the sale price, leaving a very similar book profit.[57] However, this apparently satisfactory figure makes no allowance for extended credits, which could stretch over years, and which merchants costed at 6 per cent per annum.[58] Nor did it allow for opportunistic agents, and bad debts, exacerbated in the Caribbean by very high death rates, and the problems of recovering money from a deceased debtor's estate.[59]

54 Hancock (ed.), *Letters of William Freeman*, pp. 279, 263. In 1676, after trading at Barbados for twenty years, Thomas Crundall reported that when goods were sold 'the money is and ought to be paid within 6 months after such receipt': 'Deposition of Tho. Crundall', 11 May 1676, PRO HCA 13/78.

55 Ligon, *History of Barbadoes*, p. 110; Claypoole reported from Pennsylvania in 1684 that 'English goods will sell generally for almost double money which is 60–70 per cent advance': Balderston (ed.), *Claypoole's Letterbook*, p. 232. In 1698 a West Indian factor observed that 'all their advance must be upon the sale of their goods from London which will be at 25% now upon some things'. Richard Eliot to John Usher, 28 April 1698, MHS, Jeffries Family Papers, vol. III, fo. 2.

56 'Boston Merchant's Account Book', 1688–94, MHS.

57 Brailsford Papers, PRO C 110/152.; Thomas Sandes to Charles Knight, 25 February 1703, Letterbook of John Browne and Thomas Sandes', 1701–3, BEA M 7/19.

58 'On account of the dry goods in the Abraham now 5 years past that amounted to (together with the remains of the other goods in your hands) above £2,200 sterl. principal cost; and now in 5 years you have loaden us on account of the proceeds of all those goods 60 hogsheads of sugar that produced £400. The 5 years interest of our money amounts to at 6 per cent £660. Soe that we have not received interest for our money by £260, allowing the principal lost, as I am sure it will (discompting interest) in a manner before it comes to our hands', Freeman to Westcott, 20 February 1685, Hancock (ed.), *Letters of William Freeman*, pp. 391–2.

59 Over half a sample of forty colonial cases from the 1680s were actions for debt (twenty-six) and the bulk of these (twenty) were concerned with short or non-existent returns:, CLRO, MCD, box 40; William and Francis Hall to Thomas Brailsford, 10 September 1688, 11 March 1689, 21 May 1689, Brailsford Papers, PRO C 110/152.

Illustration 7 This picture of the governor going to church
(*c.* 1695) is the first known painting of Bridgetown in Barbados. The
busy harbour, the substantial town and church, the well-ordered
fields scattered with windmills, and the ostentatious display of the
governor's carriage and retinue reflect the prosperity of the island.
Anon., Barbados Museum and Historical Society.

On obtaining payment for goods colonial correspondents were
expected to remit the net proceeds to England in commodities, bullion,
or bills of exchange, according to the best advantage.[60] The Chesapeake
lacked a central staging post for trade, but elsewhere the major port
towns (Boston, Philadelphia, New York, Bridgetown (Illustration 7), and
Port Royal) with concentrations of money, credit, expertise, and information early assumed the role of regional capitals, with informal commercial institutions developed in imitation of those in England, such

---

[60] The yearly average value of bills received by the Royal African Company between 1672
and 1687 (mainly from Barbados) was over £21,000 and matched the value of its sugar
imports: Davies, 'The origins of the commission system'. Large volumes of bullion were
exported from Jamaica: Nuala Zahedieh, 'Trade, plunder, and economic development
in early English Jamaica, 1655–89', *EcHR*, 39 (1986). For discussion of the attempt to
maximize returns 'according to the price current' see Halls to Brailsford, 22 April 1689,
Brailsford Papers, PRO C 110/152.

Illustration 8 Interior of the first Royal Exchange, 1665. The building was situated between Cornhill and Threadneedle Street and stood at the heart of London's commercial life. It was inaugurated by Sir Thomas Gresham in 1566 and built in a Flemish style with arcaded piazzas surrounding the central courtyard and two floors of shops above. Wenceslaus Hollar, Guildhall Library.

as the exchange attached to the church in Port Royal.[61] The more substantial merchants attempted to exploit their power in the small colonial markets, but were usually thwarted by the large numbers of 'little traders', and needed to pay careful attention to market conditions on both sides of the Atlantic if they were to turn a profit.[62] At times, especially in the northern colonies, it was impossible to settle balances with local commodities and merchants developed multilateral trades for the purpose. New England merchants despatched fish, timber, and provisions to Spain, the wine islands, and the Caribbean where they were exchanged for goods, money, or bills for shipment to England. Colonial merchants were engaged in a complex round of negotiations, much like those undertaken by their metropolitan counterparts, and faced similar problems of trust and poor information.

Letters, and news on the Exchange, alerted the London merchant to the arrival of goods consigned to him – either on his own or a correspondent's account – and, after visiting the Custom House to settle his dues, the trader could obtain his cargo (Illustration 8).[63] As with outward adventures, damage and leakage could give rise to serious squabbles as – although merchants took steps to restore spoilt cargoes – losses were substantial.[64] Merchants and captains tried to shift blame and costs and where neither custom, nor arbitration, could settle liability there was resort to the law, with its attendant expenses.[65] In many cases goods were insured but here, too, owners were often subjected to prevarication, tricks, and evasion before receiving a settlement. After a year of negotiations, and considerable expenditure, Claypoole persuaded the insurers to pay out £187 on a policy providing cover for lost goods valued at £250. The exasperated merchant demanded that his principal should reward him with £3 to purchase a 'beaver hat as thou promised me, besides my ordinary commission'.[66]

---

[61] For Byrd on the lack of facilities of an 'exchange or coffee house' in the Chesapeake see Tinling (ed.), *The Correspondence of the Three William Byrds*, vol. I, p. 46. 'At the north side of this church is a paved walk, built for an exchange for merchants to meet on. Over this Exchange is built a good solid gallery supported with large cedar pillars of ye Dorick order': 'Taylor's history of his life and travels in America', 1688, NLJ, MS 105, fos. 492–3.

[62] In November 1682 the Royal African Company's factors in Jamaica reported that they had agreed with other big merchants to resist buying sugar so as to reduce the price but the plan was thwarted by 'little traders'. A similar scheme failed in February 1686: PRO T 70 /10, fo. 28; T 70/12, fos. 63, 71, 75.

[63] N. H. *Compleat Tradesman*, pp. 149–50.

[64] Balderston (ed.), *Claypoole's Letterbook*, p. 59.

[65] Claypoole reported on custom: 'I having done my duty in sending them ... well conditioned aboard and sending them timely advice, I run no further hazard. And so it is in ... all commodities unless the buyer bargains that the seller shall be at hazard': *ibid.*, p. 88. For discussion of the usual allowance for damage sustained by ill stowage see PRO C110 / 1181.

[66] A beaver hat was the standard reward for extraordinary services, Balderston (ed.), *Claypoole's Letterbook*, pp. 141, 167, 187, 220.

WHISTON'S
Merchants Weekly Remembrancer,
Of the Present-Money-Prices of their Goods Ashoar in *London*,
On Monday *July*, 28th. 1686.

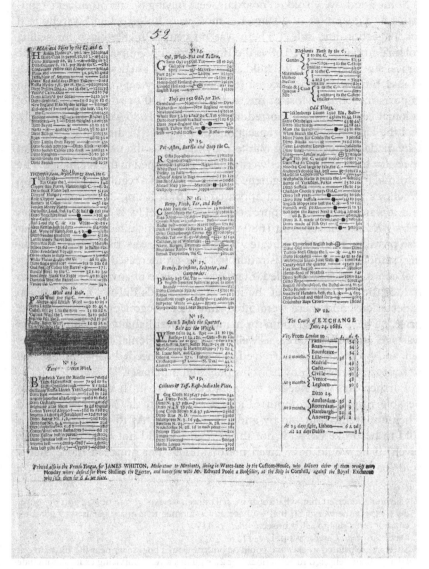

Illustration 9 *Whiston's Merchants Weekly Remembrancer*, 1686. India Office Library.

Some goods were sold on board unseen, relying on the producer's reputation as a guarantee of quality, but most were unloaded and warehoused
for inspection and sale.[67] There was no central marketplace for selling
colonial imports. In the 1680s the Royal African Company, which was the
largest single importer, did hold an average of six auctions a year at Africa
House, but the company accounted for only 5 per cent of total West Indian
imports in 1686.[68] Most of the remaining 14,000 or so consignments of
colonial commodities imported into London in 1686 were sold privately,
and the large number of transactions taking place in the tightly confined
City made it difficult to rig markets. By the 1680s there were a number of
specialist brokers and prices were quickly established in the Exchange. The
informal market was strengthened with the rise of a regular business press;
Woolley's price-current first appeared in 1671, listing 283 commodities,
and it was joined by the more sophisticated, weekly, *Whiston's Merchants
Weekly Remembrancer* from 1680 which not only included more goods but
also provided marks to indicate whether the price was 'rising, highest, falling, standing, lowest' (Illustration 9).[69] As an increased volume of colonial commodities was traded, there was more use of advance contracts to
reduce the uncertainties of the market, but goods did not always match
expectations, and there were often drawn-out negotiations to adjust the
price.[70] There was also room for manoeuvre over liability for warehousing,
wastage, and other charges as well as duties. As colonial commodity prices
fell, and profit margins narrowed, the merchant needed considerable skill
to squeeze the last penny from his potential purchaser.[71]

Further care was needed when extending credit. It was important to
be able to judge the depth of a buyer's pocket, as Claypoole retorted
when apparently outsold by another merchant. 'As to the man he then
sold to he broke twice, if not thrice, and I would not have trusted him
[even] if he would have given me 6 shillings per hundred more than I
sold for I think I know how to sell sugar as well as he or any man.'[72]

---

[67] Claypoole reported that 'what sugar we sell unseen we expect it to be bad and the buyer
does expect the worst. So that we have any assurance that our sugar is very good we
count it not equal to sell it unseen': *ibid.*, p. 117.

[68] Davies, *African Company*, pp. 179–81.

[69] Sheets were printed weekly and could be bought from a bookseller near the Exchange at
6d a piece or delivered to subscribers for 20 shillings a year. Surviving examples include
James Whiston's *Merchants Weekly Remembrancer*, 28 June 1686, BL, India Office X538;
ibid., 16 August 1697, PRO C 104/128, part 2; *Proctor's Price Current*, 28 February 1695,
PRO C 104/128, part 2. See Jacob M. Price, 'Notes on some London price currents,
1667–1715', *EcHR*, 7 (1954), 240–50; Larry Neal, 'The rise of a financial press: London
and Amsterdam, 1680–1810', *Business History*, 30 (1988), 163–78; John J. McCusker,
'European bills of entry and marine lists: early commercial publications and the origins
of the business press', *Harvard Library Bulletin*, 31 (1984), 209–55.

[70] 'Letterbook of William Freeman', NLJ, MS 134, fo. 3.

[71] Balderston, *Claypoole's Letterbook*, p. 149.   [72] *Ibid.*, p. 49.

The premium on liquidity, and the high costs of storage in the cramped port of London, encouraged quick sales rather than hoarding in anticipation of better prices.[73] Similar arguments probably explain why, although around half the tobacco and a third of the sugar brought into London in the 1680s was re-exported, most importing merchants sold supplies to a small group of specialist re-exporters, such as John Fleet and William Gore, rather than financing the additional leg of trade themselves.[74]

Writing in the 1650s Richard Ligon reported that the 'cargo being doubled at the Barbados, that returned back will produce at least 50 per cent'.[75] By the 1660s, with falling commodity prices, the inward predictions were as over-optimistic as those on the outward voyages. In the late 1670s West India merchants claimed that it was usual 'to make twenty per cent profit here running the hazard of the sea out and home'.[76] By the 1680s, with still lower commodity prices and, after 1685, very high duties, it was difficult to break even on the return leg.[77] Profits became increasingly precarious and, in 1698, a West India factor observed that even in favourable peacetime conditions, 'I observe our traders are pleased if can but make their money in England, that is if £100 in sugar cost in Barbados will make £100 in London they think themselves well.'[78] Even more than with outward trade, the small, but secure, commission of 2.5 per cent earned on sales on a correspondent's behalf seemed attractive in comparison with the risky returns on independent import trade. It is unsurprising that many merchants did all they could to expand the commission side of their business and allow colonists to shoulder a greater share of the risk; Nash has suggested that, by the 1680s, less than half London's sugar imports were imported on its merchants' own accounts. The commission system was also important in New England trade and – as suggested by the scale of business done by John Jeffreys and Thomas Lane (Table 3.3) – was becoming used in the Chesapeake trade, although it played a lesser role until the 1690s.[79]

[73] Freeman reported very low sugar prices in summer 1682 and slow payment but '[although] there may be some prospect of [the sugar price] rising in March or April but I question whether worth keeping so long, the charges of warehouse room and wastage by long lying being considerable': Hancock (ed.), Letters of William Freeman, p. 257.

[74] Nash, 'English transatlantic trade', pp. 137, 140, 143. Both Claypoole and Freeman report repeated sales to Fleet and Gore: Balderston (ed.), Claypoole's Letterbook, pp. 124, 146–7; Hancock (ed.), Letters of William Freeman, pp. 2, 3, 86, 129, 384.

[75] Ligon, History of Barbadoes, p. 111.

[76] 'Deposition of Thomas Crundall', 11 May 1676, 'Deposition of Richard Tilden', 22 June 1680, PRO HCA 13/78.

[77] Brailsford and Taylors v. Peers and Tooke, PRO C 9/177/128; C 110/152. Richard Grassby suggested that in the late seventeenth century 'the average returns of a working life in trade probably ranged from 6 to 12 per cent': Richard Grassby, 'The rate of profit in seventeenth century England', EHR, 84 (1969), 721–31.

[78] Richard Eliot to John Usher, 28 April 1698, MHS, Jeffries Family Papers, vol. III, fo. 2.

[79] Davies, 'Origins of the commission system'; R. C. Nash, 'The organization of trade and finance in the British Atlantic economy, 1600–1830', in Peter A. Coclanis (ed.), The

A commission agent was expected to provide a wide range of services: debt collection; supervision of children's schooling; assistance to visiting wives and daughters; purchase of personal clothing and household equipment. In 1683 William Byrd asked his agent, Arthur North, to buy a blackbird and to take his long periwig to be remodelled.[80] However, these tasks were charged for and did not detract from the attractions of a secure business.

Against a background of steeply falling commodity prices, and rising taxes, the merchants of Restoration London fashioned the day-to-day workings of their complex multilateral business without the comforting framework of company organization. It is plain that participants faced perils at every turn and transaction costs were high.[81] The massive rise in the volume, and value, of the trade did increase London's external economies but neither the spectacular growth in the capital's plantation trade nor the rise of re-exports would have taken place (even with the Navigation Acts) unless London's merchants had been able to improve their practices to deliver services to match those of continental rivals on price and quality. Merchant ingenuity was needed to make mercantilism work.

Commercial innovation

In the early seventeenth century England's business practices were seen as backward when compared with those on the continent. Overseas trade was heavily dominated by bilateral exchanges with Europe, conducted under the auspices of regulated companies, and there was little incentive to change customary practices. However, the needs of England's relatively open and competitive colonial commerce, and the increasingly complex web of multilateral exchanges which it spawned, presented participants with new opportunities and challenges. Colonial merchants were encouraged both to refine best-practice techniques and to innovate and, in so doing, helped London to develop the capabilities which made it the leading commercial centre in Europe.[82]

Although company organization proved ill suited to the colonization projects which underpinned the creation of England's Atlantic system – and settlement was in fact left largely to independent entrepreneurs – it was heavily used in the early period and provided an opportunity to

---

Atlantic Economy during the Seventeenth and Eighteenth Centuries (Columbia, SC., 2005), pp. 95–151.
[80] Tinling (ed.), *The Correspondence of the Three William Byrds*, vol. I, p. 107.
[81] According to Gregory King the usual mark-up on goods was 40 per cent. 'The manuscript book of Gregory King', in Laslett, *Earliest Classics*, p. 209.
[82] Peter Earle, 'The economy of London, 1660–1730', in Patrick O'Brien (ed.), *Urban Achievements in Early Modern Europe: Golden Ages in Antwerp, Amsterdam, and London* (Cambridge, 2001), pp. 81–96.

develop new ways of raising capital. Merchants in need of funds trad-
itionally relied on borrowings from a small circle of family and friends
and, although they formed companies for economic, social, and political
purposes, they did not pool capital. However, the colonization projects,
and the associated long-distance trades, tied up large capital sums over
extended periods and encouraged merchants to play a prominent role in
pioneering new types of business organization.[83] A joint-stock company,
with the right to sell shares, could draw on a large pool of strangers, as well
as friends, and could continue in business without continually repaying
its capital while, at the same time, those with funds to spare could obtain
income (dividends) without the loss of liquidity implicit in more traditional investments. It took some years of experimentation before these
mutual advantages were fully realized and, in the early seventeenth century, the East India Company's joint-stock ventures were wound up after
each voyage.[84] However, by 1689, after the formation of around twenty
joint-stock companies – including around fifteen involved in Atlantic
trade and settlement – joint-stock organization had become the accepted
way to finance expensive schemes in all areas of economic activity.[85]

During the Restoration period stocks in the three major trading companies (of which two companies were involved in Atlantic trade) began
to change hands on a regular basis and stimulated the development of an
active market in shares with transactions agreed in the Royal Exchange,
and its surrounding coffee houses, and recorded in the transfer books of
the individual companies (Illustration 10). By the 1680s the volume of
transactions had mounted to a level which supported the emergence of a
group of specialist brokers; the business press was providing regular price

[83] The initial start-up capital required to finance the transport of settlers; furnish food,
tools, and other necessities, undertake land clearance, farm building, and the creation
of basic economic and social infrastructure seemed beyond the scope of individuals
and small partnerships. Most colonies were funded in the initial stages by a joint-stock
company but most such companies did not last long, as they proved ill suited to management of colonial settlement, and made little or no profit for their shareholders: Carole
Shammas, 'English commercial development and American colonization, 1560–1620',
in K. R. Andrews, N. Canny, and P. E. Hair (eds.), *The Westward Enterprise: English
Activities in Ireland, the Atlantic, and America, 1480–1650* (Liverpool, 1978), pp. 151–74;
Richard Pares, *Merchants and Planters* (Cambridge, 1960); Zahedieh, 'Trade, plunder,
and economic development, Russell Menard, *Sweet Negotiations: Sugar, Slavery, and
Plantation Agriculture in Early Barbados* (Charlottesville, Va., 2006).
[84] K. N. Chaudhuri, *The English East India Company: a Study of an Early Joint-Stock
Company, 1600–1640* (London, 1965).
[85] William H. Scott, *The Constitution and Finance of English, Scottish, and Irish Joint-Stock
Companies to 1720*, 3 vols. (Cambridge, 1910–12); K. G. Davies, 'Joint-stock invest-
ment in the later seventeenth century', *EcHR*, 4 (1952), 283–301; Christine MacLeod,
'The 1690s patent boom: invention or stock-jobbing?', *EcHR*, 39 (1986), 549–71; Earle,
Middle Class, pp. 143–57.

Illustration 10 The Royal Exchange was destroyed in the Great
Fire and was rapidly rebuilt at a cost of £62,000 – the second most
expensive building after St Paul's. The new Exchange opened for
business in 1669 and its shops were occupied by 1671. The architects
were Edward Jerman, the City Surveyor and Thomas Cartwright,
the Master of the Masons Company. The format was similar to
that of the earlier Exchange with arcaded piazzas around a central
courtyard which provided a merchants' trading floor and fashionable
shops on the upper floors. Around it was a warren of taverns, coffee
houses, and shops which derived business from it and supported its
trade. Engraving by Johannes de Ram, *c.* 1700, Guildhall Library.

information about the three great trading companies; printed forms were
being used to make share transfers more routine and predictable; and a
body of customs was emerging which shaped what became a formal stock
market in the eighteenth century and enhanced commercial liquidity.[86]

---

[86]   Henry Roseveare, *The Financial Revolution, 1660–1760* (London, 1991), pp. 42–4; John
Houghton, *A Collection for the Improvement of Husbandry and Trade*, 12 vols. (London,
1692–8), 22 June 1694, 6 July 1694.

Although London merchants made a surprisingly limited contribution to providing the long-term funding needed for colonial settlement – only around nine of the fifty-nine big colonial merchants of 1686 are known to have owned property in the plantations – they made a massive investment in the short-term credit which lubricated the wheels of commerce.[87] Merchants involved in colonial commerce were joined in a complex web of multilateral exchanges which tied up capital for longer periods than usual in intra-European trade, and London early assumed the role of clearing house at the heart of the system. Colonial merchants and planters built up balances in London with which they could settle outstanding debts throughout the Atlantic world, using bills of exchange to avoid the transfer of money or goods. John Thomas, a Barbados merchant, and brother of Dalby, sent sugar and rum to William Byrd in Virginia, and settled the account by drawing a bill on Arthur North, Byrd's agent in London.[88] New England merchant John Usher obtained a bill drawn on London in payment for fish shipped to Bilbao.[89] The bill of exchange represented a credit transaction between at least three parties: the drawer (in this case usually a merchant or planter resident in the colonies), the drawee (his agent in London), and the payee (the drawer's creditor). It was nothing new: it was first used in medieval Italy and refined in Antwerp and Amsterdam in the sixteenth and seventeenth centuries. However, conditions in the rapidly growing colonial trade with its long credits and multilateral exchanges caused a major expansion in the volume of bills in circulation in late-seventeenth-century London and encouraged changes in practice to accommodate its needs.[90]

The use of bills involved costs and risks. John Ive complained that he called more than a dozen times on a gentleman worth '£20,000 of good estate' for a debt of £4.[91] More worrying was the fact that in the long-distance trades it was, at times, necessary to accept bills before the agent had sufficient effects in hand and careful judgement was needed in deciding whether they were likely to arrive. Efforts were made to limit risk by making the cost of 'protesting' a bill and returning it to the drawer high to both reputation and pocket. The drawer was branded as of 'unsound credit' and usually charged 25 per cent for 'the trouble'.[92] This expensive solution

---

[87] Baxter, Cary, Fowler, Lucy, Martin, Merriweather, Skutt, Starke, and Tryon are known to have owned property in the plantations. On the difficulties of absentee management of a plantation see Lynch to Lord Cornbury, 29 March 1672, BL Add. MS 11,410, fo. 532.

[88] Tinling (ed.), *Correspondence of Three William Byrds*, vol. I, p. 74.

[89] Robert Beeton to John Usher, 7 July 1685, MHS, Jeffries Family Papers, vol. III, fo. 35.

[90] For a seventeenth-century account of the use of bills see N.H. *Compleat Tradesman*, p. 7.

[91] John Ive to John Usher, 1 March 1683, MHS, Jeffries Family Papers, vol. II, fo. 109; Thomas Sandes to John Rudds, 6 May 1693, 'Letterbook of Thomas Sandes and John Browne', 1692–6, BEA, M 7/3.

[92] For lengthy discussion of the costs of protesting a bill see Thomas Sandes to Joseph Parson, 3 April 1701, 'Letterbook of Thomas Sandes and John Browne', BEA, M 7/19.

does seem to have constrained bad behaviour in good trading conditions and Davies's survey of about 1,500 bills in the African Company's records shows that few were returned between 1672 and 1688 with the largest commission agents, Bawden and Gardner, protesting only six bills drawn to pay the African Company in this period. However, the system showed signs of heavy strain when trading conditions deteriorated in the war of the 1690s and, after protesting eighteen bills between 1689 and 1694, Bawden and Gardner were accused of having 'extremely disobligeth [their] friends by exposing their reputation and bringing it into contempt'.[93]

As the volume of overseas bills increased it was possible to make scale economies and disperse risk. By the Restoration overseas bills had become negotiable instruments, usually sold at a discount reflecting the issuance (the period after sight when bills were due to be paid which varied between twenty-one days and three months), the reputation or credit-worthiness of the drawer and drawee, and the supply and demand for bills drawn on a particular location.[94] They were passed by the holder to a creditor to help settle a debt; they were sold to someone needing a remittance to the bill's place of payment; they were bought before maturity to earn interest.[95] Certain merchants began to specialize in buying bills at a discount and taking on the costs and risks of collection in order to benefit from the implicit interest charged and speculate on movements in the exchange.[96] They also introduced innovations to accommodate the particular problems in long-distance trade. It became usual to give three months' credit rather than the twenty-one days that prevailed in European trade and remained standard in Amsterdam.[97]

By the Glorious Revolution there was a well-established cadre of bill brokers in London with business to rival that of Amsterdam. It was further strengthened by the founding in 1694 of the Bank of England, which quickly became involved in discounting bills, at first subjecting all to careful scrutiny, but increasingly willing to purchase any offered.[98] Legal

---

[93] Davies, 'Origins of commission system', 98–9.

[94] Exchange rates for major commercial centres were published in the printed price currents around which real exchange rates moved and a seasonal pattern was anticipated. When William Freeman was purchasing bills in Dublin to pay for beef exports to the Caribbean he remarked that the rate in the autumn was 6 or 7 per cent whereas it was 10 or 11 per cent in the spring when bills were in high demand: Letter, September 1678, 'Letterbook of William Freeman', NLJ, MS 134, fo. 25.

[95] Jacob M. Price, 'Transaction costs: a note on merchant credit and the organization of private trade', in James D. Tracy (ed.), *The Political Economy of Merchant Empires: State Power and World Trade, 1350–1750* (Cambridge, 1991), pp. 276–97.

[96] *Ellers v. Strutt*, 1693, PRO C 24/1162.

[97] Jan de Vries and Ad van der Woude, *The First Modern Economy: Success, Failure and Perseverance of the Dutch Economy, 1500–1815* (Cambridge, 1997), pp. 130–9.

[98] Price, 'Transactions costs', p. 149. 'Minute Book of Court of Directors of Bank of England', BEA G 4, vol. I; 'Order Book of Court of Directors of Bank of England', 10 March 1697, BEA G 5.

decisions in 1693 and 1696 established (with some exceptions) free nego-
tiability, and further reduced the costs of using overseas bills and so lubricated, first the wheels of overseas commerce and later, by imitation, those
of inland trade.[99] Furthermore, as Jacob Price has emphasized, familiarity with the bill of exchange may well have encouraged acceptance of
other forms of paper (merchants' notes, insurance policies, naval bills,
warehouse receipts, and so on), which passed freely from hand to hand
in late-seventeenth-century London, and provided a valuable addition to
commercial liquidity.

The insurance business was another area of commercial activity which
had been established in the sixteenth century, and showed increasing
sophistication after the Restoration, with the greater volume, and com-
plexity, of overseas trade. London's overseas trading tonnage doubled
between the Restoration and the Glorious Revolution, and this expansion was largely driven by the growing Atlantic trade which, by 1686,
accounted for 40 per cent of overseas tonnage and it seems that a higher
proportion was insured than on safer short journeys. Premiums were
twice, or three times, as high as in European trades to reflect the bigger
risks, but also raising the capital needs of the business, and the pressure
to develop more sophisticated practices.[100] There were, as yet, no insurance corporations and the merchant, with or without specialist brokers,
had to draw on friends and associates to assemble a different group of
investors for each policy.[101] In the tradition of the bottomry loan (where
a debt was forgiven in time of loss), there was an element of the lottery
in the business: premiums reflected rules of thumb based on experience,
intuition, and the supply of funds, rather than a theoretical assessment
of risk. However, a survey of fifty policies relating to colonial trade in
the 1670s and 1680s suggests that premiums came near to the level of
assessed risk – they ranged from 3 to 7 per cent in peacetime, when
the Naval Officers' shipping returns show annual average ship losses of
around 5 per cent – although compensation covered only part of the loss,

[99] James Stevens Rogers, *The Early History of the Law of Bills and Notes: a Study of the
Origins of Anglo-American Commercial Law* (Cambridge, 1995).
[100] The Halls insured around half the consignments they sent home in 1688. Certificates
show cover for

> losses of the seas, men-of-war, fire, enemies, pirates, rovers, thieves, jettisons, letters of
> mart and counter-mart, surprizals at sea, arrests, restraints and detainments of all kings,
> princes and people ... and of all other perils, losses and misfortunes that have or shall come
> to the hurt, detriment or damage of the said goods and merchandizes or any part thereof.

Certificate of Insurance, Brailsford Papers, PRO C 110/152. In 1682 Claypoole
reported that he had insured John Spread returning from New England 'personally
against capture by the Turks at 2 percent by good men': Balderston (ed.), *Claypoole's
Letterbook*, pp. 158, 168, 170.
[101] Violet Barbour, 'Marine risks and insurance in the seventeenth century', *Journal of
Economic and Business History*, 1 (1928–9), 561–96.

and was often difficult to extract, with both insurers and insured open to a wide range of frauds and evasion of responsibilities.[102] However, by the 1680s, marine insurers had established a regular meeting place at Lloyds coffee house near the Exchange where they reaped cost savings through pooling information, greater specialization, more careful loss assessment (gaining from contemporary interest in mathematics and probability), and the development of a market in second-hand policies. All served to reduce the costs of collection and the risks of providing cover, and underpinned London's rise as a major insurance centre.[103]

The African and American trades also underpinned London's emergence as an important entrepot in the late seventeenth century and the accompanying growth in warehousing, commodity brokerage, and a commercial press. All in all, the capital demands, and complex commercial needs of Atlantic trade, with its long voyages, long credits, multilateral settlements, and prominence in the re-export trade, provided heavy pressure (more than proportional to the value of the commodity trade) to refine and improve the City's relatively backward and unsophisticated business practices, with positive effects on commercial efficiency and transaction costs, reflected in high levels of compliance with the Navigation Acts. In Josiah Child's words, the 'dwarfs' and 'pigmies' of the English commercial world were transformed into 'Samsons and Goliaths in stocks, subtility, and experience in trade to cope with our potent adversaries on the other side'.[104] London was, by the 1690s, becoming the commercial centre, not only of the English Atlantic world, but of the entire European trading system.

The merchants' training

The combination of rich rewards, and high risks, in the complex transatlantic trades encouraged aspiring entrants to invest in a solid education,

---

[102] Balderston (ed.), *Claypoole's Letterbook*, pp. 158, 168, 170; Brailsford Papers, PRO C 110/152. In 1679 Ive reported that he had 'thought to get £600 insured at £3 per cent. But Mr White and Mr Bawden gave £4 6 shillings at the same time upon another vessel the same voyage so I was forced to give £4': John Ive to John Usher, 9 August 1679, MHS, Jeffries Family Papers, vol. II, fo. 111; Naval Officers' Returns, PRO CO 33/13–14; CO 142/13; CO 5/848. In November 1663 Pepys attended a trial at Guildhall to 'hear the best story of a cheat extended by a master of a ship'. The captain had borrowed on bottomry and insured his ship and cargo for twice their worth. He bribed his crew and pilot to allow his ship to be cast away on rocks in France and returned to London to claim £3,000 compensation. One of the insurers had the ship brought home in good repair at a cost of £6. Ship and goods were worth £500: R. C. Latham and W. Matthews (eds.), *The Diary of Samuel Pepys*, 11 vols. (London, 1970–83), vol. IV, pp. 401, 403.

[103] A dispute over an insurance premium provides an insight into the business: *Samuel Spanway* v. *Herbert Alwyn*, CLRO MC 6/471. On the market in second-hand policies see *John Duddlestone* v. *Bernard Mitchell*, 31 October 1693, PRO C 24/1164, no. 35.

[104] Josiah Child, *A New Discourse of Trade* (London, 1692), pp. 23–4.

although the refinements of a thorough classical training were regarded as unnecessary for trade and, to the regret of some commentators, merchants rarely attended university. [105] A traditional education was ill suited to commercial needs and a more practical approach was preferred. As one author on trade remarked in 1686 '[a merchant] has Latin enough to understand an author or discourse a stranger ... but thinks it scarce worth the while to have seven years under the tyranny of the ferula merely to obtain the skill of hunting a Greek derivative, and capping of verses'.[106] Thomas Brailsford specified in his will that his son, destined to be a merchant, should receive a 'good education but no extravagancy'.[107] Merchants needed to write large numbers of letters: every cargo consignment in and out involved about half a dozen letters sent in duplicate and one copy held for reference and although family members, apprentices, and clerks could be used to make journal entries and copy letters, the merchant wrote many himself, as his handwriting was a guarantee of authenticity.[108] The first requirement for intending merchants was the acquisition of a good hand that combined speedy execution with legibility. The old fashioned 'set secretary', which continued to prevail in legal circles, gave way to a more modern 'neat, charming mixture of Roman and Italian flowing with a kind of artificial negligence'.[109] The second absolute requirement of the intending merchant was mastery of basic arithmetical skills – to the rule of three or better – while knowledge of double entry book-keeping was also useful; but neither was included in the traditional classical curriculum.[110] Although the grammar schools and ancient universities remained immune to change, the expansion of

---

[105] Francis Brewster, *Essays on Trade and Navigation* (London, 1695), p. iii.

[106] *Character and Qualifications of an Honest, Loyal Merchant* (London, 1686), p. 7.

[107] Will of Thomas Brailsford, 16 September 1690, PRO PROB 11/401; Brailsford Papers, PRO C 9/177/28.

[108] Contemporary best practice required a merchant to keep ten books and deal with large volumes of paperwork: see 'Directions for keeping a merchant's accounts by way of Dr and Cr after the Italian manner', CUL CH (H) papers 89/30.

[109] *Honest, Loyal Merchant*, p. 7.

[110] Arithmetic was taught as a series of rules to be learned by heart. A standard curriculum moved from addition to division in whole numbers, through denominate numbers and reduction and then to a grand finale, the rule of three which governed problems dealing with proportions, ratios or costs of multiple units of goods. This was a benchmark rule and the minimum level at which one could be considered conversant with figures. On the importance and difficulties of obtaining training in arithmetical skills see the account of John Verney's education in Margaret M. Verney, *Memoirs of the Verney Family from the Restoration to the Revolution 1660–1696*, 4 vols. (London, 1894), vol. III, pp. 366–8; Patricia Cline Cohen, 'Reckoning with commerce: numeracy in eighteenth century America', in John Brewer and Roy Porter (eds.), *Consumption and the World of Goods* (London, 1993), pp. 320–34; B. S. Yamey, H. C. Edey, and H. W. Thomson, *Accounting in England and Scotland: 1543–1800: Double Entry in Exposition and Practice* (London, 1963).

commerce (above all the complex long-distance trades) encouraged the rise of private training facilities which provided a more modern curriculum suited to its needs which served to enhance national capabilities.[111]

A good basic education was usually followed by an apprenticeship of seven years – even if the father's citizenship made the son free of a livery company. Most of London's big colonial merchants were bound at Guildhall between the ages of fourteen and eighteen and, in the tradition of the custom of London, which had long allowed a division between livery and trade, they were dispersed between a wide range of companies: cloth-makers, dyers, embroiderers, fishmongers, grocers, haberdashers, ironmongers, mercers, merchant tailors, upholders, vintners, and weavers.[112] No one company captured the open colonial trades in the way that the drapers dominated the Levant Company.[113] Jews and Quakers were barred from membership of the livery companies and made arrangements within their own ranks.[114]

Most of the big colonial traders were apprenticed to merchants and learnt about the intricacies of charter parties, bills of lading, invoices, contracts, bills of exchange, insurance policies, weights and measures, and other details of business, including a host of unwritten customary practices. It was useful, too, to acquire some familiarity with the goods traded and an eye for quality and price. In addition to commercial skills, apprenticeship sought to instil the social values regarded as vital to success: diligence, self-control, scrupulous honesty, a meticulous attention to order and detail, and a concern for reputation.[115] Some served a period abroad although, in

[111] John Parsons, in Tower Street, advertised his services.

Merchants accounts after the most exact, plain, short, full, and practical method formerly taught by Mr Thomas Nathaniel for which he had deservedly the greatest reputation of any person in England are now taught as compulsory by John Parsons only who was his scholar and hath all his books and papers of accounts and hath had considerable experience in keeping accounts for several merchants. [Pupils] may be conveniently boarded and instructed in writing and arithmetic.

BL *Tracts on Trade*, 41. Advertisements abound in Houghton's *Collection*. On the growth of mathematical writing see John Money, 'Teaching in the market place, or "Caesar adsum jam forte: Pompey aderat"': the retailing of knowledge in provincial England during the eighteenth century', in Brewer and Porter (eds.), *Consumption and the World of Goods*, pp. 335–77.

[112] Apprenticeship records were found for twenty-four of the fifty-nine big colonial merchants of 1686 giving 15.6 as the average age of indenture.

[113] T. F. Reddaway, 'Livery companies in Tudor London', *History*, 51 (1960), 287–99.

[114] For example, Claypoole took on fellow Quaker, Edward Haistwell: Balderston (ed.), *Claypoole's Letterbook*, pp. 7–8.

[115] Disputes over apprenticeship in the Mayor's Court reveal much about mutual expectations: CLRO, MC 6 / 1–554. See Christopher Brooks, 'Apprenticeship, social mobility and the middling sort', in J. Barry and Christopher Brooks (eds.), *The Middling Sort of People* (Basingstoke, 1994), pp. 52–83; Grassby, *Business*, pp. 171–203; Gauci, *Politics of Trade*, pp. 68–73.

colonial trade, this seems to have been unusual during apprenticeship and, indeed, attracted an additional premium.[116]

Although the skills taught during apprenticeship were largely generic, some branches of trade attracted higher premiums than others, which suggests that more than mere training was on offer. Apart from education in commercial skills, apprenticeship gave access to networks of tried and trusted correspondents, and most young men were allowed to exploit this opening, and cement future relationships, by starting a small trade on their own account during their service – an especially valuable asset in risky long-distance commerce.[117] In the 1650s Sir Ralph Verney was informed that he would need to pay as much as £500 to place his son in the West India, Turkey, or East India trades as, in all these areas, 'without it be some particular men that have the knack of it, not one in three of them thrives so that those which do it makes them so high'.[118] Records of over a hundred apprenticeship disputes heard in the Mayor's Court between 1660 and 1690 suggest that such high figures were indeed paid in these lucrative, but risky, sectors where experience, and trusty contacts, counted for almost all.[119] West India traders commanded a premium of around £300 – equal to King's estimate of the annual income

[116] In all other trades we are forced to seek out such men as have been abroad and as have acquired the knowledge of other foreign languages to be factors for us; such only as are so acquainted are capable of being employed in those places by us; whereas in the trade of our plantations there being no such need every man is left in the greater latitude to send whom he will so he be fit for the business that he trusts him in, and though he have no other language than his own.

BLO Rawl. MS A478, fo. 67b,. John Gould stated in his will 'I was not at taking my apprentices engaged to send them abroad but to make them merchants and instruct them in the way of merchants': Will of John Gould, 1678, PRO PROB 11/360, fos. 321–3. For an example of an apprentice sent to Maryland during service see J. M. Price, 'Sheffeild v. Starke: institutional experimentation in the Maryland trade c. 1696–1706', *Business History*, 28 (1986), 19–31.

[117] Francis Clarke, apprentice to Sir Thomas Lane, introduced himself to David Jeffreys of Boston in 1698.

Sir. I serving an apprentice with Sir Thomas Lane have been acquainted in your dealings. Though unknown to you I have made bold to consign to you 1 bale of serges as you will see by the enclosed invoice and bill of lading shipped on board the *Constant Richard* John Jacobs master. I desire your utmost endeavours for us and if I find encouragement shall employ none but yourself.

Francis Clark to David Jeffreys, 10 May 1698, MHS, Jeffries Family Papers, vol. VII, fo. 66. For Edward Haistwell's trade as an apprentice to Claypoole see Balderston (ed.), *Claypoole's Letterbook*, pp. 72, 173.

[118] Verney, *Memoirs of the Verney Family*, vol. III, p. 369.

[119] CLRO, MC 6/1–554. Discussion of premiums is often found in wills and litigation, for example, Will of Thomas Brailsford, 16 September 1690, PRO PROB 11/401; *Brailsford and Taylors* v. *Peeres and Tooke*, PRO C 9/177/28; Will of John Gould, 15 April 1678, PRO PROB 11/360, fos. 321–3; *John Booth* and *Basil Booth* v. *William Coward*, CLRO, MC 6/452A.

of a merchant family.[120] Around £200 was paid in the tobacco trades. Meanwhile, as little as £100 might be paid to a European trader – less than the usual premium of £150 paid to substantial wholesalers.

The high premium paid for an apprenticeship to a colonial merchant suggests that it was seen as giving privileged access to the trade, but it was by no means necessary, or sufficient, for success. The available evidence reveals that, in fact, among the big colonial merchants of 1686, only a handful of those who were apprenticed were bound to colonial merchants. Gilbert Heathcote, ultimately the most successful of the 1686 traders, was apprenticed to an Eastland merchant and served a period in Sweden before diversifying into Spanish and colonial trade in the 1680s.[121] Jacob Lucy and John Taylor were also apprenticed to Eastland merchants.[122] A few were apprenticed to artisans such as Bartholomew Gracedieu, son of a dyer, who was apprenticed to a salter in 1671 and retained an interest in this business.[123] Thomas Tryon trained as a hatter and emigrated to Barbados, an affluent and fashion-conscious colony, where he set up in business and accumulated the capital and contacts necessary to set up a merchant house in London.[124] Most colonial merchants were drawn from families of the middling sort, and Tryon was exceptional, but his example shows that a man with humble origins could, with hard work, determination, and luck, enrich himself through colonial trade and, in remaining open to all, and providing a broad incentive to improve skills, the sector improved not only its own 'adaptive efficiency' but also that of the nation.

Capital, credit, and reputation

A young man intending to pursue a merchant career did not need great financial resources beyond the apprenticeship premium, especially as it was common to begin trade in partnership.[125] A number stepped into their master's business, or a family firm, such as John Gardner, who went into partnership with his kinsman, John Bawden, the leading Barbados

---

[120] Laslett (ed.), *Earliest Classics*.

[121] Evelyn D. Heathcote, *An Account of Some of the Families Bearing the Name of Heathcote* (Winchester, 1899); Eveline Cruickshanks, Stuart Handley, and D. W. Hayton (eds.), *The History of Parliament: the House of Commons, 1690–1715,* 5 vols. (Cambridge, 2002), vol. IV, pp. 309–17; Astrom, *From Cloth to Iron*, pp. 141, 149.

[122] R. W. K. Hinton, *The Eastland Trade and the Common Weal in the Seventeenth Century* (Cambridge, 1959), pp. 221–5.

[123] Cruickshanks *et al.*, *House of Commons*, vol. IV, pp. 63–4.

[124] Thomas Tryon, *Some Memoires of the Life of Mr. Thomas Tryon* (London, 1705).

[125] For typical partnership arrangements in colonial trade see the case of the three Legay brothers and a cousin who made a joint investment of £4,000 with two partners living in the West Indies: Case of *Legay and Legay*, 28 May 1676, BL Add. MS 29,800, fo. 503.

merchant of the 1680s, or the Jeffreys brothers who joined their uncle.[126] The custom of allowing apprentices to begin a small trade on their own account during service helped them to accumulate the savings needed to make a start and could be expanded by a period abroad either before, or immediately after, the period of indenture.

Given that not all colonial merchants were apprenticed to traders within that sector, it is not surprising that many also served a period of factorage elsewhere. At least two merchants among the big colonial traders of 1686 served as factors in the Baltic. After finishing his apprenticeship with an Eastland merchant in the early 1670s, Heathcote, from a big family of seven brothers, was expected to make his own way in the world and set himself up as a factor in Stockholm, working with other people's capital, and charging 2 per cent for his services. The timing was fortuitous, as English traders reaped the generous rewards of neutrality, while France and Holland were embroiled in a debilitating war. In 1679 the young Heathcote was able to return to London with sufficient funds to set up on his own account and extend his operations beyond Baltic business into the linked Spanish and colonial trades.[127]

However, over two-thirds of the big colonial merchants of 1686 for whom there is evidence spent a period in the colonies (usually after apprenticeship) where, although mortality rates could be very high (especially in the Caribbean), those who took the risk and survived, benefited from higher commissions than in Europe (8 to 10 per cent against 2 per cent), and encountered many opportunities for both honest and dishonest profit.[128] They returned to England with capital, valuable connections, and a special insight into the dangers of colonial commerce which helped them to build up both their independent and commission trade.[129]

Accumulated savings were augmented with windfall gains through inheritance and marriage. Among the fifty-nine big colonial merchants of 1686 the Eyles brothers, William Baxter, John Gardner, and others inherited comfortable sums. A shrewd marriage could also transform a

---

[126] Balderston (ed.), *Claypoole's Letterbook*, pp. 173–4; *ODNB*.

[127] Astrom, *From Cloth to Iron*, p. 149.

[128] Richard S. Dunn, *Sugar and Slaves: the Rise of the Planter Class in the English West Indies, 1624–1713* (Chapel Hill, N.C., 1972), ch. 9; Trevor Burnard, 'A failed settler society: marriage and demographic failure in early Jamaica', *Journal of Social History*, 28 (1994), 63–82. On commission rates see N. H. *Compleat Tradesman*, p. 155. High rates are borne out in merchant papers.

[129] Although at least nine acquired property in the West Indies, absentee management was precarious and most preferred to avoid the risks. In the 1680s William Hall, a merchant and factor in Jamaica, took care that all his profits were remitted to England. He never intended to stay in the island longer than it took to build up a comfortable capital sum with which he could buy an estate at home and knew that it was difficult to liquidate capital invested in a plantation: William Hall to Brailsford, 24 April 1689, 23 October 1689, Brailsford Papers, PRO C 110/152.

career and played an important role in business strategies. The mean age of marriage among the big colonial merchants of 1686 was twenty-seven, by which time they had been several years out of an apprenticeship, but were in the early stages of an independent career. Almost two-thirds of the wives were London bred, and they came overwhelmingly from the merchant, and tradesman, classes which could provide them with valuable capital and skills. Marriage often established, or consolidated, a business partnership. For example, John Harwood married his master's sister; William Baxter was in partnership with his sister's husband, William Freeman; Micajah Perry's son, Richard, married Sarah, the daughter of rival tobacco merchant, George Richards; William Walker's daughter married the West Indian merchant, Stephen Skinner; Thomas Brailsford's daughter, Sancta, married his apprentice, John Taylor.[130]

Of course, portions varied with wealth and size of family. Shortly before his death, Richard Tilden calculated that his estate was worth around £3,600 and he gave his daughter, Rose, a portion of £300 and further household goods to the value of £50.[131] George Richards, who reckoned he was worth around £8,000, gave his daughter, Sarah, £1,800.[132] Girls in small or very wealthy families did much better, and marriage to an heiress, or a rich widow, gave a great boost to a career. Gilbert Heathcote, who himself married Hester Rayner, the daughter and heiress of a successful Eastland merchant in 1682, gave his daughter a portion of £6,000, and £4,000 more after her marriage, and Jacob Lucy gave his only child, Elizabeth, a portion of £10,000, which may well have contributed to his later financial difficulties.[133] But, as working merchants appreciated, women brought more to marriage than business connections and a dowry. Most wives not only managed the household (a work and family unit), but were also involved in the commercial side of the family business, especially during busy periods, or during the husband's absence, and some were able to carry on in the event of his death.[134] A diligent, shrewd, well-educated wife was recognized as a valuable asset and could, like the 'notable, stirring woman' married to one of Brailsford's correspondents, compensate for a husband's shortcomings.[135] The demands

130 'Deposition of John Harwood', 2 April 1696, PRO C 24/1186, case 59; Vere L. Oliver, *Caribbeana: Being Miscellaneous Papers Relating to the History, Genealogy, Topography, and Antiquities of the British West Indies*, 6 vols. (London, 1909–19), vol. V (1919), p. 43; Price, *Perry*, p. 21; Will of William Walker, 2 July 1708, PRO PROB 11/503; Brailsford Papers, PRO C 110/152.
131 Will of Richard Tilden, 17 December 1696, PRO PCC 261.
132 Will of George Richards, 1690, PRO PROB. 11/421 (PCC 138).
133 Will of Gilbert Heathcote, 8 Feburary 1733, PRO PCC 45; *Blackman v. St John*, 1692, PRO C 24/1142.
134 Balderston (ed.), *Claypoole's Letterbook*, p. 223.
135 Thomas Knight to Thomas Brailsford, 24 April 1690, Brailsford Papers, PRO C 110/152.

of commerce thus exerted pressure to emulate the Dutch example and provide girls with skills in literacy and numeracy.[136]

A merchant could also expand his capital base through loans, although most of the successful merchants on both sides of the Atlantic echoed William Byrd who did 'not care to be in debt' and tried to avoid long-term, heavy borrowing.[137] Secured loans played a part in financing Atlantic trade but were largely used in times of crisis, and to compound outstanding debts, as in the case of Rainsford Waterhouse, a leading Jamaica merchant, who died in 1691 with debts of £12,000–15,000, including a number of bonds and mortgages designed to extract him from difficulties.[138] Loans were largely confined to short-term credit with the London merchant and his colonial correspondent recording transactions in open book accounts, and nothing but their individual reputations as security.[139]

Although most successful merchants avoided long-term debt, all businessmen augmented their capital base through short-term credit or trust.[140] Every link in the long chain of transactions involved in transporting goods to and fro across the Atlantic was joined by credit, and in a world where it was slow and difficult to obtain commercial information, where (in the absence of modern lending institutions) loans were between family and friends, and resort to the law was slow and expensive, the first task of an aspiring businessman was to establish a good

---

[136] Josiah Child claimed that attention to the education of women as well as men was a reason for Dutch success in commerce: Child, *A New Discourse of Trade* (1692), pp. 4–6.

[137] On consigning a cargo to England, William Byrd, who did not care to be in debt and tried to avoid long-term borrowing, would enclose a list of goods for return but usually insisted that it should be 'abated' if his goods 'did not come to expectation': Tinling (ed.), *Correspondence of Three William Byrds*, vol. I, pp. 37, 41. Debt carried heavy risks. Robert Bristow, master of the *Lucitania* which was hired by the Royal African Company in 1687, borrowed to take advantage of the captain's right to carry cargo on his own account. He borrowed £100 on a bottomry loan, sold his 5/32 share of the ship for £70, and borrowed a further £100 by mortgaging the lease on his house in Stepney. The gamble did not pay off. Bristow died in Guinea and his wife was left with problems in recovering his assets, heavy debts and a law suit: *Alice Parr, George Wood and William Bristow v. Richard Holder*, 1695, PRO C 24/1168, No. 59.

[138] *Elizabeth Waterhouse v. John Cass et al.*, 27 May 1691, PRO C 24/1139, part 2.

[139] Spencer Pigott claimed that 'a very large and considerable book debt' owing by a Boston merchant 'is as justly due as the strictest bond' but his complete failure to recover the sum after fifteen years of litigation shows the lack of security in the system. Spencer Pigott to Isaac Addington, 16 January 1706, MHS, Jeffries Family Papers, vol. V, fo. 115.

[140] The definition of trust has recently received much attention from social scientists. Gambetta gave the following definition:

When we say we trust someone or that someone is trustworthy, we implicitly mean that the probability that he will perform an action that is beneficial ... is high enough for us to consider in engaging in some form of cooperation with him. Correspondingly, when

reputation, for this underpinned his credit rating. 'Wealth is the result of credit and credit the natural effect of fair dealing.'[141]

Reputation, or trustworthiness, was built on a universally accepted code of conduct, which had evolved alongside an increasingly commercial society, combining rules of reason and religion, interest, and honour. The prototype merchant of reputation appears in contemporary print literature as a paragon of prudence, wisdom, and justice.[142] He was knowledgeable about his business. He knew, understood, and abided by merchant custom. He was diligent, but careful not to overburden his mental or physical resources. He was cautious in extending and taking credit. He regulated his domestic expenses for 'expensive living ... [is] sure to kill: for it feeds upon the two most essential branches of his trade, his credit, and his cash'.[143] He kept careful accounts. He displayed 'justice' in his dealings; performed his promises, paid and demanded a fair price for his goods, gave exact weights and measures, and provided good quality. He paid his debts promptly and took especial care not to go bankrupt, 'upon design', in order to defraud creditors of their dues for here was 'stealing, notorious hypocrisy, and dissimulation; contempt of God's law and justice and injury to men'.[144] The 'rules of the game' were clear and unambiguous but this tyranny of reputation, or business culture, did not develop independently of commercial needs – it was not exogenous as some economists argue – but evolved alongside, and in response to, the needs of the merchants' increasingly far-flung and impersonal world. In the mould of economic assumptions about rational utility maximization, the commercial community – and above all long-distance traders – had drawn on common traditions of reason and religion to develop rules of behaviour which

we say that someone is untrustworthy, we imply that that probability is low enough for us to refrain from doing so.

D. Gambetta, 'Can we trust trust?' in D. Gambetta (ed.), *Trust: Making and Breaking Cooperative Relations* (New York, 1988), pp. 213–37. Nuala Zahedieh, 'Credit, risk and reputation in late seventeenth century colonial trade', in Olaf U. Janzen (ed.), *Merchant Organization and Maritime Trade in the North Atlantic, 1660–1815* (Newfoundland, 1998), pp. 53–74.

[141] *Case of the Fair Trader* (London, 1686). The theme recurs again and again in merchant correspondence. For example, in 1688 William Byrd urged his brother, 'I hope you will improve your time and acquaintance and be just and fair in your dealings, for now is your time to get credit or never. You must be diligent and careful now to get a good reputation and I will not be wanting to do all the offices of love and service that lies in my way': Tinling (ed.), *Correspondence of Three William Byrds*, vol. I, pp. 76–7.

[142] Examples include Richard Steele, *A Tradesman's Calling* (London, 1686); *Honest, Loyal Merchant; A Description of Plain Dealing, Truth and Death which all Men Ought to Mind whilst they do live on Earth* (London, 1686).

[143] Steele, *Tradesman's Calling*, p. 31.

[144] *The Case of the Fair Trader.*

would promote cooperation, and enhance overall welfare; adherents were promised wealth and honour, while deviants were consigned to serious damage to pocket and pride as well as a stinging conscience and, above all, punishment from God.[145]

The importance of trust made it vital for a merchant to advertise his 'credit' and reputation. Self-puffery was common in commercial correspondence but carried little weight without more convincing evidence of 'uniformly upright conduct'.[146] Merchants needed to be prepared to take occasional losses and to accept the arbitration of 'honest men' in cases of dispute such as that between William Freeman and John Fleet in 1678. Fleet, a major sugar re-exporter, had made an advance agreement to buy a cargo of muscovado sugar from Freeman at the price current on its arrival which, for 'good merchantable sugar', turned out to be 25.5 shillings per hundredweight. However, the goods proved such low quality that Fleet refused to comply with the contract, and Freeman referred the matter to the arbitration of 'some honest men' who supported Fleet's opinion that the goods 'could not bear the name of sugars', and that the bargain was void. None the less, in the interests of preserving a good long-term relationship and his own reputation for 'square-dealing', Fleet made a 'fair proposal' that Freeman should try the market with his sugar, and he would pay one shilling per hundredweight above the best price offered. Several sugar bakers came to look at the goods and offered, at most, 20.5 shillings per hundredweight and Fleet paid 21.5 shillings for what was agreed to be 'trash'. Freeman lamented that his Nevis agent had been 'basely abused' by his supplier, but the compromise brokered

---

[145] The idea that 'culture' was exogenous and, in the case of northern Europe, favourable to business success has a long tradition and was most famously stated in Max Weber, *The Protestant Ethic and the Spirit of Capitalism* (London, 1930). It has recently figured prominently in discussion of Japan as a 'high trust' society where the determinants of trust are reduced to a murkily defined notion of culture, which is taken as exogenous; Fukuyama states that 'community depends on trust, and trust is in turn culturally determined'. In similar vein sociologist Ron Dore has written that Japan's Confucian heritage has engendered trust in that society. Such trust builds up over time, through a series of historical experiences: Francis Fukuyama, *Trust: the Social Virtues and the Creation of Prosperity* (New York, 1995); Ron Dore, *Taking Japan Seriously* (Stanford, Calif., 1987). At the other extreme rational-thinking economists, building on the well-known 'folk theorem' assume trust to be a direct result of the traditional economic assumptions of rational utility-maximization. Trust here is essentially enforced cooperation based on repeated interaction and the possibility of punishing cheaters in the future: D. Fudenberg and J. Tirole, *Game Theory* (Cambridge, Mass., 1992).

[146] During a political crisis in Jamaica in 1688 which resulted in a substantial devaluation of sterling William Hall lamented that 'its nonsense to trade at such vast disadvantages and really what we do now is with an ill-will, but must do it that may not lose the reputation that have gained amongst my friends of selling cheap': Halls to Brailsford, 20 June 1689, Brailsford Papers, PRO C 110/152.

by 'honest men' allowed both sides to share the loss arising from inferior goods and preserve their business reputations.[147]

Public marks of probity such as parish, or City, office played an important role in underwriting reputations and no doubt contributed to the evident willingness to accept such burdens. Among the fifty-nine big colonial merchants of 1686, all those eligible for office took part (most in multiple ways), and Gauci has shown high levels of merchant involvement in vestry affairs even among non-conformists. For example Bartholomew Gracedieu, one of the managers of the Presbyterian fund in 1690, served on the parish committee of the riverside parish of St Magnus Martyr from the 1680s until 1708, shortly before his bankruptcy.[148] Thirteen of the big colonial merchants of 1686 secured election as aldermen, demonstrating to the world that they were drawn from the highest ranks of City society (with an estate worth at least £10,000). This reputational value may explain why a merchant such as John Jeffreys agreed to stand for election, as he did with success in Bread Street ward in 1660, then immediately paid a fine of £820 to avoid taking up his duties although he used the title of alderman, with all its reassuring implications of wealth and respectability, throughout the rest of his long career.[149] Involvement in charitable works such as schools and hospitals provided a similar seal of respectability and leading merchants were engaged in a busy round of philanthropic activity with the attendant opportunities to advertise Christian principles and surplus resources.[150]

Just as it was important to build, and maintain, one's own reputation in business it was equally necessary to make an accurate assessment of the credit of others. At each stage of the complex processes involved in colonial exchange the merchant needed to trust the 'fidelity, diligence, and honesty' of agents.[151] Suppliers, packers, captains, colonial correspondents, insurers, or purchasers were all in a position to undo him: overcharging invoices; providing goods of low quality; sending short supply; handling goods without proper care; reserving the better quality business for themselves; refusing to pay insurance

---

[147] 'Letterbook of William Freeman', NLJ MS 134, fo. 3.

[148] Gauci, *Politics of Trade*, p. 86.

[149] William Barnes, Thomas Clarke, John and Francis Eyles, John Gardner, William Gore, Bartholomew Gracedieu, Gilbert Heathcote, John Jeffreys, Jacob Lucy, Joseph Martin, Benjamin Skutt, Richard Tilden were elected and William Walker withdrew. On Jeffreys see Woodhead, *Rulers of London*, p. 97; *ODNB*; 'Petition of Mr Alderman Jeffreys and Mr Lucy about their debt in Sweden', 7 July 1680, PRO CO 388/1, pt 1, fo. 162.

[150] For example, Gilbert Heathcote was an original commissioner for Greenwich Naval Hospital in 1695 and President of St Thomas's Hospital 1722–33.

[151] N. H. *Compleat Tradesman*, p. 155.

claims; extending credit without proper caution; defaulting on payment. Misplaced trust was the major source of commercial loss, and Richard Steele exhorted any merchant to take pains to make diligent enquiries about those he intended to engage with in business, for 'certain it is that there is prudence in trusting some, and charity in trusting others; [but] so there are many whom it is neither prudence or charity to trust at all'.[152]

Information about character and reputation was eagerly sought, and fairly easy to obtain in the densely packed City of London. Although some merchants lived outside City jurisdiction – especially in Hackney, Stepney, Wapping, and Hoxton – most lived within the walls and, according to De Krey, 90 per cent of active merchants lived in the eastern wards.[153] Almost a quarter of the fifty-nine big colonial merchants of 1686 lived in the Thames-side parish of St Dunstan-in-the-East which incorporated a stretch of the Legal Quays (Illustration 11). Residents such as Richard Cary, Gilbert Heathcote, Richard Merriweather, Thomas Starke, Richard Tilden, Thomas Tryon, and William Paggen must have passed each other in the streets on a daily basis when moving from their home to quayside, to Custom House, and Exchange. Wives, children, apprentices, and servants must have met in streets, shops, schools, and church and exchanged gossip on a regular basis. Neighbourhood propinquity was commonly reinforced by the high levels of participation in parish business, even among nonconformists. Regular meetings and church attendance kept all abreast of local news.

Information was pooled and each man's credit was determined by talk at the merchants' meeting place, the Royal Exchange. Gresham's original bourse, built between Cornhill and Threadneedle Street, was opened by Queen Elizabeth in 1571, and destroyed by the Great Fire of 1666 and its importance to the business activities of the City was reflected in the speed with which a second exchange was built on the same site and opened in September 1669. Both were designed in the tradition of a public marketplace with four arcades built around an open courtyard intended to minimize undesirable commercial behaviour and, within this space, each group of traders had their own

---

[152] Steele, *Tradesman's Calling*, p. 68. Examples of misplaced trust abound in court records. For example, see Sir Henry Crosley on Austin and Paisley whom he had believed to be 'substantial and honest' dealers in tobacco before being sadly disabused: PRO E 112/473.

[153] Only 138 of the 1,829 merchants listed in Lee's *Directory* lived outside the City jurisdiction: Lee, *Little London Directory*. Three of the fifty-nine big colonial merchants of 1686 are known to have lived outside the City: Fowler, Johnson, and Taylor.

Illustration 11 View of the Custom House and the Legal Quays between London Bridge and the Tower of London where all overseas traders were required to unload their goods. William Morgan, *London &c Actually Survey'd* (1682).

particular position (see Illustrations 8, 10, and 12).[154] This busy concourse was at the heart of London's commercial life and the imperative
of regular attendance for monitoring, and maintaining, reputations,
was a prime reason for the continued residence of most merchants in
the City, despite high rents, crowded conditions, and dirty air. Most
merchants attended the Exchange daily and were scathing about the
less conscientious.[155]

Monitoring behaviour in London was difficult but monitoring behaviour across the Atlantic was infinitely more difficult still. The long distance and the unpredictability of colonial trade made it impractical to
constrain agents with rigid instructions and most were merely exhorted
to 'carefully, diligently, and faithfully employ [themselves] according
to the best and utmost of [their] power, knowledge and experience'.[156]
Much was of necessity left to the agents' discretion and the principal had
difficulty in assessing how well his interests had been served. As Freeman
complained to a correspondent in the Caribbean 'you know at this distance I cannot well judge of things'.[157]

Vigorous efforts were made to develop and refine strategies to promote desirable conduct and punish cheats. Bonds were taken for large
sums to secure good behaviour on the part of agents and partners.
Thomas Sadler bound himself for £5,000 to Dalby, John, and Charles
Thomas for good performance of articles of agreement 'touching a trade
and factory' to be carried on between London and Barbados, whereas
the African Company required junior factors to give security of £400,
and merchants between £800 and £1500.[158] Commission rates were

---

[154] In the interval merchants used Gresham College as a meeting place. The colonial traders
were placed together in the south-west corner; Spanish, Portuguese, and Jewish traders
were in the south-east corner; ship-brokers were in the centre with druggists, grocers,
dyers, and bay factors: Ann Saunders, *The Royal Exchange* (London, 1991); Natasha
Glaisyer, *The Culture of Commerce in England, 1660–1720* (Woodbridge, Suffolk, 2006),
pp. 27–68.

[155] Balderston (ed.), *Claypoole's Letterbook*, p. 183.

[156] 'Indenture between William Paggen and John Hardiman', 1684, BLO. MS Aubrey 4
(SC 252 79), fo.1. The Halls stressed the need for flexibility:

I must tell you I desire you to give me free liberty to do what I shall think best or else
cannot serve you nor anyone else, for if my friend thinks me not capable to manage their
affairs without tying me up, do think it best way for them so not to trust me, so that
I may take the liberty as its all reason, so that I am cautious enough of making returns
and willing to serve my friend. (Halls to Brailsford, September 1688, Brailsford Papers,
PRO C 110/152)

[157] Hancock (ed.), *Letters of William Freeman*, p. 133.

[158] 'Examination of Josiah Jones', 31 March 1686, CLRO, MCD, box 40; Davies, *African
Company*, p. 256. Merchants gave bond when entrusted with individual cargoes as did
Charles Redford for £550 when trusted by Edward Ellis, silkman, with a cargo worth
£207 4s 2d: CLRO, MCD, box 40.

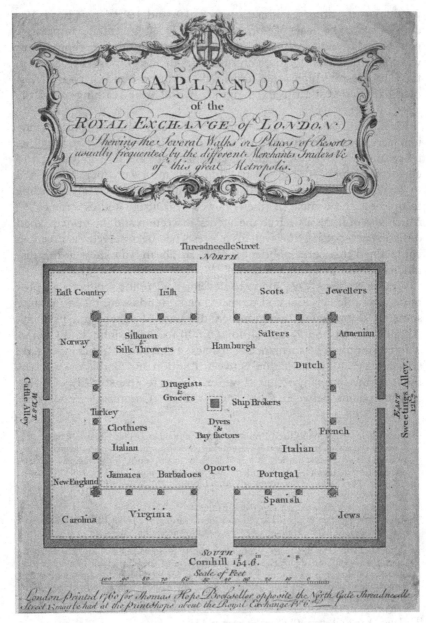

Illustration 12 The floor plan of the Royal Exchange shows how different groups of traders had their own designated meeting places inside the Exchange. Anon., Guildhall Library.

substantially higher in colonial trade than in other branches of overseas commerce and made the premium for maintaining trust, and a
good relationship, much greater and its loss more damaging. Agents
in the colonies were paid 8 to 10 per cent, against 2 or 3 per cent paid
in the Baltic, France, Spain, and Portugal and as little as 1.5 per cent
in Holland.[159] Further efforts were made to ensure loyalty and mutual
dependence through offering incentives such as repeat trade, exclusive agency, and shares in trading ventures.[160] All was cemented by the
social capital invested in the relationship. Merchants on both sides of
the Atlantic took pains to share news, exchange gifts, and other marks
of friendship, which served to enhance the cost of a breakdown in the
relationship.[161]

Unfortunately for many London merchants, the returns to cheating in the
colonies were so high, and the risk of rapid exposure so low, that generous
commissions, mutuality, and social capital often counted for little.[162] It took
William Freeman eight years to realize the extent of his losses in Montserrat
at the hands of a 'crafty, undermining sophister' who, through embezzlement, had 'raised himself to a very considerable estate'.[163] Freeman's plight
was commonplace and the law, regarded by many as a blunt instrument for
recovering losses at home, was an even blunter instrument for dealing with

---

[159] N. H. *Compleat Tradesman*, p. 155.

[160] Henry Ashurst to Hampden, 1684, BLO, Ashurst Letterbook; 'Doubt not our capacity and honesty since we intend to come in a share with you': Halls to Aylward,
21 November 1688, Brailsford Papers, PRO C 110/152. The inventories of the big
merchants reveal that it was usual to maintain a mixture of commission business and
trade on own account. For example see Richard Merriweather's inventory, PRO PROB
5/1543; Price, 'Sheffeild v. Starke'.

[161] The Halls gave friends such as Heathcote a doubloon on returning home to 'drink
with ye club mine and my wife's health': Halls to Brailsford, 25 September 1688,
Brailsford Papers, PRO C 110/152. These strategies run through all merchant correspondence. Recent work attributes the spread of institutional/organizational efficiency,
growth rates, and per capita income between Italian regions to differences in 'social
capital' defined as the additional rule-enforcing power available to communities with
an extended network of horizontal social relations: R. Putnam, *Making Democracy
Work: Civic Traditions in Modern Italy* (Princeton, 1993). The idea that cooperative social
relations facilitate cooperation in the workplace is well established. For a theoretical
explanation see Giancarlo Spagnola, 'Social relations and cooperation in organizations',
Journal of Economic Behaviour and Organization, 38 (1999), 1–25.

[162] A large body of game-theory literature considers the behaviour of players in repeated
prisoners' dilemmas under imperfect information. It is intuitive that, if players are less
able to monitor the actions of others, there will be less cooperation (and hence increased
opportunistic behaviour), since this makes it more difficult to ascertain whether or not
cheating has occurred. This intuition has been confirmed by D. Fudenberg, D. Levine,
and E. Maskin, 'The folk theorem and imperfect public information', *Econometrica*, 62
(1994), 997–1039.

[163] Letter, 14 September 1682, 'Letterbook of William Freeman', NLJ, MS 134, fo. 387.

Prospect of GUILD—HALL.   Vᵁᴱ ᴅᴱ ʟ Hôᴛᴇʟ ᴅᴇ Vɪʟʟᴇ. ᴀ Lᴏɴᴅʀᴇꜱ.

Illustration 13 Guildhall has been since at least the early twelfth
century the centre of government and civic ceremonial of the City of
London. The building also housed various courts. Gutted by fire in
1666 it was rapidly restored by Peter Mills, incorporating much of the
surviving medieval fabric, from 1667 to 1671. The cost of rebuilding
the whole complex was £37,000. Anon., Guildhall Library.

crime across the Atlantic.[164] London's colonial merchants made heavy use
of the Mayor's Court at Guildhall, 'a court of record of law and equity',
which was open to any person whether a freeman or not, where 'the gist
of an action arose within the City', and where neither plaintiff nor defend-
ant was required to be resident in the City (Illustration 13).[165] Over half a

---

[164] 'If you would grow rich be not given to law, for the quarrelling dog hath a tattered skin;
and men of strife, like too sharp a sword, cut their own scabbard' warned one pamphleteer. N. H. *The Pleasant Art of Moneycatching* (London, 1686), p. 134.

[165] For a detailed account of the Mayor's Court see Alexander Pulling, *A Practical Treatise
on the Laws, Customs and Regulations of the City and Port of London* (London, 1842). For
a flavour of the Court's business and heavy use for colonial affairs see CLRO, MCD,
boxes 30, 35, and 40.

sample of forty colonial cases from the 1680s were actions in debt (twenty-six), and the bulk were concerned with short, or non-existent, returns, but the outcome was seldom satisfactory.[166] In cases where the debtor had credit in London it was possible to attach goods belonging to the creditor (garnishee), but it was impossible to touch any money, or property, held in the colonies.[167] English law had little success in preventing, or punishing, opportunistic behaviour across the Atlantic.

A merchant needed only limited financial resources to enter colonial trade, but his success was heavily dependent on preserving his own credit and reputation and, above all, establishing strong relationships with trustworthy agents, which was difficult in nearby trades, but harder still over the long distances involved in colonial trade. Given the difficulty in maintaining such relationships, it is unsurprising that, as discussed above, the big colonial merchants of 1686 displayed very high levels of regional specialization which concentrated their trading activities and trust on one destination.[168]

Merchant associations

The difficulties encountered in establishing credit and reputation in their risky long-distance trade, exacerbated by the lack of a corporate organizing body, encouraged colonial merchants to develop a flourishing associational structure to provide information exchange and mutual support. The livery companies which had long dominated the City's economic, political, and social life did not play a major role in structuring colonial commerce. Freedom of the City was not required for entry into colonial trade, as it was in the regulated sectors, and only half the big colonial merchants of 1686 were apprenticed in a guild. Furthermore, despite the fiscal and legal privileges, only around two-thirds of those who were eligible took up the freedom, and many delayed until the stage of their careers when they wished to play an active role in politics, or at least obtain a parliamentary vote.[169] As indicated earlier colonial merchants were dispersed among a wide range of companies,

[166] The forty colonial cases included twenty-six debt cases, thirteen registration of articles of agreement or powers of attorney and five miscellaneous cases (mainly over inheritance): CLRO, MCD, box 40.
[167] Some merchants, especially those with land in the plantations, made debt-collecting journeys to the colonies: 'Deposition of Joseph Martin', 4 September 1693, PRO C 24/1161, 25.
[168] Contemporary recognition of the difficulty of dispersed trust is reflected in Claypoole's advice against trusting Charles Turner: 'he is a young man of little experience, and has too many sorts of trade to flourish', Balderston (ed.), *Claypoole's Letterbook*, p. 119.
[169] Unfreemen (such as William Freeman) could avoid higher duties by trading in partnership with a freeman (William Baxter) to whom goods were consigned: letter, 6 September 1680, 'Letterbook of William Freeman', NLJ, MS 134.

and had little scope for using the livery as a vehicle for collective action, or effective sanction of delinquency. None the less, as stressed by Gauci, the livery halls did remain important centres of sociability, useful gossip, and business support.[170] A cluster of five haberdashers among the fifty-nine big colonial merchants of 1686 joined together in several business ventures, as did the two vintners, Gracedieu and Heathcote, who were both leading Jamaica merchants.[171] A number of the big colonial merchants of 1686 were sufficiently committed to their liveries to take office – in most cases a stepping stone to a broader political stage.[172]

The City trading companies had more focused economic interests than the livery companies and played more part in structuring merchant association. Colonial merchants were, unsurprisingly, prominent in the Royal African Company and accounted for around half the original merchant investors. They included seven of the big colonial merchants of 1686 (Duck, Gardner, Hill, Jeffreys, Lucy, Skutt, and Walker), although only four (Jeffreys, Lucy, Skutt, and Thomas) were heavily involved in the core company management which, before 1688, spawned regular (sometimes daily) meetings and a number of outside partnerships.[173] Colonial merchants were also prominent in companies focused on trade outside the Atlantic. At least six of the fifty-nine big colonial traders of 1686 were members of the Eastland Company, reflecting the complementary interests of Baltic and Atlantic commerce, and again embarked on a number of joint business enterprises.[174]

However, the increased hostility to the king's use of his prerogative rights undermined the strength and value of Crown chartered privileges

[170] Gauci, *Politics of Trade*, pp. 137–43.
[171] The haberdashers were Francis Eyles, Joseph Martin, Richard Merriweather, Micajah Perry, and Thomas Starke. On the company see Ian W. Archer, *The History of the Haberdashers Company* (Chichester, 1991). Martin and Merriweather were landholders and agents for the Leeward Islands; they were both members of the New England Company. Together with Perry, Starke, and other merchants they were involved in the tobacco contract: J. M. Price, *The Tobacco Adventure to Russia: Enterprise, Politics, and Diplomacy in the Quest for a Northern Market for English Colonial Tobacco, 1676–1722* (Philadelphia, 1961).
[172] Gore was Master of the Mercers Company; Gracedieu and Heathcote both served as Master of the Vintners Company; Harwood (despite being a Quaker) of the Clothworkers; Jeffreys was Master of the Grocers, the king's company; Skutt of the Ironmongers; and Tilden of the Embroiderers.
[173] The autobiographical subscriptions are in the 'Minutes of the General Court', PRO T 70/100. Minutes of meetings are found in PRO T 70/80, T 70/81. Dalby Thomas became an assistant in 1698 and ended his career as agent general of the Company in the Gold Coast: Davies, *African Company*, p. 245; 'Petition of Mr Alderman Jeffreys and Mr Lucy about their debt in Sweden', 7 July 1680, PRO CO 388/1, part 1, fo. 162.
[174] Carleton, Gore, Heathcote, Jeffreys, Lucy, and Taylor were members: Hinton, *Eastland Trade*, pp. 221–5. A Joseph Martin was a member but not the West India merchant of the same name: see J. M. Price, 'Joseph Martin', *Notes and Queries*, 203 (1958), 440–1.

and fuelled the 'free trade' movement.[175] Barriers to entry were lowered, as in the Eastland Company where the entry fee was reduced from £20 to £2 in 1673, and membership swelled.[176] It became more difficult to exert control, or secure discipline, in the style of more exclusive associations, and functions that had been left to companies in earlier times (excluding foreigners from trade, providing protection and regulation, negotiating with foreign powers) were increasingly assumed by the state. Where privilege did remain – as in the monopolistic African and Hudson's Bay trades – it was easily flouted. In the 1680s the private slave trade was worth at least half that of the Royal African Company and exposure as an interloper inflicted neither huge financial damage or shame.[177] At least one of the big colonial merchants of 1686, William Walker, was excluded from the Royal African Company after suspicion of private trade.[178] None the less, like the guilds, the trading companies held dinners, and meetings, which provided opportunities for exchanging information and promoting mutual interests such as the campaign to secure a contract to supply the Russian tobacco monopoly, and they also acted as important channels of communication with government agencies, above all the Lords of Trade.[179]

As privileged corporations lost their bite, merchants combined in numerous informal associations with common concerns. In 1671, as the Crown stepped up its efforts to tighten control over colonial administration and extract greater revenues, a group of leading Barbados merchants, including John Bawden and Jacob Lucy, were prominent in setting up a counterweight lobby group, called the Gentlemen Planters of Barbados, with strong connections to the island's governing elite. The group met every Friday at the Cardinal's Cap tavern in Cornhill, near the Exchange, and their agent regularly attended meetings of the Privy Council committee for trade and plantations in order to represent their collective concerns.[180] Other colonial elites formed similar 'clubs' to nurture strong transatlantic bonds, disseminate information, and protect their interests.[181]

[175] Hinton, *Eastland Trade*, pp. 138–66.
[176] *Ibid.*, pp. 155–6.
[177] Davies, *African Company*, pp. 101–22.
[178] 'Minute Book of Court of Assistants of RAC of England', no. 3, 1676–1678, 12 June 1677, 24 July 1677, PRO T 70/77, fos. 34, 43b.
[179] The Lords of Trade regularly consulted the companies on a wide range of issues: PRO CO 138/4, fo. 348. Heathcote used his position as treasurer of the Eastland Company to entertain the Czar at a company banquet and promote his syndicate's efforts to obtain the tobacco contract: Price, *Tobacco Adventure*.
[180] 'Journal of the Assembly of Barbados', 1670–73, PRO CO 31/2, fos. 32–7.
[181] For a reference to the Jamaica club see Halls to Brailsford, 25 September 1688, Brailsford Papers, PRO C 110/152. Lillian M. Penson, *The Colonial Agents of the British West Indies* (London, 1924), pp. 1–78; Alison G. Olson, *Making the Empire Work: London and American Interest Groups, 1690–1790* (Cambridge, Mass., 1992), pp. 27–9.

Colonial merchants combined in numerous other associations which, at first sight, had little explicit connection with commerce. A small group of committed non-conformists, including at least three of the big colonial merchants of 1686, was involved in the New England Company, patented in 1661 as a missionary project designed to christianize the American Indians, but accused of being used to channel substantial funds into 'private men's purses', and used in the 1690s as a vehicle for obtaining naval stores contracts.[182] The Honourable Artillery Company was a 'genteel citizens' society for the private exercise of arms', which became seen as a Whig club, and reinforced bonds between like-minded individuals in ways that were likely to enhance business relationships.[183] Each of the many City associations that flourished in the period provided some economic, social, and political benefits, and examination of the big colonial merchants' lives reveals that all belonged to a handful of such clubs which combined with Church, and companies, to seal reputations, encourage exchange of information, strengthen mutual regard, and promote various business enterprises.

Trust networks

Most colonial merchants belonged to a handful of formal and informal groups with overlapping memberships and the pattern of association was regular rather than random; it was structured by family, place of origin, occupation, religion, or political convictions to construct more solid, reliable networks of trust than those that could be achieved by any lone merchant.

Most traders turned first to kin networks to structure their associations and cement the necessary bonds. Many obtained their training and initial capital from a family member, many followed kin in choosing a livery, many shared their family's religious and political beliefs. On seeking

[182] Sir Thomas Lane, Martin, and Merriweather were involved in the New England Company which was set up on the lines of an earlier society of 1649 designed for 'civilising, employing, educating, or placing out the natives or their children'. It was not to exceed forty-five members: 'Patent of incorporation of a company for the propagation of the gospel in New England', 7 Feb. 1661, *CSPC, 1661–8*, no. 223; William Kellaway, *The New England Company, 1649–1776* (London, 1961); Bailyn, *New England Merchants*, pp. 119, 183–4; *CSPC, 1693–5*, nos. 849, 851, 856, 865, 891, 940, 945, 946, 947, 957, 960, 962.

[183] This society became embroiled in the City's political quarrels when its leadership was snatched from the Tories by Whig magistrates in 1708 and prevented the Tories from gaining a complete monopoly of military resources in London after the 1710 Lieutenancy alteration. By 1713, the London Whigs regarded the company as a Hanoverian militia, and all the places on its Court of Assistants were held by reliable persons: De Krey, *Fractured Society*, p. 263; G. Gould Walker, *The Honourable Artillery Company, 1537–1947*, 2nd edn (Aldershot, 1954).

to establish a correspondence most echoed Ashurst's pleadings to his cousin Hampden that 'upon the score of relation as well as your own interest you will do what you can in the sales'.[184] James Claypoole corresponded with his brother, Edward, in Barbados; Gilbert Heathcote, the most successful merchant in the 1686 portbook database, was the oldest of seven brothers spread between Jamaica, New York, the Baltic, and London; Bartholomew Gracedieu had a brother in Jamaica; and Dalby Thomas had a brother in Barbados.[185] At least thirty-two of London's fifty-nine big colonial merchants of 1686 had similar links, some such as those of William Baxter going back a generation to the pioneer settlers, and a family that was deeply enmeshed with Leeward Island society as was that of his brother-in-law, William Freeman.[186]

However, families frequently failed to meet expectations: cousins, nephews, siblings, and even fathers and sons, proved disappointing. Moses Barrow bequeathed only £10 to his son in New York 'who has been very disobedient to me' and left all his remaining estate to his daughter, Grace.[187] Merchant records are littered with other tales of recalcitrant kin folk.[188] The pool of family members was limited (the big colonial merchants had an average of three children) and the number with talent often even more so. Sentiment was more likely to cloud judgement when dealing with family members rather than strangers and family members' fortunes were likely to be positively correlated which reduced their efficacy as a safety net in crisis. Family discipline was often undermined by inheritance arrangements, especially among those from the landed classes where primogeniture was the norm, but also among the middling sorts where, although there might be a more even division, sons often received little beyond the cost of training and apprenticeship.[189] Exclusion from

---

[184] BLO, Ashurst Letterbook, fo. 35.

[185] Balderston (ed.), *Claypoole's Letterbook*; Heathcote, *Account of some of the Families bearing the Name of Heathcote*; Dixon Ryan Fox, *Caleb Heathcote, Gentleman Colonist, 1692–1721* (New York, 1924); JA, Powers of Attorney, 1B/11/24, vol. VIII, fo. 27; vol. IX fos. 105b, 176, 183, 198; Will of Thomas Gracedieu, 21 October 1678, PRO PROB. 11/360; Tinling (ed.), *Correspondence of Three William Byrds*, vol. I, pp. 75, 95; 'Examination of Josiah Jones', 31 March 1686, CLRO, MCD, box 40.

[186] Hancock, ' "World of business to do" ', 12–13.

[187] Will of Moses Barrow, 1735, PRO PCC 1741.

[188] For example, Benjamin Skutt also effectively disinherited his eldest son, William, who had been 'very unkinde to me and hath very unjustly dealt with me': Will of Benjamin Skutt, 1697, PRO PCC 122 Pett. In 1658 Thomas Povey appointed Edward Bradbourne of the island of Barbados, a merchant, to demand his dues from William Povey, his brother: BL Egerton MS 2,395, fo. 239.

[189] Y. Ben Porath, 'The F-Connection: families, friends, and firms and the organization of exchange', *Population Development Review*, 6 (1980), 1–30. On late seventeenth-century testamentary practice among London freemen see Henry Horwitz, 'Testamentary practice, family strategies, and the last phases of the custom of London, 1600–1725', *Law and History Review*, 2 (1984), 223–39.

the family circle was not always viewed with horror. Many merchants expanded their notion of family to include all fellow countrymen. The Modyford clan drew heavily on West Country connections; Jeffreys had close links with fellow Welshmen such as Secretary Leoline Jenkins to whom he bequeathed £2,000 in his will; Jacob Lucy seems to have relied on Dutch connections early in his career.[190] However, while drawing on similar strengths as kin networks, these ethnic and regional connections also faced limits to their enforcement capabilities.

Minority religious groups used the language of kinship to describe the nature of their associations, but the lives of those in the portbook sample of 1686 suggest that they were, in fact, more effective than family networks in extracting the loyalty, mutual support, and unconditional obedience among members which promoted success in long-distance trade. Non-conformist groups such as the Presbyterians, Baptists, and Quakers drew advantage from high commitment, as did the Huguenots and Jews.[191] Information circulated rapidly in these close-knit communities, even when spread out over large areas, and members had a high stake in maintaining their social capital within the group. Religious allegiance can be ascertained for about thirty-one of the fifty-nine big merchants of 1686, and includes ten or so Quakers, and seven Jews, which are higher numbers than would be predicted from their proportion of London's population.[192] Furthermore, whereas most of the big colonial merchants of 1686 concentrated their business on one destination, the Quakers and Jews spread their trade and trust more widely, and this suggests a greater capacity to obtain good behaviour from agents; almost half the Jews (three out of seven) spread their West Indian import trade evenly between at least two destinations whereas thirty-six out of forty-one non-Jewish merchants focused overwhelmingly on one destination.

---

[190] SRO Walker Heneage MSS DD/WHh 1089, 1090, 1151; Will of John Jeffreys, 20 November 1688, PRO PCC 150 Exton; 'Deposition of Cornelis Carstens', 1669, PRO CO 1/24, fo. 41.

[191] David Ormrod, 'The Atlantic economy and the "Protestant Capitalist International", 1651–1775', *Historical Research*, 66 (1993), 197–208; Robin D. Gwynne, *Huguenot Heritage: the History and Contribution of the Huguenots in Britain* (London, 1985); Jon Butler, *The Huguenots in America: a Refugee People in New World Society* (Cambridge, 1983); J. F. Bosher, 'Huguenot merchants and the Protestant International in the seventeenth century', *WMQ*, 52 (1995), 77–102.

[192] Among the fifty-nine big merchants in the 1686 database Allestree and Tryon were non-conformists of some sort; John and Francis Eyles and Merriweather were Baptists; Gracedieu, Jackson, and Sir Thomas Lane were Presbyterians; Paggen was a Huguenot. Probable and certain Quakers include William Barnes, Thomas Clarke, William Coward, William Crouch, John Crow, Robert Curtis, John Daveson, Samuel Groome, Henry Hale, John Harwood. Jewish merchants were Moses Barrow (otherwise Anthony Lauzado), Joseph Bueno, Anthony Gomezsera, Peter and Pierre Henriques, Manuel Mendez, and Emanuel Perara.

In the export trade six out of seven Jews spread their business between several destinations whereas thirty-one out of thirty-six non-Jews focused on one destination.

The importance of Quakers in colonial commerce is well established and their business success is often attributed to unusual virtue.[193] William Crouch, a Quaker among the leading colonial traders of 1686, lauded his co-religionists as 'modest, temperate, true, and constant in their word and actions', thrifty, and eschewing any ostentation.[194] Largely recruited from the same artisan and merchant classes as the colonial traders, it is unsurprising that they espoused an ethical framework that was designed to deal with the problems presented in the world in which they lived – an increasingly impersonal world revolving around reputation and trust.[195] Quakers focused on dealing with the human frailties that were the source of ruin of many of their neighbours. Instructions were issued in 1675 'that none trade beyond their ability nor stretch beyond their compass; and that they use few words in their dealings and keep their word in all things, lest they bring through their forwardness dishonour to the precious truth of God'.[196] The advice reflected the morality embedded in the code of conduct that was promoted in contemporary advice books and discussion of commercial reputation. Quakers were not differentiated by their ethical code, but they were differentiated by their capacity to enforce it.

Crouch, son of a religious Hampshire yeoman family, who apprenticed himself in London in 1646 and was there 'convinced' by the early Quakers, has left an account of their activities which highlights a number of sources of their strength in the secular world.[197] Persecution in England, which continued sporadically between the Restoration and the reign of James II, encouraged the 40,000 or so Friends to form a tight-knit, disciplined structure.[198] There was a meeting in every county

---

[193] Frederick. B. Tolles, *Meeting House and Counting House: the Quaker Merchants of Colonial Philadelphia, 1682–1763* (Chapel Hill, N.C., 1948). Sacks provides extensive discussion of the success of Quakers and others in Bristol's Atlantic trade: David Harris Sacks, *The Widening Gate: Bristol and the Atlantic Economy, 1450–1700* (Berkeley, Calif., 1991), pp. 304–29.

[194] William Crouch, *Posthuma Christiana or a Collection of Some Papers of Wiliam Crouch Being a Brief Historical Account under his own Hand* (London, 1712), pp. 131, 182.

[195] Alan Cole 'The social origins of the early friends', *Journal of the Friends Historical Society*, 48 (1956–8), 99–118; Richard T. Vann and David Eversley, *Friends in Life and Death: the British and Irish Quakers in the Demographic Transition, 1650–1900* (Cambridge, 1992), pp. 68–72.

[196] 'Concerning trading', Friends' House, London, Yearly Meeting Minutes, vol. I (1668–93), 27th day, 3rd month 1675, fo. 19.

[197] Crouch, *Posthuma Christiana*.

[198] In 1683 Claypoole reported the difficulties in London. The civil authorities had locked the doors of all the meeting houses and put men on guard to keep members out; the

of England, and most colonies – where they were allowed freedom to practise their religion – and all were in regular communication with the London Yearly Meeting and its committees, the hub of regulation, information, and support.[199] Directives from the Yearly Meeting were copied out and sent to all other meetings exhorting not only 'self-examination and a serious consideration of the operations of the spirit' but also that all take extreme, watchful care of other Friends to ensure that 'all things proceed in good order'. All were expected to observe rules against over-trading, imprudence in business affairs, above all culpable bankruptcy, or breaking trust in any way.[200] Public remonstrations and advice were followed up with visits to miscreants and, if all failed, the ultimate sanction of disownment could be applied.

The tendency to cluster in the immediate neighbourhood of the meeting house aided the rigorous monitoring procedures. In London most Quakers lived in one of three neighbourhoods in the City: around the Bull and Bush meeting in Smithfield; in the north-east parishes near the Devonshire House meeting; and near the Gracechurch Street meeting. On the other hand the international network of meetings diffused invaluable information over long distances and ensured solid support to those in need, providing apprenticeships to the young, custom for those setting up in business, and relief to the poor and aged.[201] News of hardships, or oppression, was relayed back to the Meeting of Sufferings in London who then organized representations to the Lords of Trade although, in the repressive atmosphere of the 1670s, it was difficult to obtain access as their 'Lordships refused to take cognisance of complaints brought to them by this sort of people'.[202] Life became easier after the accession of James and a rising prospect of toleration. The business of lobbying

Quakers stood outside in the street, holding their silent meeting, 'and almost every day the informers and constables are at Friends' houses to strain': Balderston (ed.), *Claypoole's Letterbook*, p. 204. On the fines levied see Besse, *A Collection of the Sufferings of the People called Quakers for the Testimony of Good Conscience*, 2 vols. (London, 1753), vol. II, pp. 287, 290, 318.

[199] William C. Brathwaite, *The Beginnings of Quakerism to 1660* (London, 1912); William C. Brathwaite, *The Second Period of Quakerism* (London, 1919). Quakers were allowed to practise their religion in all colonies except Massachusetts Bay and before the foundation of Pennsylvania there were especially large communities in the Caribbean. The tiny island of Barbados had five meetings by the 1680s, although the Quakers did meet increasing animosity as their refusal to bear arms caused resentment in a slave society: Will of Tho. Foster, 1686, BA, Wills RB 6/10; Atkins to Lords of Trade, 17 April 1677, *CSPC, 1675–7*, no. 187.

[200] Crouch, *Posthuma Christiana*, p. 182.

[201] Thomas Story, *A Journal of the Life of Thomas Story* (Newcastle, 1747); George Welch, 'A journal of my voyage with my sundry passages thereof as I travelled in to diverse parts of the West Indies, 1671', APS, MS 917.29/W455; HSP, Norris Papers, vol. I.

[202] *CSPC, 1675–6*, no. 977.

was pursued with dogged determination and met with some success.[203] Discipline, information, sound mutual support, and the capacity to punish cheats, combined to give Quakers a competitive advantage in the risky business of Atlantic trade.

Jewish success in colonial commerce was even more striking, and again may be attributed to effective communication and trust networks underpinned by an enforceable code of conduct. The Jews had long played a prominent role in long-distance and high-value trades. Like the Quakers the community had a number of advantages when operating in high-risk enterprises. First, the universal precariousness of Jewish life favoured subjection to order and authority, and Boards of Elders could exert authoritarian, even despotic, rule in pursuit of both the moral ideals of Judaism, and also the eschewal of any behaviour which might disrupt the unity of the congregation or provoke popular hatred. Boards of Elders controlled charity, sick care, and education; exercised moral and intellectual censorship; arbitrated in business disputes; and maintained a firm grip on all aspects of Jewish life. Unless they wished to be cast adrift among the gentiles, members of the community had little choice but to comply with their rule.

Secondly, the scattered community was linked not only by religion, but also by kinship, language, culture, and commercial interest across boundaries between different empires with a hub, or focal point, in Amsterdam.[204] After the Portuguese defeated the Dutch in 1654, the Jews were expelled from Brazil, and the Sephardic transit trade between Europe and Iberian America took new shape as the community of four thousand or so fanned out all over the Caribbean. At the same time new opportunities were opening up in the English system with the establishment of sugar planting in Barbados, and the capture of Jamaica, which provided a base for contraband trade with the Spanish colonies – a trade in which Jews had long been prominent. The Navigation Acts made it illegal for foreigners to trade within England's colonial system and court records show that Englishmen used the legislation to try to exclude Jewish merchants.[205] However, arguments for re-admitting the Jews to

---

[203] Friends House, London, Cases of Suffering, Mic. 16, 1693, fos. 30, 62, 175, 196, 212; 1694, fos. 76, 96, 98, 113.

[204] Jonathan I. Israel, *European Jewry in the Age of Mercantilism, 1550–1750* (Oxford, 1985), pp. 154–8; Jonathan I. Israel, *Empires and Entrepots: the Dutch, the Spanish Monarchy and the Jews* (London, 1990); Herbert I. Bloom, *The Economic Activities of the Jews in Amsterdam in the Seventeenth and Eighteenth Centuries* (Williamsburg, 1939).

[205] Nuala Zahedieh, 'The capture of the *Blue Dove*, 1664, policy, profits and protection in early English Jamaica', in R. McDonald (ed.), *West Indies Accounts: Essays on the History of the British Caribbean and the Atlantic Economy in Honour of Richard Sheridan* (Kingston, Jamaica, 1996), pp. 29–47.

England and benefiting from their commercial capital, connections, and expertise had gained ground in the 1650s and survived the Restoration – partly in imitation of the Dutch who 'thrive best by trade and have the surest rules to thrive by [and] admit not only any of their own people but even Jews and all kinds of aliens to be free of any of their societies of merchants or any of their cities or towns corporate'.[206] Charles II was liberal in issuing patents of endenization (almost a hundred being issued during his reign) and, by the 1680s, there were firmly established communities, each numbering three hundred or so, in London, Barbados, Jamaica, and New York.[207]

The London Jews were concentrated in four parishes: St Katherine's Creechurch (where the synagogue was built); St Andrew Undershaft, the adjacent parish; St James, Duke Place; and All Hallows the Wall.[208] A court deposition made in 1672 by Anthony Gomezsera, one of the big colonial merchants of 1686, illustrates how this tight-knit community, in which social and business life were inseparable, was linked to similar communities all over the world. Gomezsera came to London in 1665 and obtained denization. He was born in Bayonne, France, and his business partners (described as 'all Jews') were born in Amsterdam, Bordeaux, and Portugal. His correspondent in Jamaica, Abraham Perara, had lived in that island since 1669, and 'before that at Barbados about two years, and before that in England for a short time, and before that in France, Flanders, and Amsterdam for about two years'. As the case unfolds it reveals the density of overlapping interests and criss-crossing paths common in the community.[209]

The other Jews among the big colonial merchants of 1686 had diffuse connections similar to those of Gomezsera. Peter and Pierre Henriques were born in Bordeaux; Moses Barrow (otherwise Anthony Lauzado) was born in Bayonne; and Emmanuel Perara in Madrid. Moses Barrow had three brothers in Barbados and Manuel Mendez had spent time in the island. All had connections with New York and Curaçao, and all had agents in Amsterdam, with links to the bullion and jewel trades. Commercial correspondence, and court records, reveal very high levels of interconnectedness and cooperation; excellent information flows;

[206] Child, *New Discourse of Trade*, p. 8. 'Freedom of religion' was advocated as a 'promoter of trade': BLO, MS Locke c30, fo.18.
[207] Maurice Woolf, 'Foreign trade of London Jews in the seventeenth century', *JHSET*, 24 (1974), 35–58; 'Census of Barbados', 1680, PRO CO 1/44 fos. 140–379; W. Samuel, 'A review of the Jewish colonists in Barbados in the year 1680', *JHSET* 13 (1932–5), 1–97; John Taylor, 'Taylor's history of his life and travels in America', 1688, NLJ, MS 105.
[208] References survive of tension when Jews would not perform tasks in St Katherine Cree and St Andrew Undershaft: GL, MS 1196/1, 4118/1.
[209] *Abraham Perara and Anthony Gomezsera v. Jacob Calloway*, 1672, PRO HCA 13/77.

a reluctance to use civil law and the efficacy of arbitration procedures internal to the community.[210] These advantages reduced risks, and allowed Jews to trade at low prices, which caused repeated complaints from English merchants in the Caribbean that they were being 'eaten out of their trade'.[211] The capacity to obtain good economic and social intelligence, and high levels of adherence to a collective code of conduct, gave the Jews, and other cohesive religious groups, undoubted competitive advantages when engaging in risky, long-distance trade and, not surprisingly, late-seventeenth-century businessmen did all they could to develop associations with similar features. Freemasonry began to develop strongly in England at this time, gathering strength after 1700 although, unfortunately, little is known about the organization in the late seventeenth century.[212]

Political networks and rent-seeking activities

While late-seventeenth-century colonial merchants took steps to harness efficiency gains in their relatively open and competitive commerce, many also attempted to use political levers to obtain privileges which would allow them to limit risk and raise profits.[213] It was customary to reward political supporters with economic favours – the 'infallible means of binding [them] to good behaviour' – and common convictions were cemented by webs of overlapping commercial interests.[214]

Political loyalties are difficult to document, other than for those taking part in formal governing institutions, and many of the fifty-nine big colonial merchants of 1686 were excluded on grounds of religion. However,

---

[210] *Ibid.*; Edgar Samuel, 'Manuel Levy Duarte (1631–1714): an Amsterdam merchant jeweller and his trade with London', *JHSET*, 27 (1982), 11–31.

[211] The Halls reported that the Jews in Port Royal charged 40 per cent advance on invoice for silk stockings – well below the 60 per cent that they sought: Halls to Brailsford, 11 March 1689, 21 May 1689, 20 June 1689, Brailsford Papers, PRO C 110/152; President and Council to Lords of Trade, 28 January 1691, PRO CO 138/7, fo.29; 'Petition of the jews of Jamaica', BLO, MS Rawl. D 924, fo. 431.

[212] Margaret Jacob, *Living the Enlightenment: Freemasonry and Politics in Eighteenth Century Europe* (Oxford, 1991), pp. 23–51.

[213] See above, pp. 41–54. Jack P. Greene, *Peripheries and Centre: Constitutional Development in the extended Polities of the British Empire and the United States, 1607–1780* (Athens, Ga., 1986).

[214] 'The present state of Virginia received from Col. Hartwell, Dr Blair, and Mr Chilton', October 1697, PRO CO 5/1309, fos. 94–98b; Dunn, *Sugar and Slaves*, pp. 96–103; Antony S. Parent, *Foul Means: the Formation of a Slave Society in Virginia, 1660–1740* (Chapel Hill, N.C., 2003), pp. 20–40; Bailyn, *New England Merchants*; J. M. Sosin, *English America and the Restoration Monarchy of Charles II: Transatlantic Politics, Commerce and Kinship* (Lincoln, Nebr., 1980), pp. 31, 79, 151, 157; J. M. Sosin, *English America and the Revolution of 1688: Royal Administration and the Structure of Provincial Government* (Lincoln, Nebr., 1982); Penson, *Colonial Agents*; Olson, *Making the Empire Work*.

more than half the remainder were clearly aligned with one of the two parties which had emerged by the 1680s.[215] A small minority could be labelled as Tories, who were broadly in support of the Stuart succession and the Crown's prerogative rights, while upholding the supremacy of the Anglican Church. A far larger group sided with the Whigs, who feared the threat of Stuart absolutism (especially in the hands of a Catholic monarch), challenged the legitimacy of the Crown's prerogative rights, championed Parliament's powers and privileges – above all its control over tax and spending – and were sympathetic to religious dissent.[216] While political allegiances did reflect religious and ideological concerns the separate business networks of the two groups suggest that, in the colonial arena, they were also shaped by a deeply material interest in the use of the Crown prerogative with its implications for the distribution of the fruits of empire.

All five Tory merchants were involved in core management of royal companies (including four in the Royal African Company) which depended for their legitimacy on the Crown's prerogative powers.[217] Four were involved in the older established royal colonies, one in Virginia and three in Barbados with their more entrenched elites. All were linked in a web of overlapping partnerships in chartered companies, ship-owning, wharf-leases, and other commercial enterprises such as a contract held by Jeffreys and Lucy to supply the Swedish tobacco monopoly – which cut across regional specializations and linked them to broader Tory networks.[218]

---

[215] Harris, *Politics under the Later Stuarts*; Nuala Zahedieh, 'Regulation, rent-seeking and the Glorious Revolution in the English Atlantic economy', *EcHR* (2009).

[216] Five Tories (Gore, Jeffreys, Lucy, Skutt, Thomas) and fifteen Whigs (Barnes, Cary, Duck, Eyles brothers, Gardner, Gracedieu, Heathcote, Sir Thomas Lane, Merriweather, Perry, Starke, Taylor, Tilden, Walker). Others, no doubt, had convictions but did not play an active role in politics and although sympathies can often be inferred they are not assumed here. For example Joseph Martin, the Leewards Island merchant, displayed strong dissenting tendencies – he was appointed agent for the Free Society of Traders to Pennsylvania in 1684 and was a member of the New England Company. He invested in the Bank of England, the New East India Company, and the Russian Tobacco contract (an overwhelmingly Whig project). He is not to be confused with a Joseph Martin who was a Levant merchant, Baltic trader and Tory MP: Price, 'Joseph Martin'.

[217] Jeffreys, Lucy, Skutt, and Thomas were involved with the Royal African Company, and Gore was primarily a German trader and became governor of the Hamburg Company (formerly the Merchant Adventurers).

[218] On various business enterprises see 'Petition of Jacob Lucy, Samuel Swinnock', April 1669, PRO CO 1/24, fo. 73; 'Deposition of Cornelis Carstens', 1669, *ibid.*, 41; 'Answers of Jacob Lucy, Samuel Swinnock, and Mark Mortimer', 15 February 1679, PRO HCA 13/131; Lucy held shares in the *Fleet* with Sir John Fleet, John Sadler (partner of Dalby Thomas) and other Tories, PRO HCA 26/1; 'Petition of Mr Alderman Jeffreys and Mr Lucy about their debt in Sweden', 7 July 1680, PRO CO 388/1, part 1, fo. 162. For example, Lucy and Thomas were linked to the lessees of the Legal Quays (with Crown-endowed

Table 3.5 *Political allegiances of London's big colonial merchants of 1686*

	Total	Aged over 40	Aged under 40
Tories	5 (25%)	4 (44%)	1 (9%)
Whigs	15 (75%)	5 (56%)	10 (91%)
Total	20 (100%)	9 (100%)	11 (100%)

Sources: PRO SP 29/415/39, 417/114, 418/199; HMC, 13th rept., part 5, p. 52;
Cruickshanks *et al.* (eds.), *House of Commons, 1690–1715*, vol. IV, pp. 46–7, 63–4,
309–17; vol. V, pp. 609–11; Basil D. Henning (ed.), *House of Commons, 1660–90*,
3 vols. (London, 1983), vol. IV, pp. 285–6; Jones, 'London overseas merchants
groups', p. 177; De Krey, *Fractured Society*, pp. 105, 139; *The Two Associations* (London,
1681); Woodhead, *Rulers of London*, pp. 66, 105, 150.

Meanwhile, the fifteen Whigs were more widely dispersed across all sectors of colonial commerce but, like the Tories, revealed a strong mutual dependence as they diversified beyond their core commodity trade.[219] Although four bought shares in the Royal African Company in 1672, and a number engaged in some business with the company, none was involved in its management while, on the other hand, at least nine were involved in the private slave trade.[220] The group had close political and economic links with the elites that had controlled colonial government before the late Stuart onslaught and acted as their political agents in London, although they did not act for the outsider governors appointed by the Crown such as Carlisle and Albemarle.[221] Like the Tories, they were connected in multiple criss-crossing partnerships which cut across regional specializations.

The age structure of the two groups suggests that calculations of advantage had shifted in the decades after the Restoration. Almost half the older men (those over forty in 1686) were Tories, which suggests that in the 1660s support was fairly evenly divided between Crown and Parliament. However, the younger merchants (who became active in

privileges) who included prominent Tories such as Child and Fleet: *Smith* v. *Ashton*, PRO C 110/181; Henry Roseveare, '"The Damned Combination": the port of London and the wharfingers' cartel of 1695', *London Journal*, 21 (1996), 97–111.

[219] The Whigs included five merchants trading predominantly to Barbados, three to the Leewards, three to Jamaica, three to New England, and two to Virginia.

[220] Charter party with Samuel Kempthorne and Thomas Duck for ship *Loyal Factor* for Angola, 20 April 1686, PRO T 70/81, fo. 46; on Duck's private slave trading see Bindloss to Lords of Trade, 8 March 1687, PRO CO 138/6, fo. 25.

[221] The partisan nature of the appointment of island agents is reflected in the career of Thomas Duck (one of the big colonial merchants of 1686) the Jamaica merchant who was agent for Modyford, Lynch, and Molesworth (all Whigs) but not for Carlisle, Morgan, or Albemarle (Tories): WAM 11,940; BL Add. MS 11,410, fo. 524; Sl. MS 2,724, fo. 246; Lords of Trade, 4 March 1684, PRO CO 138/4, fo. 204.

the 1670s and 1680s) displayed a strong preference for the opposition Whigs (ten to one). It seems that colonial merchants felt increasingly threatened by the Stuart kings' moves to undermine the independence of City, Parliament, and colonial governments and were concerned to limit Crown authority; by 1686 the balance of support was heavily in favour of the Whigs (three to one) (see Table 3.5).

At the Restoration, many merchants viewed Crown interest in the imperial project with acquiescence: they welcomed cooperation between Crown and Parliament in passing the Navigation Acts to combat foreign competition and believed that the Crown's prerogative rights might be employed to mutual advantage. Although merchant companies had been unable to exploit monopoly privileges in the business of cash-crop production, it was still hoped that exclusive rights might be put to profitable use in the extraction of resources such as fur and timber, and in supplying the colonies with necessities – above all labour. Merchants were fully aware of the buoyant demand for slaves in the English West Indies after the introduction of sugar in the 1640s but efforts to establish an English presence on the African coast were seriously thwarted by Dutch aggression. Merchants such as Jeffreys who had suffered heavy losses at the hands of the Dutch, welcomed the formation of the Royal African Company – a court project led by James, Duke of York – which would raise a joint-stock to finance a defence establishment in Africa in return for a monopoly of a trade expected to be worth more than £100,000 a year.[222] Although the Royal African Company was by far the largest Crown backed enterprise in the Atlantic, and stood at the centre of its efforts to extract a profit from empire, the king also supported the Hudson's Bay Company with a monopoly of the northern fur trade, and innumerable smaller enterprises, as well as distributing land, offices, grants, and various privileges.

However, in the decades after the Restoration, royal supporters obtained a disappointing return on Crown-endowed privileges as exemplified by the most ambitious project, the Royal African Company. After a disastrous first decade in which the company was destroyed by the Dutch, the reformed company maintained continuous trade from 1672

---

[222] A pamphlet of 1680 claimed that in the 1650s the Dutch and Danes strengthened their position on the coast of Guinea and seized English ships and goods to the value of £300,000: *Certain Considerations Relating to the Royal African Company of England* (1680), pp. 3, 8. The figure is borne out by complaints from Jeffreys and others to the Lords of Trade: PRO CO 388/1, part 1, fo. 17; part. 2, fos. 309–12. Jeffreys came from a Royalist family and built on these political credentials after the Restoration: serving as master of the Grocers company (the king's livery) in 1660, securing election as alderman in 1661 (although he paid a fine to avoid doing service), and serving as representative for the Chesapeake on the Committee of Trade set up in 1661: Committee of Trade, PRO CO 388/1, part 2, fo. 309; Woodhead, *Rulers of London*, p. 97; *ODNB*.

to 1688 but proved unable to reap monopoly rents. Despite imposing heavy costs the Crown chartered monopoly proved impossible to police in Africa or the plantations where enforcement relied on colonial governments and company agencies, which were usually staffed by the slave-owning elites who had no interest in defending privileges which would raise the price of labour – their main capital outlay.[223] Even outsider governors such as Dutton proved unwilling to seize private traders and antagonize local planters upon whose 'benevolence' they depended for their salaries and perquisites.[224] The naval presence in the Atlantic was thin and although captains had instructions and incentives to seize interlopers, they found it almost impossible to secure a conviction in a colonial court.[225] Although company agents reported the arrival of thirty-two interlopers between 1679 and 1682, only four were seized. The slave-owning elites could largely ignore what was increasingly condemned as an 'illegal' monopoly with little risk of punishment or public disgrace.[226]

However, while the company battled with the 'great inconveniencies' of proving the superiority and value of its 'exclusive' system of trade, it was forced to compete on price with interlopers who supplied at least half as many slaves as the company in the 1680s but operated with lower costs.[227] The private traders made no contribution to the expenses of the establishment in Africa and were often able to purchase slaves at lower

[223] In 1672 the company spent almost one third of its initial capital of £111,000 on forts and factories which could be used to justify its monopoly and the permanent establishment on the African coast (200–300 men) cost around £20,000 per annum: Davies, *African Company*, pp. 240–64. The company did not have the resources to police the very long African coastline. Royal interest allowed it to draft in five or six naval vessels between 1672 and 1688 but there were no more than seven or eight seizures: *ibid.*, pp. 114–15. On obtaining the Royal African Company agency for his family see Sir James Modyford to Sir Andrew King, 1672, WAM 11,348 11,689. On reluctance to enforce monopoly see Lynch to Lords of Trade, 29 August 1682, PRO CO 138/4, fo. 91; Davies, *African Company*, pp. 101–22.

[224] PRO T 70/12, fo. 8. For discussion of the problem of the governors' dependence on local 'benevolence' which 'could make their authority precarious and engage them in compliances' see 'Memo of Lords Justices', 16 July 1695, PRO CO 5/859, fo. 9.

[225] 'Report about the Dutch trading about the Leeward Islands', 7 June. 1687, PRO CO153/3, fo. 263; 'Memo upon Petition of the Royal African Company of illegal importing of negroes from Statia to Nevis', 18 July 1684, *ibid.*, fo. 270; Letter from Council to Johnson, 30 July 1687, *ibid.*, fo. 271.

[226] In 1686 the agents for Jamaica (Beeston, Duck, and Waterhouse) fitted out the *Hawke* for Africa where it picked up slaves which it delivered to Samuel Barry, a member of the Council of Jamaica, and *asiento* trader: Memo to Lords of Trade, 6 July 1686, PRO CO 138/5, fo. 156; Molesworth to Blathwayt, 2 November 1686, *ibid.*, fos. 217–19; PRO T 70/1 and 10; Davies, *African Company*, p. 113; Hancock (ed.), *Letters of William Freeman*, pp. 121, 132, 134, 150, 158–9. For the rhetoric which gained circulation see *Considerations Concerning the African Company's petition* (London, 1698).

[227] 'Report to Board of Trade', 1707–8, BL Add. MS 14,034, fo. 113; Davies, *African Company*, pp. 361–4; David Eltis, 'The British transatlantic slave trade before

prices than the company as the whole sum went into the agent's pocket (corruption with theft).[228] In fact in the 1680s, as company and private traders competed for legitimacy, slave prices fell to their lowest level in the history of the British slave trade and often barely covered company costs.[229] Low prices benefited planters and encouraged the extension of plantation agriculture, but did not allow the company to earn monopoly rents (which were effectively captured by the interlopers), or even make an operating profit, and it borrowed to pay dividends to its shareholders.[230] Although merchants who were involved in the core management of the company could direct company policies and patronage in their own interests, ordinary shareholders derived little advantage from the monopoly, investor loyalties were undermined and a number took part in private trade, despite the risk of losing stock and dividends.[231]

The Royal African Company's story fitted into a wider pattern. Although Tory interest groups continued to lobby for Crown privileges their validity was increasingly contested.[232] Efforts to exploit the Crown's prerogative through charters, monopolies, patent offices,

1714: annual estimates of volume and direction', in Robert L. Paquette and Stanley L. Engerman (eds.), *The Lesser Antilles in the Age of European Expansion* (Gainesville, Fla., 1996), pp. 185–203.

[228] Bosman, *A New and Accurate Description of the Coast of Guinea* (1721), p. 285; Davies, *African Company*, pp. 277–90; whereas the agent could only profit by charging the company above the true cost of a slave and retaining the difference (corruption without theft): Andrei Schleifer and Robert W. Vishny, 'Corruption', *Quarterly Journal of Economics*, 108 (1993), 599–617.

[229] Richard B. Sheridan, *Sugar and Slavery: an Economic History of the British West Indies, 1623–75* (Barbados, 1974), p. 252.

[230] On dividends see Davies, *African Company*, pp. 72–9.

[231] Jeffreys, Lucy, Skutt, and Thomas were all involved in management of the Royal African Company and drew benefits. For example, a policy of ship-hire was maintained in preference to purchase and charter parties allowed ship-owners to obtain very favourable access to the African trade: in 1686 Jeffreys obtained seven ship-hire contracts and surviving accounts show that he could expect an average profit of 38 per cent on his substantial cargo allowance, with the company taking the main risks: Committee of Assistants of Royal African Company, 20 April 1681, 7 June 1681, PRO T 70/81, fos. 46v, 89; Davies, *African Company*, pp. 194–5. It is perhaps unsurprising that, although Jeffreys had paid a fine to avoid the time-consuming business of serving as an alderman, he was willing to spend a substantial proportion of his week in Africa House and, no doubt, as political tensions mounted in the 1680s, his strong personal interest in upholding the Crown's prerogative rights, and the legitimacy of the company's charter, encouraged him to confirm his loyalty by accepting inclusion in the London Lieutenancy in 1685. For a summary of Jeffreys's career see *ODNB*. On shareholder involvement in interloping see 'Minute Book of Court of Assistants of RAC of England', no. 3, 1676–1678, 12 June 1677, 24 July 1677, PRO T 70/77, fos. 34, 43v.

[232] Dalby Thomas (one of the Tories among the big colonial merchants of 1686) lobbied for a Crown chartered West India Company with a stock of £500,000 and a monopoly of the sugar trade: Thomas, *Historical Account*, Dedication and pp. 48–9; BL Sl. MS 3, 984, fo. 210; Stede to Lords of Trade, 19 October 1687, *CSPC, 1685–8*, no. 1,467;

land grants, timber or mineral rights, salvage rights to Spanish wrecks, and other privileges, failed to deliver the anticipated rewards. The Restoration monarchy was unable to deliver secure rents in the colonial world.[233]

Crown efforts to tighten control over the colonial economy did not reap the expected rents but its actions did damage the interests of the regional elites who, in association with their friends and associates in the metropolis, had been accustomed to regulate colonial affairs in their own interests. For example, friends of Thomas Duck and other Whigs among the fifty-nine big colonial merchants of 1686 had used their control of government in Jamaica, and the Royal African Company agency, to secure a near monopoly of the island's Spanish slave trade. In the 1680s, this small group was selling about half the island's annual supplies of slaves to the holders of the *asiento* (a contract to provide Spanish colonies with slaves) at very high prices, with an additional 35 per cent premium charged for credit and convoy (provided at public expense), and obtained a clear profit of over £30,000 a year.[234] An observer remarked that this so-called '35 per cent trade' was a 'much easier way of making money than making sugar' but it caused considerable resentment among the smaller self-styled 'Tory' planters and traders who were excluded from the Spanish business while they were starved of slaves.[235] The king's appointment of outsider governors disrupted the business of the cosy cartel. Both Carlisle (1678–81) and the treasure-hunting Duke of Albemarle (1687–8) displaced the established 'Whig' elite, and stuffed their 'Tory'

'Address to the King as to the West India Company', Minutes of Council of Nevis, 28 August 1688, PRO CO 155/1, fos. 172–83; John Oldmixon, *The British Empire in America* (London, 1708), vol. II, pp. 47–8. Other Tories supported a New England merchant, John Wharton (an Anglican who had reaped personal advantage from his enfranchisement after the overthrow of the Massachusetts charter), in his attempt to obtain Crown support for a heavily capitalized joint-stock company, with a monopoly to exploit the timber and mining potential of the northern colonies, and a firm eye on naval contracts, the biggest business in seventeenth-century New England: Bailyn, *New England Merchants*, p. 133; Sosin, *English America and the Restoration Monarchy*, pp. 264–5; Viola F. Barnes, 'Richard Wharton, a seventeenth century New England colonial', *PCSM*, 26 (1924–6), 258–70.

[233] On Edward Randolph's heavy-handed efforts to enforce the Navigation Acts to his own advantage: PRO CO 1/46, fos. 1, 3, 60, 142, 243, 250, 258. On Albemarle's treasure hunting project see Peter Earle, *The Wreck of the Almiranta: Sir William Phips and the Search for the Hispaniola Treasure* (London, 1979); Emerson W. Baker and John G. Reid, *The New England Knight: Sir William Phips, 1651–1695* (Toronto, 1998).

[234] 'Address of Council and Assembly of Jamaica', 20 July 1689, PRO CO 138/6, fos. 287–9; Nuala Zahedieh, 'The merchants of Port Royal, Jamaica and Spanish contraband trade, 1655–1692', *WMQ*, 43 (1986), 570–93; Nuala Zahedieh, 'Regulation, rent-seeking and the Glorious Revolution'.

[235] John to William Helyar, 16 September 1688, SRO Walker Heneage MSS DD/WHh 1089. In 1683 Lynch reported that Morgan had set up a 'Loyal Club' and 'People

opponents into government, and judiciary, where they embarked on a populist, anti-*asiento* programme. They placed high taxes on re-exported slaves, seized *asiento* ships for trading contrary to the Navigation Acts, supported privateers, and renewed efforts to secure a permanent revenue bill which would allow the king's governor to largely dispense with the assembly.[236] In 1688 the *asiento* agent fled the island and leading Whigs, including Molesworth, the former governor and Royal African Company agent, returned home where, despite the buoyant trade recorded in the Naval Officers' returns, they launched a flurry of protests and petitions (in which they drew signatures from Whigs beyond the immediate circle of substantial Jamaica merchants) claiming that 'arbitrary' government had brought disaster to the island's economy.[237]

Vested interests in other parts of the empire felt similarly threatened by the 'encroachments' of Crown appointees and expressed increasing concern about the dangers of an unfettered Crown prerogative.[238] Even Tory interests were alienated by the actions of outsider governors: the Royal African Company complained about Albemarle's currency manipulations and Dudley's group, who had welcomed the overthrow of the Massachusetts charter, resented the actions of the autocratic Andros in New England.[239] Among the big colonial merchants of 1686, Benjamin Skutt was outspoken in his criticism of the execution of Henry Cornish, a fellow alderman and leading Presbyterian layman, for alleged involvement

began to think it looked as though he designed to be head of the Tories and that therefore I must be head of the Whigs': Lynch to Jenkins, March 1683, *CSPC, 1681–5*, no. 1,573.

[236] 'The humble petition of diverse of the planters and merchants trading to Jamaica', November 1688, PRO CO 1/65, fo. 373; Zahedieh, 'Regulation, rent-seeking and the Glorious Revolution'.

[237] On Castillo see F. J. Osborne, 'James Castillo, asiento agent', *JHR*, 8 (1971), 9–18; Albemarle to Lords of Trade, 11 May 1688, PRO CO 138/6, fos. 118–19. Molesworth was required to give bond for £100,000 before being allowed to leave. The list of securities reflects the membership of the *asiento* clique: PRO CO 1/65, fo. 376; Agnes M. Whitson, *The Constitutional Development of Jamaica, 1660–1729* (Manchester, 1929), pp. 70–109; 'The humble petition of diverse of the planters and merchants trading to Jamaica', 1688, PRO CO 1/65, fo. 373. For more details of grievances see 'The answers of the Jamaica merchants upon the petition of the African company', 23 August 1689, PRO CO 138/6, fo. 276. This document is signed by thirty-six merchants including five of the top colonial traders of 1686 (Cary, Heathcote, Gracedieu, Clark, Martin) and Beeston and Brailsford. All were Whigs and neither Cary, Clark, nor Martin had substantial interest in Jamaica trade. For trade records for 1688 see PRO CO 142/13.

[238] Governors were accustomed to dispose of offices and complaints that the Crown's appointment of persons 'in no way concerned with the plantations' undermined the power, and authority, of the governors came before the Lords of Trade in 1679 who recommended an inspection of the matter: Journal of Lords of Trade, 13 November 1679, *CSPC, 1677–80*, no. 1182.

[239] 'Petition of the Royal African Company', 15 July 1689, PRO CO 138/6, fo. 227. Under Dudley, from 1685 to 1686, the Council of New England had allowed the merchants

in the Rye House plot and, after being 'put on business that he did not like', he decided to flee the country for Barbados where he stayed until his death in 1697.[240]

Growing conviction among the big colonial merchants that it was in their economic interests to constrain the Crown prerogative, restore the power of Parliament and City, and regain control of colonial constitutions, was translated into financial support for the Glorious Revolution. The alacrity with which the City's Common Council (which included four of the big colonial merchants of 1686) declared unanimous support for the Lords' invitation to the Prince of Orange in December 1688, and their rapid response to the request for a large loan in January 1689, sealed William's success. Half the Whigs (and one Tory) among the big colonial merchants of 1686, made contributions; five of the thirty-one lenders who subscribed £500, or more, were among the fifty-nine big colonial merchants of 1686 and at least ten others had very substantial Atlantic interests by the 1690s.[241] Their faith was well grounded. As discussed in Chapter 2, the Revolution settlement did strengthen their political property rights on both sides of the Atlantic; it curbed the Crown's prerogative powers; it strengthened the power of Parliament, especially over economic regulation; it restored City charters; and it returned colonial government to local elites.[242] However, the Revolution did not mark a step forward in the direction of perfectly competitive markets in the Whig tradition, but rather in consolidating state power, the settlement enhanced the security and value of rent-seeking activities.

to make up for the lean years in which those who were not Church members had been excluded from office. Not only did they grant each other title to large stretches of unoccupied land, but they awarded themselves, and their friends, all offices, high and low, which promised any profit, set fees, and exempted themselves from taxation. All was disrupted by Andros who was acused of treating the New Englanders as 'slaves': Bailyn, *New England Merchants*, pp. 175–81; Sosin, *Glorious Revolution in America*, pp. 64–78.

[240] Skutt was a Common Councilman for Bishopsgate Within 1682–3, Tory alderman, Master of the Ironmongers' Company in 1682, and assistant to the Royal African Company 1672–4, 1677–9, and 1682–4: Woodhead, *Rulers of London*; PRO T 70/81, fo. 66; Sir Thomas Montgomery to Lords of Trade, 1688, PRO CO 29/4, fos. 3–6; Stede to Lords of Trade, 30 August 1688, 1 September 1688, *ibid.*, fos. 10–12, 18–19; Will of Benjamin Skutt, 28 February 1697, PRO PCC 122 Pett.

[241] A total of 1,322 lenders subscribed £185,675: CLRO, Journal of Common Council, 1682–88, no. 50, pp. 350v, 363; Loan Accounts, MS 40/34, MS 40/35, Misc. MS/133/25.

[242] See above, pp. 51–4; Julian Hoppit, *A Land of Liberty? England 1689–1727* (Oxford, 2000), p. 124; Gauci, *Politics of Trade*, pp. 205–32; Roseveare, *Financial Revolution*, pp. 2, 33–8; Richard S. Dunn, 'Glorious Revolution in America', in Canny (ed.), *Origins of Empire*, pp. 445–66; Sosin, *Glorious Revolution in America*.

Sixteen of the big colonial merchants of 1686 played an active role in partisan politics after the Revolution and their careers reflect the weight of the Whig victory in the Atlantic economy and its material value in terms of patronage and perquisites. Only two were aligned with the Tories. Dalby Thomas, a Barbados merchant, who was deeply embedded in Tory networks before the Revolution, continued to play an active role in partisan projects such as the attempt to set up a land bank in 1695 and the Royal African Company's efforts to obtain a statute charter and expressed his hostility to the 'monied' Whigs in a number of pamphlets.[243] He became a company assistant in 1698 but by 1700, he was in financial difficulties and, in 1703, he accepted appointment as agent-general of the Royal African Company on the Gold Coast, an unhealthy and not especially lucrative position, and he died in office in 1711 without seeing any great improvement in his financial position.[244] The only other surviving Tory among the big colonial merchants was William Gore, an alderman (1690–1708) and Lord Mayor (1701–2), who was first and foremost a Baltic merchant with a subsidiary interest in colonial trade and who, as Governor of the Hamburg Company, was committed to upholding the Crown's prerogative.[245] However, as a major naval contractor, with a large interest in government credit, he avoided an extreme stance and collaborated with the mainly Whig merchants who founded the Bank of England.[246]

The fourteen Whigs among the big colonial merchants of 1686 who remained politically active after 1688 drew substantial rewards from their new political strength at home and in the colonies with six serving as Common Councillors, three as Members of Parliament, and nine as agents for the colonial elites who had recovered control of the management

---

[243] See Dalby Thomas, *Historical Account*, preface; PRO HCA 26/1; *Propositions for a General Land Bank* (London, 1695); *Considerations on the Trade to Africa, Humbly Offered to the Honourable House of Commons, in Behalf of the Bill now before them* (London, 1698); *ODNB*.

[244] Davies, *African Company*, p. 245; 'London Outwards', 2 January 1701–8 July 1712, PRO T 70/1199.

[245] Gore had colonial imports valued at £3,335 in 1686 and was a major re-exporter of tobacco and sugar to Germany: Jones, 'London overseas-merchants groups', p. 176; Balderston (ed.), *Claypoole's Letterbook*, p. 124. He served as a Director of the Old East India Company (1693–6 and 1698–1703) and the Levant Company.

[246] Gore had linen imports valued at £33,227 in 1696 and was among the eight most prominent naval contractors supplying hemp and canvas: Jones, 'London overseas merchants groups', pp. 176–7, 199; Ehrman, *Navy in the War of William III*, pp. 59–66, 474. He subscribed £6,000 to the Bank of England and was one of the receivers for the first subscription in 1694 and served as a director from 1694 to 1706. He planned to stand for election to Parliament in 1701 but withdrew: Cruickshanks *et al.*, *House of Commons*, vol. IV, p. 46.

of colonial economies.[247] The Crown did retain its prerogative rights but their effective power was reduced and Crown monopolies lost all value.[248] In 1690 the Hudson's Bay Company, governed by the Whig Sir Steven Evance, managed to obtain a statute charter for eight years but Whig colonial merchants used their political platform to thwart similar efforts by the Royal African Company so that interlopers were able to continue enjoying free-rider benefits and, while the Royal African Company share price tumbled, the private slave trade flourished.[249] Only in 1698 – after a wave of revulsion against Whig corruption – was the trade opened, and the company able to impose a levy on private traders.[250] Neither side was pleased: the company lost its monopoly and the private traders lost their free-riding benefits while, with the end of the contest between 'free' and 'exclusive' trade, slave prices rose, and in 1708 planters in Barbados indicated that they would welcome a return of the monopoly.[251] The Whigs

---

[247] In the decade before 1688, five of the big colonial merchants of 1686 took civic office (three Tories and two Whigs) although four of the Whigs (all dissenters) were included in the Common Council in 1688, as James fell out with the Anglicans. None of the big colonial merchants of 1686 had taken a seat in Parliament before 1689, although Eyles was elected on an exclusionist platform in 1679 but the return was challenged and he did not take his seat. The three Members of Parliament elected after 1689 were Bartholomew Gracedieu (St Ives, 1705–8), Gilbert Heathcote (City, 1701–10 and small West Country boroughs, 1715–33), and John Taylor (Sandwich, 1695–8, 1701): Cruickshanks *et al.*, *House of Commons*, vol. IV, pp. 63–4, 763–4; vol. V, pp. 609–11. The Eyles brothers, Gracedieu, Heathcote, Sir Thomas Lane, Martin, and Merriweather were all colonial agents after 1689.

[248] I. K. Steele, *Politics of Colonial Policy: the Board of Trade in Colonial Administration, 1696–1720* (Oxford, 1968), pp. 3–41. The Royal African Company was sued by those who had suffered seizure in the 1680s: PRO T 70/82, fos. 63, 80v, 83; T 70/83, fo. 13v, 32, 36v, 46. On the case of *Nightingale* v. *Bridges* see W. Darrell Sharp, 'An economic consequence of 1688', *Albion*, 6 (1974), 26–55.

[249] For discussion of the Hudson's Bay success see K. G. Davies, 'Introduction', in E. E. Rich (ed.), *Hudson's Bay Copy Books of Letters, Commissions, Instructions Outward, 1688–96* (London, 1957). For discussion in committee see L. F. Stock, *Proceedings, and Debates of the British Parliament Respecting North America*, 5 vols. (Washington, D.C., 1924–41), *1689–1702*, pp. 20–1, 22, 23, 24–5, 32. According to Keirn, at least twenty-five of the thirty-one Members of Parliament who supported the African Company voted consistently with the Tories, whereas thirty-five of the forty-one members who opposed the Company were Whigs: Tim Keirn, 'Monopoly, economic thought, and the Royal African Company', in John Brewer and Susan Staves (eds.), *Early Modern Conceptions of Property* (London, 1996), pp. 427–66. The share price fell from 52 shillings in 1692 to 20 shillings in 1694: Davies, *African Company*, pp. 80–1. On Heathcote and Starke's private slave trading partnership see 'Deposition of Henry Mees', PRO HCA 13/82, fo. 18. For an account of Starke's slave trading to Virginia see Price, 'Sheffeild v. Starke'.

[250] Keirn, 'Monopoly, economic thought and the Royal African Company'; William A. Pettigrew, 'Free to enslave: politics and the escalation of Britain's transatlantic slave trade, 1688–1714', *WMQ*, 64 (2007), 3–38.

[251] By 1708 the price of a slave in Barbados had soared to £26.5 (almost twice the price that prevailed in the 1680s): Davies, *African Company*, p. 364; CSPC, 1708–9, no. 94.

also mounted an assault on the wharfingers' cartel set up under Tory leadership in 1695 to extract monopoly profits from the Legal Quays.[252] However, while Whig merchants (including those among the big colonial merchants of 1686) made full use of the rhetoric of 'free trade' in attacks on Crown-endowed privileges they also sought to use political influence to obtain exclusive privileges for their own projects, the Bank of England, the New East India Company, and a syndicate which sought to obtain a contract to supply the Russian tobacco monopoly at the expense of the Russia Company.[253]

As colonial charters and constitutions were restored, and governors and agents were appointed from among the ranks of the Whig trading elites, they recovered control of colonial resources and the power to resume earlier rackets and restrictive practices on the terms that had prevailed before the disruptions caused by Stuart policies.[254] The Whig merchants also used their political influence to back William's war, which not only promised to curb French commercial expansion in the Atlantic, but also opened up business opportunities for those with surplus capital and good political connections.[255] America was seen to have the capacity to provide strategic supplies which would reduce England's dependence on 'the naval stores that we are now brought from foreign parts'.[256] Whig merchants sought to use their political influence to secure advantageous contracts in New England and New York and did all they could to thwart a Tory group which had revived Wharton's ambitious schemes under the leadership of Sir Mathew Dudley.[257] War also involved expensive

[252] Roseveare, '"Damned Combination"'.
[253] Stock, *Proceedings, 1689–92*, pp. 20–1, 22, 23, 24–5, 32. A small group of twelve assigns signed the contract with the Czar in April 1698 after which it was thrown open to public subscription and they were joined by around sixty others. They were an unchartered, unincorporated joint-stock company formed by deed of co-partnership. They included a number of the big colonial merchants of 1686: Carleton, Heathcote, Martin, Merriweather, Perry, Starke, and Taylor; thirty-seven of the forty-one merchants involved in the contract whose politics can be determined were Whig: Price, *Tobacco Adventure*; De Krey, *Fractured Society*, pp. 148–9.
[254] 'Instructions to Beeston', 20 September 1692, PRO CO 138/7, fos. 84–106; 'Petition of merchants and planters concerned in Jamaica', 20 April 1693, *CSPC, 1693–5*, no. 285; 'A journal kept by William Beeston', BL Add. MS 12,430, fos. 41–7.
[255] G. H. Guttridge, *The Colonial Policy of William III in America and the West Indies* (Cambridge, 1922).
[256] 'Report on Mathew Dudley's case', 12 March 1694, PRO CO 5/859, fo. 84; Ehrman, *Navy in the War of William III*, pp. 59–66, 474.
[257] A Whig group involving the Presbyterian MP, Sir Henry Ashurst (member of the New England Company, brother of its treasurer, and agent for Massachusetts), Sir Thomas Lane (a big colonial merchant of 1686 and married to Ashurst's daughter), and Sir Steven Evance (born in New England and governor of the Hudson's Bay Company) managed to secure the placement of an ally as governor of Massachusetts (Sir William Phips); and another overlapping group involving the proprietors of Maine and New

campaigns in the Atlantic and the colonial governments combined with their Whig agents in the metropolis to secure supply contracts.[258] While war disrupted colonial commodity trade to the detriment of smaller merchants and caused a substantial contraction in the number of participants, the big colonial merchants were able to exploit their larger political and financial capital and draw handsome profits from the conflict.

As the cost of the war rose the state faced increasing difficulty in financing its activities through short-term debt, and its creditors used their strength in Parliament to develop schemes which would allow the government to borrow over the very long term or in perpetuity.[259] Although the land bank project backed by the Tories failed through lack of subscriptions, a group of predominantly Whig merchants (among whom the

Hampshire, who had long been attempting to establish monopoly control of the naval stores business, secured the appointment of John Usher, son-in-law of Samuel Allen, the proprietor, in New Hampshire. These officers employed a range of dirty tactics which undermined their rivals: John Taylor, a prominent Baltic merchant (who was also among the big colonial merchants of 1686) who had obtained a contract to supply American naval stores in 1691 and a Tory group led by Dudley. King in Council, 18 January 1693, PRO CO 5/858, fo. 10; 'Proposals humbly offered to the Lords of Trade for a patent of incorporation to trade for New England', *ibid.*, fo. 62; 'Mathew Dudley's case', 12 March 1694, *ibid.*, fo. 84; Governor, Council and Assembly of Massachusetts to Lords of Trade, 15 June 1694, *ibid.*, fo. 104; 'Petition of Mathew Dudley', PRO CO 5/859, fos. 57–9; 'Proposals of Sir Henry Ashurst and Sir Steven Evance to Lords of Trade', 29 March 1694, PRO CO 5/858, fo. 90; 'Report from Navy Office on Stores', 5 June 1696, PRO CO 5/959, fos. 46–54; 'Memo of John Taylor', 25 January 1694, PRO CO 5/859, fo. 161; 'Report of Lords of the Admiralty', 12 March 1694, *ibid.*, fo. 162; 'Proposals of Gabriel Bernon', 16 March 1694, *ibid.*, fo. 151; John Taylor to John Povey, *ibid.*, fo. 161; Bailyn, *New England Merchants*; Sosin, *English America and the Revolution of 1688*, pp. 147–9; Nathaniel Boulton (ed.), *Provincial Papers: Documents and Records relating to the Province of New Hampshire from 1686 to 1722*, vol. II (Manchester, N.H., 1868), pp. 122, 135, 142–3, 162–3. Ashurst made full use of his political position to undermine Joseph Dudley's campaign for the government of Massachusetts Bay by exposing Dudley's arbitrary proceedings as the justice presiding over Leisler's trial in New York after the Revolution. His vendetta continued into the eighteenth century: Cruickshanks *et al.*, *House of Commons, 1690–1715*, vol. III, pp. 73–6.

[258] Computation of the value of stores to be provided: PRO CO 5/859, fo. 61; invoice, June 1694, *ibid.*, fo. 74. On finance of the expedition to Jamaica see PRO CO 138/7, fos. 207–347. Contractors were notorious for supplying low quality at high prices: 'all contractors have had their valuation upon the supposition that they buy the best goods; and [theres] great difference in the value between the contract and the practice ... in a contract (however worded) will fall to the contractors profit and their Majestie's and seamans' loss': PRO T 48/49.

[259] After the Settlement of 1689 gave Parliament firm control over state taxing and borrowing, it allowed a threefold increase in government expenditures from around £1.7 million per annum in the 1680s, to £4.9 million per annum during the Nine Years' War. Taxes covered 90 per cent of wartime expenditure and it was necessary to borrow 10 per cent. The Corporation of London advanced more than 25 per cent of the loans raised on the credit of parliamentary taxes between 1689 and 1693: Roseveare, *Financial Revolution*, pp. 2, 33–8; D. W. Jones, *War and Economy in the Age of William III and Marlborough* (Oxford, 1988).

Table 3.6 *Estimated wealth at death of twenty-five of London's big colonial merchants of 1686*

Wealth	No.	Merchants
Bankrupt/in debt	3	Carleton, Gracedieu Waterhouse
Below £1,000	1	Barnes
£1–4,999	1	Tilden
£5–9,999	3	Lane, Richards, Thomas
£10–29,999	8	Gardner, Lane, Lucy, Paggen, Perry, Skutt, Starke, Walker
Over £30,000	9	John and Francis Eyles, Gore, Heathcote, Peter and Pierre Henriques, Jeffreys, Martin, Taylor

Sources: PRO PROB 4; BL Add. MS 7,421; *Elizabeth Waterhouse* v. *John Cass et al.*, 1691, PRO C 24/1139, part 2; Will of William Barnes, 1695, PRO PROB 11/427; CLRO, Orphans' Court Inventories, CSB, vol. IV, 19; Will of Richard Tilden, 1696, PRO PROB 11/435; Will of Tho. Lane, 1710, PRO PROB 11/518; Will of George Richards, 1690, PRO PROB 11/421; Will of Dalby Thomas, 1711, PRO PROB 11/521; Will of Sir Tho. Lane, 1709, PRO PROB 11/507; *Blackman* v. *St John*, 1692, PRO C 24/1142; Will of William Paggen, 1690, PRO PROB 11/398; CLRO, Orphans' Court Inventories, nos. 2200, 2124; Will of Micajah Perry, 1721, PRO PROB 11/581; Price, *Perry of London*, pp. 22–7, 51; Will of Micajah Perry, 1721, PRO PROB 11/451; Will of Tho. Starke, 1706, PRO PROB 11/487; CLRO, Orphans' Court Inventories, no. 2754; Will of William Walker, 1708, PRO PROB 11/503; CLRO, Orphans' Court Inventories, no. 2818; *ODNB*; Cruickshanks *et al.* (eds.), *House of Commons*, vol. IV, pp. 46, 316; vol. V, pp. 609–11; Dickson, *Financial Revolution*, pp. 263–4; *ODNB*; Price, 'Joseph Martin', *Notes and Queries*, 203 (1958), 440–1.

big colonial merchants of 1686 were prominent) persuaded Parliament to charter the Bank of England, which underpinned the huge expansion of long-term debt which played a central role in the 'Financial Revolution'.[260] Investors subscribed £1.2 to the Bank in perpetuity – secured by taxes on shipping and liquor – with little risk and high interest which allowed the government to pay its creditors who were, in many cases, the same people as held shares in the bank.

Family, church and education directed political loyalties in the late seventeenth century but, among London's big colonial merchants, these ties were reinforced and cemented by patronage and common

[260] All the Whigs among the big colonial merchants of 1686 subscribed and one Tory, William Gore, a Navy contractor. On the Bank see P. G. M. Dickson, *The Financial Revolution in England: a Study in the Development of Public Credit, 1688–1756* (London, 1967) pp. 54–7; Roseveare, *Financial Revolution*, pp. 34–7.

commercial interests. In the decades after the Restoration neither Crown nor Parliament could secure the political property rights needed to protect the value of rent-seeking enterprises in the colonial economy; politically endowed privileges proved of precarious value; the trade remained relatively open and free and, even in the regulated slave trade, colonial merchants were encouraged to seek efficiency gains to maintain profits. However, in strengthening the political property rights of the transatlantic trading elite, the Glorious Revolution also consolidated its capacity to enforce regulation in its own interests and enhanced the value and scale of rent-seeking enterprises at the expense of competition and efficiency.

Wealth accumulation

It is difficult to discuss levels of capital accumulation among London's colonial merchants. It is clear that there were vast differences in experience, with a high failure rate and some spectacular successes, but detailed evidence is sparse, especially for those of moderate fortune. The information in Table 3.6 shows the wealth at death of twenty-five of the big colonial merchants of 1686, but almost certainly over-represents the better-documented merchants in the lowest and highest bands. Furthermore, wealth at death is not always a good indicator of performance over a lifetime; merchants might pass on assets before old age or, like Gracedieu, fail at the end of what had earlier been a very successful career. However, it is clear that a high proportion of the fifty-nine big colonial merchants of 1686 made very large fortunes valued at over £30,000 which could not have been built on the 'punctual rotation of credit and change of commodities' alone.

Low barriers to entry, and a reputation for high profits, tempted large numbers of London businessmen to invest in trade with the colonies. However, the portbook evidence suggests that persistence rates were low and, as Verney warned, 'not one in three of them thrives'.[261] Sound training, solid experience, a good marriage, a range of strategic associations, and access to reliable trust networks, could reduce risk and enhance merchant performance. However, not even the most optimistic commentators promised that colonial commodity trade could deliver net returns in excess of 10 per cent and few of the 159 merchants importing colonial goods to the value of £1,000 and above in 1686 would have earned more than £100 or £200 a year on that part of their business. Furthermore, a substantial part of the trade was on commission and

[261] Verney, *Memoirs of the Verney Family*, vol. III, p. 369.

earning far less (the usual rate in London was 2.5 per cent). The firm of Bawden and Gardner, which was reputed to be 'the greatest dealer to the West Indies ... in England', had imports valued at £28,934 in 1686, and a commission business said to be worth £1,000 a year but this level of trade was exceptional, and even this would not have supported a high level of saving.[262]

The very heavy service needs in the long-distance Atlantic trades provided colonial merchants with attractive opportunities to diversify their business around the core commodity trade, and intensify the use of trust networks with investments in ship-owning, wharf-leases, and commercial services such as bill-broking or insurance. Some also engaged in related activities such as slave trading and manufacturing industry. Many could double, or treble, their earnings on buying and selling commodities, but even so, few trading in competitive conditions would have earned much in excess of £400 a year which was, according to Gregory King, the typical income for an overseas trader. This level of earnings provided a very comfortable living – better than that of a gentleman on King's reckoning and only exceeded by peers, knights, and esquires – but not the great riches accumulated by the most successful of the big colonial merchants of 1686.[263] Claypoole had great difficulty in realizing his assets and raising even a few hundred pounds when he emigrated to Pennsylvania in 1683.[264]

However, merchants who could command the economic, social, and political capital needed to access political power, and patronage, could raise their earnings well above the levels seen as usual in open and competitive trade. Although the Royal African Company was unable to capture the benefits of its monopoly charter, it did allow those involved in the core management to participate in the slave trade on very favourable terms through policies such as ship-hire. For example, Jeffreys took part in seven charter parties in 1686 and surviving accounts for ninety-seven ships chartered between 1680 and 1687 show that the owners could expect an average net profit of 38 per cent on the adventure, with the company taking the main risks.[265] Furthermore, Jeffreys was able to obtain good terms for a re-export trade from the Caribbean to Virginia

---

[262] Balderston (ed.), *Claypoole's Letterbook*, pp. 173, 174, 183.
[263] According to King the country had 2,360,586 families of which only 4,586 (Temporal and Spiritual Lords, Baronets, Knights, and Esquires) had incomes higher than the £400 of overseas traders and he placed a gentleman's income at £280 per annum: 'Scheme of the income', in Laslett (ed.), *The Earliest Classics*.
[264] Balderston (ed.), *Claypoole's Letterbook*, pp. 205, 219.
[265] Committee of Assistants of the Royal African Company, 20 April 1681, 7 June 1681, PRO T 70/81, fos. 46b, 89; Davies, *African Company*, pp. 194–5.

which was ill supplied by the company. Other corporations with political privileges could provide supporters with similar gains.

The best returns were made by those who could combine political power on both sides of the Atlantic and secure economic advantages through a range of rackets, restrictive practices, and government contracts.[266] Freeman and Baxter expected high returns on illicit trade in concert with the governor of the Leewards; Duck's private slave-trading ventures in partnership with Lynch, Molesworth, and other prominent Jamaicans, were more profitable than legal trade; the *asiento* business in Jamaica (valued at £50,000–£100,000 a year) allowed a small number of investors, including Beeston, Duck, and the Heathcote brothers, to double or treble their money in a few weeks. From the 1660s naval contractors such as William Warren and Josiah Child used Tory networks to obtain high prices for New Hampshire's naval stores and, after 1689, wartime contracts allowed a few individuals including William Gore, Sir Thomas Lane, Gilbert Heathcote, and John Taylor to make spectacular returns.[267] All depended on political patronage which could turn a small, risky return into bigger, more certain, profit and it is unsurprising that all of the fifty-nine big colonial merchants who left fortunes in excess of £30,000 used their commercial networks to pursue rent-seeking activities which allowed them to accumulate great wealth; three were elected as Members of Parliament (although Eyles did not take his seat), five were involved in City politics, five were colonial agents in London, and although the Jewish Henriques brothers were excluded from formal political institutions on grounds of religion they maintained good connections in the colonies and court.[268]

As colonial merchants accumulated capital balances through trade and associated activities, they sought to diversify their investment portfolios. Land was the traditional choice offering security, and liquidity, but it required careful management and yielded low returns in the late seventeenth century (around 3 per cent in the 1690s).[269] The strategies of London's big colonial merchants confirm Peter Earle's finding that land had limited appeal among the London middling sorts. Claypoole

[266] For the importance of friends at home see Henry Morgan to Jenkins, 9 March 1681, 13 June 1681, PRO CO 138/3, fo. 480; Sosin, *English America and the Restoration Monarchy*, p. 79.

[267] Contractors began to enter Stone's sample in the late seventeenth century: Lawrence Stone and Jeanne C. Fawtier Stone, *Open Elite: England, 1540–1880*, (Oxford, 1984), pp. 203, 248.

[268] John Eyles, Gilbert Heathcote, and John Taylor were elected Members of Parliament; John and Francis Eyles, Gore, Heathcote, Jeffreys, and Martin were involved in City politics; John and Francis Eyles, Heathcote, Jeffreys, and Martin were colonial agents.

[269] Earle, *Middle Class*, pp. 152–7.

and Freeman were typical in buying a country villa in the London environs to serve as a retreat from the dirt and noise of the crowded City (Stoke Newington, Hackney, Kingston, and Richmond were all popular locations) but only the richest merchants (including six of those who left fortunes above £30,000) bought country estates.[270] At least nine of the big colonial merchants of 1686 possessed land in the plantations, but this too was difficult to manage with profit; returns were low in the late seventeenth century, especially under absentee management.[271] However, whereas agricultural land was not especially popular, surviving inventories and court cases show that all but two of the big merchants for whom data is available, possessed urban property which provided an annual gross return of 10 per cent, and could be mortgaged in times of difficulty.[272]

Lending to individuals on bond or mortgage was another way to diversify investment portfolios and accounted for around a fifth of assets in the big colonial merchants' probate inventories. Returns were slightly better than those on land – those viewed as a good risk paid 6 per cent or less. Lending to the Stuart monarchs offered higher rates of interest but the volume of Crown borrowing was limited by political constraints.[273] However, after the Glorious Revolution gave Parliament greater control

[270] Claypoole was typical in owning a large house with 23 acres in Kingston: Balderston (ed.), *Claypoole's Letterbook*, p. 112. John Eyles purchased Southbroom House in Devizes in 1680; Gore purchased Tring from Henry Guy in 1705; Heathcote bought lands in six counties and Normanton Hall in Rutland in 1729; Jeffreys accumulated considerable estates in Wales and Gloucestershire; Martin left instructions to purchase a landed estate in his will; and Taylor bought Bifrons in Kent in 1694: *Wiltshire Notes and Queries*, I, 213, 265, 301, 366–7, 390–1; V 431; VI 371; VII 145–51. PRO C 8/242/138; C 7/405/40; C 7/530/76; Will of John Eyles, PCC 109 Degg; *CTB, 1689–92*, vol. V, 1972, 1974, 1983, 1984; Evelyn D. Heathcote, *An Account of Some of the Families Bearing the Name of Heathcote* (Winchester, 1899); *ODNB*; Cruickshanks *et al.*, *House of Commons*, vol. IV, p. 46; *ibid.*, vol. V, pp. 609–11; Price, 'Joseph Martin'.

[271] Baxter, Cary, Fowler, Lucy, Martin, Merriweather, Skutt, Starke, and Tryon owned property in the plantations. Success depended on close careful management and absentee landowners found it notoriously difficult to make a profit. As Sir Thomas Lynch remarked, 'servants, attorneys etc are apt to dye or remove, and this ayre I think disposes people more to covetousness than that of Europe ... those that are absent can do nothing but loose all': Lynch to Lord Cornbury, 29 March 1672, BL Add. MS 11,410, fo. 532.

[272] Leaseholds accounted for around 25 per cent of inventoried assets. On the value of urban property see *Elizabeth Waterhouse* v. *John Cass* et al., 27 May 1691, PRO C 24/1139, part 2.

[273] Before the Restoration, Parliament had sometimes demanded strict controls over its grants of additional supply – appropriation and audit – but the efforts failed to take root. By 1677–9 Charles was faced with appropriation clauses of unparalleled strictness – even the money lent to the Crown was appropriated to the uses intended and the campaign to curb the Crown's financial autonomy culminated in the resolution of the Commons on 7 January 1681 that anyone who lent money to the government or

over state finances it became willing to endorse higher levels of expenditure which almost tripled between the 1680s and 1690s, and although
almost 90 per cent was funded by taxation, the remainder was borrowed
from its own stakeholders.[274] Between 1689 and 1693 the government
borrowed over £500,000 a year, with over a quarter raised in the City,
and the big colonial merchants such as the Eyles brothers, Heathcote,
and the Henriques brothers lent generously on very favourable terms
(usually obtaining 8 to 10 per cent interest).[275] As the government got
into difficulties funding this large short-term debt the same merchants
were prominent in persuading Parliament to charter the Bank of England
in 1694 which underpinned the huge expansion of long-term debt and
further reduced the risks of government lending.[276] Not surprisingly, surviving inventories among City merchants suggest a large expansion in
investment in stocks and government debt (from below 30 per cent of
portfolios in the late 1680s to around 50 per cent in the 30 years after the
Glorious Revolution).[277]

The career of Gilbert Heathcote (1652–1733), the most spectacularly
successful of the big colonial merchants of 1686, provides a good illustration of how access to political power and rent-seeking activities could
transform a comfortable, but risky, trading income into massive wealth
(Illustration 14). Heathcote, the eldest of seven surviving sons of an ironmonger of Chesterfield, was bound to an Eastland merchant in 1667.
After serving his apprenticeship, and a period of factorage in the Baltic –
accumulating funds to trade on his own account – Heathcote returned to
London and took the freedom of the City in 1681.[278] Marriage to a rich
heiress in 1682 further expanded his capital base, and he quickly built up
a complex, far-flung, and well integrated business network. Heathcote
maintained a substantial Eastland trade, with Baltic imports valued at

dealt in government securities without parliamentary authority would be adjudged an
enemy to Parliament. The philosophy of accountability which was to shape post-Revo-
lution financial control was thus clearly articulated in the reign of Charles II: Roseveare,
Financial Revolution, p. 15.
[274] It can be argued that the desire to place public credit on a sound footing was a major
cause as well as a consequence of the Glorious Revolution. Roseveare, *Financial
Revolution*, pp. 1–32; Dickson, *Financial Revolution*; Douglas C. North and Barry R.
Weingast, 'Constitutions and commitment: the evolution of institutions governing public choice in seventeenth-century England', *JEH*, 49 (1989), 803–32.
[275] Roseveare, *Financial Revolution*, pp. 34–5.
[276] Dickson, *Financial Revolution*, pp. 46–57. All eight of the fifty-nine big colonial merchants of 1686 who left over £30,000, and died after 1688, were involved in the Bank
project.
[277] Heathcote made some £60,000 from his bank investment between 1697 and
1700: Cruickshanks *et al.*, *House of Commons*, vol. IV, p. 311.
[278] Heathcote, *Account of Some of the Families*, p. 79; *ODNB*; Astrom, *From Cloth to Iron*, pp.
161–2.

Illustration 14 Sir Gilbert Heathcote. Michael Dahl, Bank of England.

£18,590 in 1685, but also did business in Africa, Spain, Newfoundland, New York (where he had one brother), and Jamaica (where he had three brothers who gained entry to the clique that controlled the highly profitable *asiento* trade) and by 1686, he had imports from Jamaica valued at £4,600 which placed him among the leading colonial merchants.[279] By the

[279] Astrom, *From Cloth to Iron*, p. 161; Petition of Gilbert Heathcote and Arthur Shallet, Privy Council Register, February 1689–August 1690, PRO PC 2/73, fos. 168–9; 'Deposition of Henry Mees', PRO HCA 13/82, fo. 18; Halls to Brailsford, 8 June 1689, Brailsford Papers, PRO C 110/152; 'Petition of merchants trading to Madeira', 1690, PRO CO 389/16, fos. 32–3; Fox, *Caleb Heathcote*; 'Invoice of charges for goods supplied

1690s his main focus had shifted from the Baltic to the Atlantic; in 1695 he imported sugar, ginger, and indigo valued at just over £8,000 from Jamaica and goods worth £4,000 from the Baltic and he remained heavily involved in trade with Jamaica until the end of his career.[280] Like other overseas merchants he combined commodity trade with ship-owning, slave-trading, and a range of other business activities; but it was his use of political influence which opened up the most profitable opportunities.

Heathcote came from a staunch Parliamentarian background which must have predisposed him to align with the Whigs against the Crown's prerogative rights but, no doubt, these sentiments were confirmed as the rising threat of Stuart absolutism displayed in both the City and the colonies began to threaten his material interests, above all his involvement in the *asiento* trade in Jamaica. As James's efforts to tighten control over colonial government undermined the power of his friends in Jamaica, Heathcote was prominent in organizing the London protests and petitions against the 'necessitous persons' put in control of the island and gave enthusiastic support to the Glorious Revolution — subscribing £500 to the loan of January 1689, and further loans totalling £4,575 in 1690.[281] After the Revolutionary settlement and the return of Jamaican government into the hands of the local Whig elite, Heathcote lobbied to secure the appointment of a friendly pro-*asiento* governor and became island agent with a keen eye on his own commercial interests.

At the same time Heathcote was building his influence in English political circles. On the restoration of the City's charter, Heathcote became a member of the court of Common Council for Walbrook ward, and quickly established himself as a Whig leader of that assembly; he went on to take high office with a close regard for his own profit and excited various charges of corruption.[282] He maintained an active, and highly partisan, role in other City associations including the Eastland Company

to New York as presents for the Indians', 26 December 1695, *CSPC, 1693–5*, no. 2,218; JA, Powers of Attorney, 1B/11/24, vol. VIII, fos. 27; vol. IX, fos. 48b-49, 105–15b, 176, 183, 184, 198.

[280] Heathcote's total imports into London in 1695 in were valued at £14,051: Jones, 'London overseas-merchants groups', p. 263.

[281] 'Answers of the Jamaican merchants upon the petition of the African Company', 23 August 1689, PRO CO 138/6, fo. 276; John Heathcote was among those who provided security for Molesworth on his departure from Jamaica, PRO CO 1/65, fo. 376; CLRO, Loan accounts, MS 40/34; MS 40/35; Misc. MS/113/25; *CTB*, vol. IX.

[282] After 1700, he assumed high office as an alderman for Walbrook from 1702 to 1725 and Bridge-Ward-Without from 1725 to 1733; Sheriff in 1703–4; and Lord Mayor in 1710–11: Woodhead, *Rulers of London*, p. 87; Heathcote, *Families bearing the name of Heathcote*, p. 79. In the 1690s Heathcote was implicated in numerous enquiries into corruption including the passage of the Act to relieve the London orphans, the activities of the Bank of England, the arrangements for collection of plate for minting coin, and victualling contracts: Cruickshanks *et al.*, *House of Commons*, vol. IV, pp. 311–15.

(serving as treasurer between 1697 and 1699), the Vintner's Company (Master in 1700), the City's Blue Regiment, the Honourable Artillery Company; and a Whig club meeting between 1714 and 1717, which sought to extend his party's influence in the metropolis.[283] After seeking election for Parliament in 1698 without success (there was a wave of disgust against the Whig corruption and cronyism from which Heathcote had benefited) he was elected in 1700, then immediately 'expelled', being ineligible as a trustee for circulating exchequer bills.[284] After resigning as a trustee, Heathcote was elected for one of the four City seats in 1701 and sat until defeated in the Tory upsurge at the election of 1710, then returned after the Hanoverian succession as member for various West Country towns, no doubt reinforcing his long-standing interests in the Newfoundland fishery.[285]

Heathcote used his political base to good commercial effect. He played a leading part in well-organized merchant opposition to the Royal prerogative; he acted as one of the committee of interlopers in the East India trade, loudly attacked the Company's monopoly, and was active in the formation of the New East India Company in 1698; he gave evidence against the Royal African Company in the committees set up to examine its case for a statute monopoly and was able to retain his free-rider benefits as an active interloper until 1698, after which, as the costs of private trade rose, he more or less withdrew; he used his position as treasurer of the Eastland Company to promote a Whiggish syndicate's bid for an exclusive contract to supply the Russian tobacco monopoly at the expense of the Tory Russia Company; and he led an attack on a cartel set up by the Tory, John Fleet, among the Crown chartered lessees of the Legal Quays.[286]

[283] Heathcote was treasurer 1708–11; vice-president 1711–20; and president 1720–35 of the Honourable Artillery Company: De Krey, *Fractured Society*, p. 263; Henry Horwitz, (ed.), *Minutes of a Whig Club, 1714–17* (London, 1981).
[284] The new commission issued later that year featured his brother John: *CTB*, vol. XVI, pp. 47, 56, 76.
[285] He was Member for Helston (1715–22), Lymington (1722–7), and St Germans (1727–33). For Heathcote's involvement in fishing policy see Cruickshanks *et al.*, *House of Commons*, vol. IV, pp. 310–17.
[286] In 1698 he subscribed £17,000 to the New East India Company, and became a director, remaining a member of its core management until the merger with the old company in 1709: Cruickshanks *et al.*, *House of Commons*, vol. IV, pp. 309–17. On activities against the Royal African Company see Stock, *Proceedings, 1689–1702*, pp. 20–1, 22, 23, 24–5,32; Heathcote is recorded only once (11 December 1702) in the records of outward cargoes to Africa between 1701 and 1712: PRO T 70/1199. In attempting to secure the Russian tobacco contract, Heathcote used his position as treasurer of the Eastland Company to entertain the Czar to a banquet: Price, *Tobacco Adventure*; on the attack on the wharfingers see *The Case of the Traders of London. As it now Stands Since the Copartnership of the Wharfingers* (London, 1705); PRO (24/1317); Roseveare, '"Damned Combination"'.

As early as 1689 Heathcote used his political platform to advocate war with France and called for an attack on its colonies in the West Indies. He wanted to ensure that the crowns of Spain and France remained divided, and that England retained equal access to the Spanish colonial markets on which his Jamaica trade depended, as well as wanting to secure the Newfoundland trade, and northern fisheries, and he maintained this strong anti-French, pro-war stance until the end of his career.[287] Heathcote profited handsomely from the war, which not only protected his own commercial interests in the Atlantic, but also opened up lucrative contracts which, as agent of Jamaica, he was well placed to exploit. He helped persuade the government to despatch a major military expedition to the island in 1694, and obtained large supply contracts as well as using cash balances accumulated from the Spanish trade to provide the stationed forces with £5,750 a year.[288] The Heathcotes continued to benefit from large government expenditures in the War of the Spanish Succession and, between 1701 and 1706, they provided an average of £12,000 a year for the island's stationed forces as well as supplying victuals and clothing at 'high rates'.[289]

While profiting handsomely from the large wartime expenditures, Heathcote accumulated capital balances which he could lend back to the state and, in addition to supporting the Revolutionary settlement which had reduced the risks of lending to the government, he played a leading role in the formation of the Bank of England and the further strengthening of state credit.[290] Gilbert Heathcote subscribed £8,000 in 1694, £6,875 in 1697, and was reported to have made £60,000 from his investment between 1697 and 1700. He served almost continuously as a member of the Court of Directors from 1694 until his death in 1733, with two periods as governor (1709–11 and 1723–5). It is perhaps unsurprising that, in 1710, Heathcote, and three other Bank leaders, tried to

---

[287] After ejection from Parliament in 1710, Heathcote continued to lobby against peace, encouraging planters to petition and appealing before the Lords of Trade that the treaty terms should not be approved: Horwitz, *Minutes of a Whig Club*.

[288] The expedition did little for the island's welfare as it was poorly managed, and the men were ravaged by disease, *CSPC, 1691–3*, nos. 1,277, 1,278, 1,482, 1,566, 1,572, 1,946; *CSPC, 1693–5*, nos. 1,946, 1,970, 1,973, 1,980, 1,983, 2,021, 2,022, 2,026, 2,123, 2,178, 2,319, 2,329. 'Letters of Credit to Jamaica for £5,750 for subsistence of Regiment', to Josiah and George Heathcote, 17 January 1695, PRO CO 138/7, fo. 359; Heathcote to Lords of Trade, 29 November 1697, *ibid.*, fo. 155; 'Account of money furnished by Sir William Beeston and Mr Josiah Heathcote for use of men-of-war at Jamaica in 1696/7', PRO CO 138/9, fo. 159.

[289] J. Sperling, 'The International payments mechanism in the seventeenth and eighteenth centuries', *EcHR*, 14 (1962), 446–68; Curtis P. Nettels, *The Money Supply of the American Colonies before 1720* (Madison, Wisc., 1934), p.38.

[290] 'Minute Book of the Court of Directors of the Bank of England', BEA, MS G 4/1.

use the Bank's financial leverage to persuade the queen to prop up the Whig ministry and prevent peace with France.[291]

Heathcote's career combined all the ingredients needed for success in London's competitive colonial commerce: sound education, apprenticeship to an established London merchant, a period overseas in which to accumulate initial capital, a shrewd marriage, and access to an extensive kin network. However, even at the peak of his trading career, Heathcote's imports were valued at less than £25,000 and he was unlikely, even with good luck and sound judgement, to have earned more than around £2,000 a year in commodity trade alone. Heathcote did, like other merchants, use his network of trusted associates to diversify into ship-owning, the private slave trade, and other related activities which boosted his income, but it was the use of political institutions at home, and in the colonies, and rent-seeking enterprises which transformed a decent into an abundant living. During the 1680s the Crown's efforts to tighten its control over the Atlantic economy had little success but did undermine the privately profitable activities of merchants such as Heathcote and allowed relatively competitive conditions to prevail, which placed a premium on entrepreneurial efficiency. However, after the Glorious Revolution, to which Heathcote gave generous support, and the increasing alignment of Crown and City commercial interests, the security and value of rent-seeking enterprises increased. Furthermore, although the war damaged small merchants, and colonial trade stagnated, it provided lucrative opportunities in government supply and credit from which Heathcote – with capital and connections on both sides of the Atlantic – made substantial profit. In 1733, at the end of a long life, Heathcote, with a spectacular fortune of around £750,000, was hailed as the richest commoner in Great Britain and, with the acquisition of land in six counties, and the building of a large country house in Rutland, he laid the foundations of an aristocratic dynasty.[292] It is unsurprising that, in the eighteenth century, the political classes committed the country to an assertive foreign policy and a build-up of military strength which protected the empire and enhanced their wealth, and that the Tories – weighed down by land taxes – complained that it 'rained gold and silver' on the monied interest as it 'wallowed in the people's wealth'.[293]

[291] Cruickshanks et al., House of Commons, vol. IV, pp. 311–15; ODNB.
[292] Gentleman's Magazine, III (January 1733), 47; VCH Rutland, vol. II (1935) pp. xxxv, 3, 86; Heathcote, Families Bearing the Name of Heathcote, pp. 79–92.
[293] Earle, Middle Class, pp. 143–57. 'A true picture of a modern Whig set forth in a dialogue between Mr Whiglore and Mr Doubt, two under-spur-leathers to the late ministry', in Charles Whitworth (ed.), The Political and Commercial Works of the Celebrated Writer Charles D'Avenant, 5 vols. (London, 1771), vol. IV, p. 125.

4　Shipping

Seventeenth-century Englishmen shared a universal belief in the importance of maritime power. Ships and seamen provided their island with both wealth and 'walls' against invasion, both strength and safety, and it was argued that 'no trades deserve so much care to procure and preserve and encouragement to prosecute as those that imploy the most shipping'.[1] This chapter first examines the shipping demands of colonial commerce and shows that, with its large volumes of bulky goods transported over long distances, it needed a much greater tonnage than trade of equal volume and value within Europe. It then looks at how Londoners responded to the incentives offered by the expanding plantation trade to provide the capital, ships, manpower, and support services that were needed to sustain growth without undue reliance on foreign competitors, above all the Dutch. Finally, it surveys the evidence on freight rates which lends weight to the view that the growth of London's Atlantic shipping industry rested not only on the protection provided by the Navigation Acts but also on improved efficiency with associated benefits for the wider economy.

Growth of London's Atlantic freight capacity

Restoration Londoners looking at the forest of masts on the River Thames, and the piles of colonial commodities on the quaysides, could not fail to be impressed by the importance of the growing plantation trade. Just as anticipated by the first advocates of American settlement, the increasing value of colonial commerce made more than proportional demands on shipping services, 'the working tools of a trading people'.[2] Although there is no series of statistics that documents the growth of shipping tonnage with precision, there is sufficient scattered material to provide a general

---

[1] Josiah Child, *A New Discourse of Trade* (London, 1692), pp. 91–3; John Cary, *An Essay on the State of England in Relation to its Trade* (Bristol, 1695), pp. 44, 47, 68; John Evelyn, *Navigation and Commerce their Original and Progress* (London, 1674), p. 41.

[2] Charles Davenant, *Discourses on the Public Revenues and on the Trade of England in Two Parts* (London, 1698), p. 356.

picture of the plantation trade's shipping needs in the late seventeenth century. According to Davis, England's plantation tonnage almost doubled between 1663 and 1686 and as it grew faster than other shipping sectors, it accounted for around 40 per cent of overseas trading capacity by the later date, and so made a substantial contribution to England's catch-up with its Dutch rival (see Table 4.1).[3] Furthermore, the proportion of shipping engaged in plantation trade was higher in London than elsewhere as the West India and African trades were heavily concentrated on the Thames, although the outports did maintain a more sizeable share of the tobacco trade. Davis reckoned that, in 1686, 335 ships (totalling around 65,000 tons burden) entered the port from the plantations (225 from the West Indies and 110 from North America) and accounted for over half the capital's entire overseas trading fleet of around 120,000 tons burden.[4] Colonial trade had become by far the largest consumer of London's overseas trading tonnage – its share far exceeding its proportion of either the volume or value of the port's total overseas trade – and not far short of the two-thirds claimed by Josiah Child.[5]

American cargoes were bulky, which partly explains their heavy shipping needs. Davis reckoned that at the end of the seventeenth century, sugar was England's second largest import in terms of bulk (after timber and alongside wine) and required 23,000 tons of shipping stowage. Tobacco was the fifth, needing 15,000 tons of stowage. All in all, he estimated that the plantation trades accounted for around 16 per cent of the volume of English imports, which was in line with their proportion of value.[6]

[3] According to Davis, England's total merchant tonnage increased from around 150,000 tons in 1640, to 200,000 tons in 1660, and 340,000 tons in 1686. According to various estimates the Dutch fleet peaked at between 450,000 and 550,000 tons in the third quarter of the seventeenth century and then went into decline. Van Zanden suggests a wider gap but does not include coastal shipping tonnage in the English tonnage: Ralph Davis, *The Rise of the English Shipping Industry in the Seventeenth and Eighteenth Centuries* (Newton Abbot, 1962), pp. 1–21; Richard W. Unger, 'The tonnage of Europe's merchant fleets, 1300–1800', *The American Neptune*, 52 (1992), 247–61; Jan de Vries and Ad van der Woude, *The First Modern Economy: Success, Failure, and Perseverance of the Dutch Economy, 1500–1815* (Cambridge, 1997), pp. 296–300; Jan Luiten van Zanden, 'Early modern economic growth: a survey of the European economy, 1500–1800', in Maarten Prak (ed.), *Early Modern Capitalism: Economic and Social Change in Europe, 1400–1800* (London, 2001), pp. 81–2.

[4] The tonnage is tons burden, deadweight tonnage, carrying capacity which are nearly synonymous terms. This was the figure that interested the ship-owner, and almost invariably recorded tonnages are tons burden. It was used in all commercial contracts for hire of ships, and until 1773 in government records of merchant shipping. Measured tonnage – measured by rules which the shipwrights had developed – was used only as a basis for the shipwright's selling price, and in government contracts. In ships of conventional build during most of the seventeenth century carrying capacity was usually about three-quarters of measured tonnage: Davis, *Shipping Industry*, pp. 7, 298–9, 395.

[5] Josiah Child, *Trade and Interest of Money Considered* (London, 1692), p. 176.

[6] Davis, *Shipping Industry*, p. 184; Ralph Davis, 'English foreign trade, 1660–1700', *EcHR*, 7 (1954), 150–66.

Table 4.1 *Tonnage of shipping required to serve England's overseas trade*

	1663		1686	
	000 tons	%	*000 tons*	%
North Europe	13	10	28	15
Nearby Europe	39	31	41	22
South Europe	30	24	39	21
Plantations	36	29	70	37
East India	8	6	12	6
Total	126	100	190	100

Source: Davis, *Shipping Industry*, p. 17.

However, the bulk of cargoes is only one factor in determining the demand for shipping, which also depended on distance. As Davis stressed when calculating the total volume of goods carried, 'it is unnecessary to elaborate on the fact that carrying 1,000 tons of goods from one place might create a much smaller demand [for shipping] than carrying the same volume from elsewhere'. Carrying 1,000 tons of wine a year from France created a far smaller need for shipping than transporting the same volume of timber from the Baltic or sugar from the West Indies. The French trade might employ one ship of 130 tons in eight round trips a year, the Baltic trade of identical volume might employ three ships, and the West India trade of identical volume required eight ships of the same size for a year or more. As Davis warned 'a deliberate effort' must be made to remember distance when calculating the size of the merchant fleet as distinct from the volume of goods carried.[7]

Of course, in the days of sail different weather conditions caused huge variations in voyage times on all routes. In 1676 the *Constant Martha*, hindered by 'contrary winds and stress of weather', took sixteen weeks to cross the Atlantic to the Chesapeake, whereas in 1688 William Byrd took a mere four weeks to come in sight of the American shore, although it was another four weeks before he came to anchor in Chesapeake Bay.[8] However, the patchy Naval Officers' returns combine with the London portbooks to suggest that typical sailing times in Atlantic commerce

[7] Davis, *Shipping Industry*, p. 175. The point was made at length in a report to the Treasury, of 1721, 'Report on the plantations', CUL, CH (H) Papers 89/11.
[8] 'Deposition of Nicholas Oliver', 28 June 1678, PRO HCA 13/78; Marion Tinling (ed.), *The Correspondence of Three William Byrds of Westover, Virginia, 1684–1779*, 2 vols. (Charlottesville, Va., 1977), vol. I, p. 81.

changed little during the late seventeenth century. The longest outward voyage was that to Jamaica and took around ten weeks. Barbados and the Chesapeake were usually reached in around eight weeks, and the shortest haul to New England took six weeks or so. Homeward trips took a week or two less.[9]

Sailing times alone suggest that Hakluyt was correct in claiming that the passage was 'neither too long nor too short, but easie and to be made twise in the year'.[10] Two voyages were indeed possible, even on the longest haul to Jamaica, as demonstrated by a packet service to the island in the war of the Spanish succession.[11] But, in fact, even on the shortest haul to New England, it was unusual to undertake two voyages.[12] Hakluyt had ignored the imperatives of the weather, and crop cycles, which imposed a slower rhythm on Atlantic trade than sailing times alone.

By the time Richard Ligon visited Barbados in the 1640s, the islanders had developed a regular planting schedule with new sugars available in the dry season between February and May.[13] London merchants were advised to despatch their vessels in the final months of the year. This allowed them to arrive at 'crop time' and secure a cargo before the 'hot, sultry, rainy, sickly' summer months when mortality soared, especially among newcomers, to the intense detriment of many ships' crews. Furthermore, it was advisable to be away from the Caribbean before the onset of the 'merciless storms' that regularly caused damage in the hurricane season between August and October.[14]

The relative shortness of the crop season made it difficult for London ships to obtain two sugar loads a year, especially as turnaround times were long. Both Barbados and Jamaica had substantial port towns with good loading and warehouse facilities (Illustration 15). Port Royal, Jamaica, was built at the mouth of a magnificent, deep-water harbour which provided sheltered moorings for 200 ships and even 'the largest [London]

---

[9] The expeditionary force sent to the West Indies in 1655 reached Barbados in a mere six weeks but the supply vessels took much longer: Francis to John Barrington, BL Egerton MS 2,648, fo. 245; Naval Officers' returns, Barbados, Jamaica, New England, PRO CO 33/13–14, CO 142/13, CO 5/848. For a more detailed account of sailing times see Ian K. Steele, *The English Atlantic, 1675–1740: an Exploration of Communication and Community* (Oxford, 1986).

[10] Richard Hakluyt, 'A particular discourse concerning the great necessitie and manifold comodyties that are like to grow to this realme of England by the western discoveries lately attempted' (1584) reprinted in *Maine Historical Society Collections*, vol. II (1877), p. 152.

[11] Steele, *English Atlantic*, pp. 168–88.

[12] John to Nathaniel Higginson, 29 August 1700, MHS, Higginson Family Papers.

[13] Richard Ligon, *A True and Exact History of the Island of Barbadoes* (London, 1657), pp. 85–94.

[14] Henry Blake to John Bawden, 4 November 1674, PRO HCA 15/10.

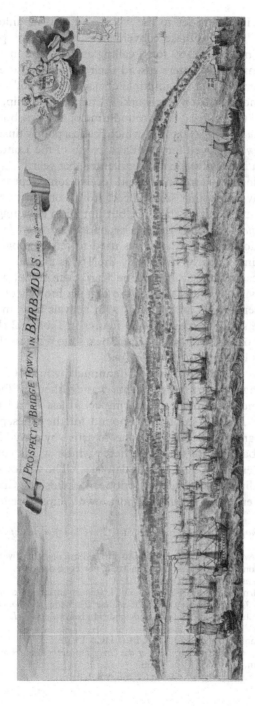

Illustration 15 A sketch prepared from the deck of a ship by Samuel Copen and engraved by Johannes Kip shows Bridgetown in Barbados, 1695. The waterfront is lined with wharves and well-built brick warehouses with substantial houses behind. High levels of economic activity are reflected in the crowded harbour and large numbers of windmills. Samuel Copen, Library of Congress, Washington

ships could lay their broadsides to the wharf and load or unload from a plank on shore'[15] Despite these conveniences, the average port time for London ships (mean size 180 tons) calling at the island in 1686 was 117 days. Merchants and planters spread their cargoes between different ships to reduce risks and the multiple consignments, collected from all around the island, made for slow work.[16] The smallest ship, the *John* (40 tons), achieved the shortest turnaround time of 41 days, but another fairly small ship, the *William* (80 tons), which made a poorly timed arrival in October 1685, was delayed for 173 days. None of the London ships arriving in Jamaica in 1686 made a second entry that year.[17]

Barbados was closer to London and did receive some repeat voyages. Nine of the fifty-five ships that sailed direct from London to Barbados in 1686 made two trips during the year, but not all to advantage.[18] The island-owned *Friends Adventure* made a second entry from London in October, too late to load sugar, and was used to fetch timber from St Lucia until crop time in early 1687.[19] By the 1680s a regular shipping pattern was well established in peacetime Caribbean trade, with most London ships arriving in the islands in the first six months of the year, and leaving between March and August, with arrivals back in London peaking in the late summer months. The figures in Table 4.2 show that almost 60 per cent of arrivals from the Caribbean into Wiggins' Key were in the four months between July and August.

The weather and crop cycle also shaped the annual rhythm of Chesapeake trade. Transplanting young tobacco plants was finished by the end of May, cutting by mid-September, and curing could last until late winter and early spring.[20] Most London ships bound for the Chesapeake left between mid-July and late September so as to arrive by early November for, although the bay seldom froze, the fierce winter winds could deny entry for weeks on end and cause serious damage.[21] The winter was spent unloading and loading but, unlike the Caribbean islands, the Chesapeake lacked the convenience of a substantial port town. Ships were obliged to

---

[15] 'Diary of Francis Rogers', in B. S. Ingram (ed.), *Three Sea Journals of Stuart Times* (London, 1936).

[16] A mean number of twenty-seven merchants (and a maximum of eighty-five) loaded on ships bound from London to the West Indies in 1686, portbook database.

[17] Naval Officers' returns, Jamaica, PRO CO 142/13.

[18] Naval Officers' returns, Barbados, PRO CO 33/14. Repeat entries were made by the *Hopewell* (Aubony), *James and Mary* (Hill), *Katherine* (Emberley), *Arabella* (Manby), *Friends Adventure* (Chinery), *Isabella and Katherine* (Hudson), *Loving Hand* (Parrott), *Elizabeth* (Martin).

[19] 'Deposition of Benjamin Humphreys', 1690, PRO HCA 13/79.

[20] T. H. Breen, *Tobacco Culture: the Mentality of the Great Tidewater Planters on the Eve of Revolution* (Princeton, N.J., 1985), pp. 46–58.

[21] Tinling (ed.), *Correspondence of Three William Byrds*, vol. I, p.18.

Table 4.2 *Records of monthly arrivals from the plantations at Wiggins'*
Key, 1686

	J	F	M	A	M	J	J	A	S	O	N	D
West Indies	1	2	1	2	5	2	6	5	6	5	3	2
North America	–	–	2	1	2	–	1	3	–	–	–	
All arrivals	2	4	4	6	9	3	10	8	6	6	7	5

Source: PRO C 113/14, box 1, journal G.

'vie up and down straggling ... riding below that gentleman's door where
they find the best reception'.[22] Merchants carried tobacco to convenient
landing stages where they had to wait for the right conditions for it to
be shipped. 'If the seamen roll it in bad weather or dirty ways it is much
damaged.'[23] Long turnaround times were inevitable, especially as ships
trading to the Chesapeake were around 30 per cent larger than those
in the sugar trade, averaging 240 tons in 1686.[24] However, most of the
tobacco ships did try to clear the Chesapeake by late spring so as to avoid
the 'vast beds of seedling worms' which rose up in early June and devoured
the ships' bottoms.[25] Arrivals back in London peaked in July and August
alongside the sugar traders (almost half the entries to Wiggins' Key from
the Chesapeake were in these two months).

The direct trade between London and other parts of North America
was far smaller than that to the West Indies or the Chesapeake as, without an enumerated staple, they engaged in an increasingly complex network of trades supplying fish, grain, and lumber to southern Europe and
the West Indies where they obtained goods and bills of exchange to settle
their accounts in London. None the less, as the Caribbean provided over
70 per cent of the value of New England's direct shipments to London,
it was linked to West Indian seasonality.[26] Furthermore, although New
England's ports were rarely frozen up, the bitterly cold winters and winds

[22] Louis B. Wright (ed.), *The History and Present State of Virginia by Robert Beverley* (Chapel Hill, N.C., 1947), p. 121.
[23] Account of the Present State of Virginia, 20 October 1697, PRO CO 5/1309, fo. 88b.
[24] 'The ships wait long for their freight being collected in such a scrambling manner and are detained three or four months while they might be despatched in a fortnight if the tobacco was ready in certain ports. Thus the cost of freight is doubled.' *Ibid.* For size of ships see Naval Officers' returns, PRO CO 33/13–14, CO 142/13, CO 5/848, and Privy Council Register, PRO PC 2/73 pp. 356–7, 364–5.
[25] Wright, *History and Present State*, p. 121; Thomas Sandes to Henry Sutton, 30 October 1695, 'Letterbook of Thomas Sandes and John Brown', BEA, M 7/3.
[26] Arthur Tanner left Boston in the *President* on 9 August 1686 with a cargo of Caribbean commodities. He reached London in September where he loaded for Barbados where he arrived on 19 January and returned to Boston: PRO CO 5/848; portbook database, 1686.

made merchants advise against arriving in the 'dead of winter', and they preferred the months between April and November. As a result, two round trips a year were 'seldom done' and only two of the twenty-one ships entering London from New England in 1686 made two entries in the year (Captains Foy and Fairweather).[27]

Weather and crop cycles imposed a slow seasonal rhythm on London's plantation trade and raised the demand for shipping above the large needs already dictated by distance. However, the limited scope for undertaking two shuttle voyages a year, and long periods of idleness, raised carrying costs and encouraged ship-owners to develop ways to ensure that freight capacity could be more intensively used and earnings increased. London ship-owners, like their New England counterparts, developed a complex web of multilateral exchanges incorporating Africa, the Atlantic Islands, Ireland, Newfoundland, Portugal, and Spain, in addition to the American colonies, with the Caribbean playing a pivotal role.[28] The introduction of sugar planting into the Caribbean in the 1640s raised the islanders' purchasing power and their dependence on outside suppliers for food, fuel, horses, manufactured goods, and slaves. Ligon reckoned that, by 1650, the tiny island of Barbados, similar in size to Anglesey, attracted a hundred ships a year.[29] By 1661 it was reported to receive two hundred ships a year and, in 1686, the naval officer recorded 422 entries, totalling 26,986 tons, making it the busiest port in English America and busier than Bristol, England's second port (Table 4.3).[30] Fewer than half (55) of the 127 ships entering the island from London came direct and 72 ships had sailed via Africa, Ireland, or the wine islands. Jamaica's shipping returns display a similar pattern.[31] Such ships could, with good management, perform a three-sided trip from London within a year, which allowed more intensive use of shipping capacity and higher earnings than in the slacker shuttle voyages, but also reinforced the very heavy shipping needs of plantation trade.

Ship-owners

The expansion of England's merchant marine to accommodate the demands of long-distance trade required a very large capital investment.

---

[27] John to Nathaniel Higginson, 29 August 1700, MHS, Higginson Family Papers.
[28] The correspondence of John Paige throws these complex networks into sharp focus: George F. Steckley (ed.), *The Letters of John Paige, London Merchant, 1648–1658* (London, 1984).
[29] Ligon, *History of Barbadoes*, p. 40.
[30] Naval Officers' returns, Barbados, PRO CO 33/14. In 1700, 240 ships arrived in Bristol from overseas ports and the total tonnage of ships entering was 19,878: W. E. Minchinton, *The Trade of Bristol in the Eighteenth Century* (Bristol, 1957), pp. ix–x.
[31] Naval Officers' returns, Jamaica, PRO CO 142/13.

Table 4.3 *Last port of call of ships entering Barbados, 1686*

Last port	London	Outports	West Indies	Bermuda	Chesapeake	New England	Wine islands	Ireland	Africa	Other	Total
No.	55	38	49	17	19	108	48	35	12	41	422
Tons	6,973	3,027	1,766	432	669	6,023	1,483	2,441	1,192	2,980	26,986
Average tons	127	80	36	25	35	56	31	70	99	73	64
% tonnage	26	11	7	2	2	22	5	9	4	11	100

Source: Naval Officers' returns, Barbados, PRO CO 33/14.

At a time when most industrial production was carried on in small workshops using rudimentary equipment, and even a great colliery or a brewery cost no more than a few thousand pounds, Gregory King's figures suggest that it cost £1,980 to build an average West India trader (180 tons at £11 per ton), and £3,480 to build an average tobacco ship (240 tons at £14.5 per ton).[32] At King's rates, London's plantation fleet of 1686 with around 65,000 tons would have had a capital cost of over £780,000. Assuming, as suggested by King, that a ship had a life of eleven years, the annual replacement cost would have been over £70,000 without allowing for further growth in tonnage. Furthermore, annual refitting expenses averaged between £1 and £3 per ton. In 1686 the value of London's entire foreign trade was around £5 million, and the value of its plantation trade was, at most, £1 million. At a time when the fixed capital stock in the country's coal industry was between £250,000 and £450,000, the 'working tools' of Atlantic commerce required an unusually large fixed capital investment which was almost entirely drawn from within the sector.[33]

The Navigation Acts required that all ships involved in England's plantation trade should be English owned, and although foreign ships were often welcome in the colonies, it seems likely that most of the 335 ships entering London from the plantations in 1686 did comply with the Acts and that English investors had successfully risen to the challenge imposed by the legislation.[34] Ship-ownership was not registered, which makes it impossible to obtain a detailed picture of the structure of the business between 1660 and 1700. However, there is scattered information in surviving bills of sale, court records, African Company records, and probate inventories. Furthermore, the records of letters of marque issued to

[32] 'Seventeenth-century manuscript book of Gregory King', in P. Laslett (ed.), *The Earliest Classics: John Graunt and Gregory King* (Farnborough, 1973), p. 208. This is broadly in line with Navy Board figures which suggest a building cost of £13–14 per ton for naval ships of around 250 tons burden, 'The dimensions and burden of His Majesty's ships when, where, and by whom built with the price of their hulls', NMM, CAD/B4. Appraisals of sixty-three ships (hull, mast, and yards) in the High Court of Admiralty between 1685 and 1687 provide a mean second-hand value of £2.3 per ton, suggesting that London's Atlantic hulls would have had a current market value of around £126,500, with a similar sum needed to fit the ships for sea: High Court of Admiralty, Instance Court, Appraisement files, 1685–7, PRO HCA 4/14.

[33] The largest production unit to be destroyed in the London weavers' riots of 1675 was a workshop with ten looms valued at £120; an iron forge with all the necessary buildings and equipment cost less than £500 and there were perhaps seventy or eighty such installations in the country: John Hatcher, *The History of the British Coal Industry*, vol. I (Oxford, 1993), p. 336.

[34] For a summary of the Acts see above, pp. 36–8. For full discussion see Lawrence A. Harper, *The English Navigation Laws: a Seventeenth Century Experiment in Social Engineering* (New York, 1939).

twenty-four of the seventy-nine ships sailing in the Atlantic convoys in
1689–90 include lists of all the ships' owners and provide an unusually
detailed insight into ship-owning in colonial commerce; a small number
of ships were in sole ownership (8 per cent) but most were owned by
partnerships (ranging from three to sixteen owners with a mean of eight)
which shared the costs and risks of the venture and divided the proceeds
of each voyage in proportion to their investment.[35] Shares were usually
divisors of four, following a long established international pattern.[36]

Ship-owning has been portrayed as an attractive passive investment
but the letters of marque suggest that in 1689, although 4 per cent of
the shares were owned by women, London's Atlantic fleet was mainly in
the hands of those people who were active in the capital's colonial commerce. Funds were drawn mainly from within the capital itself; 85 per
cent of the 163 owners were Londoners.[37] Provincial interest was tiny,
although colonial investors made a more substantial contribution: 29 per
cent of the ships with commissions in the colonial convoys of 1689–90
had at least one colonial owner whereas only 4 per cent of the ships had
provincial involvement.[38] At least two-thirds of the owners were involved
in colonial trade and over half were listed among the 170 big merchants
in the 1686 database. At least thirty-two of the fifty-nine big colonial
merchants of 1686 were involved in ownership of one ship or more and
many spread risks between a number of vessels like the tobacco merchant,
William Paggen, who on his death in 1694 had shares in seven ships
ranging from three-sixteenths of the *Young Prince*, to five-sixteenths of
the *Antelope* and the *William*.[39] Ship-owning allowed merchants, marine-
related tradesmen, and mariners to use their existing business networks
to diversify investment, spread risk, and secure a range of bargaining
tools in the fiercely competitive Atlantic commercial world.

It was common for major colonial merchants to name ships after themselves, or their partnership – the ships which obtained letters of marque
in 1689 included the *Lucy*, *Fleet*, *Booth*, *Jeffreys*, *Perry* and *Lane* – but
the interests of merchants as owners and as traders were not always
aligned and they did not routinely use their own ships to carry their own
goods.[40] The top thirty-seven West Indian importers into London in 1686

---

[35] 'A list of ships bound for Virginia and Maryland', 25 January 1690; 'A list of ships
bound for the West Indies', 27 January 1690, PRO PC 2/73, fos. 356–7, 364–5; Letters
of Marque, 1689–90, PRO HCA 26/1.

[36] Davis, *Shipping Industry*, pp. 82–3, 87.

[37] Letters of Marque, PRO HCA 26/1.

[38] Davis, *Shipping Industry*, pp. 82–4, 88–9; Letters of Marque, PRO HCA 26/1.

[39] 'Inventory of William Paggen', 22 April 1691, CLRO, Orphans' Court Inventories, 2124.

[40] Letters of Marque, 1689–90, PRO HCA 26/1; Davis, *Shipping Industry*, p. 90.

imported an average of 88 consignments spread between an average of twenty-eight different vessels. Thomas Duck received 48 consignments on fifteen different vessels, of which he had shares in only three.[41] As traders, merchants wished to ship goods at the first possible opportunity, at the lowest possible price, and to spread their risks between vessels whereas, as ship-owners, they wished to maximize freight earnings.[42] At times merchants did hope to obtain special treatment as owners, but they were often disappointed. The merchant planter, William Byrd, complained bitterly that as freight rates soared in 1689 his purchase of a sixteenth share in Captain Bradley's ship did not secure any favours from his grasping captain, who insisted on the prevailing freight rate.[43] However, owners did obtain some commercial advantages as in 1690, when freight was short in the Chesapeake, and Captain Tatnall would accept only goods consigned to his ship's owners.[44]

In some major branches of Atlantic commerce, including the Newfoundland fish trade, the Hudson's Bay trade, the slave trade, and contraband trade in the Spanish empire, it was usual for merchants to charter entire vessels and this often provided high profits for the ship-owners. The Royal African Company relied heavily on hired ships for its trade to Africa and America where they were usually discharged. Three-quarters of the 165 ships sent out from England by the company between 1680 and 1685 were hired, and most of the company-owned vessels were small craft used for service on the African coast. Before 1689 the company would have had little difficulty in borrowing money to purchase ships and Davies concluded that the preference for hire was deliberate policy and reflected the private interests of company managers.[45] The company allowed the owners of hired ships (who included company directors) an interest in part of the outward cargo from England, which was typically turned at high profit; both Jeffreys and Bawden mention expectation of a 26 per cent net return and company accounts suggest a figure of 38 per cent.[46] At least six of the seven original shareholders among the fifty-nine big colonial merchants of 1686, hired ships to the Royal African Company, including Jacob Lucy, a member of the company's committee of shipping.[47]

[41] Portbook database, 1686; PRO HCA 26/1.
[42] In 1685 Byrd asked his agent to send his goods on the first ship 'but not where Mr Perry and Lane have ship my other cargo': Tinling (ed.), *Correspondence of Three William Byrds*, vol. I, p. 37.
[43] *Ibid.*, pp. 31–2, 46, 48, 101.
[44] *Ibid.*, pp. 114, 133.
[45] K. G. Davies, *The Royal African Company* (London, 1957), pp. 194–6.
[46] 'Minutes of Court of Assistants', 20 April 1686, PRO T 70/81, fo. 46b.
[47] Thomas Duck, John Gardiner, John Jeffreys, Jacob Lucy, Benjamin Skutt, and Dalby Thomas all hired ships: PRO T 70/81.

The case of the *Rose and Crown*, owned by Lucy in partnership with Samuel Swynock and Mark Mortimer (another Royal African Company shareholder and lessee of Wiggins' Key), reveals how ownership of a vessel could exploit complex sets of overlapping, mutually supportive business interests. The ship was hired to the African Company for a slaving voyage and, after discharge in Barbados, carried company goods to London where it berthed at Wiggins' Key. In fact, thirteen ocean-going vessels part-owned by the wharfingers berthed at the key in 1681 and together they accounted for over 24 per cent of the wharf's import earnings in that year. Roseveare suggests that ownership was used to direct a ship's choice of berth, and that this business was more valuable to the partnership than freight earnings which were 'generally unimpressive'.[48]

Other businessmen, such as ships' suppliers and victuallers, could use a share in a vessel to gain advantages beyond freight earnings from a share in a vessel.[49] Above all it was usual for aspiring captains to buy a share in a ship to help gain a command. Almost a tenth of the owners securing letters of marque for the Atlantic crossing in 1689 were captains and three-fifths of the ships were part-owned by their captain (three captains had shares in more than one ship).[50] This investment was more than mere purchase of influence, being seen as security for good behaviour.[51]

Gregory King reckoned that in peace time ship-owners made an annual return of 10 per cent on their capital investment, but a handful of surviving account books suggest that the *Friend's Adventure* was typical among Atlantic traders in producing a much more modest net return of around 5 per cent a year between 1679 and 1684.[52] With luck, good management, and above all, a careful, competent, and trustworthy master, reasonable earnings were realized; but it is also clear that

[48] Mark Mortimer owned the *Rose and Crown* with Jacob Lucy and Samuel Swynock, PRO HCA 13/131; Matthews and Mortimer owned shares in twenty-one ocean-going vessels. 'Inventory of John Matthews', CLRO, Misc. Inventories, roll 155, box 55. The *Rose and Crown* berthed at the key in July 1681, PRO C 113/14, box 1, journal E, fo. 31. On the partnership see Henry Roseveare, '"Wiggins' Key" revisited: trade and shipping in the later seventeenth century', *Journal of Transport History* (1995), 10–11.

[49] For example, the *Cadiz Merchant* was part owned by a cooper and a baker, as well as the captain: CLRO, 'Interrogatory of Philip Designy', MC 6/511; Richard Pares, *Merchants and Planters* (Cambridge, 1960), p. 6.

[50] Letters of Marque, 1689–90, PRO HCA 26/1.

[51] For example, Freeman persuaded Captain Clayton to buy an eighth share in the *Batchelor* to 'make him more diligent': Hancock (ed.), *Letters of William Freeman*, p. 103.

[52] 'Seventeenth-century manuscript book of Gregory King', Laslett (ed.), *The Earliest Classics*, p. 55. Davis suggested that a ship of 250 tons in Virginia trade with a full cargo made a return below 4 per cent on capital in 1680: Davis, *Shipping Industry*, pp. 363–87; 'Account book of *Friend's Adventure*', PRO HCA 30/864.

low returns, or losses, were commonplace. However, freight dividends were only one part of the return on a shipping investment. The business records of merchants such as Lucy and Mortimer show that a share in a vessel fulfilled a range of ambitions and was often part of a complex business strategy, exploiting overlapping interest networks in the slave trade, fishing, wharfingering and warehousing, the provision trade, and other activities. Even in a period of falling freight rates, overall returns in the business were sufficiently good to attract the very large annual investment needed to purchase, and maintain, London's expanding merchant marine and provide the ships needed to secure compliance with the Navigation Acts.

Ship-building

The Navigation Acts not only required that ships involved in colonial carrying trade should be English or colonial owned but also that they should be English or colonial built. Precisely how far London's expanding Atlantic fleet complied with this aspiration cannot be established, as there was no ship registration in the seventeenth century. However, scrappy evidence in the colonial Naval Officers' returns, the Register of Passes kept in the 1680s, and the High Court of Admiralty supports Davis's conclusion that a dwindling proportion of London's overseas shipping tonnage was foreign built (a third or more between 1654 and 1675 and less than a fifth by 1688).[53]

Contemporaries claimed that the new prosperity of England's ship-building could be attributed to the protection of the Navigation Acts.[54] No doubt the Navigation legislation did encourage those involved in Atlantic commerce to use English-built shipping where all things were equal, or nearly equal. Furthermore, the legislation provoked a series of wars with the Dutch in which the English made a substantial net gain of between 1,000 and 1,700 ships (heavily concentrated in the 1650s). These prize ships were naturalized so that they were treated as English-built and Davis argues that 'these are the years which reconstituted the English fleet with Dutch fly-boats'.[55] However, as will be discussed below, fly-boats were not heavily used in long-distance trades which needed heavier, well-armed vessels and, furthermore, as the addition was concentrated in the 1650s, and a ship had an average life of eleven years, the windfall cannot explain the

[53] Book of Passes, PRO ADM 7/75–6; Davis, *Shipping Industry*, p. 52. Foreign-built ships were often prize vessels.
[54] Child, *New Discourse of Trade*, p. 94.
[55] Davis, *Shipping Industry*, pp. 12–15, 51, 316.

sustained expansion of the fleet.[56] In any event, the gains were offset by net losses in the wars with Spain in the late 1650s and France in the 1690s.[57]

Meanwhile, although the Acts might have encouraged use of English shipping where all things were fairly equal, they were not alone sufficient to force its use in adverse circumstances. It was easy to flout the law. The state did not have the resources to fund a strong or effective enforcement agency and instead relied on colonial governors and other local officials, who were inclined to protect their own interests rather than those of the state. Individuals such as Randolph, who did attempt to uphold the law, were easily thwarted. Merchants who chose to use foreign-built ships had little difficulty in doing so as, without ship registration, it was hard to establish a vessel's provenance. In 1686 the naval commander, Captain St Loe, seized the *Good Intention* at the Leewards on grounds that 'it was commonly reported to be foreign-built', and the ship was condemned in the colonial Admiralty Court. However, on the ship's return to London the original owner petitioned for restoration as he claimed that the ship was, in fact, built in Lancashire. St Loe, who had purchased the ship for himself, stood to lose all his disbursements on the vessel, and although in this case the king did uphold his seizure, the incident highlighted the difficulties, and risks, in enforcing the legislation.[58] The legal waters were further muddied by the extreme ease with which foreign ships could obtain naturalization in the colonies. As reported by the Commissioner of the Customs in 1687, it was usual for the owners of foreign-built ships 'to procure the condemnations at any easy and cheap rates by begging of or compounding with the governor'.[59] Captains, crews, planters, colonial officials, and reputable London merchants were linked in webs of subterfuge which suggest widespread toleration of illegal activity (even among Londoners who had most to gain from the system). The Acts did not, as suggested by Adam Smith and many later historians, have the strength to divert traders away from low-cost foreign-built ships to high-cost alternatives and if, as revealed in the figures, English merchants were increasingly persuaded to use English-owned and English-built ships, it can be assumed that their ships were able to compete with those of foreign rivals.[60]

[56] 'Seventeenth-century manuscript book of Gregory King', in Laslett (ed.), *Earliest Classics*, p. 208.

[57] Davis, *Shipping Industry*, pp. 12–15, 51, 316.

[58] PRO HCA 13/27; HCA 24/122; *CSPC, 1685–8*, nos. 1,293, 1,303, 1,313, 1,350.

[59] Davis, *Shipping Industry*, p. 14; Molesworth to Lords of Trade, 17 April 1687, PRO CO 138/6, fos. 32–6; 'Letter from Mr Guy with report from the Commissioners of the Customs', 28 April 1687; *ibid.*, fos. 6–10.

[60] Adam Smith, *An Inquiry into the Nature and Causes of the Wealth of Nations* (London, 1776; 1812 edn), pp. 360–1; Lawrence A. Harper, 'The effect of the Navigation Acts on the thirteen colonies', in Harry Shreiber (ed.), *United States Economic History: Selected Readings* (New York, 1964), pp. 42–78; Robert P. Thomas, 'A quantitative approach to

How was this catch-up achieved? Mid-seventeenth-century Englishmen had viewed the Dutch shipping industry with awe. The superiority of Dutch vessels, in terms of both building and running costs, was taken as given in writings of the time and used to justify the need for the protection provided by the Navigation Acts.[61] However, the Dutch advantage had been established in the northern bulk trades where they had developed the flat-bottomed, round-sterned fluite (fly-boat). Earlier ships had been designed to carry armament and needed gun platforms, portholes, and reinforced construction, whereas fly-boats did not carry guns, and could be lightly built providing speed, and greater stowage capacity, as well as simple rigging. They were both cheap to build and to operate as they needed only small crews. As the demand for timber increased, and imports rose, the Dutch began to develop saw-milling technology in the 1590s which reduced raw material costs (although this was partly offset by high labour costs).[62] By the early seventeenth century Dutch shipyards were producing a large number of these ships to a standard design, allowing extensive division of labour, and specialization which further reduced unit costs (Illustration 16).[63] English ship-builders made little effort to imitate these designs, and when such boats were used in English trade, they were usually purchased or captured from the Dutch.[64]

However, fly-boats were little used in Atlantic commerce, which had very different needs from the Dutch-dominated northern trades. The long, dangerous voyages across the ocean, and the prevalence of piracy and privateering on the African coast and in the Caribbean, established a preference for substantially built, heavy masted, well-armed ships in the English tradition (Illustration 17). The Naval Officers' returns for Jamaica show that between 1679 and 1688 over 60 per cent of the ships entering the island from London were these broad stern vessels, whereas fly-boats

the study of the effects of British imperial policy on colonial welfare: some preliminary findings', *JEH*, 25 (1965), 615–38.

[61] Worsley complained that the Dutch undercut English freight rates by as much as 20 per cent: Benjamin Worsley, *The Advocate: or, a Narrative of the State and Condition of Things between the English and Dutch Nation in Relation to Trade* (London, 1651), p. 4; Child, *New Discourse*, p. 4.

[62] De Vries and van der Woude, *First Modern Economy*, pp. 300–3, 637.

[63] Violet Barbour, 'Dutch and English merchant shipping in the seventeenth century', *EcHR*, 2 (1930), 261–90; Richard W. Unger, *Dutch Shipbuilding before 1700* (Assen, 1978); de Vries and van der Woude, *First Modern Economy*, pp. 296–9; Jaap R. Bruijn, 'Productivity, profitability and costs of private and corporate Dutch ship ownership in the seventeenth and eighteenth centuries', in J. D. Tracy (ed.), *The Rise of Merchant Empires: Long Distance Trade in the Early Modern World, 1350–1750* (Cambridge, 1990), pp. 174–94; Unger, *Dutch Shipbuilding before 1700*.

[64] In 1670 Williamson remarked that if no ships of this type were being built in England it suggested that there was no demand: PRO SP 29/281a/252.

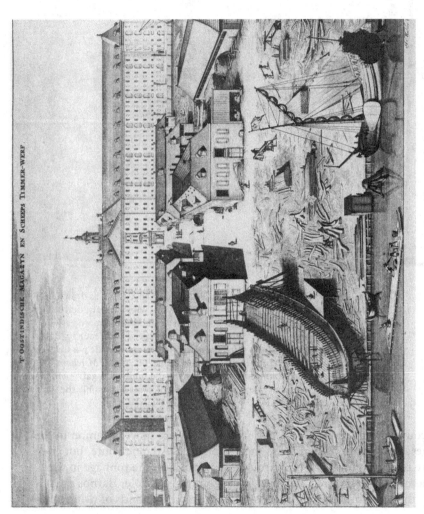

Illustration 16 The Dutch East India Company's storehouse and yard at Amsterdam. The building slips, piles of sawn timber, pieces of grown shaped pieces (knees), and a ship under construction with the access ramp and staging around the hull were features common in England as in Holland. Engraving by J. Mulder.

Illustration 17 The *Cadiz Merchant* in the Jamaica trade, 1682, as drawn in
'Edward Barlow's Journal of his Life at Sea', NMM. Most vessels, down to
50 or 60 tons, had three masts but the sail plan was becoming more varied
in the late seventeenth century allowing for greater speed and security (due
to better manoeuvrability) and some reduction in crew size made possible
by breaking up the total sail area into smaller units. The *Cadiz Merchant*
was well up to modern standards except that she did not have a gaff – which
replaced the lateen mizzen after mid century – which made possible the
setting of a mizzen topsail.

accounted for a mere 5 per cent.[65] Fly-boats were more common in the
Chesapeake trade, which used the safer North Atlantic route, but even
here they accounted for only around 20 per cent of the tonnage in use.[66]
These figures reinforce the point long ago made by Violet Barbour that it
was the structural shift in English trade, with the demands of rising long-

[65] In 1686 twenty-one ships arrived in Jamaica direct from London. They included thirteen
broad stern, one flyboat, two ketches, five pinks: PRO CO 142/13.
[66] Berkeley noted, 'our ships once past the landsend are in no danger of pirates, rocks or
leeshores til they come to their port – fewer ships miscarry going to Virginia than to any
port at that distance in the world': BL Egerton MS 2,395, fo. 354.

distance commerce, rather than the protection of the Navigation Acts, which revived the prosperity of the English ship-building industry in the late seventeenth century.[67]

English ships were used because they suited Atlantic conditions and, furthermore, they could be built in England at prices which competed with those of their rivals. Timber accounted for over half the cost of building a ship and both the English and the Dutch relied on foreign supplies. In the early seventeenth century England imported supplies from Norway and the Baltic via the Dutch entrepot but, after the passing of the Navigation Acts, they were brought direct. As the English did not develop a saw-milling industry, and imported sawn lumber, they reduced their transport costs below those paid for the bulkier unprocessed wood imported by the Dutch.[68] Furthermore, labour was around 40 per cent cheaper in south-east England than in the western Netherlands, and although some of England's new merchant ships continued to be built on the Thames (at Shadwell, Rotherhithe, and Blackwall), it is clear that growing demand was straining the capital's capacity, and encouraged merchants to arrange construction in the provinces where wages and other costs were still lower.[69] Meanwhile, Dutch ship-builders were slow to diversify and allowed their industry to descend into technical conservatism. By 1700 Englishmen had ceased complaining about Dutch superiority and were producing ocean-going ships which could compete on cost and quality.[70]

While England's ship-building industry responded with vigour to the stimulus of increased Atlantic trade in the late seventeenth century, the nation's shipping capacity was further enhanced by extensive growth in America which offered the English an important new source of supply – a bounty not enjoyed by their Dutch rivals who, after the loss of New York, did not maintain permanent settlements in North America. Timber grew

[67] Barbour, 'Dutch and English merchant shipping', 253.

[68] In 1669 Benjamin Worsley estimated that raw materials accounted for almost 90 per cent of ship-building costs and half these costs were for timber: Barbour, 'Dutch and English merchant shipping', 238; J. R. Tanner (ed.), *Pepys' Memoires of the Royal Navy, 1679–88* (London, 1906), p. 38.

[69] Davis, *Shipping Industry*, pp. 55–6; Basil Lubbock (ed.), *Barlow's Journal of his Life at Sea in King's Ships, East and West Indiamen and other Merchantmen from 1659 to 1703* (London, 1934), p. 327; Rupert C. Jarvis, 'Eighteenth century London shipping', in A. E. J. Hollaender and W. Kellaway (eds.), *Studies in London History* (London, 1969), pp. 403–25; Leo Noordegraaf and Jan Luiten van Zanden, 'Early modern growth and the standard of living: did labour benefit from Holland's Golden Age?', in Karel Davids and Jan Lucassen (eds.), *A Miracle Mirrored: the Dutch Republic in European Perspective* (Cambridge, 1995), pp. 410–37.

[70] 'In fact, towards the end of the seventeenth century, complaints of inferior Dutch ship-building techniques became frequent, especially with respect to English and French products': de Vries and van der Woude, *First Modern Economy*, p. 298.

close to the shore all along the North American seaboard 'costing nothing but labour' and these forests also provided abundant tar, pitch, and rosin while the islands of Jamaica, and Bermuda, possessed good supplies of cedar.[71] It was not cost efficient to transport these low-value, bulk commodities across the ocean and, despite the staunch desire of contemporaries to promote a division of labour in which colonies concentrated on producing raw materials, and the mother country on manufacture, the need for ships was such that the English authorities acquiesced in the growth of a colonial ship-building industry and the Navigation legislation gave colonial-built ships the same status and protection as those produced in England.[72]

Although local timber was abundant and cheap, the colonial industry did have to rely on imported iron, cordage, and sail-cloth.[73] The benefits of American resource abundance were also somewhat reduced by the scarcity, and expense, of skilled labour. In the 1660s the wage level for shipwrights in the colonies was more than double that in London, and this gap was maintained throughout the Restoration period.[74] However, this disadvantage did help to dissolve traditional barriers to skill dissemination, and whereas early-seventeenth-century London shipwrights maintained their trade as a 'mystery', to be learned only through apprenticeship, the late seventeenth century saw the publication of manuals, such as Edmund Bushnell's *Compleat Shipwright,* targeted directly at 'those removed to Virginia or New England ... where timber is plenty for their use, yet through their ignorance they dare not undertake such a

---

[71] Thomas Budd, *Good Order Established in Pennsylvania and New Jersey in America* (Philadelphia, 1685), p. 13. Jamaica and Bermuda were renowned for the very high quality of their brigantines and sloops which were lauded as 'the best sailors in the world': Russell to Lords of Trade, 30 August 1694, *CSPC, 1693–5,* no. 1,266.

[72] Robert Greenhalgh Albion, *Forests and Sea Power: the Timber Problem and the Royal Navy, 1652–1862* (Cambridge, Mass., 1926); William Avery Baker, 'Vessel types of colonial Massachusetts', *PCSM,* 52 (1980), 3–29.

[73] The letters of John Ive, London agent for several Boston merchants, are full of details about the supply and price of these materials: John Ive to Charles Lidgett, 20 April, 7 June 1686, MHS, Jeffries Family Papers, vol. VI, fos. 46, 48.

[74] 'No persons to mend and calk vessels except those employed by Robert Aves, shipwright- 5 shillings per diem, 4 shillings for each of the men': Proclamation, 20 August 1661, *CSPC, 1661–8,* no. 159. In the same year the navy allowed 40 shillings a month for shipwrights: Report to Navy Commissioners, 21 March 1662, *ibid.,* no. 261. A London assessment of 1655 indicated that 30d should be the maximum daily wage for a master, 24d for a journeyman: Jeremy Boulton, 'Wage labour in seventeenth century London', *EcHR,* 44 (1996), 268–90. Davis gives the London shipwrights' daily wage as 30–36d in the late seventeenth century: Davis, *Shipping Industry,* pp. 374–5. In 1697 the Agents of Jamaica reported that 'there being so great a scarcity of handicraftsmen, that we give for carpenters, bricklayers and smiths from 5 shills to 10 shills per day and their victuals and for a cawker and ship carpenter 10 shills to 15 shills per day'; in the 'Opinion of the agents of Jamaica upon Mr Wellowton's proposals', 8 March 1697, PRO CO 138/9, fo. 79.

work'. The author provided 'instructions sufficient for moulding of any
ship or vessel whatever ... in a very plain and exact method which I am
confident will be understood by the meanest of capacities if they can but
read English and have the benefit of a little arithmetic'.[75] Conditions on
England's frontier encouraged investment in a sound general education
(including reading, writing, and arithmetic) and worked to promote the
broader diffusion of the information needed to accumulate important
skills.

America's resource endowment also encouraged a greater enthusi-
asm for technological solutions to labour scarcity. Englishmen did not
establish sawmills at home until the eighteenth century (despite the
example of the thriving Dutch industry), and chose to saw their small
domestic supplies by hand while importing processed timber. However,
in America, with abundant wood, and high labour costs, they adopted
a different strategy, and mills were used from the first days of settlement; the industry relied on foreign craftsmen in the early years but, by
the late seventeenth century, the mills were equipped with English made
blades.[76] Furthermore, America's resource abundance and labour scarcity also helped stimulate organizational efficiency. By the 1680s records
of ship-building in New England reveal that the industry was highly
organized with division of labour, specialization, and time penalties for
late completion of contracted work serving to reduce costs below those
in England.[77]

Although we do not have reliable figures for colonial tonnage, con-
servative estimates suggest that, by the 1670s, it was between 30,000

[75] Edmund Bushnell, *The Compleat Ship-wright* (London, 1662). Anderson lists works on
ship-building in English and other western European languages in 'Early books on ship-
building and rigging', *Mariner's Mirror*, 10 (1924), 53–64.
[76] Victor S. Clark, *History of Manufactures in the United States*, 3 vols. (Washington, 1929).
[77] In Boston Captain Arthur Tanner and the merchants Charles Lidgett and Benjamin
Davis commissioned the *President*, a square-sterned ship of 130 tons, from shipwright
William Greenhough in July 1685 for completion in May 1686. He was given detailed
instructions on the dimensions of the ship, and while it was being built on the stocks
in his yard, the owners contracted the smith, Thomas Hunt, to make anchors, grapnels,
bolts, chain plates, rudding irons, and other iron work; Edmund Budd to undertake all
the carved work; and John White to do the joiner's work of planing, making rails, doors,
shutters, beds, tables, close stools and so on: 'Articles of Agreement between Arthur
Tanner and Thomas Hunt, Edward Budd, and John White', July 1685, MHS, Jeffries
Family Papers, vol. VI, fos. 10, 12 13. The goods of William Henderson to value of £300
were attached in 1679 'being just damage the said Waldron and his employers have
sustained by said Henderson not fitting, furnishing and completing a ship built by him
for the said Waldron burden about 127 tons with all ship's carpenters work whatsoever
fitting for the sea not causing it to be done according to his obligation': *ibid.*, vol. VI, fo.
146. On low ship-building costs in the colonies see document in G. N. Clark, *Guide to
English Commercial Statistics, 1696–1782* (London, 1938), pp. 103–5.

and 40,000 tons – half as big as London's Atlantic tonnage and larger than that of the outports combined.[78] By the early eighteenth century it was reported to be 100,000 tons (including the fishery).[79] This strength allowed the colonies to relieve the mother country of the need to supply shipping to service the large inter-colonial trade, which played an essential role in maintaining the sealed Atlantic system envisaged in the Navigation code. The Naval Officers' returns for Barbados show that, between 1679 and 1686, around 70 per cent of Barbados's very large inter-colonial trade was carried in plantation-built ships and Jamaican records reveal a similar story.[80] However, the colonies also provided an increasing proportion of transatlantic shipping: available records reveal that 10 per cent of the tonnage arriving in Barbados and Jamaica from London was plantation built, as were half the ships entering London from New England in 1686.[81] Furthermore, by the 1680s, London merchants had begun to commission ships to be built in the colonies rather than relying on *ad hoc* purchases in England.[82] American shipbuilders were already making a small, but important, contribution to the transoceanic fleet, a contribution which grew strongly in the eighteenth century.[83]

Child warned that dangerous consequences would arise from the strength of colonial ship-building: 'there is nothing more prejudicial, and in prospect more dangerous to any mother kingdom than the increase of

---

[78] Petty gave a figure of 14,000 tons for New England (which probably accounted for half or so of colonial tonnage) in 1674 and Randolph gave a figure of 20,000 or so for 1676: Henry Lansdowne Fitzmaurice (ed.), *The Petty Papers: Some Unpublished Papers of Sir William Petty*, 2 vols. (London, 1927), vol. II, pp. 100–1.

[79] In 1717 Massachusetts alone had 8,000 tons: CUL, CH (H) Papers 89/11.

[80] Naval Officers' returns, Barbados, 1679–86, PRO CO 33/14; Naval Officers' returns, Jamaica, PRO CO 142/13; 'Observations on the Present State of Jamaica', 14 December 1675, PRO CO 138/2, fo. 96; Lynch to Jenkins, 6 November 1682, NMM, MS GOS/5–6.

[81] Naval Officers' returns, Barbados; Jamaica; New England, PRO CO 33/14, 142/13, 5/848. For an example of an island built ship in Atlantic trade see the *Content*, PRO HCA 13/155. Henry Martin reckoned that, by the 1690s, about a fifth of plantation imports were shipped in plantation-built ships and, after two or three voyages, these ships were commonly sold in England: Henry Martin quoted in Clark, *Commercial Statistics*, pp. 103–5. For a New England example see the *President*, MHS, Jeffries Family Papers, vol. VI.

[82] A report of 1721 claimed that the Massachusetts Bay colony launched ships amounting to 6,000 tons a year 'And the greatest part was built for account of or sold to the merchants of this kingdom or other plantations': CUL, CH (H) Papers 89/11.

[83] According to the Bailyns' survey over 19,000 tons of Massachusetts shipping were sold in England between 1697 and 1714 and 29.9 per cent of 75,267 tons known to have been built in Massachusetts before 1715 had ended up with home ports in Britain or its possessions outside the mainland colonies: Bernard Bailyn and Lotte Bailyn, *Massachusetts Shipping, 1697–1714: a Statistical Study* (Cambridge, Mass., 1959), p. 53; Jacob M. Price, 'A note on the value of colonial exports of shipping', *JEH*, 36 (1976), 704–24.

shipping in their colonies, plantations, or provinces.'[84] In fact, without
the resources of the frontier it is unlikely that England could have provided anything approaching the large carrying capacity needed to supply
the sealed, self-contained, trading system projected in the Navigation
Acts. Freight rates would have been forced upwards (as they were during
wartime shortages), essential plantation inputs would have been more
expensive and, no doubt, Atlantic traders would have turned to foreign
carriers on a greater scale.[85]

The Navigation Acts may well have been unnecessary, and were
certainly not sufficient, to ensure that the benefits of the increased
demand for ships that accompanied colonial expansion were reserved for
Englishmen. However, the suitability of ships in the traditional English
style for Atlantic commerce, the conservatism of foreign ship-builders, and the successful exploitation of abundant American resources,
combined to allow the English to produce an increasing proportion of
London's, and England's, Atlantic tonnage at a competitive price, and
ensured that the aspirations of the architects of the Navigation legislation
were largely fulfilled.

Manpower

Colonial commerce not only created a large demand for ships but also
served as a 'nursery of [the] seamen' that 'great princes' needed to swell
the ranks of their small standing navies in time of war, skilled workers
who could not 'be nourished in few days nor a few years'.[86] High mortality rates on long-distance voyages, and the defence needs of transatlantic
trade, demanded generous manning levels. The Naval Officers' returns
indicate that ships carried one man for 9 tons on Atlantic voyages, which
was twice the level Davis calculated for North European trade, and suggests that London's Atlantic fleet would have employed around 3,240
sailors in the 1660s and around 6,300 in 1686 of whom at least three-

[84] Child, *A New Discourse*, p. 223.
[85] P. C. Emmer, ' "Jesus Christ was good but trade was better": an overview of the transit
trade of the Dutch Antilles, 1634–1795', in Robert L. Paquette and Stanley L. Engerman
(eds.), *The Lesser Antilles in the Age of European Expansion* (Gainesville, Fla., 1996),
pp. 206–22; Jan de Vries, 'The Dutch Atlantic economies', in Peter A. Coclanis (ed.),
The Atlantic Economy during the Seventeenth and Eighteenth Centuries (Columbia, S.C.,
2005), pp. 1–29.
[86] Hakluyt, 'A particular discourse', p. 155. The ranks of the country's merchant marine
grew from just over 10,000 in 1615, to around 40,000 in 1688: John Ehrman, *The Navy
in the War of William III, 1689–1697* (Cambridge, 1953), pp. 109–36; *CSPC, 1693–6*, nos.
479, 931, 1,121, 2,261; *CSPC, 1696–7*, nos. 639, 1,166; 'Seventeenth-century manuscript book of Gregory King', in Laslett (ed.), *The Earliest Classics*, p. 209.

quarters were required by the Navigation legislation to be English or colonial subjects.[87] The expansion took place in a context of generally stable wage rates in London and recruits were successfully drawn from the capital's pool of unskilled labour with fairly modest increases in pay from around 20 shillings a month in the 1660s to 25 shillings in the 1680s.[88] Men such as the diarist Edward Barlow, who were attracted to the capital by its reputation for high wages, abundant opportunities, glamour, and excitement were often drawn to the sea by a desire 'to see strange countries and fashions'.[89]

Men such as Barlow, who survived the extreme ardours of life at sea, stood a good chance of promotion to quartermaster, boatswain, gunner, or mate with increases in pay reaching 70 shillings per month.[90] However, an increasingly bitter Barlow reckoned that even the ships' officers were 'little better than slaves' and concluded that the only place worth having was that of master. A captain in colonial trade was well rewarded. It was usual to receive £6 per month in peacetime, against £3–4 in the domestic and north European trades. With living expenses paid during the voyage, and an allowance for freight on his own account, a master in colonial trade could earn a substantial income of several hundred pounds a year.[91] In 1686 over half the captains entering Jamaica from London carried goods on their own account, and there were six captains among London's hundred largest plantation importers: Aubony, Bristow, Hudson, Knapman, Strutt, and Stubbs. Others such as the New England captains Foy, Jenner, and Piggot had very substantial trade. By the late seventeenth century, there was keen competition for a command in colonial trade and few rose through the ranks to these lucrative positions, which were increasingly appropriated by sons of the middling sorts with access to patronage and capital to buy a share in a ship.[92] Among the fifty-nine big colonial traders in the 1686 portbook database, at least one was son of a captain (Dalby Thomas), and another saw his son work as

[87] Naval Officers' returns, Jamaica; Barbados, PRO CO 142/13, 33/14; Davis, *Shipping Industry*, pp. 59–61; Harper, *Navigation Laws*, p. 55.

[88] Jeremy Boulton's figures for London labourers' wages show stability in the three decades after the Restoration (at 30d per day), whereas the modal wage rate for common sailors on Atlantic traders rose by 25 per cent: Boulton, 'Wage labour in seventeenth-century London'.

[89] Lubbock (ed.), *Barlow's Journal*, p. 60.

[90] 'Account book of *Cadiz Merchant*', PRO HCA 30/664, fo. 44.

[91] 'Deposition of Francis Neagle', 16 June 1684, PRO HCA 13/79; Case of *Swallow*, PRO HCA 13/78; Case of *Lucitania*, PRO C 24/1168.

[92] The mate might assume temporary command in an emergency but was seldom retained unless he had influence. For example, John Mingham, master of the *Jonas* died on a voyage to Jamaica in late 1685. Molesworth (governor) and Wiliam Mingham, administrator of the deceased, appointed the mate to take command of the ship, and agreed wages of

a master for a number of years (Peter Paggen), while three-fifths of the Atlantic traders with letters of marque in 1689 were part-owned by their captains.

However, although patronage, and capital, were usually needed to obtain a command they were not sufficient to ensure a successful career at sea. A good reputation and personal contacts were further vital ingredients. In 1675 Robert Little, mate on the *Nevis Factor*, reported the difficulty in hiring a crew, owing to 'the bad reputation of ship and master' which proved 'not without cause'. After a series of mishaps with a leaky ship, and a number of desertions, the mate concluded that 'she never was fit for the work', being badly manned and badly sailed.[93] The masters who dominated the London portbooks of 1686 followed regular routes, building networks of good contacts, and merchants such as William Byrd of Virginia dealt with the same captains year after year.[94]

A master's reputation rested on a wide range of skills. Any captain needed the leadership qualities required to maintain order and discipline among a crew of up to forty men. This was not easy on the long voyages with bouts of tedium alternating with extreme danger. Men became drunk, insolent, and incapable.[95] Some were shirkers, thieves, deserters, even mutineers, if rations ran short, or masters crossed the thin line between acceptable discipline and unwarranted violence.[96] Real ability was needed to maintain courage among the ranks in a violent storm, or an encounter with pirates, and the stakes were high, as demonstrated by Thomas Simms, master of the *Revenge*, who in 1695 saved his ship from loss to pirates at the cost of his own life.[97]

Of course, any master needed a reputation for navigational competence. Those sailing in European waters might manage with little in the way of technical training, employing few instruments, and often relying on little more than an intuitive feel for the sea and the elements, familiarity with the coastline, and good pilotage to reach the intended destination. More was needed for the long, difficult, and dangerous transatlantic crossing.[98] Knowledge remained fairly rudimentary and there was, as yet,

---

£6 per month, for the return trip to London, where he was replaced: PRO HCA 24/122, fo. 115. Barlow had a similar experience: Lubbock (ed.), *Barlow's Journal*, p. 60.

[93] 'Deposition of Robert Little', 13 October 1677, *CSPC*, no. 1,641.

[94] Tinling (ed.), *Correspondence of Three William Byrds*, vol. I, pp. 14, 30, 37, 48, 57.

[95] The account of the *Encrease*'s voyage from London to Antigua in 1677 provides a colourful example of drunkenness, violence, and dishonesty on an ill-disciplined ship: 'Deposition of John Ransley', 15 December 1677, PRO HCA 13/78.

[96] 'Relation of ye unhappy and unparalleled revolt of ye Hannibal on ye Coast of Guinny, 1696', BL Sl. MS 3,986, fo. 10.

[97] 'Deposition of Henry Mees', PRO HCA 13/82, fo. 18.

[98] Lubbock (ed.), *Barlow's Journal*, pp. 327–8; J. B. Hewson, *A History of the Practice of Navigation*, 2nd edn (Glasgow, 1963).

The Great and Newly Enlarged
SEA ATLAS or **WATERWORLD,**
Containeing, Exact descriptions of all the
SEA COASTS of the **WHOLE WORLD,**
According to theyre true scituation uppon the Globe in longitude & latitude as well as in Plano
many Errors which were in the former Charts , with much care and Industrie corrected & amended according
to good Informations gathered from Many able & experienced Navigators both English & Holanders sundry shoalds & dangers not formerly knowne (especially in the West Indies) here descovered, very usefull & nessasary for all such
as Practize the Art of Navigation.

In A M S T E R D A M,
By JOHANNES van KEULEN , Bockseller & Instrument maker at y east end of the
New Bridge at the signe of the Crowned Steerman. MDCLXXXII.

Illustration 18 The exended title of Johannes van Keulen's *Great and Newly Enlarged Sea Atlas or Waterworld*, published in Amsterdam in 1682, credits the new improved information it provides to English as well as Dutch navigators. 'Sundry shoalds and dangers not formerly knowne (especially in the West Indies) [are] here discovered.' The image includes Neptune and personified continents studying a celestial globe and an Atlas of sea charts. The Zodiac and the wind are shown above them. NMM.

no practical way to measure longitude so that it was common to over-shoot one's destination.[99] When travelling to Barbados in 1700 Father Labat warned against over-reliance on geographers or astronomers 'who are usually about as sure of their theories as the makers of almanacs and horoscopes'. Labat reckoned that good sight was the best defence against shipwreck.[100] But despite Labat's scepticism, the thirst for the knowledge, and the understanding, to cross the oceans and unlock the riches of distant lands had stimulated important advances on both the practical and theoretical fronts. Maps and charts were becoming more detailed and accurate (Illustrations 2 and 18) and London craftsmen made a number of small improvements in navigational instruments which placed them at the forefront of the European industry.[101]

By the late seventeenth century most masters on Atlantic voyages carried a waggoner, backstaff (or Davis quadrant), and compass among their effects (Illustration 19).[102] Practical use of instruments was best learned at sea, but some mathematics was required for the necessary calculations, and as this was not included in the traditional classical curriculum private schools and tutors were encouraged to offer training that filled the gap.[103] In 1673 the king's interest in maritime affairs led him to endow a foundation within Christ's hospital for forty poor boys who had already attained a 'competence in the Grammar and common Arithmetic to the Rule of Three' to be instructed 'in the art of navigation and the whole science of arithmetic' with the stipulation that they would later be apprenticed to ships' captains.[104] Similar institutions were set up elsewhere.

[99] 'Deposition of Benjamin Humphreys', 1690 PRO HCA 13/79.
[100] Neville Connell, 'Father Labat's Visit to Barbados in 1700', *JBMHS*, 20 (1957), 160–74.
[101] Joel Mokyr, *The Lever of Riches: Technological Creativity and Economic Progress* (Oxford, 1990), pp. 85, 103–4; Kenneth Pomeranz, *The Great Divergence: China, Europe, and the Making of the Modern World Economy* (Princeton, 2000), p. 67; Karel Davids, 'Shifts in technological leadership in early modern Europe', in Davids and Lucassen (eds.), *A Miracle Mirrored*, pp. 338–66.
[102] The fourth volume of John Seller's *Sea Waggoner for the Whole World*, by John Thornton and William Fisher, became the standard marine atlas of the English Atlantic from its appearance in 1689. Labelled for pilots rather than learned navigators this book included profiles to help identify islands sighted, channels and soundings of significant ports, and descriptions of routes and approaches. It was an aid to any practical mariner sailing the Atlantic: Steele, *English Atlantic*, pp. 143–59.
[103] Advertisements are seen in John Houghton, *A Collection for the Improvement of Husbandry and Trade*, 12 vols. (London, 1692–8).
[104] In the 1690s Isaac Newton was consulted about the curriculum for the 'mathematics' (as the king's scholars were known) and provided a report of eight pages outlining a systematic and practical training in trigonometry, geometry, use of instruments and globes, and chart-making: E. H. Pearce, *Annals of Christ's Hospital* (London, 1901), pp. 99, 123–6; the king to the Royal African Company, 11 January 1676, *CSPC, 1675–8*, no. 780; 'Petition of Ann Fisher', November 1684, *CSPC, 1681–5*, nos. 1,839, 1,940. A German tourist visited Christ's Hospital in 1710:

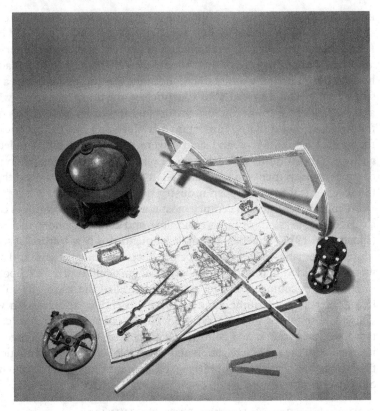

Illustration 19 Instruments including a globe, backstaff (Davis quadrant), an hour glass, a folding ruler and a compass arranged around an atlas of the seventeenth century, NNM.

A modern education was also needed to equip a master with the accounting and management skills he needed in Atlantic trade, for he took charge of a ship, and cargo, together worth several thousand pounds. 'Good husbandry' was important in managing the ship's stores and provisions with minimum waste and embezzlement, and in organizing the

Next the hall is the new school of mathematics which is very fine. In it there stood several cupboards with glass doors, in which various globi and a certain number of mathematical instruments, though for the most part geometrical. There stood also here a couple of fairly large wooden models of ships of most elegant and curious workmanship: these can be taken to pieces, so that the children, who make a special study of ship-building, may be shown all the parts of a ship. In a great cupboard near the door were some 400 mathematical books.

W. H. Quarrell and Margaret Mate (eds.), *London in 1710 from the Travels of Zacharius Conrad von Uffenbach* (London, 1934), p. 87.

repair, refitting, and revictualling of the ship at the destination port.[105] Although by the late seventeenth century it was uncommon for captains to be responsible for selling goods they did have to secure freight in both directions.[106] They advertised the ship's intended voyage in the Custom House, the Exchange, and coffee houses.[107] With a large number of competing and uncommitted ships there was a single freight market in each port, and each master took part in fixing prices but had little scope for divergence without alienating his customers. Loading, and unloading, cargoes involved dealing with very large numbers of individuals, especially in the West Indian trade, with ships sailing direct to Jamaica in 1686 carrying goods for between fifteen and eighty-five separate merchants. There was copious paperwork, as each consignment needed receipts and multiple bills of lading, for which many masters took on an apprentice to help.[108]

In view of the wide range of demands made on masters it is not surprising that many failed to meet expectations, especially as patronage and wealth played a part in securing a command. Complaints of laziness or dishonesty were commonplace.[109] In 1683 Claypoole ranted against Jeffries, the master of the ship that took him to Philadelphia, condemning him as 'a base imperious fellow', unable to control his quartermaster and crew who were the 'veriest rogues and thieves to be found in Newgate'.[110] Even worse were captains such as Joseph Bannister, the commander of

---

[105] 'Instructions to Samuel Morley commander of *Coast Frigate*', 13 October 1692, BL Sl. MS 3,986, fo. 21. Fitting and provisioning the *Cadiz Merchant* for a voyage from London to Jamaica cost £362. On arrival in Port Royal, the ship required refitting and minor repairs (such as mending the cabin windows) costing £84, and revictualling with turtle meat, biscuit, and other stores costing £77: 'Account book of *Cadiz Merchant*', PRO HCA 30/664.

[106] This system was used for small-scale opportunistic ventures: account book of *Friend's Adventure*, 1680, PRO HCA 30/654, fos. 4–5. However, it was viewed with increasing disfavour. In 1686 John Usher's agents in Madeira had little sympathy for the Boston merchant when a captain proved a 'very knave'. They roundly asserted that 'those that prefer masters of ships before merchants in the consignments of their concerns are not much to be pitied, if they run away with your goods or otherwise cheat them': letter to John Usher, 1 February 1686, MHS, Jeffries Family Papers, vol. II.

[107] It cost about 1.5 shillings to put a bill in the London Exchange: 'account of the *Swiftsure*', 5 October 1674, PRO HCA 15/14.

[108] 'The master's business when the ship is in harbour, is most on shore, to receive and take care of goods, from and amongst the merchants, to send aboard for the loading of the ship and likewise for the signing of receipts and bills of lading for the goods transported': Lubbock (ed.), *Barlow's Journal*, p. 327. Advertisements stress the need for an apprentice who 'hath his pen well and understands arithmetic, to assist ... in keeping of books and doing of business': Houghton, *Collection* 17 January 1695/6; 13 December 1695.

[109] Tinling (ed.), *Correspondence of Three William Byrds*, vol. I, pp. 68–9.

[110] Marion Balderston (ed.), *James Claypoole's Letter book, London and Philadelphia, 1681–84* (San Marino, Calif., 1967), p. 241.

the *Golden Fleece*, a large ship which traded at Jamaica for many years. Bannister turned pirate in 1685, and caused substantial damage to English trade until captured, and hanged, on orders of the governor.[111] However, some masters met high praise. In 1671 a Quaker merchant sailing to Jamaica applauded Captain John Kent as a 'very careful man', who had not slept in his cabin at night but 'rather upon the table or deck, wind or no wind, rain or otherwise through all weathers'.[112] By the time Kent died in port in 1687 his probate inventory shows that his reputation for care and skill had allowed him to establish trade on his own account and a modest prosperity.[113]

The expansion of the Atlantic fleet offered employment for a large pool of unskilled labour and provided the nation with experienced seamen in time of war. It also provided a ladder of opportunity for those with the skills, capital, and patronage needed to secure a command. In company with other aspects of commercial expansion, the rewards of command in long-distance voyages provided Englishmen with an incentive to invest in a range of mathematical, mechanical, and managerial skills which encouraged wider provision of a modern educational curriculum that served to enhance not only the shipping industry but also the nation's overall adaptive efficiency.

Port of London

By the Restoration the scale of overseas trade was such that the Port of London was becoming seriously congested and further commercial expansion served to exacerbate the situation. The loading and unloading of dutiable goods in London was, in the interests of controlling smuggling, confined by Act of Parliament to twenty-one Legal Quays crowded along a short stretch of the river between London Bridge and the Tower of London and, by the 1680s, they serviced around two thousand ships a year including almost 350 from the plantations (Illustration 11 and Map 5).[114] At peak times in the summer, the vessels were three or more deep along the shore. Smaller ships could load at the quayside but those above about 80 tons (including most Atlantic traders) needed to be served by lighters and provided employment

---

[111] The *Golden Fleece* is listed as coming into London from Jamaica on 8 October 1681: 'Account of goods imported from the plantations', 19 January 1681, PRO SP 29/418. Molesworth to Blathwayt, 9 February 1687, PRO CO 138/5, fo. 323.

[112] George Welch, 'A journal of my voyage in 1671', APS, MS 917.2a/w455.

[113] 'Inventory of John Kent', 1687, JA, Inv IB/11/3, vol. III, fos. 60–4.

[114] For the Elizabethan demarcation and naming of the wharves see Brian Dietz (ed.), *The Port and Trade of Early Elizabethan London* (London, 1972), pp. 156–67.

1	Fresh	6	Lyon's	11	Wiggin's	16	Custom House
2	Grant's	7	Somers'	12	Young's	17	Wool
3	Cox's	8	Smart's	13	Sabb's	18	Galley
4	Hammond's	9	Dice	14	Bear	19	Chester
5	Botolph's	10	Ralph's	15	Porter's	20	Brewer

Map 5 Part of two sheets of a map surveyed by William Leybourn between 1672 and 1675 and published by William Morgan in 1676 as *A Large and Accurate Map of the City of London, by John Ogilby and William Morgan* (1676). The superimposed numbers indicate the location of the Legal Quays.

for hundreds of small boats. A large West Indian trader, such as the *Guanaboa,* documented by Edward Barlow, occupied eight or more freights of a lighter, and took two weeks or more to unload its cargo of 375 hogsheads and 39 barrels of sugar, 112 bags of cotton, 14 puncheons of lime juice, 42 tons of ebony, and 23 hundredweight of ivory.[115] As ships, lighters, hoys, and barges jostled for space, collision damage was commonplace.

The congestion and confusion on the water extended to the quay. In the early 1660s Evelyn deplored the 'deformities' of the dock. He was filled with disgust at the noise, filth, and inconvenience of men and horses picking their way through piles of 'wood, boards, coal, and other coarse materials' in the very heart of this 'glorious and ancient city' and advocated moving the warehouses and docks downstream on the south bank to make way for noble palaces at the City's waterside. After the area was razed to the ground by the Great Fire of 1666, he antici- pated radical transformation, but in fact the commercial importance of the quays, and the strength of vested interests, meant that the area was rebuilt in haste, and the working port remained in the very heart of the capital, a short walk from St Paul's, Guildhall, the Exchange and, of course, the Custom House.[116] The commissioners appointed to regu- late the port did order small improvements. Nothing was to be built within 40 feet of the shore, apart from cranes, and there were to be no posts or rails between quays as before, but only unobtrusive denter stones in the pavement. The waterfront was raised about three feet and the wharves brought to a common level. The alterations allowed the cre- ation of a broad, undivided concourse before the Custom House, with easier exit to the lanes up to Tower Street, which were widened to at least 11 feet and made less steep.[117] Pepys welcomed the changes which made the descent down Fish Street and Gracious Street 'very easy and pleasant'. However, as wharfingers and customs officials defended their own interests, and successfully resisted any extension of the landing area (which would have brought increased competition for the former, and greater trouble and inconvenience for the latter), the minor changes were not enough to compensate for the disamenities suffered by traders on account of the increasing crowding and inconvenience of the port.[118]

[115] Lubbock (ed.), *Barlow's Journal*, p. 326; PRO C 113/14, part 1, journal E.
[116] E.S. De Beer (ed.), *John Evelyn. London Revived. Considerations for its Rebuilding in 1666 (Londinium Redivivum, or London Restored not to its Pristine, but to far greater Beauty, Commodiousness and Magnificence)* (Oxford, 1938), pp. 43–4.
[117] T. F. Reddaway, *The Rebuilding of London after the Great Fire* (London, 1940), pp. 221–43.
[118] R. C. Latham and W. Matthews (eds.), *The Diary of Samuel Pepys* (11 vols., London, 1970–83), vol. IX, p. 285.

London merchants complained that the lessees of the Legal Quays exploited their monopoly by exacting great charges. The second great rebuilding Act of 1670 included provisions to regulate wharf levies, but they were never acted on, and only competition between wharves acted to restrain prices. Colonial merchants were especially loud in their complaints as heavy charges were laid on plantation goods. Henry Roseveare's reconstruction of the import earnings of the three central quays (known as Wiggins' Key) in 1681–2 reveals that, whereas European traders generated a modest £2–3 apiece, the ten Virginia ships yielded an average of £11.60 per ship, and the forty ships from the West Indies yielded an average of £21.80. Individual East Indiamen produced still higher sums but, as they were few, their aggregate earnings were much less than those in the plantation trade. The business of colonial ships accounted for 30 per cent of the wharf's import earnings which, in turn, accounted for 45 per cent of total earnings. Warehousing charges, which also fell heavily on colonial trade with its large re-export sector, accounted for a further 24 per cent of earnings in 1681, and 33 per cent in 1682.[119] Wharf-leases attracted some of the city's most prominent merchants, including Josiah Child and John Fleet, and were clearly viewed as an attractive business opportunity, and the plantation trade's contribution to port prosperity was far more than proportionate to its value.[120]

In 1689 war brought the long trade boom to an end and entries to the port of London more than halved. Plantation trade was especially badly hit. In 1695 the Tory alderman, John Fleet, a leading sugar re-exporter, and lessee of Sabb's Dock, and Bear Key, led the fourteen wharfingers who managed the twenty-one Legal Quays in a collective response to the depression. Articles of association set up a secret partnership by deed poll – a legal device which allowed them to avoid registration and keep both articles and signatories secret. Joint management of the wharves was agreed for a term of twenty-one years with a capital stock of £12,000. The wharfingers had created a powerful cartel capable of dictating terms to users of the quays and joint management was expected to save between £12,000 and £13,000 per annum through economies in labour and equipment, control of bad debts and theft, and an end to competitive bidding.[121]

Merchants were soon aware of changes. Charges were raised, choice of quay was removed, credit was curtailed, and ships were obliged to use the

[119] Roseveare, '"Wiggins' Key"', 1–20.
[120] 'Lease to be made to Sir Josiah Childe of Bottolph's Wharfe and of her things to contain', 19 May 1686, CLRO, MCD, box 40.
[121] Smith v. Ashton, PRO C 110/181; Henry Roseveare, ' "The Damned Combination": the port of London and the wharfingers' cartel of 1695', London Journal, 21 (1996), 97–111.

wharves' own small fleet of lighters rather than the hundreds competing with one another on the river. In 1705, 294 merchants led by the Whig, Gilbert Heathcote, petitioned Parliament against the abuses of the predominantly Tory wharfingers and followed with a long pamphlet complaining about the 'insufferable treatment they daily met with from the wharfingers since their confederacy'.[122] However, these efforts failed to dislodge the vested interests in control of the quays, or to secure the reforms needed to stem the rising costs of congestion, delay, and poor management in the port. It is surprising that, although the colonial trade of the outports grew faster than that of London in the eighteenth century, the capital retained its overwhelming dominance of Atlantic trade down to the American Revolution.[123]

Although the loading and unloading of plantation cargoes was confined to a short stretch of the river, the refitting and repair work needed between voyages stretched far down both banks of the Thames. Ships' accounts show that it was usual to spend between £1 and £3 per ton in refitting for each voyage and the estimated 65,000 tons of shipping engaged in London's plantation trade in 1686 would have provided welcome work for blacksmiths, carpenters, carvers, compass-makers, glaziers, ropemakers, sailmakers, shipwrights, and other craftsmen, as well as encouraging investment in new docks and equipment.[124]

Ocean navigation also provided instrument makers with an important market for clocks, telescopes, and new tools as producer goods rather than consumer luxuries. The stimulus of rapidly expanding long-distance commerce, and the damage inflicted on the competing French industry by large-scale emigration of Protestant craftsmen after 1685, combined to

---

[122] *Journal of the House of Commons*, vol. XIV, pp. 473, 475; *The Case of the Traders of London. As it now Stands since the Copartnership of the Wharfingers* (London, 1705); Henry Roseveare, 'Property versus commerce in the mid eighteenth century port of London', in John J. McCusker and Kenneth Morgan (eds.), *The Early Modern Atlantic Economy* (Cambridge, 2000), pp. 65–85.

[123] In 1699/1701 London accounted for 77 per cent of imports from British colonies and 80 per cent of exports to British colonies: PRO CUST. 3/3–5, 72–4; Christopher J. French, 'Crowded with traders and a great commerce: London's domination of overseas trade, 1700–1775', *London Journal*, 17 (1992), 27–35; Rupert C. Jarvis, 'The metamorphosis of the port of London', *London Journal*, 3 (1977), 55–72.

[124] For example, the cost of fitting the *Cadiz Merchant* (280 tons) for a voyage to Jamaica in 1680 was £362 including payment to fifteen different craftsmen. Almost as much was spent on turnaround in Jamaica: PRO HCA 30/664. In 1663, Robert Clayton advanced £300 at 6 per cent for one year, or longer, on security of property for the purpose of investment. The property consisted of 5 acres of land adjoining the shipyard at Deptford and held of 'squire Evelyn'. On the land there was built 33 feet of 'new strong wharf', a large house, two cranes, a dock and various buildings. The loan was required for 'inlarging the wharfs and buildings': D. C. Coleman, 'London scriveners and the estate market in the later seventeenth century', *EcHR*, 4 (1952); also see D. C. Coleman, 'Naval dockyards under the later Stuarts', *EcHR*, 6 (1953), 134–55.

make England the leading European instrument-maker by 1700, with the industry concentrated in London. A cluster of mechanics, entrepreneurs, inventors, and other men of learning, interacted to promote a continuous cross-fertilization of ideas through discussion, spying, copying, and improving. These mechanical skills turned out to be a major ingredient in the new technology that encouraged innovation and economic growth. In fact, Mokyr concluded that Europe's real technical edge in the eighteenth century, and Britain's within Europe, was in instrument-making.[125]

Victualling the Atlantic traders for long voyages imposed further heavy demands on the capital's resources. In the 1680s the plantation traders needed provisions for around 8,000 crew, and hundreds of passengers (equivalent to the population of a substantial town) for three months or more. Given limited space, and the durability of food, the return victuals were obtained in the colonies.[126] Ships' accounts show per capita expenditure of 16 or 17 shillings a month between the Restoration and the 1680s, with the rate rising well above 20 shillings in the war of the 1690s. This suggests annual peacetime expenditure of between £17,000 and £34,000 on the bread, beef, saltpork, stockfish (air-cured Iceland cod which was more lasting than salt fish), cheese, peas, and beer which comprised the ordinary sailor's meagre, and often intensely unappetising, diet. With luck the stale, salty diet could be varied a little with fresh fish caught at sea.[127] Additional food taken on board for officers and quality passengers further inflated demand. In 1685 a promotional tract suggested that an emigrant to Pennsylvania would pay £5 for his passage, and was advised to allow an additional £1 for 'fresh provisions above the ship's rations as rice, oatmeal, flower, butter, sugar, brandy, and some odd things more'.[128] In 1697 the charge for transportation had increased

---

[125] Mokyr, *The Lever of Riches*, pp. 111–12, 240–1; Davids, 'Shifts in technological leadership'.

[126] For an account of victualling in the colonies see 'Deposition of Abraham Langford', 6 July 1669, PRO HCA 13/77. The ability of North American ports to victual their ships is unsurprising but, in the 1680s, Caribbean port towns were also providing hundreds of ships with turtlemeat, jerkt pork, yams, salt beef, and other local, as well as imported, provisions.

[127] For a typical list of provisions see the accounts of the *Cadiz Merchant* at London on 25 March 1680: PRO HCA 30/664, fo. 36. The trade in stockfish is described in *Reasons Humbly Offered to the Consideration of Parliament why Stockfish and Live Eels should be Imported into England* (London, 1695). Barlow complained about his meagre diet on an Atlantic voyage. Each man was allowed less than a pound of bread a day with a little dry stockfish and two teaspoons of oil on four days in a week and, on the other three, a little salt beef and a few peas, or a little old musty rice: Lubbock (ed.), *Barlow's Journal*, pp. 35–6, 51, 53–4, 60, 83.

[128] Budd, *Good Order Established*, p. 24. In 1685 the apprentice Francis Hanson complained that on being taken to Jamaica he was enforced to 'eat the ordinary provisions of the ship which were very unwholesome and often stale': CLRO, MC 6/452.

to around £6 'and if the passenger would have any fresh meat on the voyage he must find it himself. The usual way for the better sort is to lay in 40 or 50 shillings for fresh meat.'[129]

The size of London's ship-provisioning needs encouraged the development of large, specialized firms with well-organized supply networks in the capital's hinterland: fishmongers, such as Goffe and Kent of Wapping, butchers Fryer and Holland, bakers, Peesley and Fletcher, and the brewers Philip and Bond all operated on a large scale.[130] Economies of scale and specialization underpinned a well-developed central purchase and distribution system which also supplied the navy and was able to respond to wartime needs with great profit.[131] A report to the victualling office in 1694 indicated that it was usual for naval contractors to charge a 25 per cent premium for victuals, and that they further increased profits by substituting low-quality goods, although they faced none of the uncertainties of the peacetime provision trade.[132]

Crews needed refreshment on shore as well as at sea. A high proportion of the wage bill for the plantation trades was spent in London between voyages. Between their hiring and the ships' departure from Gravesend the men were given half pay and then (apart from those on the slavers who were paid off in the colonies) the crews had to wait for the remainder of their wages until their return to England.[133] On disembarking in London in 1680, the twenty-eight-man crew of the *Cadiz Merchant* received wages for ten and a half months totalling £439.[134] Each man had between £10 and £20, which was a large lump sum for a common labourer. Many had incurred debts on board ship and on shore. Those with wives and children needed to provide for their families. All needed to support themselves until their next voyage. But after the hardships and deprivations of months at sea there was a strong temptation to indulge in a spending spree. Excessive eating and drinking were commonplace, and spawned a plethora of inns and lodging houses in Shadwell and Wapping near the docks. Many of these businesses were small scale and allowed both men and women with limited resources to survive, and even flourish as in the case of Mary Hill, a tripe-woman on Tower Hill, or the wife

---

[129] James Blair to William Popple, 25 October 1697, *CSPC, 1696–7*, no. 1,411.
[130] PRO T 70/81, fos. 10b, 34, 57, 66; T 70/82, fo. 57; 'Account book of *Cadiz Merchant*', PRO HCA 30/664.
[131] Ehrman, *Navy in the War of William III*, pp. 144–57.
[132] 'Richard Gibson, his reasons for keeping the victualling of their Majesties' navy in a regulated commission', 27 February 1694, PRO T 48/89, fo. 176; Letters from Victualling Board, 1703–4, NMM, ADM/D/2.
[133] 'Answers of William Greene', 20 September 1683, PRO HCA 13/132.
[134] 'Account book of *Cadiz Merchant*', PRO HCA 30/664, fo. 44.

of Barlow's captain.[135] Provisioning plantation traders, in peacetime and war, on board and on shore, offered opportunities to a wide range of entrepreneurs and helped fuel the stimulus to agricultural improvement and commercial food production created by the rapid growth of the capital in the seventeenth century.[136]

It has been suggested that by 1700 a quarter of London's population depended directly on employment in the various port trades and, allowing for the multiplier effect of this employment, it has been claimed that the 'greatness of London depended before everything else on activity in the port of London'.[137] The rapidly expanding plantation trades, with their heavy shipping needs, played a prominent part, more than proportional to the value of their imports and exports, in promoting the full range of loading, unloading, warehousing, repairing, refitting, and victualling activities that supported this greatness in the seventeenth century.

Freight rates

Contemporaries were impressed by the expansion of the English shipping industry to cope with the demands of Atlantic trade after the Restoration and later historians have echoed their admiration. However, many (including Adam Smith) have attributed this maritime success to the protection provided by the Navigation Acts and, drawing on little more than the assertions of mid-century polemicists, it has been argued that, with the exclusion of foreign shipping, the achievement was at the expense of overall efficiency: trade was diverted from low-cost Dutch carriers to high-cost English carriers to the detriment of both producers and consumers of colonial produce.[138] However, as indicated in the earlier discussion of ship-building, the gap between Dutch and English freight rates was certainly always smaller in the Atlantic trades than in the northern bulk trades and evidence drawn from the Restoration period suggests that the English made efficiency gains which allowed them to compete with their rivals. If the English had not provided a competitive service then a weak state could not have forced English colonists to use English shipping on the scale reflected in surviving figures and they would have turned to foreigners – as they did in war when English shipping was scarce and expensive.

---

[135] The tripe woman, Mary Hill, on Tower Hill made £80 per year from her business: November 1663, CLRO, MC 6, 166; Lubbock (ed.), *Barlow's Journal*, p. 39.

[136] E. A. Wrigley, 'A simple model of London's importance in changing English society and economy, 1650–1750', *Past and Present*, 37 (1967), 44–70.

[137] Davis, *Shipping Industry*, p. 390.

[138] Worsley, *The Advocate*, p. 4; Harper, *Navigation Laws*.

Unfortunately, the statistical evidence with which to weigh these arguments is both limited and difficult to interpret. Records of freight rates are scattered, and there were wide fluctuations within a single season, making it difficult to determine an average freight rate. The uncertainties of the weather, and the harvest, made it hard to match supply and demand for shipping. Merchants did not obtain information about likely crop yields in time to adjust the volume of shipping despatched across the Atlantic and, by the end of the season, it was usual to face short or surplus capacity. In Jamaica in 1680 (a bad crop year), the rate for sugar fell by 50 per cent between the beginning of the season and the end.[139] In a good crop year such as 1686, with bumper harvests, the move would be in the opposite direction, freight rates would soar, and planters would be left with crops on hand.[140] None the less, the scrappy statistical evidence supports claims that in the late seventeenth century the English merchant fleet expanded to cope with rising demand at a declining, and increasingly competitive, cost.[141]

The dry goods that dominated exports from London were not bulky, and surplus capacity was reflected in lower outward receipts, with shipowners expecting to make around two-thirds of their earnings on return voyages.[142] However, there was little change in the level of outward freights which stood at around £2 per ton from the Restoration until the 1690s.[143] Charges tended to be higher for voyages to new colonies where there was risk of underlading on return.[144] The impression of stability is reinforced by evidence drawn from a sample of thirty-four invoices, which in a period of stable prices show a freight burden of 3 or 4 per cent on the invoice price of dry goods, and around 15 per cent for bulkier goods such as flour and wine.[145] Passengers provided an important

---

[139] 'Royal African Company freight books', PRO T 70/962; 'Account book of *Cadiz Merchant*', PRO HCA 30/664.

[140] In July 1686 Byrd was expectant of 'mighty crops' in Virginia. By the time his letter reached England it was too late to arrange additional shipping to take advantage of the glut. Byrd complained that freight rates soared and he was left with 100 hogsheads of tobacco on hand without shipping. Tinling (ed.), *Correspondence of Three William Byrds*, vol. I, pp. 63, 69, 70.

[141] On the eve of the war in 1688 Cary claimed that sugar freight rates were at 30 per cent of the level prevailing in the 1660s: Cary, *An Essay on Trade*, p. 147.

[142] In the case of the *Cadiz Merchant,* outward receipts were 46 per cent of total earnings in 1680–81, and 33 per cent of those on a more successful voyage the following year: 'Account book of *Cadiz Merchant*', PRO HCA 30/664.

[143] 'Account book of *Swiftsure*', 1676, PRO HCA 15/14; 'Account book of *Cadiz Merchant*', PRO HCA 30/664; Balderston (ed.), *Claypoole's Letterbook*, p. 189; 'Memo of Lords of Trade', 2 September 1692, PRO CO 138/7, fo. 113; Clark, *Commercial Statistics*, p. 92.

[144] *Ibid.*, p. 197.

[145] CLRO, MCD, boxes 38, 39, 40.

source of additional revenue, accounting for 65 per cent of the outward freight earnings on the *Cadiz Merchant* in 1680, and 54 per cent in 1681, and fares remained at £5 per head between the 1660s and the outbreak of war in 1689.[146]

However, there is evidence of declining freights on return cargoes, although the practice of levying charges on tobacco and sugar (which together accounted for around 80 per cent of the value of home cargoes) by volume rather than weight makes it difficult to translate nominal rates per ton into real freight rates. It was customary to pay freight for tobacco and sugar accounting four hogsheads to the ton 'be they lighter or heavier, bigger or less', and the pressure to both increase the size of the cask, and pack it more tightly, was irresistible.[147] Although the peacetime charge for shipping one ton of tobacco stood at around £6 or £7 throughout the late seventeenth century, the amount carried in an average cask certainly increased, and Menard suggests that the price of transporting one pound of tobacco from the Chesapeake to London was reduced from around 1.5d per pound in the 1660s to 1d in the 1680s (with a low point of 0.75 d in 1688) before soaring up to pre-Civil War levels after the outbreak of hostilities in 1689.[148] The decline did not match that of the farm price of tobacco (which fell from 2d to 1d per pound) but none the less, falling freights made an important contribution to falling retail prices.[149]

In the sugar trade peacetime freights from Barbados changed little between the 1660s and the 1680s, and fluctuated between £3 and £5 per ton. In Jamaica, more recently settled, and further from England, freights were £7 or £8 in the 1670s but were brought down to £5 or £6 in the 1680s, as sugar planting became firmly established in the island and volumes increased.[150] As in the tobacco trade, the stability of nominal rates reveals little as casks became bigger, and sugar was better processed and packed. In 1663 Willoughby established rules for collecting the 4.5 per cent duty on Barbados exports and established that butts of sugar should be entered at 1,250 lb, and hogsheads at 625 lb, and freight continued to be charged on the traditional ton despite subsequent increases in the sizes of casks; in the period 1678–82, the average hogshead imported by

[146] 'Account book of *Cadiz Merchant*', PRO HCA 30/664.
[147] 'Deposition of Robert Bigg', 14 November 1695, *Starke* v. *Seagoe*, PRO C 24/1181.
[148] Russel R. Menard, 'Transport costs and long-distance trade, 1300–1800: was there a European transport revolution in the early modern era?', in James D. Tracy (ed.), *The Political Economy of Merchant Empires: State Power and World Trade, 1350–1750* (Cambridge, 1991), pp. 254–6.
[149] Russell R. Menard, 'The tobacco industry in the Chesapeake colonies, 1617–1730: an interpretation', *Research in Economic History*, 5 (1980), 146–7.
[150] 'Royal African Company freight books', 1678–1700, PRO T 70/962–72; Davies, *African Company*, p. 202.

the Royal African Company contained 896 lb of sugar, and by 1683–8, the weight was 1050 lb in Barbados and 966 lb in Jamaica.[151] Between 1660 and 1688 Menard suggests that the mean peacetime price of shipping a pound of sugar from Barbados to London fell from around 0.3d to 0.26d.[152] The Royal African Company records indicate that, in Jamaica, the price was around 0.42d per pound in 1678–82, and was reduced by 25 per cent to 0.32d per pound in 1683–8.[153] The falls did not match reductions in the farm price of sugar (from 2d per pound in the 1660s to just over 1d per pound in 1686) and the freight burden on each pound slightly increased. None the less, as with tobacco, the fall did make a contribution to bringing consumers cheaper sugar.

The scrappy statistical evidence of falling freight rates is supported by qualitative material. Efficiency gains in shipping owed little to new technology although, according to Cary, there were minor improvements in ship design which enhanced stowage and safety, while better charts and navigational instruments reduced risks and voyage times.[154] Overall input costs were also fairly stable. As discussed in the section on shipbuilding, capital costs changed little, although the trend was probably downward. A ship's running expenses were fairly evenly divided between refitting, victualling, and wages.[155] Assuming that refitting costs reflected Boulton's evidence on craft wages in Restoration London, these costs would have fallen by between 10 and 15 per cent between 1660 and 1689, and provisions would have fallen by a similar amount, but the mariners' wage rate rose by around 20 to 25 per cent between the 1660s and 1680s and cancelled out some of the gains.[156]

However, although technology and unit input costs were fairly stable, the higher charges levied on voyages to new colonies such as Carolina and Pennsylvania illustrate how increased volumes, and growing experience, furnished scope for organizational improvements which made for more efficient use of inputs.[157] Greater awareness of seasonality, and careful

---

[151] CUL, CH(H) Papers 84/1; 'Royal African Company freight books', PRO T 70/962–72.

[152] Menard, 'Transport costs', p. 265.

[153] 'Royal African Company freight books', PRO T 70/962–72; Davis, *African Company*, p. 202.

[154] Cary, *Essay on Trade*, p. 147.

[155] Examples include *Cadiz Merchant*, PRO HCA 30/664; *Friends Adventure*, HCA 30/864.

[156] Boulton, 'Wage labour in seventeenth-century London'; Jeremy Boulton, 'Food prices and the standard of living in London in the century of revolution, 1580–1700', *EcHR*, 53 (2000), 455–92.

[157] Gary M. Walton, 'Sources of productivity change in American colonial shipping', *EcHR*, 21 (1968), 268–82.

timing, reduced the risks of damage caused by bad weather and delays in securing a cargo, while the development of multilateral voyages (such as in the slave trade) made fuller use of shipping capacity.[158] As Menard emphasized, substantial savings were achieved 'by the rather simple practice of using standard containers and taking care to pack them tightly'.[159] Furthermore, the practice of shipping loose tobacco declined, and was outlawed in the 1690s, in an effort to reduce customs fraud.[160] All served to improve earnings.

Ship-owners also became increasingly adept at managing the high risks in Atlantic trade. The Naval Officers' returns for Jamaica show that one in twenty ships sailing between London and Jamaica between 1679 and 1688 was entirely lost through storm, fire, or plunder and many others suffered some damage.[161] Insurance became more widely available, and better managed, and it became customary to force crews to share any losses through deductions from their wages, which reduced the risks of damage and embezzlement.[162]

Plunder remained an ever present danger and was a major reason for heavy manning and armament on colonial traders. Although England was at peace in Europe for all but very brief intervals in the three decades after the Restoration, there was almost continuous war with one of the Barbary states (Illustration 20). Diaries and logbooks reveal the fear and trepidation with which vessels approached the African coast and the plight of hundreds of white slaves held in North Africa was a frequent cause of national lament.[163] Neither naval or diplomatic activities made much impression on the danger, which raised commercial costs through necessitating convoys and heavy manning.[164]

However, although the Barbary threat remained little diminished the English were able to take advantage of their strategic settlements on the east coast of the mainland and well-placed islands to gain the upper hand in managing violence in American waters. The Caribbean had long swarmed with freebooters of all nationalities, drawn by the fabled wealth of the Indies

[158] The *Cadiz Merchant* made a 20 per cent saving on wages and secured a 30 per cent increase in freight earnings through better timing of a voyage in 1681/2 than the year before: 'Account book of *Cadiz Merchant*', PRO HCA 30/664.
[159] Menard, 'Transport costs', p. 263.
[160] BL Sl. MS 2,717, fos. 57–57b.
[161] Naval Officers' returns, Jamaica, PRO CO 142/13.
[162] 'Deposition of Richard Tilden', 16 December 1680, PRO HCA 13/78; Lubbock (ed.), *Barlow's Journal*, pp. 376, 341, 350, 83.
[163] George Welch described an encounter with a Sally Man in 1671: APS, Journal of George Welch.
[164] 'Allegation of Thomas Beacon', 1681, PRO HCA 13/131.

Illustration 20 An English ship in action with Barbary corsairs, *c.* 1680. Willem van de Velde the Younger, NMM.

and the reputed weakness of their Spanish masters and, as in the seventeenth century, English governors had little naval support (a frigate or two at Jamaica and Barbados) they generally pursued policies of collusion which promoted mutual dependence and security for their own trade rather than attempting eradication, which was seen as likely to alienate the predators and expose English trade to attack.[165] Privateers were generally allowed to come in and out of England's well-placed colonial ports to fence their loot, and refit their ships, without fear of molestation on the tacit understanding that they did not damage English trade or shipping. Those who crossed this line such as Joseph Bannister, an English captain who took four vessels bound for Jamaica in the first few months of 1686, were treated as pirates and punished accordingly.[166] The governor sent HMS *Drake* in vigorous

---

[165] Violet Barbour, 'Privateers and pirates of the West Indies', *American Historical Review*, 16 (1911), 529–66; Nuala Zahedieh, ' "A frugal, hopeful and prudential trade": privateering in Jamaica, 1655–89', *JICH*, 18 (1990), 145–68; Nuala Zahedieh, 'The capture of the *Blue Dove*, 1664 policy, profits and protection in early English Jamaica', in R. McDonald (ed.), *West Indies Accounts: Essays on the History of the British Caribbean and the Atlantic Economy in Honour of Richard Sheridan* (Kingston, Jamaica, 1996), pp. 29–47.

[166] Joseph Bannister had a long-standing career as a merchantman captain in the Jamaica trade before he turned pirate, Naval Officers' returns, Jamaica: PRO CO 142/13.

pursuit of Bannister and the pirate was brought into Port Royal hanging on the yard arm, 'a spectacle of great satisfaction to all the better sort'.[167] English governors reported that policies of patronage, and collusion, with privateers allowed them to reduce their costs below those of their Dutch competitors who did not have a strategic base in the heart of the Caribbean, and Eltis's finding that English ships in the slave trade operated with lower manning levels than their competitors tends to support their claims.[168]

Evidence of falling freight rates in England's Atlantic trade casts doubt on Smith's assertion that the Navigation Acts reduced efficiency by diverting English merchants away from low-cost carriers. In fact Dutch rates may well have been higher in late seventeenth-century Atlantic trade as they did not have the same edge on capital and running costs as in the northern bulk trades. Nominal wage rates were around 10 per cent higher in Amsterdam than in London (raising refitting costs), and bread (revictualling) costs were also higher.[169] Meanwhile, although hard evidence is lacking, it is unlikely that the Dutch could sail with fewer men or guns than the English, who were generally acknowledged to have the upper hand in managing violence in the Caribbean.

However, the strongest evidence that the Navigation Acts did not impose a heavy burden on English trade lies with the high rates of compliance reflected in rising trade volumes and shipping tonnage. As indicated in Chapter 2, the state had limited power to enforce the legislation, especially in the colonies where, as widely reported by the king's agents, it was a simple matter to load or unload foreign ships in remote bays or nearby entrepots.[170] An illegal cargo could easily be concealed by legal fish or flour. Records of illicit trade such as the cargo picked up in France on account of Freeman and Baxter in 1678, or in Hamburg on account of the Halls in 1688, indicate that fear of seizure was slight, and precautionary expenses were minimal; the vessels were not manned above the usual complement, and nor were the crew paid premium wages, although Freeman did provide generous brandy rations to maintain crew morale.[171] Evasion of the Navigation legislation carried low risks and costs and this suggests that the high levels of peacetime compliance also imposed low

---

[167] Molesworth to Blathwayt, 9 February 1687, PRO CO 138/5, fos. 323–4.

[168] Molesworth to Blathwayt, 15 May 1685, PRO CO 138/5, fo. 68; David Eltis, *The Rise of African Slavery in the Americas* (Cambridge, 2000), pp. 114–36.

[169] Noordegraaf and van Zanden, 'Early modern economic growth and the standard of living', 410–37.

[170] Report about the Dutch trading about the Leeward Islands: 7 June 1687, PRO CO 153/3, fo. 263.

[171] William Freeman to Robert Helmes, 19 September 1678, 'Letterbook of William Freeman', NLJ, MS 134, fo. 21.

costs.[172] If English shipping charges had been substantially greater than those of their rivals, and compliance had imposed a heavy burden, there can be little doubt that the legislation would have been widely ignored or the growth of the plantation economy would have stalled.

The suggestion that the Navigation legislation was not sufficient to push English commerce into high-cost channels was tested, and confirmed, by the wartime experience of the 1690s when the downward trend in freight rates was dramatically reversed but the Acts were not suspended. Although merchant ships were not used in the line of the fleet in the 1690s, they were needed as transport, fire, and hospital ships; in 1690, 54,000 tons of shipping were hired for the Irish campaign. Trade was regulated to give priority to naval needs, and the Atlantic trades were allowed barely half the tonnage employed in 1686 while, at the same time, owners were offered tempting contracts for state service – with premium rates and payment even in the event of loss or damage.[173] Routine commerce was starved of shipping as reflected in the collapse in the legal tonnage entering Port Royal after 1689 (Table 4.4) and widespread complaints that the inhabitants of the plantations were 'ready to perish for extreme want of provisions and forced to go naked for want of clothing'.[174] In June 1694 the governor of Barbados reported that half the crop remained unladen on account of 'the great want of shipping' and the agent for the Leewards complained that 'not one ship had gone thither this winter from the port of London'.[175] The substance in their complaints is borne out by a very substantial fall in West Indian trade as measured by a large decline in the receipts for the 4.5 per cent duty on legal exports from the islands.[176] Meanwhile, in the Chesapeake, Byrd also grumbled that, given the shortage of ships, 'truly there is no coming near a master without great observance'.[177]

[172] In 1675 the master of the *Newfoundland Merchant* reported that freight rates from Barbados to London had soared from £3 or £4 a ton in peace to £14. The Acts were suspended: 'Deposition of master of *Newfoundland Merchant*', 1675, PRO HCA 13/78.
[173] 'Lord President concerning next year's trade and convoy', 22 September 1690, PRO CO 1/68, fos. 23–53; BL Add. MS 28,878, fo. 47. Political connections and patronage were important in securing business and bribes were commonplace. On attractions of state service see Tho. Sandes to Capt. John Davison, 19 May 1692, 'Letterbook of Thomas Sandes and John Browne', BEA, M 7/3; Davis, *Shipping Industry*, pp. 324–5, 332; Jones, *War and Economy*, pp. 145–55.
[174] Naval Officers' returns, Jamaica, PRO CO 142/13; 'Petition of merchants of Barbados', 1690, PRO CO 1/68, fo. 149.
[175] *CSPC, 1693–6*, nos. 1,926, 1,675.
[176] The median receipt was reported to be £7,000 in the peace years between 1673 and 1688 and £5,000 in the war of 1689–97. 'Some considerations in behalf of the auditor of the plantations right to audit the account of the 4.5 per cent duty arising in the Caribbee Islands': CUL, CH(H) Papers 84/1–27.
[177] Tinling (ed.), *Correspondence of William Byrd*, vol. I, p. 114.

Table 4.4 *Tonnage of ships entering Port Royal, Jamaica, 1686–91*

	1686	1687	1688	1689	1690	1691
From London	2,666	4,330	4,393	1,502	2,110	1,740
From England	3,605	4,955	5,785	3,460	2,590	2,780

Source: Naval Officers' returns, Jamaica, PRO CO 142/13.

Ship-owners who did maintain their usual trade faced spiralling costs. Manpower was in short supply as the navy expanded from 12,714 men in 1688 to a peak of 48,515 in 1695 and fear of impressment drove many regular sailors away from the ports, which exacerbated the shortage.[178] In the Dutch wars of the 1660s and 1670s the Navigation laws were suspended to allow the employment of foreign sailors, but permission was piecemeal in King William's war and wages rose steeply in the 1690s.[179] Victualling costs also increased, especially in the Caribbean islands which relied heavily on imported food supplies that were easily intercepted by enemy ships.[180] In Barbados the price of Indian corn increased from 1 shilling to 7.5 shillings per bushel in the first year of King William's war, and the price of meat trebled.[181] The situation was exacerbated by profiteering: in Jamaica, the governor reported that 'moneyed men' in Port Royal 'bought up by wholesale all the [imported] provisions and in two or three days more made the country pay 50 per cent and more'.[182]

Risks rose with costs. Unfortunately there are no comprehensive listings of ships captured in seventeenth-century wars, and the situation is complicated by the usual practice of ransom, but there is no doubt that losses were great. Between 1689 and 1697 the Royal African Company alone lost sixty-four ships on the homeward journey from the West Indies.[183] Some ships were seized more than once in the same season and passed back

[178] The number of men that could be employed in the Atlantic trades was carefully regulated so that trade did not encroach on military needs, and they were allowed 2,596 men in 1691, as compared to the 7,500 or so employed in peace time: PRO CO 1/68, fos. 1–253; Davis, *Shipping Industry*, pp. 323–4; Jones, *War and Economy*, pp. 145–55; Ehrman, *Navy in the War of William III*, pp. 109–13.

[179] Tho. Sandes to Charles Knight, 14 April 1701, 'Letterbook of Thomas Sandes and John Browne', BEA, M 7/19.

[180] *CSPC, 1689–92* , nos. 1,746, 1,931, 1,934, 1,941.

[181] Kendall to Lords of Trade, 22 August 1690, *CSPC, 1689–92*, no. 1,034.

[182] Beeston to Lords of Trade, 7 August 1696, PRO CO 138/9, fo. 48

[183] Davies, *African Company*, pp. 206–7.

and forth between French and English owners.[184] Heavy risk of capture led to huge increases in insurance premiums and other efforts at improving security – such as increased manning levels or sailing in convoy – also raised operating costs. Fleets awaiting convoy were delayed for months in the Thames 'which in respect of the perishableness of a considerable part of the lading of the said ship what with money laid out in fitting men and advances to the seamen will be a loss of at least £40,000'.[185] Furthermore, they reached the colonies long after crop time and, in the southern colonies, late arrival in the sickly summer season meant that unseasoned crews suffered heavy mortality and risk of storm loss from hurricanes.

In conditions of scarce shipping, and spiralling costs, freight rates soared. The Halls reported that in Port Royal sugar freight rates almost trebled between 1689 and 1691 (Table 4.5) and charges remained high in all the plantations until the end of the war. Colonists complained bitterly about the 'exorbitant' rates charged by 'grasping' captains but were powerless to resist their demands and efforts to use colonial assemblies to regulate this tight market were doomed to failure.[186] Despite Parliament's refusal to suspend the Navigation Acts, the regulatory system crumbled as settlers throughout the colonies complained that '[it] makes them think themselves to be but a sort of slaves and all that they labour and hazard for to be but precarious'. Governors felt no shame in turning a blind eye to illegal trade and although English commentators warned of the 'dangerous consequences' of such breaches of discipline, and Parliament reaffirmed the Navigation legislation in 1696, it was to no avail until peace was restored and the supply of English shipping recovered.[187] Legislation alone could not control the direction of English trade and it could not be enforced without the support of a competitive native shipping industry.

In the decades after the Restoration, London's commercial classes, and their colonial correspondents, went a long way in meeting the aspirations of the Navigation Acts in creating an English Atlantic system serviced

[184] The French-built *Swallow* was captured by two English privateers and made a free English ship after condemnation in the Court of Admiralty. However, in 1697, it was seized by an American privateer, William Bumble, near the coast of Carolina and condemned as prize, being a French ship, by a local jury condemned by the captain as 'butchers, tailors, carpenters and shoemakers': 'Deposition of George Harris', PRO HCA 13/82, fo. 23.

[185] 'Petition of merchants and traders of Virginia and Maryland to Parliament', 9 December 1690, PRO CO 1/68, fos. 145–7.

[186] In 1691 the Barbados Assembly passed an Act limiting the rate for muscovado sugar to 7 shillings per hundredweight (about £14 per ton of four hogsheads) but to no avail: *CSPC, 1693–6*, nos. 692, 693, 709, 718, 892–3, 917.

[187] Beeston to Lords of Trade, 5 April 1694, 7 August 1696, PRO CO 138/7, fo. 191; CO 138/9, fos. 47–8; Davenant, 'On the plantation trade', p. 397.

Table 4.5 *Annual mean freight rates paid by the Halls at Port Royal, 1688–91*

	1688	1689	1690	1691
Cotton (lb)	–	–	2.5d	3.0d
Indigo (lb)	1.25d	1.25d	2.0d	3.0d
Logwood (ton)	–	47 shillings	45 shillings	–
Muscovado (ton)	–	£7	£13	£20
Pimento (lb)	–	1.5d	2.5d	3.25d

Source: Brailsford Papers, PRO C 110/152.

largely by English and colonial shipping. They were able to provide the capital, men, and port services needed to double the plantation tonnage and service the heavy demands of the long-distance, high-volume, colonial carrying trades; and they did so at a declining cost which ensured that consumers were supplied with a range of colonial commodities at prices that they could afford. In responding positively to the incentives offered by successful settlement in the New World, and finding solutions to the problems posed in expanding shipping capacity, London's business classes made an important contribution to enhancing the nation's commercial capabilities and, as witnessed by peacetime adherence to the Navigation code, this was not achieved at the expense of national efficiency.

5   Imports

Early English settlement in America was projected on the promise that nature would prove 'amicable in its naked kind' and expectations were largely fulfilled. England's New World territories did not, as many hoped, provide easy wealth based on vast resources of gold and silver. However, they did offer abundant supplies of fish, furs, and forest products which permitted the initial survival of the settlements and also allowed the pioneers time to work out how to combine 'art and industry' with nature to produce tobacco, sugar, and a wide range of other desirable commodities which enhanced national self-sufficiency.[1] London's plantation imports doubled in value between the Restoration and the end of the century, and by 1700 they accounted for not only around a fifth of the capital's inward trade but also a third of its re-export trade to Europe, which greatly strengthened the national balance of payments.[2]

However, a large addition to the nation's resource base was not by itself sufficient to raise productivity or promote sustained economic development. 'Affluence of money' warned Charles Davenant in the 1690s, might merely encourage a 'lazy temper'. Drawing on the case of Spain, he asserted that 'it is not the taking in a great deal of food but it is good digestion and distribution that nourishes the body.' The Spaniards had neglected arts, labour, and manufactures so that all the riches of the New World had passed through the country undigested without providing any 'spirits, strength, or nourishment'.[3]

---

[1] R. J., *Nova Brittania. Offering Most Excellent Fruits by Planting in Virginia* (1609); Carole Shammas, 'English commercial development and American colonization, 1560–1620', in K. R. Andrews, N. P. Canny, and P. E. H. Hair (eds.), *The Westward Enterprise: English Activities in Ireland, the Atlantic, and America, 1480–1650* (Liverpool, 1978), pp. 151–74; K. G. Davies, *The North Atlantic World in the Seventeenth Century* (Oxford, 1974).

[2] In 1700 plantation imports into London were valued at £838,812 and total imports into London were valued at £4,777,277: PRO CUST. 2/9; Ralph Davis, 'English foreign trade, 1660–1700', *EcHR*, 7 (1954), 150–66.

[3] Charles Davenant, *Discourses on the Public Revenues and on the Trade of England in Two Parts*, in Charles Whitworth (ed.), *The Political and Commercial Works of the Celebrated Writer Charles D'Avenant*, 5 vols. (London, 1771), vol. I, pp. 381–3.

By contrast, in the late seventeenth century London's commercial classes responded with vigour to the economic stimuli provided by the influx of resources from the New World. Participants in the novel plantation sector operated in an intensely competitive environment, with low barriers to entry, and limited scope for rent-seeking activities, while neither Crown nor Parliament could secure its right to control regulation. Merchants eagerly sought efficiency gains and, as they accumulated capital and commercial expertise, they succeeded in making improvements in the sorting, marketing, processing, and distribution of colonial commodities in ways that lowered costs. As a result they strengthened London's industrial and commercial base, consolidated the city's position as hub of an increasingly integrated national economy, and established its role as a leading emporium in Europe.

Early expectations and experiments in the New World

The colonial policy that started to take shape in Elizabethan England reflected a range of political, intellectual, and commercial concerns.[4] Wartime disruption to supply networks, and heavy price inflation, raised English awareness of the dangers of dependence on expensive foreign imports and continental entrepots. Dutch wealth and strength, based on trade, displayed 'how exceedingly it mounts the state of a Commonwealth' to secure supplies which could furnish its own wants and also supply those of others.[5] America's vast lands, in varied climatic conditions, were expected to offer precious natural bounty, just as they had done for the Spaniards, but there was also a novel interest in 'improvement' fostered partly by the increased circulation of classical texts on agricultural innovation after the development of the printing press and reinforced in England by a Protestant preoccupation with pursuing a Christian duty to survey and tame nature – a step towards the millennial condition.[6] According to one writer, husbandry was both the most 'natural and holie' occupation of man and also the most profitable as 'no man

[4] A statement of Elizabethan colonial policy is found in Richard Hakluyt's 'A particular discourse concerning the greate necessitie and manifolde commodities that are like to grow to this realme of England by the westerne discoveries lately attempted' (1584) reprinted in *Maine Historical Society Collections*, vol. II (1877).
[5] *Nova Brittania*; 'Advantages of trading with our plantations', BLO, MS Rawl. A 478, fos. 67b-68; Thomas Leng, *Benjamin Worsley (1618–1677):Trade, Interest and the Spirit in Revolutionary England* (Woodbridge, Suffolk, 2008), pp. 62–4.
[6] Ambrosoli shows how the 'new agriculture' of seventeenth- and eighteenth-century Europe was necessarily preceded by a period of learning, supported and spurred by a reorganization of ancient and medieval botany: Mauro Ambrosoli, *The Wild and the Sown: Botany and Agriculture in Western Europe, 1350–1850* (Oxford, 1997).

of any art or science (except an alchemist) ever pretended so much gain any other way... the usurer doubles but his principle with interest upon interest in seven years; but [the improver will teach you] how to do more than treble your principle in one years compass'. This enthusiast showed how, in seven years, an industrious man could convert the value of barren heath land from £5 to £7,000 per year.[7] Interest in agricultural improvement was sharpened as Baconian experimental science gained ground in the seventeenth century.[8] Farming practice, and the returns on an acre of land, were at the heart of discussions absorbing the intelligentsia, for good husbandry served God, the nation, and the individual improver.[9]

Many from the gentry and merchant classes, infused with the spirit of improvement, embarked on agricultural experiment on marginal or unused land at home.[10] For example, in the 1650s, a London merchant, Sir Nicholas Crispe, with interests in Ireland and the Atlantic was involved in various home-based improvement schemes, including a madder plantation in Deptford, and it was a small intellectual step to promoting similar undertakings on newly available lands in Ireland and America.[11] General aspirations were clearly reflected in the final instruction to the Council of Trade established in 1650. Members were exhorted to see 'how the commodities [of plantations] may be so multiplied and improved, as [if it be possible] those plantations alone may supply the Commonwealth of England with whatsoever it necessarily wants'.[12] It was seen as both eminently desirable, and feasible, to use extensive growth in the New World to boost national self-sufficiency.

[7] *A Discourse of Husbandry used in Brabant and Flanders showing the Wonderful Improvement of Land there; and Serving as a Pattern for our Practice in this Commonwealth* (London, 1652).

[8] 'Nothing ever did, or will come to perfection without great experiences, constant practices, and great scrutiny into the bowels of it, and that will draw forth the mystery, and that is the profit and glory of all trade and merchandise': Walter Blith, *The English Improver Improved or The Survey of Husbandry Surveyed. Discovering the Improveableness of all Lands* (London, 1653).

[9] Introduction and chapter 11 in Mark Greengrass, Michael Leslie, and Timothy Raylor, (eds.), *Samuel Hartlib and Universal Reformation: Studies in Intellectual Communication* (Cambridge, 1994); Leng, *Benjamin Worsley*.

[10] Joan Thirsk, *Alternative Agriculture: a History* (Oxford, 1997), pp. 27–8. Merchants, who combined foreign experiences with capital surpluses, played an important role in financing new agricultural projects.

[11] Blith, *English Improver*, p. 235. For an example of Irish promotional literature of the period see Robert Payne, *A Brief Description of Ireland made in this Year, 1589* (London, 1589); T. C. Barnard, 'Planters and policies in Cromwellian Ireland', *Past and Present*, 61 (1973), 31–69; T. C. Barnard, 'The Hartlib circle and the cult and culture of improvement in Ireland', in Greengrass *et al.* (eds.), *Samuel Hartlib*, pp. 281–97. On Crispe see Robert Brenner, *Merchants and Revolution: Commercial Change, Political Conflict and London's Overseas Traders, 1550–1653* (Cambridge, 1993), pp. 163–4, 174, 404, 451.

[12] 'Instructions to Council of Trade', BL Egerton MS 2,395, fo. 268.

However, although England's new lands in America did, in the end, fulfil the promoters' hopes, and yield almost every 'known commodity', not all could command a price sufficient to cover the high costs of production in the experimental stage, or the permanently large overhead costs of long-distance trade, and without such yields it was impossible to attract sufficient labour and capital to extend output.[13] Even natural bounty was only partly exploited: furs and fish found ready markets in Europe but most timber, with low value to bulk, could not be delivered across the Atlantic at a price which would allow it to compete with supplies which were nearer to hand.

Meanwhile, early English efforts to improve on nature and promote imperial self-sufficiency largely met with failure.[14] Despite the discovery of natural vines in America, and repeated trials with plants from Europe, all colonial attempts at viniculture were thwarted by the cold winters and England remained dependent on continental wine producers.[15] Efforts at silk cultivation were similarly abortive. The growth of a silk-weaving industry in England made the supply of the raw material a matter of concern and, after wartime disruptions in the late sixteenth century, there were vigorous attempts to establish production in England with royal support.[16] The discovery of red mulberry trees native to Virginia diverted attention to America. Silkmen and wormseed were despatched with the early supply vessels, along with French handbooks on production, in hopes that the colonists would establish an industry that would supplant the Italians in the European silk trade.[17] After some years the colonists realized that the red mulberry was unsuitable for silk production but, by the 1640s, the white mulberry was introduced into Virginia and, after

[13] Hakluyt, 'Discourse'. In 1623 the Virginia Company complained that a return of 25 per cent was inadequate to attract investment in their colony: Susan M. Kingsbury (ed.), *The Records of the Virginia Company of London*, 5 vols. (Washington, DC, 1906–35), vol. IV, p. 264.

[14] Attempts at diversification are discussed in Philip A. Bruce, *Economic History of Virginia in the Seventeenth Century*, 2 vols. (New York, 1896), vol. I, ch. 6; Lewis Cecil Gray, *A History of Agriculture in the Southern United States to 1860*, 2 vols. (Washington, DC, 1933), vol. I, ch. 8; Robert Beverley, *The History and Present State of Virginia* (Chapel Hill, N.C., 1947), pp. 556–71; *A Perfect Description of Virginia* (London, 1649).

[15] Beverley, *History and Present State*, pp. 134–7. When Claypoole emigrated to Pennsylvania in 1683 he sought advice on transporting vines to the new colony: Marion Balderston (ed.), *James Claypoole's Letterbook, London and Philadelphia, 1681–1684* (San Marino, Calif., 1967), p. 182. In the 1680s a number of French Protestants were assisted in emigration to English colonies in hopes that they would teach skills in wine, silk, and oil production: *CSPC, 1681–5*, nos. 823, 835, 883, 903, 913, 924.

[16] William Stallenge, *Instructions for the Increasing of Mulberry Trees and the Breeding of Silkworms* (London, 1609); Thirsk, *Alternative Agriculture*, pp. 118–30.

[17] *Nova Brittania*; Kingsbury (ed.), *Records of the Virginia Company*, vol. III, pp. 260–1, 291, 389, 397–400.

the Restoration, Berkeley was enthusiastic about the prospects: 'We can experimentally say that within seven years if we are assisted and commanded we shall bring in yearly as much silk into England as now costs the nation £200,000 sterling at least'.[18] These hopes did not materialize. Sericulture needs little land but is labour- and skill-intensive, and did not suit America's factor endowment, or allow it to compete effectively with eastern or European producers. Despite continued interest in mulberries, and silkworms, the industry did not take root in early English America.[19]

However, alongside many failures and disappointments early English settlers did establish production of two relatively novel commodities which secured the success of the colonial project: tobacco, which was introduced into Virginia around 1612, and sugar, which was produced in Barbados from the 1640s. Both commodities shared certain characteristics which contributed to their success. Both tobacco and sugar commanded a high price in the early years of experimentation, with its heavy costs, and delivered profits sufficient to attract the capital and labour needed to ensure continued cultivation. Once established, both commodities were produced and distributed at steeply falling cost and, despite being targeted for high taxation, were sold at a lower and lower price which promoted increased use. Income distribution was heavily skewed in early modern Europe and even though in the late seventeenth century England's population fell and real wages rose, few could afford luxury goods in large quantities.[20] Lower price increased the breadth of use of both tobacco and sugar down the social scale, and out from London, to provincial centres and the countryside, but demand was still further

[18] Charles E. Hatch, 'Mulberry trees and silkworms: sericulture in early Virginia', *VMHB*, 65 (1957), 3–61; William Berkeley, 'A discourse and view of Virginia', 1662, BL Egerton MS 2,395, fo. 354; Samuel Hartlib, *The Reformed Virginian Silk-Worm* (London, 1652); Warren M. Billings, 'Sir William Berkeley and the Diversification of the Virginia Economy', *VMHB*, 104 (1996), 443–54.

[19] The efforts in Virginia seem to have been abandoned by the 1670s: Thomas Glover, *An Account of Virginia, its Scituation, Productions, Inhabitants and the Mannor of Planting and Ordering Tobacco* (London, 1676), pp. 12–16. For the high hopes of the industry in Georgia in the eighteenth century see 'Account of the design of trustees for establishing the colony of Georgia in America', BL Sl. MS 3,986, fo. 38.

[20] E. A. Wrigley and R. S. Schofield, *The Population History of England, 1541–1871: a Reconstruction* (Cambridge, 1981); E. H. Phelps-Brown and S. V. Hopkins, 'Seven centuries of the prices of consumables compared to the builders' wage rates', in E. M. Carus-Wilson (ed.), *Essays in Economic History*, 3 vols. (London, 1954–62), vol. II, pp. 179–96. Gregory King suggested that even in 1688, a peak of prosperity before a decade of war, almost 3 million of England's 5 million people were 'decreasing the wealth of the country'. There were 4,526 families (containing 57,520 people) with an annual income of £450 or more: Gregory King, 'Natural and Political Observations and Conclusions upon the State and Condition of England, 1696', in P. Laslett (ed.), *The Earliest Classics: John Graunt and Gregory King* (Farnborough, Hants., 1973).

Table 5.1 *Recorded imports into London from the plantations 1663/9, 1686, and 1701*

	1663/9 quantity	price	value (£)	1686 (quantity)	price	value (£)	1701 value (£)
Tobacco	8,196,600 lb	6d	204,915	14,924,300 lb	2.4d	149,243	154,533
Muscovado	148,388 cwt	27s	200,324	403,911 cwt	27s	537,201	501,616
Whites	19,860 cwt	56s	55,608	23,014 cwt	39s	45,852	5,780
Cotton	6,986 bags	£6	41,916	2,337 bags	£6.33	14,782	25,402
Cocoa	1,732 cwt	£10	11,920	202 cwt	£4	1,013	13,164
Beaver	14,250 skins	10s	7,125	41,899 skins	4s	8,380	3,943
Otter	3,795 skins	5s	1,318	3,791 skins	4s	758	293
Ginger	2,659 cwt	22s	2,924	17,394 cwt	25s	21,742	8,288
Indigo	15,000 lb	2s	1,500	131,814 lb	1.4s	9,961	10,370
Other			17,538			95,244	115,425
			545,088			884,176	838,814

Source: BL Add. MS 36,785; London portbook database, 1686; PRO CUST. 2/9, fos. 25–32.

enhanced with greater intensity of use. Tobacco moved from being a therapeutic to a recreational drug, and sugar could be consumed in myriad ways, with Londoners playing a prime role in establishing new tastes and fashions.[21] Both commodities also found buoyant markets in Europe and helped establish London as a major entrepot.

The growing taste for smoke and sweetness in seventeenth-century Europe secured the success of England's settlement project. By the Restoration, tobacco and sugar combined to account for over 80 per cent of direct trade with the mother country (Table 5.1) and they maintained this overwhelming dominance until the American Revolution.[22] However, in attracting the investment in the commercial infrastructure that made Atlantic trade possible, and profitable, they also supported production of a wide range of minor staples including cotton, ginger, hardwoods, indigo, logwood, and other exotic commodities which could not, on their own, have sustained large-scale trade but which, none the less, made an important contribution to satisfying contemporary aspirations for increased national self-sufficiency.

[21] F. J. Fisher, 'The development of London as a centre of conspicuous consumption in the sixteenth and seventeenth centuries', *TRHS*, 30 (1948), 37–50;. E. A. Wrigley, 'Urban growth and agricultural change: England and the continent in the early modern period', *JIH*, 15 (1985), 683–728. The theme of London as fashion capital is prominent in Restoration drama, for example see William Wycherley, *The Country Wife* in Robert G. Lawrence (ed.), *Restoration Plays* (London, 1976), pp. 85–160.

[22] BL Add. MS 36,785; Davis, 'English foreign trade, 1660–1700'; John J. McCusker and Russell R. Menard, *The Economy of British America, 1607–1789* (Chapel Hill, N.C., 1985), pp. 81, 130, 160.

Natural bounty

Although Englishmen were disappointed that their colonial settlements did not yield the gold or silver mines which underpinned Spanish wealth, they did draw profit from America's natural bounty and, above all, its abundant supplies of fish, furs, and forest products. Fishermen based in West Country ports, and drawing heavily on London capital and marketing networks had by 1600 developed a migratory fishing trade in Newfoundland.[23] After the Civil War, local settlers took control of a similar trade in New England waters but Newfoundland's migratory trade survived into the eighteenth century although a permanent plantation also developed after the Restoration.[24] Large numbers of English fishermen arrived in Newfoundland in June when they found vast supplies of cod around the coast which, being rich and glutinous without being fatty, were (unlike salmon and herring) easily cured by salting and drying in the sun.[25] The fishermen went out daily, three men to a boat, working ten hours or more with their lines. After being landed, the fish were split, salted, and laid on 'hakes' to dry until they were thoroughly cured, which took about six weeks (Illustration 21). A large part of the catch was taken away by the so-called 'sack ships' (fitted out only for freight and not to process the fish) which left England after the price of fish was 'broken' on Easter Monday and arrived in Newfoundland in late summer. They exchanged manufactures, food, and drink for fish and train-oil.[26] At the end of the season, as the hard winter set in, the fishermen returned home to England leaving behind some boats and equipment for the following year.[27]

The Newfoundland fish trade was big business. Scattered figures suggest that, throughout the seventeenth century, the Newfoundland catch fluctuated between 200,000 and 300,000 quintals a year except during

[23] For the role of London merchants with West Country connections see George F. Steckley (ed.), *The Letters of John Paige, London Merchant, 1648–1658* (London, 1984), pp. xii, 106, 122–4, 126–8.

[24] 'An account of the colony and fishery of Newfoundland and the present state thereof taken about the year 1678': PRO, CO 195/2, fos. 1–28; Peter E. Pope, *Fish into Wine: the Newfoundland Plantation in the Seventeenth Century* (Chapel Hill, N.C., 2004).

[25] Harold A. Innis, *The Cod Fisheries: the History of an International Economy*, rev. edn (Toronto, 1954), pp. 1–10; Gillian T. Cell, *English Enterprise in Newfoundland, 1577–1660* (Toronto, 1969).

[26] 'Sack' derives from *vino de saco*, or wine set apart for export: 'A list of sack ships in St Johns Harbour and in other parts of Newfoundland', 1677, PRO CO 1/43, no. 112. For the charter party of the *Friends Adventure* let to freight to three London merchants in 1681 for a voyage from London to Newfoundland and then Lisbon, see PRO HCA 30/ 653; Pope, *Fish into Wine*, p. 96; Steckley (ed.), *Letters of John Paige*, pp. 117, 122, 127–8.

[27] 'Further answers to Lords of Trade of Commodore Leak', 26 October 1699, PRO CO 195/2, fo. 323; Pope, *Fish into Wine*, pp. 15–38.

A View of a Stage & also of y manner of Fishing for, Curing & Drying Cod at NEW FOUND LAND.
A. The Habit of y Fishermen B. The Line C. The manner of Fishing D. The Dressers of y Fish E. The Trough into
which they throw y Cod when Dressd. F. Salt Boxes G. The manner of Carrying y Cod H. The Cleansing y Cod I. A Press
to extract y Oyl from y Cods Livers. K. Casks to receive y water & Blood that comes from y Livers. L. Another Cask to receive
the Oyl. M. The manner of Drying y Cod.

Illustration 21 'A view of a stage and also of the manner of fishing for, curing, and drying cod at Newfoundland', *c.* 1712. Herman Moll, NMM.

the Civil War and Interregnum (marked by war with the Dutch Republic and Spain) when both ships and men were in short supply and the trade collapsed.[28] Unlike other colonial staples the price of fish increased over the seventeenth century: a quintal fetched 8 shillings in 1615, 20 shillings during the Civil War disruption, and 12 or 13 shillings between the Restoration and 1700, and the Newfoundland fishery was an increasingly valuable asset. It produced a catch worth around £120,000 in 1615, and almost £180,000 in 1699, which was almost three times the value of that sold by the New England fishery at this time, and exceeded the value of London's tobacco imports in 1700 (Table 5.1).[29]

Although dried cod was not popular in England, it was important in victualling ships and so part of the catch was taken to London and

[28] A quintal was 112 lb and 20 quintals made a ton.
[29] 'An account of the fishing trade in the year 1615 and 1677', PRO CO 195/2, fo. 23; 'Report of Lords of Trade on fishery', 30 March 1699, *ibid.*, fo. 280; 'An account of the fishery at Newfoundland in 1700 by Capt Stafford', *ibid.*, fo. 384. In 1719 Martin estimated the Newfoundland catch was worth £300,000 at 20 shillings per quintal and the trade employed 150 ships a year: Clark, *Commercial Statistics*, p. 99; Pope, *Fish into Wine*, pp. 35–9.

other home ports. However, above half the fish was consumed in foreign markets, and given the perishability of this important product, it was not – like other staple goods – enumerated in the Navigation Acts and could be delivered direct to the final destination. Furthermore, in the interests of cost competitiveness, the fisheries were allowed to obtain salt direct from foreign suppliers rather than via England. Most of the 'good merchantable fish' was taken to southern Europe and the wine islands, where it provided an inexpensive alternative to meat, and the 'refuse fish' that was broken, undersized, oversalted, or damaged in any way, was taken to the West Indies where it provided cheap protein for the rapidly expanding slave population.[30]

London merchants such as Gilbert Heathcote played a major part in the Newfoundland trade as fish helped England finance its deficit in bilateral trade in a number of regions.[31] Although England was able to export large quantities of light woollen cloths to southern markets they did not match the value of wine, oil, dried fruits, wool, and bullion imports.[32] Fish helped fill the void.[33] A list of 138 sack ships which traded at Newfoundland in 1677 shows that 28 (34 per cent of the tonnage) were London based, and these London ships loaded 57,887 quintals of fish valued at £34,734 (36 per cent of the total), which was similar in value to the entire New England catch at this time, and exceeded the value of any plantation product imported directly from America into London apart from tobacco and sugar (Table 5.1).[34] Most of the twenty-eight London sack ships sailed for Spain (seven to Alicanti, seven to Barcelona, one to Bilbao, and five to southern ports) with five making for Italy, and three for Lisbon. London merchants also played an

---

[30] 'Humble address of divers merchants, owners and masters of ships and others of the towns of Plymouth, Dartmouth, and the western ports concerned in the fishing trade of the Newfoundland', PRO CO 195/1, fo. 42; Daniel Vickers, *Farmers and Fishermen: Two Centuries of Work in Essex County, Mass., 1630–1850* (Chapel Hill, N.C., 1994), p. 99.

[31] 'Proposals from merchants of Bristol', 2 December 1696, PRO CO 195/2, fos. 44–5; 'Memo of Newfoundland traders of London', *ibid.*, fos. 45–6; 'Report of Council of Trade', 29 January 1697, *ibid.*, fo. 77. Eveline Cruickshanks, Stuart Handley, and D. W. Hayton (eds.), *The House of Commons, 1690–1715*, 5 vols. (Cambridge, 2002), vol. IV, pp. 309–17, 343–7; 'Charter party of *Friends Adventure*', 1681, PRO HCA 30/653; 'Petition of Gilbert Heathcote and Arthur Shallett, of London, merchants, that *Southampton*, laden for Newfoundland, be permitted to sail notwithstanding the embargo', 1689, PRO PC 2/73.

[32] Imports from Spain to London in 1663/69 were valued at £503,628 and exports were valued at £448,022: BL Add. MS 36,785.

[33] 'An account of the colony and fishery of Newfoundland and the present state thereof taken about the year 1678', PRO CO 195/2, fo. 10.

[34] 'A list of sack ships in Newfoundland', 1677, PRO CO 1/43, no. 112; Vickers, *Farmers and Fishermen*, pp. 100, 154. The London ships often sailed from western ports. The portbook database for 1686 lists three ships departing for Newfoundland.

Table 5.2 *Imports to London from North America, 1686 (£sterling)*

	Hudson's Bay	New England	Middle colonies	Chesapeake	Lower South	Bermuda	Total
Tobacco		82	533	136,974		3,422	141,011
Skins	3,431	8,146	4,833	2,698	1,564		20,672
Molasses		19,867	304				20,171
Sugar		15,242	679	244	492		16,657
Misc	9	5,074	1,282	1,266	61	315	8,007
Total	3,440	48,411	7,631	141,182	2,117	3,737	206,518
Total in 1701	5	29,001	18,802	155,021	12,108	1,079	216,016

Source: London portbook database, 1686; PRO CUST. 2/9, fos. 25–32.

important role in the trades between Newfoundland, the Canaries, and the West Indies.[35]

Skins, like fish, were in abundant supply in early English America although Europeans relied heavily on native American middlemen and supply networks. Beaver was the most valuable but they also included coney, deer, elk, fox, mink, moose, otter, sable, and others. Part of the trade was concerned with fancy fur used on the pelt, valued for its beauty and warmth, and much in demand in northern Europe. Part was concerned with staple fur, such as beaver, which had a barbed character that gave it qualities of cohesion that made it suitable for felting and it was in increased demand as the fashion for felt hats spread in the late seventeenth century, and a new English industry developed in London.[36] Furs were important in all early mainland settlements, but as animal stocks were depleted, the hunters needed to move over longer distances, and the trade ran into steeply rising costs and diminishing returns. Furthermore, after the formation of the Hudson's Bay Company in 1668, England secured access to the vast northern territories and beaver shipments rose to dizzy levels which could not be absorbed in the English market, and prices tumbled.[37] Difficult market conditions encouraged the

---

[35] The rhythm of Newfoundland trade allowed for convenient delivery of cod during Tenerife's vintage. John Paige cooperated with Devon men in the trade as did Gilbert Heathcote: Steckley (ed.), *Letters of John Paige*, pp. xix–xx, 11–12, 38–9, 41–2, 43, 55; 'Paige's Invoices', PRO C 105/12.

[36] David Corner, 'The tyranny of fashion: the case of the felt-hatting trade in the late seventeenth and eighteenth centuries', *Textile History*, 22 (1991), 153–78; 'Journal of Thomas Sandes', 30 August 1699, BEA, M 7/4.

[37] Harold A. Innis, *The Fur Trade in Canada: an Introduction to Canadian Economic History* (New Haven, Conn., 1930). Hudson Bay is the one area of English colonial enterprise in which there was lasting involvement of a joint-stock company. The English fur trade on Hudson Bay began with the establishment of Charles Fort in 1668 and a charter was granted to the company in 1670.

development of a re-export trade to Europe, above all Russia.[38] However, although skins did remain the second most valuable direct import from North America into London, as shown in Table 5.2, they were a long way behind tobacco in value. Even in New England, which sustained the biggest fur trade in 1686, it was outweighed in value by re-exports of sugar and molasses from the Caribbean.

Forest fringed America's entire Atlantic coast and included a profusion of timbers. The supply was fundamental to colonial survival as it furnished the material for buildings, bridges, landing stages, carts, boats, barrels, tools, and equipment of all sorts, besides providing fuel and charcoal for smelting. Given resource abundance, and the scarcity of labour, most settlements set up a sawmill as soon as possible, although in the early seventeenth century they needed to draw on continental craftsmen to provide the necessary expertise as in England timber was generally sawn by hand.[39] The mills produced plank, deals, and pipe staves for their own use and some, especially those in the northern regions, began to produce lumber for other colonial markets, above all in the Caribbean where demand was very strong.[40] However, although colonial promoters had enthused about the possibilities of using American forests to solve England's apparent wood shortage, the low value to weight of timber imposed a very heavy transport burden.[41] The cost of Baltic timber delivered in England's dockyards was twenty times the value of a tree on the stump, and the distance of England from America was three times that from the Baltic, and five times that from Norway. Even with the heavy export taxes imposed by the north European states, it was impossible for most colonial timber to compete with Baltic supplies in the English market.

An exception was the trade in mast trees. Few woods possessed the necessary height, shape (a cylindrical straightness), elasticity, strength

[38] E. E. Rich, 'Russia and the colonial fur trade', *EcHR*, 7 (1955), 307–28. The Hudson's Bay Company recorded sales varying between around £2,000 and £12,000 in the 1680s but they collapsed in the 1690s: PRO CUST. 2/9, fo. 27

[39] Victor S. Clark, *A History of Manufactures in the United States*, 3 vols. (Washington, DC, 1929). The Virginia Company of London despatched materials for setting up sawmills and German millwrights to supervise the job: Edmund S. Morgan, *American Slavery, American Freedom: the Ordeal of Colonial Virginia* (New York, 1975), p. 95.

[40] By the 1660s commercial sawmilling was well established in New England. In 1671 Robert Mason reported that New Hampshire exported 20,000 tons of deal and pipe staves a year and that the income of the sawmills at Nawichewanock was 'considerable', paying £200 for 'privilege of common': *CSPC, 1669–74*, no. 687. In 1700 there were reported to be fifty sawmills in 'the little province': *CSPC, 1700*, no. 841. On regulating the trade see Governor and Council of New Hampshire, 4 October 1683, PRO CO 1/53, fo. 59; Richard Pares, *Yankees and Creoles: the Trade between North America and the West Indies before the American Revolution* (London, 1956), pp. 37–43.

[41] *Nova Brittania*; Robert Greenhalgh Albion, *Forests and Sea Power: the Timber Problem and the Royal Navy 1652–1862* (Cambridge, Mass., 1926), pp. 200–13.

and durability. The choice was confined to fir, pine, and spruce and none grew in England. Fir was grown in Scotland but was markedly inferior to its foreign rivals.[42] Thus, the national wealth and security provided by England's masted marine was already dependent on overseas supplies. America's white pine belt reached the coast from Nova Scotia to New Hampshire and stretched westwards across Connecticut and the Hudson and along the St Lawrence. The virgin forest furnished massive trees (as large as 120 feet long and 40 inches in diameter), which were no longer found in Europe, and could be used to form single stick masts for a large man-of-war at much lower cost than the composite alternative.[43] Masts had a higher value to volume than other timber (a tree worth £100 as a mast would produce £15 worth of plank) and consequently, were able to bear high transport costs.[44]

A consignment of mast trees was shipped from Virginia in 1609 and occasional ventures followed in the next few decades but it was in the 1650s, when the navy faced a supply crisis during the first Dutch war, that the trade was put on a regular footing.[45] Nehemiah Bourne, who had begun his career as a merchant in New England, and had become a Navy Commissioner on his return to London, undertook to provide three cargoes of American masts.[46] By the late 1650s American masts began to appear with greater regularity. Some of the first were installed in the great new ship, the *Naseby*, renamed the *Royal Charles*, the flagship carried off in triumph by the Dutch from the Medway in 1667 (Illustration 22).

The colonial mast trade was centred on Portsmouth in New Hampshire and London naval contractors such as Pepys's friend William Warren, and Josiah Child had agents there.[47] By 1670 Portsmouth had a small fleet of specially designed long, flat-bottomed ships which carried around ten mast cargoes a year to England, including two or three for the navy.[48] London dealers with sufficient capital began to stockpile reserves so that, on the eve of war in 1670, Warren had 259 New England masts (priced between £12 and £135 a piece) ready for sale at his yard in Wapping.[49]

[42] Albion, *Forests and Seapower*, p. 151.
[43] According to Navy Board papers from the 1680s, a composite mast for a first rate warship cost £235 whereas 'in case be of 1 tree' the cost was reduced to £120: 'Victualling, proportions and wages of H. M. Navy, 1684', NMM, CAD B/4.
[44] Albion, *Forests and Seapower*, pp. 30–4, 232–4. 'Computation of volume and value of masts and other naval stores to be supplied from New England, 1696', PRO CO 5/859, fo. 60.
[45] *CSPC, Addenda, 1574–1674*, nos. 75, 76.
[46] Albion, *Forests and Seapower*, pp. 207–13.
[47] *Ibid.*, pp. 235–7; Bernard Bailyn, *The New England Merchants in the Seventeenth Century* (Cambridge, Mass., 1955), pp. 133–5; *CSPC, 1661–8*, nos. 1149, 1336, 1337.
[48] 'Account by Robert Mason of the commodities of New Hampshire', 11 December 1671, *CSPC, 1669–74*, no. 687.
[49] Bailyn, *New England Merchants*, p. 132.

Illustration 22 In June 1667 the Dutch carried out a daring raid up the River Medway and captured one of the finest ships in the fleet, the *Royal Charles*, which is here seen being taken into Dutch waters. The Commonwealth warship had been built with a single stick mainmast provided by a New England pine. It was named the *Naseby* and renamed the *Royal Charles* after it was used to bring Charles back to England in 1660. Ludolf Bakhuizen, NMM.

The trade was sufficiently well organized to allow big colonial merchants, such as John Taylor (one of the fifty-nine big colonial merchants of 1686) to maintain mast supplies in the early 1690s at the prices prevailing before the outbreak of war, whereas the prices of other naval stores soared.[50]

It was apparent from the first days of colonization that tar, pitch, and rosin could be produced in American forests from Carolina to Maine but, as with lumber, the economics of the trade delayed its growth.[51] John Taylor, who described himself as 'bred in the trade of naval stores', outlined the difficulties to the Lords of Trade in 1694. 'I would gladly see this kingdom independent of Sweden and Denmark but I must speak out as a merchant who judges his trade by the measure of profit and then

[50] Commissioners of the Admiralty, 30 January 1694, PRO CO 5/858, fo. 84; John Ehrman, *The Navy in the War of William III, 1689–1697* (Cambridge, 1953).

[51] In 1628 it was stated that pitch and tar and pipe staves could not be produced profitably because of high labour costs and freight rates and that settlers lacked the expertise to make potash: 'The Randolph Manuscript', *VMHB*, 17 (1909), 34.

arises the difficulty how we shall bring bulky goods from a remote part as cheaply as from countries near us.'[52] One voyage to New England cost four or five times as much as one to the Baltic and there was a similar gap in labour costs.[53] However, as demand rose in the war of the 1690s, and Baltic supplies were interrupted, the price of tar doubled between 1689 and 1693, and that of pitch rose by 50 per cent, and the Commissioners of the Navy encouraged experiments with production, in the New World.[54] Taylor ordered his mast agent to embark on trial production and he and others provided stores which the Navy office declared 'good and fit'.[55] A number of powerful merchant partnerships (including many with Baltic connections) competed for contracts but it was not until the next war that, with bounties and other encouragement, the American trade was firmly established.[56] In the seventeenth century America's raw forest products made a limited contribution to transatlantic trade. It was generally accepted that, given the barrier of transport costs, it was sensible to manufacture essential timber products near the source of the raw materials, and despite the general mercantilist dislike of colonial industry, the settlers were allowed to produce ships and barrels, which do not appear in the official import statistics, but without which the English Atlantic economy would not easily have met the demands imposed by the Navigation Acts.

Tobacco

The promoters of early English colonization envisaged more than mere extraction of natural resources to enhance national self-sufficiency. They were also intent on using 'art and industry' to improve nature and produce cash crops for export.[57] Commercial success came with the cultivation of tobacco in Bermuda, and then Virginia, after John Rolfe's experiments with Caribbean varieties in 1612.[58] As tobacco could be

[52] 'Memo of John Taylor', 25 January 1694, PRO CO 5/859, fo. 161.
[53] *CSPC, 1693–5*, no. 967.
[54] Instructions for John Budger and Benjamin Firmin appointed agents to New England for rendering to His Majesty a true account of the condition in that colony with relation to the product of [ships stores], 22 October 1696, PRO CO 5/859, fos. 84–5.
[55] 'Report of the Navy Office', 5 June 1696, PRO CO 5/859, fo. 46.
[56] For competition for contracts and discussion of product quality see PRO CO 5/858, fos. 10, 62, 74, 80, 90–2, 104; PRO CO 5/859, fos.46–74; Joseph J. Malone, *Pine Trees and Politics: the Naval Stores and Forest Policy in Colonial New England, 1691–1775* (Seattle, Wash., 1964).
[57] *Nova Brittania*.
[58] Wesley Frank Craven, 'An introduction to the history of Bermuda', *WMQ*, 17 (1937) 176–215; Bruce, *Economic History of Virginia*, vol. I, pp. 194–5; Gray, *History of Southern Agriculture*, vol. I, pp. 213–76; Morgan, *American Slavery, American Freedom*, pp. 90–1, 108–10.

grown in northern Europe, and was introduced into England with considerable profit, it did not fit mercantilist ideals of colonial complementarity but it did possess a number of attributes necessary for success in transatlantic trade.[59]

The Spaniards had supplied the European market in the sixteenth century and established a taste for the weed but, as output was small, prices were high and, after 1605, vigorous efforts to curb the very substantial English, French, and Dutch contraband trades forced them up further; it was a good moment to enter the market.[60] Furthermore, tobacco was an excellent beginner's crop as it required only a small patch of cleared land and a few simple tools to start production and, in the pioneering years, a Virginian planter could obtain high prices while experimenting with different soils, plant varieties, cultivation methods, curing, and packing techniques.[61] In 1620 John Smith reported that a single hand could tend 1,000 plants, and produce around 250 pounds of tobacco a year, grossing (at the boom price of 3 shillings per pound) £37.5.[62] High profits made it possible for a relatively poor man who combined hard work, and good health, to become rich and attracted the immigration needed for rapid extension of the area under cultivation in the Chesapeake, Bermuda, and the West Indies.[63] England's imports of its own plantation tobacco rose from around 1,250 lb in 1616 (a tiny proportion of annual consumption of 100,000 lb) to around 12 million lb by the Restoration, 28 million

---

[59] C. T. *An Advise How to Plant Tobacco in England* (1615). After the first Virginia boom demonstrated that very high profits could be made from the novel crop, a number of London merchants were active in promoting cultivation at home. A small farmer on a traditional 30-acre holding in England could expect an annual income of about £14.5 whereas in 1620 a Gloucestershire farmer documented by Thirsk earned a net return of £26.5 on an acre of tobacco, and the profit on a high quality crop could easily be four times as much – riches indeed: Joan Thirsk, 'New crops and their diffusion: tobacco growing in seventeenth century England', in Joan Thirsk, *The Rural Economy of England* (London, 1984), pp. 259–85.

[60] Kenneth R. Andrews, *The Spanish Caribbean: Trade and Plunder, 1530–1630* (New Haven, Conn., 1978), pp. 179, 196, 213–16, 224–34. A Spanish observer of 1611 asserted that England consumed 100,000 lb of tobacco yearly and that only 6,000 lb was obtained in Spain, suggesting that the remainder came through contraband channels: see Joyce Lorimer, 'The English contraband trade from Trinidad and Guiana, 1590–1617', in Andrews *et al.* (eds.), *The Westward Enterprise*, pp. 124–50.

[61] Russell R. Menard, 'The tobacco industry in the Chesapeake colonies, 1617–1730: an interpretation', *Research in Economic History*, 5 (1980), 109–77.

[62] Edward Arbor (ed.), *Travels and Works of Captain John Smith* (Edinburgh, 1910), vol. II, pp. 541, 564–5; Kingsbury (ed.), *Records of the Virginia Company*, vol. III, pp. 581–8; vol. IV, pp. 37–9.

[63] Richard S. Dunn, *Sugar and Slaves: the Rise of the Planter Class in the English West Indies, 1624–1713* (Chapel Hill, N.C., 1972), pp. 8–9, 46, 49–51; Carl Bridenbaugh and Roberta Bridenbaugh, *No Peace Beyond the Line: the English in the Caribbean, 1624–1690* (New York, 1972), pp. 51–5.

Table 5.3 *Estimated revenues from tobacco duties 1663/9 and 1686*[a]

	Retained tobacco (lb)	Duty per lb	Revenue	Re-exported tobacco (lb)	Duty per lb	Revenue	Total revenue
1663/9	8,000,000	2d	£66,666	4,000,000	0.5d	£8,333	£74,999
1686	14,000,000	5d	£291,667	14,000,000	0.5d	£29,167	£320,834

Source: Menard, 'The tobacco industry', pp. 113, 137, 141; Price, *Tobacco Adventure*, pp. 5–6.
[a] These are upper bound estimates as discounts were given for large (unspecified) quantities of damaged tobacco and cash payment: Marshall (ed.), *Autobiography of William Stout*, p. 106.

lb in 1686, and 30 million lb in 1700 with around two-thirds entering through London.[64]

Tobacco sealed the success of early English settlement in both mainland America, and the Caribbean, and demonstrated that new lands could provide profits for producers, merchants, and manufacturers. Furthermore, the state soon realized that it was easy to tax the large quantities of tobacco entering through a handful of ports and, given the weed's addictive qualities, it had a low elasticity of demand which allowed rates to be increased without causing a matching fall in consumption.[65] Despite the Stuart monarchs' dislike of the noxious substance, the fiscal imperative encouraged the Crown to protect the colonial cashcow by outlawing domestic production in 1619, and as tobacco imports raised tax revenues of around £75,000 a year in the 1660s and (with the additional imposition of 1685) over £320,000 in 1686, the policy of prohibition was maintained throughout the century with the Privy Council issuing regular orders to destroy domestic crops (Table 5.3).[66]

[64] BL Add. MS 36,785; portbook database, 1686; Menard, 'Tobacco industry'; PRO CUST. 2/9, fos. 27–32.

[65] Sugar and tobacco both yielded additional revenue of £5,000 in 1618 when total receipts from the Great Customs were £140,000: Gray, *History of Agriculture in the Southern United States*, vol. I, pp. 235–58. In 1670, Dering described the temptation to tax sugar and tobacco as 'things we could not do without': B. D. Henning (ed.), *Sir Edward Dering: the Parliamentary Diary, 1670–73* (New Haven, Conn., 1940), pp. 24–5; Jacob M. Price, 'The tobacco trade and the treasury, 1685–1733: British mercantilism in its fiscal aspects', unpublished doctoral thesis, Harvard University (1954), ch. 2; Jacob M. Price, 'Tobacco use and tobacco taxation: a battle of interests in early modern Europe', in Jordan Goodman, Paul E. Lovejoy, and Andrew Sherratt (eds.), *Consuming Habits: Drugs in History and Anthropology* (London, 1995), pp. 165–85; C. D. Chandaman, *The English Public Revenue, 1660–1688* (Oxford, 1975), pp. 156–7.

[66] James I, 'A counterblaste to tobacco', in J. Craigie (ed.), *Minor Prose Works of King James VI and I* (Edinburgh, 1982); David Harley, 'The beginnings of the tobacco controversy: Puritanism, James I and the royal physicians', *Bulletin of the History of Medicine*, 67 (1993), 28–50;. Order of the Privy Council, 9 July 1680, PRO PC 2/69, fo. 32. According to Chandaman the government's total income in 1686 was £2,113,644: Chandaman, *Public Revenue*, p. 200.

Table 5.4 *Imports to London from the West Indies, 1686 (£ sterling)*

	Barbados	Jamaica	Antigua	Montserrat	Nevis	St Christophers	Total
Sugar	317,663	131,579	30,106	8,482	68,623	14,962	571,415
Ginger	19,306	3,727	—	—	—	—	23,033
Cotton	10,073	4,641	654	20	124	—	15,512
Molasses	11,466	1,995	778	3	391	479	15,112
Indigo	293	7,033	22	594	1,940	35	9,917
Dyewoods	264	9,335	155	—	—	—	9,754
Tobacco	149	52	7,174	—	2	—	7,377
Cocoa	1	547	—	465	—	—	1,013
Miscellaneous	4,703	18,807	177	19	774	45	24,525
Total in 1686	363,918	177,716	39,066	9,583	71,854	15,521	677,658
Total in 1700	242,824	193,674	66,294	28,494	69,882	20,625	621,793

Source: London portbook database, 1686; PRO CUST. 2/9, fos. 25–32.

The huge increase in tobacco output in seventeenth-century English America was accompanied by increased efficiency at every stage of production and distribution. With greater experience planters learned to improve the growing and curing of tobacco so that, by the 1660s, one man could produce around ten times as much tobacco a year as in 1620 and there were further small gains until the 1680s.[67] Reductions in costs did not entirely compensate for the fall in farm price from 2 or 3 shillings (24d to 36d pence) per pound in the boom of 1619, to a shilling or so in the 1620s, to well below 2d in the 1660s, and less than a penny in the 1680s, as the market became increasingly well stocked.[68] By the 1660s a planter's tobacco earnings were a quarter of what they had been in the boom of 1619 and had fallen further by the 1680s.[69] However, as profit margins were squeezed, producers in regions with other choices abandoned tobacco production, and by 1686, only one island in the English Caribbean, Antigua, exported sizeable quantities and these were tiny besides the Chesapeake's exports (Tables 5.2 and 5.4). After considerable social unrest and rebellion in the Chesapeake region, tobacco production was, by the 1680s, becoming concentrated on the best soils with the most successful units raising the higher value sweet-scented tobacco (which could only be grown in the rich bottom lands of lower tidewater Virginia and Maryland) with slave labour, while on the poorer, less fertile soils there were signs of economic diversification which gathered strength in the eighteenth century.[70]

[67] According to John Scott, by 1666 (a low point for prices) one man could produce 2,500 lb of tobacco a year: BL Sl. MS 3,662. In 1697 it was reported that one man could produce 3,000 lb of oronoco and 4,500 lb of sweet-scented: Journal of Council of Trade, 1 September 1697, *CSPC, 1697–8*, no. 1,285; Menard, 'Tobacco industry', pp. 145–6.

[68] *Ibid.*, pp. 157–9. That which 'will be the speedy and certain ruin of the colony is the low price of tobacco. The thing is so fatal and desperate that there is no remedy; the market is overstocked and every crop overstocks it more. It is commonly said that there is enough in London to last all England for five years. Too much plenty would make gold itself a drug': Culpepper to Lords of Trade, 12 December 1685, PRO CO 1147, no. 105.

[69] 1 September 1697, *CSPC, 1697–8*, no. 1,285; Lois Green Carr, Russell R. Menard, and Lorena S. Walsh, *Robert Cole's World: Agriculture and Society in Early Maryland* (Chapel Hill, N.C., 1991), pp. 12–17.

[70] The most extreme demonstration of discontent was Bacon's rebellion of 1685 but there were also repeated campaigns of tobacco destruction (in which women were prominent): PRO CO 1/48, nos. 69, 72, 88, 89, 97; CO 1/49, no. 25. The sweet-scented strain was discovered in the 1640s and became common along the York valley in the 1650s. It was favoured by English consumers and produced high prices on the London market. The leaves were denser than those of the lower value oronoco strain which reduced freight costs: Lois Green Carr and Lorena S. Walsh, 'Economic diversification and labour organization in the Chesapeake, 1650–1820', in Stephen Innes (ed.), *Work and Labour in Early America* (Chapel Hill, N.C., 1988), pp. 144–88; Anthony S. Parent, *Foul Means: the Formation of a Slave Society in Colonial Virginia, 1660–1740* (Chapel Hill, N.C., 2003).

Apart from reductions in production costs there were, as described in Chapter 4, efficiency gains in packing, shipping, and handling tobacco as greater volumes were traded, and the commerce settled into more regular and predictable channels. Tobacco was cured in America but, before consumption in Europe, much required further 'picking, stripping, cutting, and rolling' in England where it spawned a new manufacturing industry (Illustration 23). In a drive to reduce labour costs, engines were developed to replace knives for cutting leaves from the stalks and further engines were devised for flattening and shredding the stalks to reduce waste.[71] Some tobacco was smoked in leaf, but most was bathed in a liquor of sugar, water, and additives which caused fermentation, and increased its weight by as much as 10 per cent, ready for spinning and rolling on great wheels and reels.[72] The roll combined different grades of tobacco and the flavour and durability of the product depended heavily on the skill of the manufacturer and his own special (often secret) recipe which allowed some, such as John Linton, to build elevated reputations.[73] The roll usually weighed above 100 lb and could be cut off and used as a smoking mixture or as a chewing tobacco. Some was processed further by pressing and rolling into a shape known as a 'carotte', mainly ground into snuff.[74] Many retailers – especially those in the provinces such as Stout – employed their own spinner and roller, but the labour-intensive nature of the processes, and increasing use of machines, created economies of scale that encouraged investment in large workshops which were concentrated in London and other entry ports: John Linton, of Watling Street, employed over a hundred people in the 1680s and the industry as a whole may have employed two or three thousand workers.[75] According to Cary, the general surge in ingenuity in tobacco processing (drawing heavily on merchant capital) resulted in large improvements in labour productivity and falling costs.[76]

[71] Letter to Earl of Sunderland enclosing a representation regarding the tobacco trade, 1 July 1707, PRO CO 5/ 1362, fos. 241–3.

[72] Liquoring was in fact a form of adulteration and was later prohibited by legislation. Stout reveals much detail about tobacco processing: J. D. Marshall (ed.), *The Autobiography of William Stout of Lancaster, 1655–1752* (Manchester, 1957), pp. 106, 145, 161–2.

[73] Linton was reported to have 'brought that art to such perfection as to keep tobacco manufactories sound for 10 or 12 years, as many merchants can demonstrate by rolls of tobacco so long kept by them'. Others were unable to produce a roll that would keep sound above eighteen months: 'Memo from Mr Linton', 3 May 1706, PRO CO 5/1362, fos. 64–5; 'Letter from Mr Quary', 29 April 1706, *ibid.*, fos. 54–5.

[74] Jordan Goodman, *Tobacco in History: the Culture of Dependence* (London, 1993), pp. 222–3.

[75] Marshall (ed.), *Autobiography of William Stout*, pp. 80, 162; 'Memo from Mr Linton', 3 May 1706, PRO CO 5/1362, fos. 64–5. Debts to John Linton 'role-maker' are listed in the inventory of Francis Levitt, grocer, of 1705, CLRO, Orphans' Court Inventories, no. 2,817.

[76] John Cary, *An Essay on the State of England in Relation to its Trade* (Bristol, 1695), pp. 145–6.

Illustration 23 Tobacco is sorted. The best and biggest leaves are used as wrappers which are carefully soaked. The bulk is humidified then stripped of its fibrous ribs. The spinning work is done either by hand or by a reel (left) which works the leaves into a rope. The tobacco is drawn off a reel and wound around a bobbin into a tight roll several layers thick. The rolls are then compressed, closely wrapped and aged in a warehouse until fit to be sold as pipe tobacco. Snuff required further pressing. Denis Diderot, *Encyclopaedia* (1751–71).

Although around two-thirds of the tobacco imported into England was entered through the port of London, archaeological findings of the long clay pipes used to smoke tobacco, and records of their production, show that the addictive habit had quickly diffused out from the metropolis, along the main trade routes, to the large provincial towns from where it found its way into remote rural corners.[77] Beresford has shown that, as early as 1637, London and Middlesex held only 10 per cent of the licences to retail tobacco, and yielded but 16 per cent of total rents, and as increased volumes of tobacco were traded, there were savings in distribution costs which further enhanced diffusion of the smoking habit.[78] Even at the end of the century some provincial retailers, such as William Stout, journeyed to London to purchase supplies of tobacco. However, with the accumulation of expertise in dealing with the crop, greater sophistication in sorting and grading the many different types of tobacco, with Whiston's price current of 1686

[77] D. Atkinson and A. Oswald, 'London clay tobacco pipes', *The Journal of the British Archaeological Association*, 3rd ser. 32 (1969), 171–227; A. Oswald, 'The archaeology and economic history of English clay tobacco pipes', *The Journal of the British Archaeological Association* (1960), 40–102. Houghton provides a contemporary account of the clay-pipe industry, John Houghton, *A Collection for Improvement of Husbandry and Trade* (London, 1692–1703), 12 vols., 12 January 1694.

[78] M.W. Beresford, 'The beginnings of retail tobacco licenses', *Yorkshire Bulletin of Economic and Social Research*, 7 (1955), 139.

listing thirteen varieties priced from 7.75d to 3 shillings per pound, and wider access to such detailed information, it became increasingly common to use advance contracts or sell by sample at fairs (Illustration 9).[79] The inventory of Francis Levett, a large London grocer, reveals a far-flung distribution network with sales by sample at Gainsborough, Boston, Beverley, LentonWhitson, and Houlden fairs. At his death in 1705, provincial tradesmen accounted for 85 per cent of those who owed him debts amounting to £5,429.[80] London wholesalers benefited from being at the hub of a national transport system which, as Willan has shown, had developed in the sixteenth century to distribute imports from England's premier port.[81] As a growing volume of tobacco entered the port in the seventeenth century, it played a prominent part in the rapid rise of traffic out of the capital. In 1686, 70 per cent of outward bound coastal cargoes contained tobacco and the trade helped to stimulate additional investment in coastal, river, and road transport which reduced transaction costs and prices and, in turn, fuelled further consumption of the 'weed'.[82]

Efficiency improvements in the production and distribution of tobacco were translated into a massive reduction in retail price from over £1 (240d) per pound in the first days of plantation production, to a low point of around 6d per pound in the early 1680s, after which the additional tax imposed in 1685 pushed it up to a shilling or more.[83] As noted by the Lancaster grocer, William Stout, falling price stimulated 'great consumption', especially as real wages were rising after the Restoration. In the late sixteenth century tobacco was in limited use and was seen, above all, as a therapeutic drug which could expel phlegm and warm the body, although its virtues were strongly contested.[84] Tobacco was also long thought to provide protection from plague, and was sold as a cure for venereal disease although, of course, it was merely a palliative which disguised the odour of infection.[85] Even though a pipe consumed tiny amounts of

[79] *Whiston's Merchants Weekly Remembrancer*, 28 June 1686, BL India Office, X538, fo. 51.
[80] 'Inventory of Frances Levett', 30 April 1705, CLRO, Orphans' Court Inventories, no. 2,817. Levett was one of three tobacco manufacturers that worked up tobacco for the Russia Company: J. M. Price, *The Tobacco Adventure to Russia: Enterprise, Politics, and Diplomacy in the Quest for a Northern Market for English Colonial Tobacco, 1676–1722*, Transactions of the American Philosophical Society, 51 (Philadelphia, 1961), p. 48.
[81] T. S. Willan, *The Inland Trade: Studies in English Trade in the Sixteenth and Seventeenth Centuries* (Manchester, 1976).
[82] London portbook, coastal trade outwards, 1686, PRO E 190/137/5.
[83] According to Stout tobacco which he purchased for 2d a pound in 1681 retailed for 6d per lb. In the early 1690s Haggerstone paid between 1 and 3 shillings per lb for chewing tobacco: BL Harleian MS 1,238, fos. 13–20; Marshall (ed.), *Autobiography of William Stout*, p. 80; Ann M. C. Forster (ed.), *Selections from the Disbursements Book of Sir Thomas Haggerstone Bart. (1691–1709)* (Gateshead, 1969), pp. 5, 8, 26.
[84] Harley, 'The beginnings of the tobacco controversy'.
[85] When Pepys saw a door marked with a red cross in 1665, he immediately purchased and chewed some roll tobacco which 'took away the apprehension': Latham and Matthews,

Illustration 24 Gentlemen smoking tobacco and drinking rum
punch sweetened with sugar. Anon., private collection.

tobacco (one pound provided about 192 pipefuls), recreational use at
a price of £1 per pound was confined to the social and economic elite
(perhaps used as a symbol of their colonial ambitions) and groups with
favoured access to supplies such as sailors. By the 1620s, as the price of
tobacco had tumbled, a pipe could be had for less than a farthing and
could be shared by a group of friends lower down the social scale. With
its capacity to assuage hunger, cold, and fatigue, tobacco appealed to a
wide range of men and women, and with its addictive qualities, it fast

(eds.), *Diary of Samuel Pepys*, vol. VI, p. 120; Margaret Pelling, 'Appearance and reality: barber surgeons, the body and disease', in A. L. Beier and Roger Finlay (eds.),
London 1500–1700: the Making of the Metropolis (London, 1986), p. 95. For contemporary efforts to improve tobacco's image see *The Virtues and Excellency of the American
Tobacco Plant for the Cure of Diseases and Preservation of Health* (London, 1712).

took hold of unwary consumers (Illustrations 24 and 27).[86] By the 1660s it was ubiquitous in urban life: Pepys took a pipe at the coffee house and with supper before bed; he met a friend in a tobacco shop under Temple Bar Gate, and passed some hours smoking and drinking Lambeth Ale; he purchased chewing tobacco to ward off plague; and he blew tobacco up his sick horse's nose 'upon which the horse sneezed and by and by grows well'.[87] Although Sir Ralph Verney's refusal (in 1679) to hire a gardener who was 'popish, or phanatical, or takes tobacco', suggests that smoking retained a slightly disreputable image, the 'vicious weed' was so well established that although consumption did not increase after the tax hike of 1685, it did hold steady even at prices above a shilling a pound and remained 'a custom, the fashion, all the mode … so that every plow man has his pipe'.[88]

Recorded retained imports of tobacco into England and Wales increased from 100,000 lb in 1611, to 8 million lb in the 1660s and 14 million lb in 1686 (Table 5.3).[89] This volume would have allowed annual per capita consumption to increase from insignificant quantities in the 1620s, to 1.57 lb in 1669, and 2.87 lb in 1686 which was more than sufficient to furnish half the population of the country with a pipeful of tobacco a day and make it an item of 'mass consumption'.[90] In fact, consumption levels must have been higher than indicated in the trade records, as the increasingly punitive tax regime encouraged smuggling and domestic production, despite repeated prohibitions and destruction of crops.[91]

The London merchants who had promoted early experiments with tobacco in the West Country seem to have responded to falling prices and repeated prohibitions by withdrawing from direct involvement in domestic production. However, having familiarized themselves with

[86] Goodman, *Tobacco in History*, pp. 58–89. Tryon commented that 'nor is it become infrequent for women not only to drink brandy but also to smoke tobacco': Thomas Tryon, *Health's Grand Preservative or the Women's Best Doctor* (London, 1682), p. 11.

[87] Latham and Mathews (eds.), *Diary of Samuel Pepys*, vol. II, p. 117; vol. VI, p. 120; vol. VIII, p. 390.

[88] Susan E. Whyman, *Sociability and Power in Late Stuart England: the Cultural Worlds of the Verneys, 1660–1720* (Oxford, 1999), p. 14; Thomas Tryon, *The Way to Health, Long Life and Happiness* (London, 1691), pp. 126–8.

[89] Figure for 1611 in 'Information as to the great trade in tobacco', BL Sl. MS 36,319, fo. 268 as quoted in Lorimer, 'English contraband trade', p. 136.

[90] According to Wrigley and Schofield the population in 1663/9 was 5,070,620 and in 1686 it was 4,864,762: Wrigley and Schofield, *The Population History of England*, pp. 532–3. Shammas gives lower figures for consumption in the seventeenth century: Carole Shammas, *The Pre-Industrial Consumer in England and America* (Oxford, 1990), pp. 78–9.

[91] On the smuggling trade see R. C. Nash, 'The English and Scottish tobacco trades in the seventeenth and eighteenth centuries: legal and illegal trade', *EcHR*, 35 (1982), 352–72.

tobacco growing techniques, many landlords and tenants persevered with what, despite the risks of it being 'spoiled' by troops, remained a profitable enterprise in a period of low grain prices.[92] Carew Reynal may not have been romancing when he claimed in the 1670s that marginal land, otherwise worth 10 shillings per acre, was worth six times as much under tobacco and that the grower could make a net profit of £30 per acre after all charges were paid. If an acre of land could produce anything like the 2,500 lb of tobacco it produced in the colonies then as the wholesale price of the American product (burdened with freight and tax) was at that time around 4d or 5d a pound, an English producer could make a very satisfactory gross return of £40/50 per acre (when the return on wheat was around £6).[93] In the 1650s English domestic output was reported to match Chesapeake imports which suggests that around 28,000 acres might have been under tobacco cultivation (0.5 per cent of the total arable acreage suggested by King) and in 1670, tobacco was grown in twenty-two counties.[94] It was especially popular in pastoral areas in the West Midlands where there was surplus labour and loose manorial control and continued orders for destruction from the Privy Council show that it was still cultivated in the 1690s.[95] The urge to 'improve' found expression in England, as it did in the New World, and in addition to extensive new land, America provided novel crops that could raise the return on marginal lands at home and employ slack labour.

Although domestic consumption rose steeply until the 1680s, it did not keep pace with increased imports – especially after the massive tax rise of 1685 – and, to the great satisfaction of contemporary commentators, there was a growing surplus for sale in European markets. The extent to which the state valued the promotion of entrepot trade beyond even fiscal considerations was seen in its decision to reduce duties on re-exported tobacco from 12d to 2d in 1631, and 0.5d in 1661, after which all further increases in duty were rebated on tobacco shipped out of England (see Table 5.3).[96] With the encouragement of a rebate of 75 per cent of the duty, around a third of total tobacco imports were apparently re-exported in 1671, half in 1686, and over two-thirds in the years

---

[92] Thirsk, 'New crops and their diffusion'. The complicity of local landowners in tobacco growing was revealed in the failure of JPs to take action and the king's reliance on troops: Latham and Mathews (eds.), *Diary of Samuel Pepys*, vol. VIII, p. 442.

[93] Carew Reynal, *The True English Interest* (London, 1674), pp. 32–3; John Scott, 'History of Barbados', BL Sl. MS 3,662.

[94] King, 'Natural and political observations', in Laslett (ed.), *The Earliest Classics*, p. 52.

[95] *Acts of the Privy Council of England, Colonial Series, 1680–1720*, pp. 7, 35, 299, 535.

[96] J. M. Price, *France and the Chesapeake: a History of the French Tobacco Monopoly, 1674–1794, and its Relationship to the British and American Tobacco Trades*, 2 vols. (Ann Arbor, Mich., 1973), ch. 2.

from 1698 to 1701, by which time the home tax on tobacco was about six times the market value of the leaf, and the rebate amounted to 90 per cent.[97] By the end of the century tobacco accounted for around 16 per cent of the value of recorded re-exports from London to Europe, second to calicoes, and slightly ahead of sugar.[98] Tobacco was thus one of three commodities identified by Ralph Davis as defining the 'new character' of English trade after the Restoration when re-exports increased from virtually nothing in the 1640s to over a third of England's exports by 1700.[99]

There was intense competition in continental markets, especially at the end of the century when wartime disruptions raised the price of American tobacco and cultivation in northern Europe expanded to match Chesapeake levels.[100] As indicated in Chapter 3, the re-export trade was concentrated in fewer hands than the import trade, and large-scale merchants with the capital resources to hold stock in hand, such as the naval contractors, Gore and Taylor, could reduce transactions costs through specialization in particular markets, use of advance contracts, and the integration of import and re-export trade to cut out middlemen. It became common for those supplying France or Amsterdam to pass their tobacco through south coast ports or the Channel Islands in compliance with the Navigation Acts and so avoid the costs of unloading in the Thames. In 1686 Perry and Lane, the second largest firm in the Chesapeake trade, were primarily concerned with the domestic market, and imported most of their tobacco through London, but a sizeable proportion was destined for the continent, and around 16 per cent was passed through Cowes, at the Isle of Wight.[101] William Paggen, another of the fifty-nine big colonial merchants of 1686, had a sufficiently large re-export trade to warrant the lease of a warehouse in the Isle of Wight.[102]

Even in 1700 the Dutch staple took two-thirds of English re-exports but competitive conditions had encouraged merchants to seek new markets, and to attempt to supply them direct. Trade with the Baltic expanded during the years of English neutrality in the Franco-Dutch war of the 1670s

---

[97] An increase in 1697 raised the nominal duty from 5d to 6d per pound.

[98] Price, *Tobacco Adventure*, p. 5. The drawback on duties created a large incentive to make false entries and contemporary reports suggest that a large (but, of course, unquantifiable) proportion of the tobacco was smuggled back into the home market especially in the outports: Nash, 'The English and Scottish tobacco trades'.

[99] Davis, 'English foreign trade', p. 153.

[100] PRO CO 5/1362, fos. 14–19, 26–9, 240–7; Price, *Tobacco Adventure*; H. K. Roessingh, 'Tobacco growing in Holland in the seventeenth and eighteenth centuries: a case study of the innovative spirit of Dutch peasants', *The Low Countries History Yearbook*, 12 (1978), 18–54.

[101] Jacob M. Price, *Perry of London: a Family and a Firm on the Seaborne Frontier, 1615–1753* (Cambridge, Mass., 1993), pp. 45–6.

[102] 'Inventory of William Paggen', 1693, CLRO, Orphans' Court Inventories, no. 2,200.

and tobacco accounted for about a fifth of the value of London exports to the region in 1700.[103] Success was spread unevenly and for some reason exports to Sweden remained low, and efforts by Jeffreys and Lucy to corner this market through a deal with the state monopoly in the 1670s resulted in nothing but very large losses.[104] Meanwhile, the closed Russian market with its large (if poor) population offered tempting prospects for British colonial tobacco tapped only by a flourishing smuggling trade through the Russia Company's factory at Narva. As tobacco prices fell to a low point in the 1680s, merchants outside the Russia Company lobbied hard for help in gaining access to this trade with claims that 'free importation into Russia will revive our drooping spirits for we want nothing but vent'.[105] In the 1690s Peter the Great decided to flout Church opinion and end his country's prohibition on tobacco, which would allow the state to raise new revenues. On the Czar's visit to London in 1698 a syndicate (including, at least, five of the fifty-nine big colonial merchants of 1686) pulled political strings to obtain an exclusive contract to supply the Russian market, at least partly at the expense of the Russian Company.[106] Although at first sight tobacco did not fit mercantilist ideals, it not only allowed the English to establish viable settlements in the New World, but also provided a tradeable surplus which contributed to a significant strengthening of the balance of trade.

Sugar

Sugar was the most important of England's colonial staples. Sugar imports exceeded those of tobacco in value by the Restoration and were at almost four times the level by 1686 (see Table 5.1). Sugar also conformed more closely to mercantilist ideals. The crop was not native to either Europe, or America, and as it needed warmth and abundant water, it could not conceivably be produced in their northern regions. It was brought from Asia to the Mediterranean in the early middle ages but, even here, growing conditions were far from ideal.[107] Not until the fifteenth century,

---

[103] Tobacco exports to the Baltic were valued at £40,730 in 1699 (15 per cent) and £54,564 in 1700 (19 per cent): Sven-Erik Astrom, *From Cloth to Iron: the Anglo-Baltic Trade in the Late Seventeenth Century* (Helsingfors, 1963), pp. 56, 68.

[104] 'Petition of John Jeffreys and Jacob Lucy', 7 July 1680, PRO PC 2/69, p. 34.

[105] Culpepper to Lords of Trade, 12 December 1681, PRO CO 1/47, no. 105.

[106] A small group of twelve assigns signed the contract with the Czar in April 1698 after which it was thrown open to public subscription and they were joined by about sixty others. They included Gilbert Heathcote, Joseph Martin, Richard Merriweather, Thomas Starke, and John Taylor: Price, *Tobacco Adventure*; Astrom, *From Cloth to Iron*.

[107] William D. Phillips Jr., 'Sugar in Iberia', in Stuart B. Schwartz (ed.), *Tropical Babylons: Sugar and the Making of the Atlantic World, 1450–1680* (Chapel Hill, N.C., 2004), pp. 27–41. For a history of sugar production very different from the New World experience see Sucheta Mazumdar, *Sugar and Society in China: Peasants, Technology and the World Market* (Cambridge, Mass., 1998).

when the Portuguese extended cultivation to their Atlantic islands, was supply sufficient to allow this 'king of sweets' to become firmly established in European diets.[108] Columbus carried sugar to Hispaniola on his second voyage but the Spaniards showed little interest in the crop until the eighteenth century. On the other hand, the Portuguese successfully transferred cane technology from their Atlantic islands to Brazil where they were able to expand production and provide the bulk of Europe's supplies until the mid seventeenth century.[109]

English settlers made attempts at commercial sugar production as early as 1619 but, as with vines, experiments in Virginia and Bermuda were thwarted by unsuitable climate and doomed to fail.[110] The small Caribbean islands which were settled by the English in the 1620s did offer ideal growing conditions but lacked the levels of capital needed for sugar production. Unlike tobacco, sugar was not a poor man's crop. It needed a substantial investment in labour, livestock, and processing plant (mills, boiling equipment, and curing houses).[111] The promoters of early English colonization were unwilling to sink such large funds in risky absentee investments and, in the early stages, West Indian planters focused their energies on tobacco, which still offered good returns.

In the late 1630s tobacco prices collapsed and, although they recovered a little in the mid 1640s, the shock seems to have encouraged island planters to attempt diversification. Some switched to cotton production which, like tobacco, had low entry costs. Others had accumulated sufficient funds through 'Barbados custom' – starting out with small staples that required little labour or capital and gradually accumulating enough to engage in more ambitious operations – to experiment with canes and take advantage of the soaring sugar prices caused by rebellion in Brazil.[112]

---

[108] Thomas Tryon, *Tryon's Letters, Domestick and Foreign to Several Persons of Quality Occasionally Distributed in Subjects* (London, 1700), p. 221.
[109] For an excellent account of the early Atlantic sugar economies see chs. 3, 4, 5, 6 in Schwartz (ed.), *Tropical Babylons*; Noel Deerr, *History of Sugar*, 2 vols. (London, 1949–50), vol. I, pp. 112, 193–9; Frederick Mauro, *Le Portugal et l'Atlantique au XVII siècle (1570–1670)* (Paris, 1960), p. 165; Stuart B. Schwartz, *Sugar Plantations in the Formation of Brazilian Society, Bahia, 1550–1835* (Cambridge, 1985).
[110] Deerr, *History of Sugar*, vol. I, pp. 162–4.
[111] It was generally held to cost £4,000 or more to establish a sugar plantation in the English West Indies: Dalby Thomas, *An Historical Account of the Rise and Growth of the West India Colonies and the Great Advantage they are to England in Respect of Trade* (London, 1690), pp. 14–15; Dunn, *Sugar and Slaves*, pp. 188–223. Leases and inventories confirm the high figures, for example, in 1686 Codrington scheduled two plantations (containing 750 acres with four stone windmills, one stone watermill, two boiling houses with twenty-nine coppers, two still houses, and 250 working negroes) which was leased for £2,200 per annum: 'Indenture between Major General Christopher Codrington and Daniel Browning of Sussex', BA, Deeds RB 3/14.
[112] Scott reported that, in the 1650s, the farm price for muscovado was 4d per pound although during the Luso-Dutch war the price of Amsterdam whites reached 2 shillings

Historians (following contemporaries such as Scott and Thomas) have often told a story in which the Dutch played the central role in providing the necessary capital and expertise, but recent research has found little evidence to support the long-established 'myth' of heavy Dutch investment.[113] The rapid expansion in the early years rested largely on high profits and substantial ploughback of earnings, although Menard has established that London merchants such as the Noell brothers, and Civil War refugees such as Thomas Modyford (who purchased a half share in a working plantation in partnership with William Hilliard and Thomas Kendal, a London grocer), played a significant role in financing sugar production. He has identified seventy-five merchants who owned land in Barbados between 1640 and 1650 although most withdrew from direct investment by the 1660s and only seven of the fifty-nine big colonial merchants of 1686 owned property in the West Indies.[114]

Although the pioneers of English sugar production did not draw heavily on Dutch capital, Richard Ligon describes how they did look to Brazil for the plants and the practical know-how needed to establish the tricky business: 'bending all their endeavours to advance their knowledge... which though they studied hard, was long a learning'. In the early days, Barbados sugars were low-quality muscovadoes, and 'scarcely merchantable, being moist and ill-cured' and the industry only survived because of the unusually favourable market conditions during the Luso-Dutch war. However, with a decade of 'daily practice' and 'new directions' brought from Brazil, the planters began to produce saleable goods.[115] The Barbadian pioneers absorbed the available information and modified it to suit their own island's conditions; they slowly learned how best to plant the crop, how to make and operate the machinery needed to process the sugar, and how to perfect the boiling and curing techniques needed to convert the cane into semi-processed muscovado or fine white

per pound: John Scott, 'History of Barbados', BL Sl. MS 3,662; Richard Ligon, *A True and Exact History of the Island of Barbadoes* (London, 1657), p. 43; 'The true state of the manufacture of sugars within our plantations', BL Egerton MS 2,395, fo. 636; J. H. Bennett, 'Cary Helyar, merchant and planter of seventeenth century Jamaica', *WMQ*, 21 (1964), 53–76.

[113] John Scott, 'The description of Barbados', BL Sl. MS 3,662, fo. 60; Thomas, *Historical Account*, pp. 13–14; Peter C. Emmer, ' "Jesus Christ was good, but trade was better": an overview of the transit trade of the Dutch Antilles, 1634–1795', in Robert L. Paquette and Stanley L. Engerman (eds.), *The Lesser Antilles in the Age of European Expansion* (Gainesville, Fla., 1996), pp. 206–22; Russell R. Menard, *Sweet Negotiations: Sugar, Slavery, and Plantation Agriculture in Early Barbados* (Charlottesville, Va., 2006); John J. McCusker and Russell R. Menard, 'The sugar industry in the seventeenth century: a new perspective on the Barbadian sugar revolution', in Schwartz (ed.), *Tropical Babylons*, pp. 289–330.

[114] Menard, *Sweet Negotiations*, pp. 49–65; Ligon, *History of Barbadoes*, pp. 22–3.

[115] Ligon, *History of Barbadoes*, pp. 24–5, 85–7.

Illustration 25 The map of Barbados provided in Richard Ligon's *True and Exact History of the Island of Barbados* (1657) shows that the island is already densely populated along the coast. Camels were used as draft animals.

sugar.[116] They expanded the labour force by shifting to black slaves, who had become cheaper and were worked more intensely than white servants, and they developed a regulatory framework for managing this new labour force which became the model in other English colonies.[117] By the 1650s, the Barbadian planters had developed a blueprint for a sugar and slave system that remained the standard English mode of production for almost two hundred years (Illustrations 25 and 26).

The high sugar prices of the early years provided the pioneer planters with spectacular returns.[118] By the late 1650s one worker could tend two acres and, according to Ligon, produce 6,000 lb of sugar a year which, even though prices had fallen to 3d per pound (half their peak level in the mid 1640s), gave a gross income of £75. All planters with sufficient capital and labour were drawn into cane cultivation while other commodities were 'slighted and neglected'. Sugar became the 'whole soul of trade' in Barbados and accounted for around 90 per cent of the island's exports by 1686.[119] As planters in other English islands secured sufficient funds, they followed the Barbadian example although, as reflected in Table 5.4, the larger island of Jamaica retained a little more diversity than others. Sugar imports into London, the main port of entry, rose from around 150,000 in the 1660s, to around 400,000 cwt in 1686 (Table 5.1), although they fell back to 320,000 cwt in 1700 largely because of a substantial decline in Barbados (Table 5.1).[120] By the 1680s the English Caribbean was producing as much sugar as Portuguese Brazil and – despite Colbert's measures to encourage production – substantially more than the French islands (around 183,000 cwt in 1683) or the Dutch in Surinam (50,000 cwt in 1683) and the Far East (10,000 cwt).[121] Although sugar bore a far lighter

---

[116] *Ibid.*, pp. 84–95; John Scott, 'History of Barbados', BL Sl. MS 3,662.

[117] Barry Higman, 'The sugar revolution', *EcHR*, 53 (2000), 213–36.

[118] Ward Barrett, 'Caribbean sugar-production standards in the seventeenth and eighteenth centuries', in John Parker (ed.), *Merchants and Scholars: Essays in the History of Exploration and Trade* (Minneapolis, 1965), pp. 147–70; J. R. Ward, 'The profitability of sugar planting in the British West Indies, 1650–1834', *EcHR*, 31 (1978), 197–213. Ligon claimed that a clear annual profit of £7,517 could be made on a plantation costing £14,000: Ligon, *History of Barbadoes*, pp. 115–16.

[119] Ligon, *History of Barbadoes*, p. 86.

[120] Large quantities were also exported to the northern colonies. Eltis calculated that in 1688–9, 40 per cent of Barbados' sugar output was exported to North America: David Eltis, 'New estimates of exports from Barbados and Jamaica, 1665–1701', *WMQ*, 52 (1995), 631–48.

[121] Deerr, *History of Sugar*, vol. I, pp. 38–43, 112, 193–9; Neils Steensgaard, 'The growth and composition of the long distance trade of England and the Dutch Republic in the early modern world', in J. D. Tracy (ed.), *The Rise of Merchant Empires* (Cambridge, 1990), pp. 102–52; Joseph E. Inikori, *Africans and the Industrial Revolution in England: a Study in International Trade and Development* (Cambridge, 2002), p. 175; Robert Louis Stein, *The French Sugar Business in the Eighteenth Century* (Baton Rouge, La., 1988), pp. 1–10.

Illustration 26 A sugar plantation, Denis Diderot, *Encyclopaedia* (1751–71).

Table 5.5 *Duties on sugar in England, 1651–98 (shillings per cwt)*

		1651	1660	1685	1698
Of English	Muscovado	1.5	1.4	3.5	2.8
plantations	Clayed	5.0	4.75	11.0	9.5
Of foreign	Muscovado	3.0	3.8	8.0	7.6
plantations	Clayed	10.0	7.0	17.5	13.8

Source: Deerr, *The History of Sugar*, vol. I, p. 427.

fiscal burden than tobacco, it did provide the state with an important additional source of revenue with the tax-take amounting to around £5,250 in the 1660s and, after the additional imposition, over £50,000 in 1685 (Table 5.5).[122]

As with tobacco, increased output of sugar was accompanied by efficiency gains in both production and distribution. The costs and risks of sugar planting fell steeply as the 'secrets' of cultivation were learned, techniques improved, and production was more efficiently organized.[123] The yields per acre did not rise after the initial experimental period (in fact planters claimed that they fell as soils were depleted) but the cost of labour was reduced as the slave trade became better organized and slave prices fell to a low point in the 1680s.[124] The turn from servants to slaves allowed planters to extract maximum labour from their workforce at minimum cost (with high participation rates, long hours, and miserable levels of food, shelter, and clothing). Mill technology improved, with

[122] In 1668–9 Chesapeake planters sold tobacco to the value of £50,000 and paid duty of £75,000 whereas West Indian planters sold sugar for around £180,000 and this paid customs of £18,000. In the late 1670s tobacco was paying over £100,000 in customs and West Indian sugar paid less than £25,000: Dunn, *Sugar and Slaves*, pp. 206–7. The additional duty of 1685 (alongside that on tobacco) more than doubled the tax burden: retained sugar sold by the planter for a penny a pound in 1686 paid 0.4d duty, giving the state over £50,000. Between Michaelmas 1687 and Michaelmas 1688 the additional imposition on sugar and tobacco produced £148,861 (customs in the same year were £551,497). Sugars from Barbados and the Leewards were subjected to an additional tax of 4.5 per cent on export from the islands after they were taken into Crown control in 1663. According to the portbook database of 1686 the 4.5 per cent duty yielded £17,658 in that year (John Thrale's imports 'per rege') and it produced over £81,000 for the royal exchequer between 1670 and 1688: Thornton, *West India Policy Under the Restoration*, p. 258.

[123] Ligon, *History of Barbadoes*, pp. 85–92; John Scott, 'History of Barbados', BL Sl. MS 3,662.

[124] According to Barrett yields fell from 1.35 tons per acre in 1649 to less than a ton in the 1690s: Barrett, 'Sugar-production standards'; Menard, *Sweet Negotiations*, p. 78; David Eltis, *The Rise of African Slavery in the Americas* (Cambridge, 2000), p. 53.

better machinery, and a gradual substitution of wind and water power for animals (Illustration 29).[125] By the 1680s large integrated units, with sufficient land and labour to justify their own mill and processing plant, had almost entirely replaced dispersed production with large numbers of small-holders sharing fixed capital costs.[126] Although larger supplies placed downward pressure on price, cost reductions accounted for much of the fall in the farm price of muscovado from 7d per pound (58 shillings per cwt) in the early 1640s, to 3d in 1657, around 2d at the end of the 1660s, and just over a penny a pound (9.25 shillings per cwt) in 1686, a low point for sugar prices.[127]

As with tobacco, sugar freight rates fell as packing improved, voyages were better timed, and with greater volumes, shipping space was more fully used.[128] Greater volumes of sugar, and more experience in production, also stimulated efficiency gains and cost reductions in the processing stage. While Brazilian planters produced large quantities of white refined sugar, the figures in Table 5.5 show how the English state used the customs regime to encourage their planters to export semi-processed muscovadoes which conformed more completely to mercantilist ideals: they needed greater shipping stowage (having twice the bulk) and generated greater numbers of manufacturing jobs at home.[129] In the 1660s trade records suggest that muscovadoes accounted for 90 per cent of the volume, and 78 per cent of the value, of London's sugar imports and, by 1686, the portbooks indicate that brown sugar accounted for 95 per cent of the volume, and 92 per cent of the value, of London's sugar imports (Table 5.1). Only Barbados shipped a significant quantity of white sugar (14 per cent of the island's recorded sugar exports to London), whereas whites accounted for only 1 per cent of Jamaica's recorded exports, and

[125] Richard B. Sheridan, *Sugar and Slavery: an Economic History of the British West Indies, 1623–1775* (Barbados, 1974), pp. 145–6; Otis P. Starkey, *The Economic Geography of Barbados* (New York, 1939), pp. 73, 89.

[126] Menard, *Sweet Negotiations*, pp. 71, 91–5.

[127] 'The true state of the manufacture of sugar within our plantations', BL Egerton MS 2,395, fo. 636; Ligon, *History of Barbadoes*, p. 112; David Eltis, 'New estimates of exports', 631–48; K. G. Davies, *The Royal African Company* (London, 1957), p. 341. Sugar from the more recently settled, and more distant, colony of Jamaica cost a little more and probate inventories show a fall from 16 shillings per cwt in the early 1670s to 12.5 shillings in the mid-1680s: JA, Inventories, 1B/11/I–III.

[128] London wholesale prices fell from around 80 shillings for a hundredweight of muscovado in 1650 (9.6d per pound), to around 35 shillings by the Restoration, and below 17 shillings (2d per pound) by 1686. In April 1685 (just before the additional imposition) the African Company reported that 'Barbados sugars put up at 17 shillings per cwt but not selling at that price they were set again at 16 shillings per cwt. The Company paid duty': PRO T 70/81.

[129] Sugar refining was forbidden in Lisbon with the consequence of stimulating refining in Brazil: Davies, *North Atlantic World*, p. 185.

almost none from the Leewards.[130] Although merchant records reveal that, after bribing the officers in the Custom House, false entries were made to reduce the tax burden, it is clear that the bulk of imports were semi-processed muscovadoes.[131]

Large-scale, specialist refineries which drew on the technical expertise of immigrants were first established in London in the late sixteenth century in response to the surge of prize sugars that were imported in the war years.[132] However, there was only a handful of such houses until the massive increase in muscovado imports after the 1640s encouraged London merchants to invest in expanding domestic refining capacity rather than allowing the benefits of improved supplies to accrue to the Dutch.[133] By the 1690s Child reported that there were around fifty sugar houses in England, of which most were in London.[134] The City of London poll tax returns of 1692 listed nineteen sugar bakers, with around two-thirds of them in riverside wards, where they could be easily supplied with raw sugar and coal and, no doubt, there were as many in Southwark, and eastern riverside places.[135] Meanwhile, Amsterdam, which had had fifty or sixty houses in 1661, was reduced to thirty-five by 1700, as it lost ground to London and Hamburg.[136]

Sugar refining was not labour intensive (each house employed one sugar-baker and a handful of support staff) so that, even in the 1690s, the industry employed only a few hundred people. However, it did need a highly skilled labour force. The raw sugar was treated with clarifying agents (usually lime juice), boiled in large coppers, stirred, and skimmed. The liquid swelled and was controlled by addition of oil, or another agent, and rapid stirring. The boiling took about 45 minutes and ascertaining

---

[130] John Fleet reported in 1686 that a high proportion of Barbados sugars were clayed or 'cleansed from their brownness at the first juice' and were 'almost white' but were not refined and were sold as muscovado Barbados sugars, 'Deposition of John Fleet', 21 September 1686, CLRO, MCD, box 40.

[131] Balderston (ed.), *Claypoole's Letterbook*, p. 49.

[132] K. R. Andrews, 'The economic aspects of Elizabethan privateering', unpublished doctoral thesis, University of London (1951), p. 154; BL Landsdowne MS 83, fo. 6.

[133] 'Petition exercising the mystery of the refining of sugar', 1661, BL Add. MS 25,115, fos. 301–3.

[134] Child, *Discourse on Trade*, p. 37.

[135] Three were in Castle Baynard ward, six in Queenhithe ward, and three in Dowgate ward, the three wards alongside the river above London Bridge: 1692 poll tax database, CMH. The assessors of the 1694 aid listed 140 manufacturing enterprises including two sugar-houses (one assessed with a rent value of £15 and the other near the Thames waterfront assessed for stock to the value of £200). The sugar-houses and one dye-house were the only industrial installations that the assessors recorded within the City walls: Craig Spence, *London in the 1690s: a Social Atlas* (London, 2000), pp. 115–18.

[136] Eddy Stols, 'The expansion of the sugar market in western Europe', in Schwartz (ed.), *Tropical Babylons*, pp. 237–88.

the moment that the sugar was 'done' by testing between finger and thumb required careful judgement. When cool the liquor was poured into earthenware pots and taken to the curing house where the sugar was matured for several months. When ready the pots were turned upside down and the sugar was knocked out, the top and bottom were scraped away, leaving the refined sugar in the centre.[137] Products varied greatly in quality, depending on the goodness of the raw material but, above all, on the skill and care applied to the boiling and curing processes.

Although each sugar-house employed few staff, it did need an investment of several thousand pounds in the workshop with rooms for boiling and curing hundreds of pots at a time; equipment including ovens, coppers, ladles, and other tools; stocks of sugar (in various stages of processing); and enough coal to ensure that the works were kept in continuous operation.[138] In 1703 a survey of London's coal stocks revealed that a Southwark refiner held one of the biggest supplies in the city with 300 chaldrons, some 400 tons.[139] The industry made a sizeable contribution to the 'prodigious clouds of smoke' that, to the disgust of Evelyn, 'so universally and so fatally infest[ed] the air of London'.[140] An individual artisan was unlikely to command the large capital resources needed to support a sugar-house and surviving records suggest that merchant investment played a key role in expanding production. Many sugar-bakers were partners, or salaried employees, of merchants such as John Matthew (associate of Jacob Lucy), sugar importer, ship-owner, and lessee of Wiggins' Key, who had a quarter share in a sugar-house in Gardner's Alley, in Dunghill Lane, appraised at almost £4,000. Shrewd entrepreneurs such as Matthew reduced transactions costs by integrating overlapping branches of their business.[141]

As with tobacco processing, there were no major technological breakthroughs in sugar refining in the seventeenth century. However, greater

[137] Ligon, *History of Barbadoes*, pp. 90–2; Benjamin Moseley, *A Treatise on Sugar*, 2nd edn (London, 1800), includes a description by Mr Francis Willoughby of making sugar, written during a visit to Spain in 1644; *Tryon's, Letters, Domestick and Foreign*, letter 34.

[138] Inventories suggest that around 12 per cent of the investment was fixed capital and the rest was in stocks of sugar and coal. Vanderpost had utensils worth £327 in a sugar works valued at £2,836; Matthew had utensils valued at £411 in a sugar-house valued at £3,922: 'Inventory of Adrian Vanderpost', 25 January 1675, CLRO, Orphans' Court Inventories, 1057 a and b; 'Inventory of John Matthew', 10 February 1680, CLRO, Misc Inv., roll 155, box 55.

[139] John Hatcher, *The History of the British Coal Industry*, 5 vols. (Oxford), vol. I, p. 447.

[140] E. S. Beer (ed.), *John Evelyn. London Revived. Considerations for its Rebuilding in 1666 (Londinium Redivivum) or London Restored not to its Pristine, but to far greater Beauty, Commodiousness and Magnificence)* (Oxford, 1938), pp. 43–4.

[141] 'Inventory of John Matthew', 10 February 1680, CLRO, Misc. Inventories, roll 155, box 55; 'Inventory of Abraham Hickman, Cheesemonger, Cripplegate', 1706, CLRO, Orphans Court Inventory, box 41.

volumes offered opportunities to reap economies of scale, and greater
experience stimulated minor improvements in organization, and tech-
nique, which reduced unit costs: work schedules were better planned
so that labour was kept in continuous operation and fuel was more efficiently used; boiling techniques were improved; the manufacture of refining equipment became a specialized branch of the instrument-making
industry and the design of tools and utensils was modified to suit the
special needs of sugar – even giving rise to its own vocabulary. As in
the late sixteenth century, the industry was able to draw on continental
best practice as a wave of immigrants brought new skills. London sugar-
bakers failed to gain corporate privileges which would have allowed them
to exclude the foreigners, and the trade remained open and 'free' so that
new workers were able to put the skills of their 'mystery' to work.[142]
Furthermore, although some craftsmen sought to maintain the 'mystery'
of their skill, merchants such as Claypoole played an active role in organizing training, practical demonstrations, and the dissemination of written
instructions in, and beyond, the capital which further raised the overall
level of competence.[143] Cary's claim in the 1690s that 'the ingenuity of
the manufacturer and the improvement he makes in his ways of working'
had allowed sugar refiners to halve the retail price of their produce in
twenty years was, perhaps, not too far from the mark.[144]

Increased volumes of sugar also encouraged improvements in the marketing and distribution of the product. Merchants gained greater expertise in sorting and grading sugar. Whiston's price current of 1686 listed
eighteen grades of sugar with a price of 45 shillings per hundredweight
for 'first whites' and 8.25 shillings for molasses (Illustration 9).[145] Such
detailed information facilitated advance contracts and other marketing
innovations which reduced transaction costs. Like tobacco, sugar was
distributed throughout the country, and placed heavy demands on the
national transport network which stimulated investment in improved
capacity which, in turn, reduced unit costs.

[142] Native refiners petitioned for a charter to set up a society for regulating the trade in
London and its environs for 21 miles. Their claims that the foreigners had reduced
quality and undermined the trade were ignored and sugar refining remained open to
all with sufficient skills and capital allowing rapid expansion of capacity: BL Add. MS
25,115.
[143] John Hodgson, a Lancaster merchant, employed London refiners in the sugar-house he
set up in the 1680s and his neighbours reckoned that, being kept in ignorance of their
techniques, he suffered loss: Marshall (ed.), *Autobiography of William Stout*, pp. 95, 145.
In the 1680s Claypoole arranged for George White, a sugar baker, to allow another
refiner to observe his operations for a month on payment of a fee. On another occasion,
White was paid to provide written instructions for an Irish refinery: Balderston (ed.),
Claypoole's Letterbook, pp. 61–2, 66, 70, 115.
[144] Cary, *State of Trade*, p. 145.
[145] *Whiston's Merchants Weekly Remembrancer*, 28 July 1686, BL, India Office X538, fo. 51.

The English were fast developing a very sweet tooth as efficiency improvements in the production and distribution of sugar allowed a reduction in the retail price from around a shilling a pound (which provided 100 level teaspoons) in 1660, to 6d or 7d in the early 1680s although, as with tobacco, the trend was reversed after the additional imposition of 1685. In a seventeenth-century world of stable, or rising, food prices, sugar's exceptionalism was startling and aggregate domestic consumption trebled in the three decades after 1660 despite stable population.[146] By 1700 retained imports of sugar provided Englishmen with an annual intake of around 7lb a head, allowing two teaspoons a day, a long way short of the 84lb or so consumed by each Briton in 2006, but none the less a significant presence in the diets of all Englishmen.[147] Although only accounting for a tiny proportion of a household's calorific intake (2 per cent or less as compared with 12.5 per cent in 1962) sugar took, according to Gregory King's reckonings, around 4 per cent of its annual expenditure on food in 1688.[148] Of course, sugar consumption was, as yet, unevenly spread, for in a world where a skilled craftsman earned 36d a day, sugar that cost 6d a pound remained a 'treat', enjoyed, above all, by the 'rich and opulent people of the nation'. None the less, sugar's growing accessibility, and the sweet's 'infinite capacity to delight' was making it increasingly 'useful to all degrees of man'.[149]

Sugar was not only consumed by more and more people but also used in an ever-increasing number of ways. Sugar was long established as a decorative material: it could be mixed with other substances such as gum arabic, water, or ground nuts to form a claylike solid which could be moulded before hardening, then decorated and displayed.[150] Sugar was also an important ingredient in a wide range of manufacturing processes such as tobacco production, brewing, and distilling.

---

[146] Sugar was the one really consistently deflationary commodity in the cost of living in the capital, the price of which fell by 56 per cent between 1574 and 1700; Jeremy Boulton, 'Food prices and the standard of living in London in the "century of revolution", 1580–1700', *EcHR*, 53 (2000), 455–92.

[147] Sydney W. Mintz, *Sweetness and Power: the Place of Sugar in Modern History* (New York, 1985), p. 37. In 2007 DEFRA reported that the UK consumed around 2.25 million tons of sugar per year, approximately 75 per cent of which was sold to industrial users such as soft drinks and confectionary manufacturers. Consumption remains more or less constant. (www.defra.gov.uk/farm/crops/sugar).

[148] 'Natural and political observations of Gregory King', in Laslett (ed.), *The Earliest Classics*, p.51; J. P. Greaves and Dorothy F. Hollingsworth, 'Changes in the pattern of carbohydrate consumption in Britain', *Proceedings of the Nutrition Society*, 23 (1964), 136–43.

[149] Thomas, *An Historical Account*, p. 8; Forster (ed.), *Disbursements Book of Sir Thomas Haggerston Bart.*, pp. 25, 58.

[150] Robert May, *The Accomplished Cook* (London, 1671); Mintz, *Sweetness and Power*, pp. 87–96.

Molasses (the refuse of the sugar boiling process) was an important raw material in the most dynamic sector in the production of alcoholic beverages, the distilling of British spirits as a substitute for brandy.[151] But, above all, sugar was used as medicine, preservative, and sweetener.

Sugar played an important role in medical texts from the middle ages and in 1708 Oldmixon remarked that it was indispensable to apothecaries 'there being nearly 300 medicines made up with sugar'.[152] Sugar's preservative powers were also long established and the lower price allowed delicacies such as candied and syruped fruits, marmalade, and jam to enjoy increased popularity. By the late seventeenth century there were around forty confectioners in the City supplying such goods and many housewives, such as Elizabeth Pepys, invested time and money in learning to make them at home.[153] The taste for such delicacies spread out from London, and further and further down the social scale. Gregory King remarked that, although 'country people and the poorer sort' consumed little meat, they ate substantial quantities of fruit and vegetables which were usually flavoured, or preserved, with sugar and in farmers' houses 'scarce a day passes without apple or pear pies'.[154] Tryon reported that sugar stimulated demand for fruits, 'that were hardly thought of or, at leastwise, but little valued formerly', and encouraged farmers with good access to markets to diversify production, away from cereals (in which prices were languishing), and into market gardening with a massive improvement in earnings.[155] Sugar

[151] John Chartres, 'No English calvados? English distillers and the cider industry in the seventeenth and eighteenth centuries', in John Chartres and David Hey (eds.), *English Rural Society: Essays in Honour of Joan Thirsk* (Cambridge, 1990), pp. 330–42. Stout reported that after the outbreak of war with the French in 1689 'abundance of stills set up for extracting good and strong spirits from malt, molasses, fruit, and other materials instead of brandy': Marshall (ed.), *Autobiography of William Stout*, p. 94.

[152] John Oldmixon, *The British Empire in America*, 2 vols. (London, 1708), vol. II, p. 159.

[153] 1692 poll tax database, CMH. Inventories show that confectioners sold a wide variety of goods, including wet and dry sweetmeats, comfits and assorted biscuits. They supplied the provinces and overseas as well as metropolitan consumers: 'Inventory of William Medley', 1667, CLRO, Orphans' Court Inventory, 302; Latham and Matthews (eds.), *Diary of Samuel Pepys*, vol. III, p. 53.

[154] Forster (ed.), *Disbursements Book of Sir Thomas Haggerstone*, p. 65. King reckoned that, in 1688, the market for fruit and vegetable stuff (closely linked to sugar) was worth £1 million of which £100,000 was spent within the Bills of Mortality: 'Seventeenth century manuscript book of Gregory King', in Laslett (ed.), *Earliest Classics*, p. 213.

[155] How many acres of land are by the use of this noble plant [sugar], made of five times the value and more than otherwise they would have been? As having brought a great number of fruits, grains and seeds into use, that were hardly thought of or at leastwise but little valued formerly such as apples, pears, plumbs, apricots, gooseberries, currants and many more of the like nature; which do all increase the consumption of grain. To which may be added the many brave and exhilarating drinks that are made of the juices of our fruits ... Cherry wine, currant wine. (Tryon, *Tryon's Letters*, p. 219)

was also used to preserve and glaze meat, to disguise the taste of low quality – even rotten – food, and to sweeten beer and wine.[156] Sugar made it possible to make more intensive use of existing resources and so enhanced national self-sufficiency.

Recipes in early English cookbooks suggest that sugar was widely used as a spice in main dishes before the rise of the 'new' French cuisine in the late seventeenth century which advocated a stricter separation between sweet, salty, and bitter flavours.[157] However, by the late seventeenth century there were an increasing number of recipes in which sugar was a principal ingredient. It was common to serve cakes, biscuits, or pastries with beer, or wine, at funerals, weddings, and other feasts and, in London, it was becoming increasingly usual to serve tarts and tansies (a type of syllabub) with the second-course meat dishes of more elaborate meals.[158] By the 1680s, the French habit of serving a succession of courses, with a sweet one to finish, was becoming fashionable among the capital's affluent classes, although the custom of a 'pudding' or 'dessert' to finish meals day after day did not permeate the provinces, or down the social scale, until well into the eighteenth century.[159]

By 1700 the availability of cheaper and cheaper sugar had also allowed a range of hot beverages – tea, coffee, and chocolate – to become firmly established as desirable substitutes for beer (which, according to King, absorbed a third of the nation's grain output in the 1680s). Although consumption of hot drinks was, as yet, confined to the upper and middle income groups they became very important among all classes over the next century.[160] Tea drinking was introduced at court by Catherine of Braganza (reflecting her country's long-standing global connections) and became established as a fashionable practice among the metropolitan elite, with accompanying rituals and tea services, but does not seem to have spread to the provinces until after 1713, when Britain firmly established a trade with China and imports rose; the household accounts

Blith claimed that farmers could earn £100 per acre by market gardening: Blith, *The English Improver*. Benjamin Worsley and others devoted considerable attention to the problems of fruit preservation: Leng, *Benjamin Worsley*, pp. 103–4.
[156] A grocer accused his apprentice of stealing sugar to put in stale beer while drinking with his friends: *George Harper v. Granado Chester*, May 1685, CLRO, MC 6/442.
[157] Mintz, *Sweetness and Power*, pp. 82–7. Stols, 'The expansion of the sugar market', in Schwartz (ed.), *Tropical Babylons*, pp. 237–88.
[158] Forster (ed.), *Disbursements Book of Sir Thomas Haggerstone*, p. 65; Latham and Matthews (eds.), *Diary of Samuel Pepys*, vol. IV, p. 361.
[159] Mintz, *Sweetness and Power*, pp. 131–3.
[160] King, 'Natural and political observations', in Laslett (ed.), *The Earliest Classics*, p. 43. Peter Mathias, *The Brewing Industry in England, 1700–1830* (Cambridge, 1959), p. 375; John Chamberlayne, *The Manner of Making of Coffee, Tea and Chocolate as it is used in most parts of Europe, Asia, Africa and America with their Virtues* (London, 1685).

Illustration 27 A London coffee house, *c.* 1700. Anon., Ashmolean Museum.

of a Northumberland gentleman who consumed both tobacco and sugar in the 1690s make no reference to the purchase of tea.[161]

Coffee drinking became very popular in Restoration London, and other urban centres, although it was usually taken in specialist coffee houses rather than at home (Illustration 27). By the early 1660s the City boasted eighty-two houses selling coffee and chocolate, an American delicacy made by combining cocoa beans with sugar and spices, which was valued as a 'great healer of bad stomachs'.[162] As reflected in Pepys's regular visits, 'the coffee [house]' had become an important institution in urban life for those who could afford a penny a dish and was used, not only for sober refreshment, but also for

---

[161] K. N. Chaudhuri, *The Trading World of Asia and the English East India Company, 1660–1780* (Cambridge, 1978), pp. 538–9; Mintz, *Sweetness and Power*, pp. 110–11; Shammas, *Pre-Industrial Consumer*, pp. 83–4; Forster (ed.), *Disbursements Book of Sir Thomas Haggerstone*.

[162] It is usually claimed that the first coffee house was set up in Oxford in 1650: Aytoun Ellis, *The Penny Universities: a History of the Coffee Houses* (London, 1956); Earle, *Making of the Middle Class*, pp. 53–4; S. D. Smith, 'Accounting for taste: British coffee consumption in historical perspective', *JIH*, 27 (1996), 183–214. In 1661, Pepys records waking with a bad hangover after heavy drinking to celebrate the coronation and took his morning draught 'in chocolate to settle my stomach': Latham and Matthews (eds.), *Diary of Samuel Pepys*, vol. II, p. 88.

obtaining information, engaging in all sorts of improving discourse, and listening to the stories of travellers and thinkers.[163] A picture of comfort and convenience is presented by an advertisment placed in Houghton's *Collection* by Walsall the 'coffee man against the church in Leadenhall'. Walsall kept a library, advertised jobs, property for sale, schools, and ships for freight.[164] In Woodruffe Smith's words 'it was fitting that venues designed for consumption of exotic beverages sweetened with New World sugar should become a significant part of the infrastructure of commercial capitalism giving tangible form to what classical economists call the market'.[165]

As the utility and desirability of sugar became firmly established in English diets, its per capita consumption increased more rapidly than imports and, unlike with tobacco, an increasing proportion of London's rising sugar imports was retained for home consumption. As with tobacco, merchants were allowed to draw back almost all the duty on re-exports so that they were not unnecessarily burdened in European markets, but prices were usually higher in London than in either Amsterdam or Hamburg.[166] While around half of London's muscovado imports were re-exported in the 1660s, the proportion had fallen to less than a third by 1700, putting them slightly behind tobacco in value.[167] None the less, even at the end of the seventeenth century they played an important role in strengthening the national balance of payments.

Sugar, more than tobacco, allowed Englishmen to reap rich rewards from extensive growth in America. Although it would have required only around 150,000 additional acres of wheat to substitute for the calories provided by retained sugar imports in 1686 (a mere 1.4 per cent of King's estimate of arable land in England) such calculations of the 'ghost' acres provided in the New World do not capture the full

---

[163] For Pepys's use of the coffee house see the diary for a few weeks in 1663, Latham and Matthews (eds.), *Diary of Samuel Pepys*, vol. IV, pp. 361–3, 371, 378, 390, 395, 401, 412, 434; Brian Cowan, *The Social Life of Coffee: the Emergence of the British Coffee House* (New Haven, Conn., 2005).

[164] Houghton, *Collection*, 8 February 1695.

[165] Woodruff D. Smith, 'From coffee house to parlour: The consumption of coffee, tea and sugar in north western Europe in the seventeenth and eighteenth centuries' in Goodman *et al.* (eds.), *Consuming Habits*, pp. 148–64.

[166] For competition and prices in European markets see Henry Roseveare (ed.), *Markets and Merchants of the Late Seventeenth Century: the Marescoe–David Letters, 1668–1680* (Oxford, 1987), pp. 208–27, 238.

[167] As with tobacco, there were efficiency gains in the sugar re-export business as it became heavily concentrated, with seven merchants accounting for 83 per cent of London's re-exports in 1686, and increasingly integrated with the import trade (six of the re-exporters were also major sugar importers) and able to reduce transaction costs. The re-exporters were John Fleet, John Bawden, John Jelly, Woodhouse, Wright, William Gore, and Peter Joy. The last did not import sugar.

usefulness of sugar.[168] A spoonful of sugar contained only 16 calories but went a long way to extend resources: raw materials were available for the new distilleries and a range of industrial processes; the durability of meats, fruits, and vegetables could be prolonged; inferior, even rotten, foods were rendered palatable and saved from waste; hot beverages became established as substitutes for beer – allowing a halving of per capita consumption in the eighteenth century – which relieved pressure on cereal supplies.[169] Furthermore, during the seventeenth century, there was a surplus of sugar above domestic consumption which could be used to pay for imports and strengthen the balance of trade. In addition, the prospects of profit in the business of marketing, processing, and distributing sugar spawned investment in a wide range of skills, and a commercial infrastructure which increased the nation's adaptive efficiency and strengthened the economy beyond a mere addition of resources.

Minor staples

The strong growth in England's imports of tobacco and sugar in the late seventeenth century necessitated the construction of increasingly efficient transport and distribution networks which could be used by other valuable commodities. Many of these goods proved to have strategic significance for England's economic development but were not traded in volumes that alone could have supported the necessary commercial infrastructure.

England's woollen cloth industry faced difficulties in the late seventeenth century. Intense foreign competition, rising tariff barriers, stagnant markets, and falling prices combined to damage the industry's export strength. A revival in the textile industry's fortunes depended on the diversification of products and processes and, although colonial attempts at sericulture met repeated failure, planters did provide a range of other necessary raw materials. The success of Asian cottons in European and African markets had demonstrated strong demand for lightweight, colourful cloths and encouraged efforts to provide home-produced substitutes.[170] Early European settlers in Brazil and Guiana

---

[168] Retained imports of 300,000 cwt of sugar would have taken about 15,000 acres. One acre of sugar produced nine to twelve times as many calories as one acre of wheat and four times as much as one acre of potatoes. Using a multiplier of 10, sugar imports substituted for 150,000 acres of wheat out of a total of 10 million.

[169] Mathias, *Brewing Industry*, p. 375.

[170] Chaudhuri, *Trading World of Asia*; A. P. Wadsworth and J. de la Mann, *The Cotton Trade and Industrial Lancashire, 1660–1780* (Manchester, 1931).

found cotton grown by American natives and were able to learn the secrets of cultivation. In the 1630s English planters in Barbados began to experiment with the crop which could be grown on small plots, offered a quick return, and provided an attractive alternative to tobacco as its price collapsed.[171] In the 1660s plantation-grown cotton, valued at around £40,000, was the third most important colonial import into London (after sugar and tobacco) and exceeded the value of cotton imports from the Levant, the traditional supplier. Although cotton gave way to other crops in subsequent decades, colonial cotton imports were valued at £23,107 in 1700 and remained an important source of supply.[172] In supplying raw materials and credit, London's colonial merchants played a crucial role in nurturing the manufacture of new cotton mixtures in London and the provinces. For example, Richard Holt imported cotton from Jamaica and employed a factor in Manchester to supply it to local linen-drapers who, in turn, put out materials for making fustians (linen and cotton mixes) which Holt took in payment for the raw cotton and exported to the Caribbean.[173] American lands provided a secure 'domestic' supply of the raw material needed to establish a new branch of the textile industry.

The triumphs of British textiles during the eighteenth century depended not only on diversification in the product range but also improvements in the finishing sectors which accounted for as much as half of the final value of the cloths. In 1600 a high proportion of English cloth exports were undyed, and the domestic finishing industry was dispersed and backward. By 1700 the finishing trades were concentrated in London and almost all exported textiles were dyed.[174] Progress depended partly

---

[171] Bridenbaugh and Bridenbaugh, *No Peace Beyond the Line*, pp. 55–61. For a description of cotton cultivation see Hans Sloane, *A Voyage to the Islands Madeira, Barbados, Nieves, St Christopher's and Jamaica*, 2 vols. (London, 1707–25), vol. II, p. 68. Even in the later seventeenth century each Caribbean island did (contrary to myth) retain an important small farm sector: vital in producing a large part of the provisions needed to victual both the plantations and the ships that transported the sugar to market. Cotton provided an attractive cash crop for these poorer farmers. A map of Jamaica in 1684 marks 299 cotton/provision farms alongside 246 sugar plantations and 145 others: Dunn, *Sugar and Slaves*, p. 169.

[172] BL Add. MS 36,785; in 1700, London imported cotton to the value of £13,153 from Jamaica and £8,879 from Barbados: PRO CUST. 2/9, fos. 29–32.

[173] 'Account book of *Cadiz Merchant*', PRO HCA 30/664, fo. 37; Holt also purchased cotton at the Royal African Company sales, 9 August 1683, PRO T 70/80, fo. 37; 'Case of Joshua Browne and Nathaniel Walker against Richard Holt and Thomas Heyrick', PRO E 134/2 Jas 2/Mich. 30; Wadsworth and Mann, *Cotton Trade*, pp. 29–96.

[174] Susan Fairlie, 'Dyestuffs in the eighteenth century', *EcHR*, 17 (1965), 488–510. A breakdown of the costs of textile manufacture is provided in 'The importance of the manufacture of Turkey raw silk in this kingdom', *The British Merchant*, 22–5 June 1714; J. Hellot, *The Art of Dyeing Wool and Woollen Cloth* (London, 1789).

228 The Capital and the Colonies

on improved technical know-how, but also on improved supplies of raw materials, and dry-salters were heavily dependent on overseas trade. The only important dyestuff grown in Britain was woad, and that was viewed as inferior to the French product.[175] Madder was attempted but was never established.[176] Meanwhile, American lands provided the English industry with 'domestic' supplies of a wide range of dye-stuffs.

Indigo, which yielded a fast blue dye, originated in Asia and was imported into London by the East India Company.[177] The West Indies offered appropriate growing conditions and English settlers began to experiment with the crop in the 1630s. Capital needs were fairly modest – a few hundred pounds – and returns were quick so that indigo fast took hold and, as supplies increased, the price fell from 5 shillings per pound in the 1620s to around 2 shillings per pound in the 1670s, at which price the East India Company reduced their imports.[178] However, as sugar established itself as the leading West Indian staple, indigo was increasingly neglected in the smaller islands, and by 1692, the Committee for Trade and Plantations reported that Jamaica supplied 70 per cent of England's indigo imports, and by 1700 the island provided 92 per cent of London's imports valued at £10,370.[179]

Logwood, which provided black, red, and rust colours, grew in the low-lying marshy ground along the coast of Yucatan and Campeche and, despite fetching £100 per ton in the early seventeenth century, it was neglected by Spanish colonists.[180] However, Jamaican vessels began frequenting the logwood coasts in the early 1660s, landing and cutting a full lading of wood which they took back to Port Royal and sold to merchants for shipment to Europe.[181] By the 1670s there were permanent settlements of logwood cutters, which attracted men such as William Dampier from the same pool of restless fortune hunters as the privateers and, as

[175] Thirsk, *Alternative Agriculture*, pp. 79–96.
[176] *Ibid.*, pp. 104–18.
[177] Chaudhuri, *Trading World of Asia*, pp. 331–5.
[178] Indigo production is described in detail in Pere Labat, *Nouveau Voyage*, vol. I, pp. 268–310; Bridenbaugh and Bridenbaugh, *No Peace Beyond the Line*, pp. 60, 284–5; Davies, *North Atlantic World*, pp. 191–2.
[179] 'Report of Committee for Trade and Plantations', 11 October 1692, PRO CO 138/7, fos. 124–5; PRO CUST. 2/9, fo. 25.
[180] Sandwich reported from Madrid in 1668 that Spain imported only 500 tons of Campeachy wood a year. Thornton, *West India Policy Under the Restoration*, p. 125. On the logwood trade see Arthur M. Wilson, 'The logwood trade in the seventeenth and eighteenth centuries', in Douglas McKay (ed.), *Essays in the History of Modern Europe* (New York, 1936), pp. 1–15.
[181] 'A memorial of what I observed during my being in ye island of Jamaica, 1670–1673', BL Sl. MS 4,020, fo. 22b; 'Affidavits concerning logwood at Yucatan', BL Egerton MS 2,395, fos. 481–482b.

the trade was put on a regular footing, the price of logwood was brought down to £30 per ton by 1670.[182] The English argued that, as the coasts were uninhabited, they were covered by a clause in the Treaty of Madrid which allowed the King of England to retain any territories that were in English hands by 1670. Spain stubbornly resisted such claims into the eighteenth century and ordered regular reprisals against the settlements but, none the less, they survived, and continued to attract ships from Jamaica and the North American colonies. In 1700 logwood imports into London were valued at £45,945, with two-thirds coming from Jamaica and further large quantities from New England, New York, and Carolina.[183] In addition to indigo and logwood, the Caribbean supplied small quantities of other dye-stuffs including anotto, braziletto, fustick, and redwood, as well as re-exports of the highly prized cochineal from Spanish America.[184]

The increased supply of dye-stuffs in London, along with ample quantities of coal, and a skilled workforce enhanced by immigration from Europe, combined to encourage the growth and development of London's finishing sector at the expense of smaller-scale, less well-capitalized provincial competitors. An increasing proportion of cloths were despatched to London in unfinished condition and merchant firms such as the Royal African Company, which both imported the raw materials, and exported the finished cloths, played an important role in financing and organizing their dyeing, setting, drawing, pressing, and packing before shipment overseas.[185] As the industry grew it benefited from economies of scale with more specialization, and division of labour, as well as various improvements in techniques, equipment, and the use of fuel which all served to raise productivity and widen the product range.

Extensive growth in America provided England with a wide range of other useful commodities: foodstuffs such as cocoa (combined with sugar and spices to make chocolate), ginger, lime juice, pimento, an array of spices, drugs, gums, spermaceti oil, hardwoods for furniture, and exotic

[182] William Dampier, the famous buccaneer and explorer, spent three years as a logwood cutter and described his life in his diary: Anton Gill, *The Devil's Mariner: a Life of William Dampier, Pirate and Explorer, 1651–1715* (London, 1997), pp. 40–68.

[183] PRO CUST. 2/ 9, fos. 25–32.

[184] Composed of dried insect carcasses, this brilliant red dye-stuff was second in value only to silver as a Mexican import. The high price reflected the fact that a pound of this quality dye-stuff by the salter's estimate would 'strike a better colour and go further than 4 lbs of campechena': R. Lee, 'American cochineal in European commerce 1526–1624', *Journal of Modern History*, 23 (1951), 205–24.

[185] 11 January 1686, PRO T 70/81, fo. 76b; Committee of Goods, 19 May 1691, PRO T 70/127, fo. 36. Thomas Sands to William Lloyd, 10 June 1692, 'Letterbook of Thomas Sandes and John Browne', BEA, M 7/3.

commodities such as tortoiseshell.[186] All extended England's raw material base, and reduced reliance on foreign imports while leaving a surplus to pay for those imports that did remain indispensable, or merely desirable. By 1700 London had become an international emporium to rival Amsterdam. However, the additional product of 'ghost' acres in the New World did more than merely extend resources, it also provided incentives to invest in improving the skills, tools, and the organization of industry, in ways that greatly intensified the use of resources and strengthened the nation's commercial and manufacturing capacities.

Bullion

From the days of the first discoveries America was seen, above all, as a source of gold and silver, 'the measure and standard of all riches', providing both a standard for the national unit of account and the ultimate means of settling international debts. Spain's bullion imports dazzled contemporaries and the English were disappointed that their own new lands in America did not yield similar supplies. In the early seventeenth century England obtained most of its bullion through commerce with Spain, including underhand participation in the American trading fleets controlled by the Carreras de Indias in Seville.[187] But Englishmen did also obtain some bullion direct from America through plunder or peaceful contraband commerce.[188] Direct trade offered scope for reducing transactions costs by avoiding the high charges, and delays, experienced when loading goods on the increasingly irregular fleets but was hampered by England's lack of a convenient base in the Caribbean. The capture of Jamaica, in the heart of the Indies, greatly extended the possibilities of profit.[189]

During the first fifteen years of English rule privateering was actively encouraged at Jamaica with the connivance of the home authorities. It was widely believed that only force would persuade the Spaniards to allow

---

[186] In Jamaica the English inherited a few cocoa walks from the Spaniards and, in the first years of settlement, cocoa was considered Jamaica's 'principal and most beneficial commodity'. Cocoa imports into London almost doubled from 1,200 cwt in 1663, valued at £12,000, to 2,264 cwt in 1669, valued at £22,640. However, a mysterious blight destroyed the crop at the end of the 1660s and, in the south of the island, it never recovered. In 1700 total imports into London were valued at £12,7770: BL Add. MS 36,785; Richard Blome, *A Description of the Island of Jamaica* (1672), pp. 9, 16–21; Sir Thomas Lynch, 'A description of the cocoa', BL Egerton MS 2,395, fos. 643–8; PRO CUST. 2/9, fos. 25–32.

[187] C. H. Haring, *Trade and Navigation between Spain and the Indies in the Time of the Habsburgs* (Cambridge, Mass., 1918).

[188] Kenneth R. Andrews, *The Spanish Caribbean: Trade and Plunder, 1530–1630* (New Haven, Conn., 1978).

[189] Nuala Zahedieh, 'The merchants of Port Royal, Jamaica, and the Spanish contraband trade, 1655–92', *WMQ*, 43 (1986), 570–93.

open access to their American trade and, although most of the profit accrued to local interests, much of the loot did find its way home.[190] In 1669 the Spanish ambassador raged with anger as he reported the arrival in London of the *George and Samuel* laden with bullion, and other rich Spanish goods, taken in Morgan's spectacular raid on Portobello which yielded prize valued at £100,000.[191] After the Treaty of Madrid in 1670 there was no official sanction of privateering but the lucrative business was so well entrenched that it could not be easily suppressed and continued to flourish (more or less openly) in the English islands (especially Jamaica, the Bahamas, and Bermuda) and in ports on the mainland coast.[192]

Despite the relentless plunder, and the inevitable hostility it engendered, merchants in the colonies and the metropolis also combined to finance an increasingly well-organized peaceful trade, using Jamaica as their main base. Manufactured goods and slaves were exchanged for Spanish colonial goods including large amounts of bullion.[193] As Cary noted, a substantial portion of the trade which had been driven via Cadiz (worth £378,000 in 1670) was redirected to Jamaica, especially in years when no fleet sailed.[194] While the French continued to focus on the Cadiz trade (neglecting direct trade until the 1690s), and the Dutch lacked a base sufficiently westward in the Caribbean to pursue trade in the major Spanish ports, the English had the 'governing trade'.[195] Various estimates suggest that, in the 1680s, Jamaica's contraband commerce was worth in excess of £100,000 a year and, in 1691, governor Inchiquin reported that '[Spanish] trade and the asiento are the life of this place'.[196]

Salvage was another source of bullion. Wreck-hunting had become a major occupation by the mid-seventeenth century, especially in Bermuda and the Bahamas, where treacherous rocks and waters ensured frequent wrecks. In the early 1680s a Spanish treasure ship found off New Providence provided rich pickings, especially for those with the most up-to-date diving tubs. The windfall gains stimulated a good deal of speculative interest in

---

[190] Nuala Zahedieh, 'Trade, plunder, and economic development in early English Jamaica, 1655–89', *EcHR*, 39 (1986), 205–22; Nuala Zahedieh, ' "A frugal, prudential and hopeful trade"; Privateering in Jamaica, 1655–89', *JICH*, 18 (1990), 145–68.

[191] 'Memorial of the Spanish Ambassador', 7/17 July 1669, *CSPC, 1669–74*, no. 1.

[192] Zahedieh, ' "A frugal, prudential and hopeful trade"'.

[193] In the 1680s around half the slaves delivered to Jamaica by the Royal African Company were resold to Spaniards and high prices were paid in bullion: Zahedieh, 'Merchants of Port Royal', 589–92.

[194] And [this] 'I take to be the true reason why our vent for [manufactures] at Cadiz is lessened': Cary, *Essay on the State of England*, pp. 115–16.

[195] The prevailing winds made it very difficult to sail from west to east in the Caribbean: Letter to Nottingham, March 1689, NLJ, MS 390. On the Dutch in Curaçao and St Eustatius, Wim Klooster, *Illicit Riches. Dutch Trade in the Caribbean, 1648–1795* (Leiden, 1998).

[196] Zahedieh, 'Merchants of Port Royal', 589–92.

treasure hunting which seized even the king and court. Information about a Spanish flagship that had been wrecked off Hispaniola in 1641, and sank with an immense treasure, drew particular interest and, after a few years of search and disappointment, the wreck was discovered by William Phips, a New England captain (later governor of Massachusetts), with '[no] better than a carpenter's education' who had obtained London backing for the project.[197] Phips became the talk of the nation when he returned to London in 1687 with a shipload of treasure valued at a spectacular £210,000.[198] The backing syndicate of six merchants and courtiers (including the Duke of Albermarle, later governor of Jamaica) was handsomely repaid for its combined 'hazard' of £3,000 in the venture, and although James II resisted pressure to make a direct investment, he must have been well pleased with the receipt of over £20,000 as the Crown's tenth share.[199]

Trade, plunder, and salvage allowed English settlers in America to obtain substantial supplies of bullion. Although some was used as coin in the colonies most was remitted home, either direct or via North America but, as it was not recorded in either the portbooks or the customs accounts, it cannot be computed with precision and is often overlooked.[200] Thomas Stubbs, commander of the *Richard and Sarah*, sailed from Jamaica in January 1688 and the Naval Officers' returns show that he carried a typical cargo of sugar, cotton, logwood, pimento, hides, indigo, ivory, lime juice, and ebony.[201] However, the returns do not record the ninety-three consignments of bullion listed in the captain's own notebook.[202] This

---

[197] Molesworth to Blathwayt, 18 November 1684, PRO CO 138/5, fo. 12. For a detailed account of the treasure hunt see Peter Earle, *The Wreck of the Almiranta: Sir William Phips and the Search for the Hispaniola Treasure* (London, 1979). On Phips see Emerson W. Baker and John G. Reid, *The New England Knight: Sir William Phips, 1651–1695* (Toronto, 1998).

[198] *London Gazette*, no. 2249, 6–9 June 1687; Daniel Defoe, *An Essay Upon Projects* (London, 1697).

[199] C. H. Karraker, 'Spanish treasure, casual revenue of the crown', *Journal of Modern History*, 5 (1933), 301–18.

[200] Preface in Francis Hanson, *The Laws of Jamaica, Passed by the Assembly and Confirmed by His Majesty in Council, February 1683. To which is Added, a Short Account of the Island and Government Thereof* (London, 1683). The Commissioners of the Mint reported on one of many efforts to retain coin through revaluation in Nevis in 1684,

As to the Act of Nevis for raising the price of money. It can be no possible advantage and of great possible prejudice to the trade of the island to raise the piece of eight from 4s 6d to 6s for the price of commodities will rise in proportion to the money. Trade is not balanced by notions and names of money and things but by intrinsic values. Nor will the law attain its end of hindering the exportation of money for prices will rise in proportion to the money and the conditions will be the same.

Commissioners of the Mint to Lords of the Treasury, 27 September 1684, *CSPC, 1681–4*, no. 1,876.

[201] Naval Officers' returns, Jamaica, PRO CO 142/13, fo. 119.

[202] 'Book belonging to Thomas Stubbs', 19 September 1688, PRO HCA 30/664.

treasure included 5,383 pieces of eight (worth £1,345 at 5 shillings per piece), over 5,000 ounces of silver (worth over £1,250 at five shillings per ounce) and miscellaneous coin, plate, gold, and jewellery, and may well have been worth more than the rest of the commodities put together. The Royal African Company's records show receipt of a steady stream of silver from the West Indies, and there are a number of credible reports claiming that, in the 1680s, Jamaica exported between £100,000 and £200,000 worth of bullion each year.[203] Smaller amounts were brought from other English colonies – including those in the north which lacked a staple crop – and all combined to make a sizeable contribution to mint output which averaged £447,000 a year in the 1680s and helped balance trade with the Baltic and the East.[204] Plentiful supplies of bullion meant that silver could be obtained for 5.25 shillings an ounce in London in the 1680s, and the East India Company could furnish its large needs at home until 1695 when wartime disruption to trade, and heavy government remittances, caused prices to soar and drove the company to make purchases in Amsterdam.[205] Despite the disappointment of failing to find reserves of precious metals in their own New World settlements, the English were able to exploit territorial bases to secure cheaper, more regular supplies direct from America and, above all, Jamaica. The island earned its reputation as the nation's 'silver mine' and assumed central importance in the imperial vision of the commercial and political elite.[206]

The impact of the colonial import trade

The appropriation and improvement of new lands in America enhanced both England's supply base and also its adaptive efficiency. Even at the end

[203] Inchiquin to Committee of Trade, 12 August 1691, PRO CO 138/7, fo. 19. In 1700 Beeston claimed that bullion exports were worth £150,000 a year: 'An estimate of what is shipped every year from Jamaica to England', BLO, MS Locke c30, fo. 129. Merchants' letters and inventories make frequent reference to bullion exports. For example, the inventory of a Jewish merchant, Joseph de Costa Alveringa, of Kingston, mentions silver consignments to his son in London amounting to £970 in 1699–1700: JA, Inv 1B/11/3, vol. V, fo. 55. John Newton's inventory of 1702 indicates trade with Jamaica and lists 400 pieces of eight from Jamaica valued at £91 lbs 6d: CLRO, Orphans' Court Inventories, no. 2,501. Estimates of annual import into Europe from the Americas vary. Inikori gives a figure of £3,355,925 per annum in the period 1676–1700: Inikori, *Africa and the Industrial Revolution*, p. 487.

[204] Claypoole reported receiving barrels of silver from New England: Balderston (ed.), *Claypoole's Letterbook*, pp. 162, 164; Ive to Usher, MHS, Jeffries Family Papers, vol. III, fo. 109.

[205] PRO T 70/81, fo. 6b. Exports to the east were valued at £1,091,613 in 1680–2 and £320,779 from 1686–8: Chaudhuri, *Trading World of Asia*, pp. 153–90; Jones, *War and Economy*.

[206] Hanson's account, *The Laws of Jamaica* (1683); 'Jamaica', CUL CH (H) Papers 80/74, fo. 6.

of the seventeenth century the 'ghost' acreage provided by extensive growth in the New World was small.[207] In any case, following a period of population stability, the country was able to supply itself with grain, and even had a small amount for export. However, by 1700 colonial imports had become firmly established in English diets and had changed consumption patterns in ways that, more than proportionate to their value, relieved pressure on domestic resources. The use of tobacco assuaged hunger and tiredness and diverted demand from other foodstuffs. The use of sugar promoted more intensive use of domestic resources by preserving fruit, vegetables, and meat and also allowed hot beverages to be substituted for beer. The new habits became increasingly important as population resumed its rise, and broke through its medieval peak, in the eighteenth century.

By 1700 America was also providing a 'domestic' supply of industrial raw materials: cotton, dye-stuffs, furs, hardwoods, ships' masts, and other products with a high value to weight.[208] The colonies also furnished growing numbers of merchant ships. As yet high transport costs precluded drawing on American supplies of bulky, low-value goods such as sawn timber or iron, but the growing surplus of more exotic colonial commodities was re-exported to pay for these essential imports from Europe, as well as a range of foreign luxuries such as calicoes, linens, silks, spices, and wines, which were needed to satisfy the 'spendthrift' humour which had taken hold of Englishmen and which contemporaries appreciated was unlikely to be reformed.[209] With active encouragement from the state, which refunded duties on re-exports, London emerged as a major European entrepot to rival Amsterdam, with sugar and tobacco re-exports valued at around £531,000 in 1700, and accounting for a third of London's re-exports to Europe, and almost 12 per cent of London's total commodity exports. Where there remained a deficit in the balance of trade, it was settled in bullion, and here also, colonial settlement allowed England to improve its supply.

As early as 1700 England's New World resources were providing strategic relief to the pressures imposed by a finite supply of land at home. However, colonial settlement not only provided room for extensive growth but also encouraged entrepreneurs to invest in improving skills, techniques, and commercial infrastructure in ways which stimulated intensive growth, or gains in efficiency. Although part of the large gap between the plantation value of imports and their retail value can

[207] For recent discussion of the contribution of American 'ghost' acres to English economic development see Pomeranz, *Great Divergence*, ch. 6; E. A. Wrigley, 'The transition to an advanced organic economy: half a millennium of English agriculture', *EcHR*, 59 (2006), 435–80.
[208] Wrigley remarks that 'it is easy to overlook the fact that output of animal and vegetable products set limits to the expansion of manufacturing industry as firmly as it constrained population growth': Wrigley, 'Transition to an advanced organic economy', 459.
[209] Davenant discussed luxury consumption:

be attributed to high taxation (especially on tobacco) there were clearly opportunities for very substantial earnings in the transport, processing, and distribution of colonial commodities. The 'affluence of money' arising from colonial commerce might well have encouraged the 'lazy temper' which Davenant discerned in Spain but, in fact, in the competitive conditions which prevailed in Restoration England, the City's commercial community had a strong incentive to pursue efficiency gains, and did respond positively to the opportunities provided by colonial expansion.

During the late seventeenth century London's merchants extended port and warehouse facilities to cope with growing imports of bulky colonial commodities and the burgeoning re-export trade, while also developing increasingly sophisticated sorting and marketing skills. The heavy concentration of the trade in London reinforced its role as key point of entry for foreign imports and strengthened its pivotal role in the nation's distribution system. Willan shows that, between 1628 and 1685, the volume of London's outward bound coastal trade trebled, and matched the growth rate of colonial commerce, but far outstripped that of the city's population, or its total overseas commerce.[210] A survey of the London portbooks of 1686 suggests that colonial groceries figured prominently in the coastal trade with 70 per cent of outward cargoes containing tobacco, 59 per cent containing grocery ware (including sugar), and 11 per cent containing confectionery.[211] Better coastal shipping facilities were accompanied by improvements in inland waterways, with England possessing around 685 miles of navigable rivers in 1660, and around 960 by 1700.[212] The road network also underwent major extension and improvement with increased numbers of regular carrying services available from the capital.[213] A virtuous circle was established: investment and improvement in transport out of London did, of course, also reduce the costs of bringing goods into the metropolis and better access to the large market encouraged increased specialization in the provincial economy.[214]

> Kingdoms grown rich by traffic will unavoidably enter into a plentiful way of living; but so long as this is universal ... When the inferior rank of men have their share of plenty as well as the better sort; when tillage, labour and manufactures go on well ... In such a nation some excess of luxury is rather the sign and effect of future poverty ... To banish luxury by a long series of steady government and wisdom is certainly the most advisable; but if the people is not to be reformed, and if this spendthrift humour is not to be cured, care must be taken to entail on the prodigal a vast estate, and to get him such wealth as may weary out and baffle his vanities. (Davenant, *Discourses on the Public Revenues*, p. 390)

[210] Willan, *Inland Trade*, p. 101.

[211] London portbook, coastal outwards, 1686, PRO E 190/137/5.

[212] T. S. Willan, *River Navigation in England, 1600–1750* (London, 1936), p. 133.

[213] T. de Laune, *The Present State of London* (London, 1681); Dorian Gerhold, 'The growth of the London carrying trade, 1681–1838', *EcHR*, 41 (1988), 392–410.

[214] E. A. Wrigley, 'A simple model of London's importance in changing English society and economy, 1650–1750', *Past and Present*, 37 (1967), 44–70. Van Zanden, after reviewing

Improvements in the national transport network reduced transaction costs beyond those of carriage. Faster and more regular postal services, together with the rise of a commercial press, improved the quality, reliability, and speed of the circulation of information. Better information, in turn, encouraged the spread of practices such as buying by sample, and advance contracts, which further lowered transaction costs and smoothed risk; it accelerated the diffusion of news about product innovations and changes in fashion which stimulated changes in consumption patterns; and it assisted the spread of information about process innovations and technical expertise beyond the capital.[215]

The lower costs of producing, marketing, and distributing colonial commodities also stimulated changes in retailing patterns which further encouraged consumption. Tobacco, sugar, and other imported goods could be purchased from travelling salesmen, markets, and fairs, as well as by mail order as shown in advertisements placed in Houghton's *Collection*.[216] However, given the durability of the goods, and the preference among consumers for buying very small quantities on a regular basis, they were also attractive stock items in permanent shops. Stout, the Lancaster grocer, who sold goods to the value of £600 in his first year of trade, reported that tobacco accounted for one-quarter of his sales and 'that the most profitable part' and Shammas has suggested a strong causal link between the consumption of new groceries and the rise of shops which, in turn, encouraged a further shift away from subsistence production to an increasingly commercialized economy.[217]

The growing taste for imported goods which could not be produced in the home increased the perceived need for cash. In the 1690s, a Northumberland gentleman, such as Sir Thomas Haggerston, continued to substantially self-provision his household – producing all the bread,

data from a large number of European countries, both over the whole early modern period and cross sectionally in about 1800 has recently remarked that 'the breakthrough of agricultural systems with markedly higher levels of productivity must be primarily attributed to the strong growth of urban demand in the region concerned': J. L. van Zanden, 'The development of agricultural productivity in Europe, 1500–1800', in B. J. P. van Bavel and E. Thoen (eds.), *Land Productivity and Agro-Systems in the North Sea Area (Middle Ages–20th Century)*, CORN publication ser. 2 (Turnhout, 1999), pp. 357–75.

[215] 'Inventory of Frances Levett', 30 April 1705, CLRO, Orphans' Court Inventories, no. 2,817; Fisher, 'The development of London', 37–50; Lorna Weatherill, *Consumer Behaviour and Material Culture in Britain, 1660–1760* (London, 1988); Balderston (ed.), *Claypoole's Letterbook*, pp. 61–2, 66, 70.

[216] Houghton sold coffee powder at 6 shillings per pound and 5d per ounce for any quantity below a quarter pound 'whoever will send money by penny post or other wise shall be sure of fair dealing and if they send their letters in tin pots twill keep it better than paper which is apt to suck out': Houghton, *Collection*, 19 March 1694, 16 July 1697.

[217] By 1691 Stout reckoned that tobacco accounted for at least a third of what he sold and it was especially profitable if it could be bought on board, paying custom himself and getting good allowance for damage: Marshall (ed.), *Autobiography of William Stout*, pp. 96, 106, 151, 161; Shammas, *Pre-Industrial Consumer*, pp. 225–65.

beer, meat, and dairy products needed – but he spent a pound or so a year on rolled or chewing tobacco, and his wife spent around £40 a year on groceries supplied from London by a Newcastle merchant. Lower down the social scale, people also wanted cash to pay for tobacco or a sweet treat. The desire for money encouraged both a reallocation of labour away from self-provisioning towards the market, and also an intensification of work schedules – an 'industrious revolution'.[218] In short, the desire for New World groceries expanded aggregate demand and changed the way that producers behaved.

Many of the New World goods needed processing before consumption, and the tax regime encouraged this to be done in England rather than America, despite high transport costs for bulky raw materials. London entrepreneurs not only had easy access to colonial raw materials, but also capital, skills (reinforced by immigration from Europe), and cheap fuel. Sugar refining, dyeing, clay-pipe production, and other industries stimulated by plantation imports were fuel-intensive processes and London's well-organized domestic coal supply from the north-east gave it a cost advantage which helped it catch up with its Dutch rivals who faced higher fuel prices. At the Restoration London was already England's largest manufacturing centre and the surge of colonial imports encouraged investment in improved production techniques which contributed to a major strengthening and diversification of its industrial base.[219]

New lands in America provided England with abundant resources that supplemented domestic supplies as well as providing a surplus for re-export. However, as Davenant warned, additional resources might be wasted and were not alone sufficient to stimulate economic development. Trade and industry were needed to draw full benefit from the windfall gains in the late seventeenth century and London entrepreneurs responded well to the challenge. Operating in a competitive environment, and in quest of real efficiency gains, London entrepreneurs invested in the accumulation of skills, and improved techniques, that allowed the metropolis to reinforce its role as hub of an increasingly commercial economy; to emerge as a major emporium to rival Amsterdam; and to strengthen and diversify the country's industrial base. In ensuring that more and more people were able to consume more and cheaper tobacco, sugar, and other desirables, London's colonial merchants combined to enhance the nation's adaptive efficiency and strengthened the economy in ways that underpinned economic development in the eighteenth century.

[218] Jan de Vries, 'Between purchasing power and the world of goods: understanding the household economy in early modern Europe', in John Brewer and Roy Porter (eds.), *Consumption and the World of Goods* (London, 1993); Jan de Vries, 'The industrial revolution and the industrious revolution', *JEH*, 54 (1994), 249–70.

[219] Brian Dietz, 'The engine of manufacture: the trades of London', in Beier and Finlay (eds.), *London*, pp. 141–67.

6   Exports

Historians of early English expansion and the commercial revolution have neglected the colonial export trade. Attention has focused on the 'revolutionary' changes in the import, and linked, re-export trades.[1] Yet contemporaries prized the American colonies as markets for English goods and services at least as much as they valued them as sources of raw materials.[2] At a time when English cloth exports faced stagnant demand and fierce competition in Europe, exports of cloth and other commodities to the New World would prevent the country from 'negligently and steepingly' sliding into 'beggary', and maintain industrial employment. In Hakluyt's view this alone was sufficient to justify investment in overseas expansion.[3] Close examination of London's colonial commerce in the late seventeenth century suggests that American markets fulfilled Hakluyt's expectations and provided an important quantitative and qualitative stimulus to growth.

[1] Historians have followed Fisher who, while he focused attention on the drive to find new markets for woollen cloths, none the less asserted that 'in the early seventeenth century as in the nineteenth century the merchant looked upon colonies less as markets in which it might one day be possible to make substantial sales than as sources from which primary commodities might be speedily obtained for resale elsewhere': F. J. Fisher, 'London's export trade in the early seventeenth century', *EcHR*, 3 (1950), 151–61; Ralph Davis, 'English foreign trade, 1660–1700', *EcHR*, 7 (1954), 162; Robert C. Nash, 'English transatlantic trade, 1660–1730: a quantitative study', unpublished doctoral thesis, University of Cambridge, 1982; Robert C. Brenner, *Merchants and Revolution: Commercial Change, Political Conflict, and London's Overseas Traders, 1550–1653* (Cambridge, 1993), pp. 3–50; David Ormrod, *The Rise of Commercial Empires: England and the Netherlands in the Age of Mercantilism, 1650–1770* (Cambridge, 2003), pp. 39, 181.

[2] According to Shammas, the first colonial projectors had no plans for cash crop production in America and expected to make gains through supplying the colonies: Carole Shammas, 'English commercial development and American colonization, 1560–1620', in K. R. Andrews, N. P. Canny, and P. E. H. Hair (eds.), *The Westward Enterprise: English Activities in Ireland, the Atlantic, and America, 1480–1650* (Liverpool, 1978), pp. 151–74.

[3] Richard Hakluyt, 'A particular discourse concerning the great necessitie and manifold commodities that are like to grow to this realme of England by the Western discoveries lately attempted', reprinted in *Maine Historical Society Collections*, vol II (1877), p. 5; William Penn, ' The benefits of plantations and colonies', 1680, in *Select Tracts Relating to Colonies* (London, 1732); John Cary, *An Essay on the State of England in Relation to its Trade* (Bristol, 1695), pp. 47, 84, 131.

Despite the recent emphasis on 'import-led' growth in the seventeenth century, the statistics provided by Davis show that between the 1660s and the end of the century London's total exports grew at a slightly faster rate than imports and, in the case of colonial commerce, exports grew substantially faster than imports.[4] Unlike suppliers in the east, the producers of American commodities displayed a voracious demand for European goods and services and, aided by the protection offered by the Navigation Acts, a growing proportion was provided by England. It is true that the value of direct commodity exports fell short of that of imports but, apart from allegations that this was partly caused by the over-valuation of imports, both contemporaries and later historians have shown that the gap was largely filled by earnings in multilateral trades (in which English manufactures were used to pay for colonial supplies of labour, food, and drink), freight and other commercial services which were essential to the smooth operation of the plantation system.[5] A near balance of trade is reflected in the very small exports of bullion from the mother country to the colonies (Table 6.1).

In addition to weak quantitative support for the import-led explanation of growth there are other reasons for allowing at least equal weight to the export sector in driving expansion and change. First, as discussed in Chapter 3, the export sector proved to be the most profitable branch of colonial commerce and played a central role in attracting the investment needed to sustain expansion.[6] Secondly, colonial demand extended well beyond woollen cloths, and English merchants were encouraged to diversify and invest in a wide range of new export industries whose growth, as Davis acknowledged, was as fast as that of the 'revolutionary' re-export trade.[7] Thirdly, production for distant markets encouraged merchants to focus on different priorities

[4] According to Davis's figures, between 1663/9 and 1699–1701, London's total exports grew by 35 per cent and exports to the colonies by 250 per cent, whereas total imports grew by 33 per cent and imports from the colonies by 200 per cent: Davis, 'English foreign trade 1660–1700', 164–5.

[5] For discussion of the overvaluation of imports and the value of exports see 'An essay towards finding the balance of our whole trade annually from Christmas 1698 to Christmas 1719', PRO CO 390/14; S. D. Smith, 'Prices and the value of English exports in the eighteenth century: evidence from the North American colonial trade', *EcHR*, 48 (1995), 575–90.

[6] Richard Ligon, *A True and Exact History of the Island of Barbadoes* (London, 1657), pp. 109–11; Shammas, 'English commercial development', 159–60. Despite his focus on import-led growth, Brenner notes that English merchants – including prominent 'new merchants' such as Maurice Thompson – made a killing through supply of provisions: Brenner, *Merchants and Revolution*, pp. 25, 118–19.

[7] Davis reported that miscellaneous manufactures exported from London rose from £223,000 in 1663/9 to £420,000 in 1699–1701, above all serving colonial markets: Davis, 'English foreign trade', 154.

Table 6.1 *England's plantation trade, 1698–1701 (£ sterling)*

	1699	1700	1701
Exports			
Manufactures	559,055	517,538	552,841
Slaves and wine	82,512	139,886	122,254
Provisions	41,256	69,943	61,127
Bullion	1,558	4,985	7,054
Freight	122,160	163,560	139,972
Total	806,541	895,912	883,248
Imports			
Total	866,698	1,155,607	991,313

Source: PRO CO 390/14.

from those needed in smaller local markets. Economies of scale could be reaped by those who organized bulk production at low unit cost, and with minimal variance in product quality. While colonial imports did have some minor impact on English industry, the drive to supply the lucrative colonial market encouraged a substantial restructuring of industry and channelled investment, innovation, and enterprise in directions that turned out to be very important for England's long-term economic development.

White servants

A large proportion of colonial export earnings was used to pay for the labour needed to expand cash-crop production. Until the last quarter of the seventeenth century no region in British America, except New England, achieved natural increase in population and all relied on supplies from outside. Given the abundance of land, and the high returns to labour in the staple producing regions, free workers could command high wages and quickly accumulate sufficient resources to farm on their own account. As a result, planters favoured bound workers from the days of first settlement and merchants adapted the traditional English system of service-in-husbandry to suit New World needs by enabling potential emigrants to pay for their passage by effectively selling their labour for a fixed term (usually four years).[8]

---

[8] For a discussion of service in husbandry see Ann Kussmaul, *Servants in Husbandry in Early Modern England* (Cambridge, 1981). On the development of indentured servitude see Abbot E. Smith, *Colonists in Bondage: White Servitude and Convict Labour in America, 1607–1776* (Chapel Hill, N.C., 1947); David W. Galenson, *White Servitude in Colonial America: an Economic Analysis* (Cambridge, 1981); Hilary McD. Beckles, *White Servitude and Black Slavery in Barbados, 1627–1715* (Knoxville, Tenn., 1989). For discussion of the length of service in the Caribbean see BL Sl. MS 2,724, fo. 250.

In the early years of colonization conditions at home favoured the recruitment of servants. After rapid population growth in the sixteenth century, real wages were falling, and the prospects for advancement in the New World seemed enticing. However, the environment changed in the second half of the seventeenth century as the population level stabilized, unemployment fell, real wages rose, and the push to emigrate lost strength.[9] At the same time the pull of the colonies waned as there was growing awareness of the harsh treatment and high mortality experienced by servants, especially in the Caribbean: '[The servants'] bodies and souls are used as if hell commenced here and continued in the world to come.'[10] Furthermore, as wages rose, the ruling classes became increasingly hostile to what was described as a 'drain' on labour, charging the colonies with depriving the mother country of valuable workers, and pressing for steps to regulate the trade.[11]

Unfortunately the portbooks do not list servants, and other quantitative evidence about the trade is patchy, but it is apparent that, although the indenture system continued to account for the bulk of white migration to America, the number of servants transported from London declined between the 1660s and the registration period between January 1683 and March 1686 for which there are fairly detailed lists – although London ships did load additional servants in Scotland and Ireland.[12] John Wareing's

[9] E. A. Wrigley and R. S. Schofield, *The Population History of England, 1541–1871: a Reconstruction* (Cambridge, 1981), pp. 219–28.

[10] Sir Thomas Montgomery to Lords of Trade, 3 August 1688, PRO CO 29/4, fo. 6; Ligon, *History of Barbadoes*, pp. 43–4; Richard Blome, *A Description of the Island of Jamaica* (London, 1672), pp. 26–7; J. S. Handler, 'Father Antoine Biet's visit to Barbados in 1654', *JBMHS*, 32 (1967), 66; Richard S. Dunn, *Sugar and Slaves: the Rise of the Planter Class in the English West Indies, 1624–1713* (Chapel Hill, N. C., 1972), p. 88.

[11] Dalby Thomas, *An Historical Account of the Rise and Growth of the West India Colonies and the great Advantage they are to England in Respect of Trade* (London, 1690), p. 1. Josiah Child, *A New Discourse of Trade* (London, 1692), pp. 183, 185; John Wareing, 'The regulation and organisation of the trade in indentured servants for the American colonies in London, 1614–1718, and the career of William Haveland, emigration agent', unpublished doctoral thesis, University of London (2000). In 1682, forty-one merchants signed a petition complaining about the damage done to the servant trade by Crown office prosecutions and emphasizing that the labour transported was surplus to requirements, 'Petition of sundry merchants possessing estates in America', 7 November 1682, PRO CO 1/49, no. 90.

[12] For estimates of total numbers see Nicholas Canny, 'English migration into and across the Atlantic during the seventeenth and eighteenth centuries', in Nicholas Canny (ed.), *Europeans on the Move: Studies of European Migration, 1500–1800* (Oxford, 1994), pp. 39–75; Trevor Burnard, 'European migration to Jamaica, 1655–1780', *WMQ*, 53 (1996), 769–94. Davies suggests that the colonies needed to be supplied with 3,000–4,000 servants a year down to the last quarter of the seventeenth century: K. G. Davies, *The North Atlantic World in the Seventeenth Century* (London, 1974), p. 97. On registration see order of the king in council designed to regulate the transportation of white servants to the colonies, 13 December 1682, PRO CO 1/47, pp. 87–91; the

analysis of the 2,107 indentures from the registration period indicates that 55 per cent of the servants were taken to mainland America (25.3 per cent to Maryland and 23.1 per cent to Virginia) and 45 per cent to the West Indies (22 per cent to Jamaica and 18.6 per cent to Barbados).[13] About a quarter of the migrants were below twenty-one years of age, around three-quarters were male, and 95 per cent were unskilled.[14] Business letters show that, even in the 1660s, 'artificers and mechanics' were in such high demand that they could negotiate a salaried contract and white skilled tradesmen increasingly worked for wages rather than a term.[15]

Wareing's survey shows that less than 5 per cent of the 661 individuals who were bound servants in the registration period lived in the colonies. Over half the masters were mariners and they transported a similar propor-tion of the servants.[16] Ships' officers were allowed to carry servants on pay-ment of their passage and many availed themselves of the opportunity: in 1680, Charles Johnson, captain of the *Cadiz Merchant*, bound for Jamaica, shipped thirty-four servants on his own account, and the chief mate carried two.[17] Most of the remaining servants were shipped by merchants, includ-ing a number of specialist emigration agents, but only a small proportion of London's commodity merchants took part in the servant trade and most were involved in a small, irregular way. The trade was heavily concentrated, with under 6 per cent of the masters (including ships' captains, merchants, and large-scale emigration agents) binding ten servants or more, and accounting for over 40 per cent of all the servants shipped.[18]

Servants were procured in a number of ways. Some were found through family and business networks.[19] Some were tempted by advertisements

---

Lord Mayor's waiting lists cover the whole period. Most of the entries are abstracted in Michael Ghirelli, *A List of Emigrants from England to America, 1682–92* (Baltimore, Md., 1968). A second collection is held at the Greater London Records Office (Middlesex Section, as 'Plantation Indentures', MR/E); a third list of 406 names is filed among the Fishmongers Company's records in the GL, MS 6,679. All three lists are com-bined for use in John Wareing, 'The emigration of indentured servants from London, 1683–86', *Genealogical Magazine*, 19 (1978), 199–202; John Wareing 'Trade in inden-tured servants'.

[13] *Ibid.*, p. 167.
[14] *Ibid.*, pp. 154–8.
[15] J. H. Bennett, 'Cary Helyar, merchant and planter of seventeenth century Jamaica', *WMQ*, 21 (1964), 70–1. In 1678 William Freeman reported, 'If I can procure such servants as you desire will send them. I shall do my best but tradesmen are dear, I could not get one this two years to send and those I sent formerly on high wages': William Freeman to Thomas Warner, 28 September. 1678, NLJ, MS 134, fo. 35.
[16] Wareing, 'Trade in indentured servants', 143–5.
[17] 'Account book of *Cadiz Merchant*', PRO HCA 30/664, fo. 38.
[18] Wareing, 'Trade in indentured servants', 222.
[19] Bennett, 'Cary Helyar', 70–1; J. C. Jeaffreson (ed.), *A Young Squire of the Seventeenth Century from the Papers of Christopher Jeaffreson*, 2 vols. (London, 1878), vol. I, p. 186; Ghirelli, *List of Emigrants*, pp. 8, 12, 20, 41, 48, 49, 57.

in newspapers, taverns, and coffee houses.[20] Some were obtained from gaols.[21] Large consignments – such as the nineteen servants purchased by John Bawden in 1686 – were supplied by emigration agents, such as William Haveland and John Dykes, commonly known as 'spirits', who also traded in servants on their own account.[22] The emigration agents did manage to maintain supplies at a price of around 40 shillings per head in peacetime – in war they were diverted into supplying the army and navy – but often resorted to thoroughly disreputable, even illegal, practices.[23] Most agents were located near the port, or in the eastern riverside parishes, and the big operators, such as Haveland (who bound eighty servants on his own account in the twenty months from January 1683 to December 1684) employed gangs of crimps to roam the streets and taverns looking out for newly arrived countryfolk, the unemployed, homeless, and anyone down on their luck.[24] A mixture of golden promises, drink, and violence was used to 'spirit' the naïve or desperate into agreeing to service for themselves, or their children, after which they were taken to a secure place.[25] Those who repented their decision usually found that they had no escape and that they had been effectively kidnapped.[26] Others were straightforwardly duped or violently seized. In

---

[20] By 1657 sheets such as *The Publick Advertiser* and *The Weekly Information from The Office of Intelligence* contained advertisements from both potential employers and employees: BL Thomason Tracts, E 919, nos. 2, 3, 4. Others followed and, in the 1690s, Houghton's *Collection* performed a similar role.

[21] In 1664 Sir James Modyford obtained the privilege of sending all pardoned felons to his brother in Jamaica for the next five years 'for better improving of the island': PRO SP 44/14, fo. 46. On the drawn-out efforts to obtain 300 malefactors for the Leewards in St Christophers see *CSPC, 1677–80*, nos. 280, 404; *ibid., 1681–85*, nos. 716, 717, 800, 1,668, 1,723, 1,729; Jeaffreson (ed.), *Young Squire*, pp. 142–7. The most famous group of prisoners were the 850 Monmouth rebels ordered to be transported to Barbados and Jamaica in 1685: Peter Earle, *Monmouth's Rebels: the Road to Sedgemoor, 1685* (London, 1977), pp. 178–82.

[22] PRO KB 9/10, 21, 37, 39. 'Affidavits against William Haveland generally called him a spirit', January 1671, PRO CO 389/2.

[23] 'You advis for servants to bee sent giving an account of the incuridgement that is given for their payment, but they are neither to bee procured in England nor Ireland at this time, the army entertaining all these kind of loose fellows': William Freeman to Robert Helmes, in David Hancock (ed.), *The Letters of William Freeman, London Merchant, 1678– 1685* (London, 2002), pp. 11, 17.

[24] Edward Barlow describes an encounter with a man he guessed was a 'spirit' or kidnapper and his inveigling methods: Basil Lubbock (ed.), *Barlow's Journal of his Life at Sea in King's Ships, East and West Indiamen and Other Merchantmen from 1659 to 1703* (London, 1934), pp. 26–8.

[25] Details of the trade in children are revealed in a case concerning Thomas Platt, a joiner in Wapping, who bound his son to Robert Llewellin, a broker for servants in crafts, for service in Barbados on promise of payment of £10 per year to himself. Llewellin claimed, falsely, that Platt had died and did not make the promised payments: CLRO, MC Interrogatories, March 1657, MC 6/92.

[26] 'Affidavits against spirits', PRO CO 389/2.

244 The Capital and the Colonies

the aftermath of Monmouth's rebellion, Daniel Manning moved from Devon to London in search of work. The stranger fell into the company of 'one John Peirson living on Tower Hill who pretended to help him to an employment – telling him he should go four mile over the river to serve a gentleman'. After grateful acceptance of the offer, the illiterate Manning put a cross on an indenture that he was unable to read. He embarked on a vessel in the Thames and it is easy to imagine his horror when weeks later he was taken ashore in Barbados.[27]

Haveland, who operated as a spirit from the 1660s until his death in 1710, was brought to court on thirty-eight occasions on kidnapping or assault charges and, when found guilty, was subjected to fines, pillory, and imprisonment. Prosecution, conviction, and public disgrace were clearly inevitable hazards in the trade but, as long as he found customers willing to pay 40 shillings per head, Haveland (who paid his suppliers around 25 shillings) was left with a tidy profit and chose to remain in business.[28]

Meanwhile, interest among commodity merchants was limited and intermittent: Wareing found that less than 5 per cent of the merchants consigning goods to the colonies in 1684 were also listed in the servant registration documents. After paying an agent around £2 for a servant, the charge for a passage to the colonies stood still throughout the Restoration period at around £5 per head. However, the colonial end of the servant trade was increasingly speculative and the prices fetched often fell far short of expectations, especially in the Caribbean where slaves were becoming cheaper and increasingly preferred.[29] In 1686 the diarist, John Taylor, paid the Newgate gaoler £2 for each of three convicts (one man and two women) for service in Jamaica. On arrival in the island, he obtained a good price of £12 for the man, but the women fetched only around £8 which barely covered transport and other expenses. However, although he claimed that his final profit of £3.75 sterling 'was not so considerable profit as he had expected' it was not a bad return on his original outlay of £6.[30] Until the difficulties of wartime in the 1690s, the London servant trade probably provided America with an annual supply of between one and two thousand workers which must have grossed between £10,000 and £24,000 per year, and there

---

27 'Examination of Daniel Manning', 1686, PRO CO 1/59, fo. 75; Stede to Lords of Trade, 3 February 1686, *ibid.*, fo. 82.
28 Wareing, 'Trade in indentured servants', 195–212; PRO KB 9/10, 21, 37, 39; Jeaffreson (ed.), *Young Squire*, vol. I, pp. 318–19.
29 Galenson, *White Servitude*; Hilary McD. Beckles and A. Downes, 'The economics of transition to the black labour system in Barbados, 1630–1680', *JIH*, 18 (1987), 225–47.
30 'Taylor's history of his life and travels in America', 1688, NLJ, MS 105, fos. 137, 180–1.

was plainly still money to be made in trading men. Although the servant trade was increasingly marginalized, labour was needed in the colonies, and the individual liberty of the voiceless 'loose vagrant people, vicious and destitute of means to live at home' who were tempted and traduced into service was widely seen as a price worth paying to ensure the prosperity of the plantations.[31]

Slave labour

London's trade in white servants was, after the Restoration, increasingly overshadowed by the slave trade which by the 1680s probably absorbed around six to eight times as much colonial purchasing power.[32] English colonists employed black slaves from the first years of settlement in America, but numbers were low until the 1640s, and when sugar was first introduced into Barbados the planters used black and white labour for unskilled work in the fields.[33] The heady profits earned in the early years of sugar production created a huge demand for labour that coincided with increased difficulties in obtaining white servants during the Civil War, and improvements in the supply of slaves (especially by the Dutch) that encouraged a shift towards black labour.[34] By the 1660s an adult male slave who worked for life could be purchased for £20, whereas a white servant bound for four years cost around £12; it is unsurprising that, where returns to labour were high, more and more work was done by slaves, and white labour was increasingly reserved for skilled jobs and supervision.[35] As the governor of Barbados observed in 1680, 'since people have found out the convenience and cheapness of slave

[31] In 1682, interested merchants argued that 'the generality of volunteers for transportation are the scum of the world, brought to volunteer by their own prodigality; if they do not go to the colonies they will probably go to Tyburn': 'Petition of sundry merchants possessing estates in America', 3 November 1682, PRO CO 1/49, no. 90; Child, *New Discourse*, pp. 183, 185.

[32] In the 1680s colonists are estimated to have purchased one to two thousand servants a year at £10–£12 per head and an average of 4,500 slaves a year at around £18 each.

[33] Russell R. Menard, *Sweet Negotiations: Sugar, Slavery, and Plantation Agriculture in Early Barbados* (Charlottesville, Va., 2006), pp. 31–5; Philip D. Curtin, *The Atlantic Slave Trade: a Census* (Madison, Wis., 1969) pp. 52–60; Beckles, *White Servitude and Black Slavery*.

[34] Sugar production is very labour intensive. It is usually reckoned that it required at least one man per acre: Ward Barrett, 'Caribbean sugar-production standards in the seventeenth and eighteenth centuries', in John Parker (ed.), *Merchants and scholars: Essays in the History of Exploration and Trade* (Minneapolis, 1965), p. 165. On the Dutch in the slave trade see Johannes M. Postma, *The Dutch in the Atlantic Slave Trade, 1600–1815* (Cambridge, 1990); Menard, *Sweet Negotiations*, pp. 40–6.

[35] David W. Galenson, 'White servitude and the growth of black slavery in colonial America', *JEH*, 41(1981), 39–49; Beckles and Downes, 'The economics of transition to the black labour system'.

labour they no longer keep white men who used to do all the work on the plantations'.[36] The white population of the English Caribbean declined from 44,000 in 1660 to 33,000 in 1700, whereas the black population climbed from 15,000 in 1660, to 115,000 in 1700 and as almost all blacks were enslaved this allowed seven slaves for two whites (Table 2.1).

In North America, where the returns to labour were lower than in the Caribbean, the shift towards slave labour was later and less extreme. According to figures provided by McCusker and Menard, the white population numbered almost 250,000 in 1700 and it owned only around 21,000 slaves (Table 2.1). However, the aggregate figures hide sharp regional differentials. Even in the last quarter of the seventeenth century there were very few slaves in New England or the middle colonies, but large Chesapeake planters had become dependent on slave workers, although the lesser planters continued to rely heavily on servants. In the 1660s less than a fifth of the region's bound labourers were slaves and, by the early eighteenth century, the proportion was two-thirds.[37] Meanwhile, the planters who began to establish rice cultivation in the lower south in the 1690s depended on slave labour from the start.

English merchants had been drawn into the African trade since the reign of Elizabeth but their efforts had been heavily overshadowed, first by the Portuguese, and then the Dutch.[38] However, with the end of the Civil War, and rising demand for slaves in Barbados, the Dutch were alarmed to see English merchants making serious encroachments on the trade.[39] According to a Dutch governor on the Gold Coast there were nineteen English ships buying slaves in El Mina between February 1645 and 1647 and, according to Gragg's use of Dutch sources, there were at least eighty-four English ships trading for slaves between 1652 and 1657.[40] The Dutch responded with the violent tactics that had served

---

[36] Atkins to Lords of Trade, 26 October 1680, PRO CO 29/3, pp. 92–3; Dunn, *Sugar and Slaves*, pp. 96–8.

[37] Russell R. Menard, 'From servants to slaves: the transformation of the Chesapeake labour system', *Southern Studies*, 16 (1977), 355–90; John J. McCusker and Russell R. Menard, *The Economy of British America, 1607–1789* (Chapel Hill, N.C., 1985); Anthony S. Parent, *Foul Means: the Formation of a Slave Society in Virginia, 1660–1740* (Chapel Hill, N.C., 2003).

[38] P. E. H. Hair and Robin Law, 'The English in Western Africa in 1700', in Nicholas Canny (ed.), *The Oxford History of the British Empire*, 5 vols. (Oxford, 1998), vol. I, pp. 244–54.

[39] The trade was mainly conducted by illegal traders operating in breach of the Guinea Company's monopoly: Hair and Law, 'English in West Africa', p. 255; John C. Appleby, 'A Guinea venture, c. 1657: a note on the early English slave trade', *Mariner's Mirror*, 79 (1993), 84–7; John C. Appleby, ' "A business of much difficulty": a London slaving venture, 1651–54', *Mariner's Mirror*, 81 (1995), 3–14.

[40] Larry Gragg, ' "To procure Negroes": the English slave trade in Barbados, 1627–60', *Slavery and Abolition*, 16 (1995), 65–84.

them well in the Spice Islands, and tension mounted between the two nations.[41] In 1656 a group of London merchants (including William and Maurice Thompson, John Jeffreys, the major tobacco importer, and his partner, Thomas Colclough) despatched four ships to load slaves in Guinea; these were seized by the Dutch, costing the partnership, on its own reckoning, over £50,000. An appeal for diplomatic assistance from the newly formed Council of Trade in 1661 (of which Jeffreys was a member), and the hopelessness of trying to obtain compensation through the Dutch courts, highlighted the real attractions of joint-stock enterprise with strong state backing.[42]

In 1660 a group of courtiers led by James, Duke of York (always alert to the possibilities of profit in the Atlantic), and a handful of merchants, including Jeffreys, established a new London-based Company of Royal Adventurers into Africa which was given Crown chartered monopoly trading rights on the west coast of the continent. The rights were extended after negotiations with other commercial interest groups, and incorporated in a new Crown charter in 1663, with the Duke of York as governor.[43] In 1662 the company undertook to supply 3,000 slaves a year to the West Indies at prices below £25 per head and it made an ambitious start, claiming to have established eighteen factories in Africa, and to have despatched over forty ships to trade there in the first year of operation. It also created a network of agents in the Caribbean, and took steps to gain entry to the valuable, and highly coveted, Spanish imperial market.[44] Once again, there were violent clashes with the Dutch, leading to war in 1665, and the company was ruined.[45]

After the war an enfeebled company licensed private traders and, in 1669, leased part of the trade to a separate group of Gambia Adventurers. After the Treaty of Madrid promised peace and friendship between Spain and England in the Indies, and renewed hopes of being able to sell slaves in Spanish markets, the first company was liquidated in 1672 and replaced by a new London-based Royal African Company with combined court and City support and a chartered monopoly.[46] The Dutch

---

[41] Postma, *The Dutch in the Atlantic Slave Trade*; Hair and Law, 'English in West Africa', pp. 241–63.

[42] PRO CO 388/1, fos. 389, 48, 18.

[43] G. F. Zook, *The Company of Royal Adventurers Trading to Africa* (Lancaster, Penn., 1919).

[44] The Spaniards were reputed to pay two or three times the price paid in the English islands. Thomas to James Modyford, 30 March 1663, PRO CO 1/17, fos. 28–9; 'Minute Book of the Royal Adventurers', 20 June 1663, PRO T 70/75, fo. 11; Nuala Zahedieh, 'The merchants of Port Royal, Jamaica, and Spanish contraband trade, 1655–1692', *WMQ*, 43 (1986), 570–93.

[45] K. G. Davies, *The Royal African Company* (London, 1957), pp. 42–3.

[46] *Ibid.*

were embroiled in war with France until 1678 and so the new company benefited from a more auspicious environment than its predecessor and, despite planter complaints about short supplies, it delivered numbers well in excess of those projected in the 1660s. The English took their place as Europe's leading slave traders, a position they maintained until the abolition of the trade in 1807.

Slaves were obtained in Africa (alongside gold, ivory, and dyewoods) in exchange for manufactured goods and, in the 1670s and 1680s, Davies reckoned that the company shipped cargoes with a mean annual value of £52,360 (Table 6.2).[47] The goods were more diverse than those exported to Europe: woollen cloths accounted for around a quarter of the value, and the remainder consisted of other textiles and miscellaneous manufactures. In the days of the first company around two-thirds of the goods were produced abroad and re-exports of Swedish copper, Baltic voyage iron, Italian beads, and Indian textiles continued to be important. However, partly owing to deliberate import substitution policies, an increasing proportion of the goods despatched to Africa were produced in England and, by the early eighteenth century, they accounted for two-thirds of the total – a substantial addition to the demand created by direct colonial purchases of English manufactures. The trade was a mercantilist's ideal: it provided labour for the plantations, without draining the mother country's population, and provided profitable manufacturing employment at home.

According to Davies, around half the manufactured goods were exchanged for slaves, and the company delivered 55,526 blacks to the West Indies between 1673 and 1688.[48] However, this annual average of 3,470 slaves fell far short of the company's undertaking to supply 5,600 a year and as around a third were re-exported to the buoyant markets in Spanish America, it left tempting opportunities for private traders to profit from unfulfilled demand.[49] Hired ships took freight earnings in slaves; captains were given an allowance on their own account; a number of vessels traded outside the company's monopoly area at places such as Madagascar; privateers brought in prize slaves.[50] Above all in importance was a sizeable illicit commerce.

[47] According to Davies, the company imported gold to provide 354,661 guineas between 1673 and 1688, an annual average of 22,166: Davies, *African Company*, p. 360.

[48] Davies, *African Company*, p. 363. Inikori raised Davies's figures for slave deliveries to 73,863 for 1672–90 and 19,299 for 1691–1700 making a total of 93,162 for the whole period between 1672 and 1700: Joseph E. Inikori, *Africans and the Industrial Revolution in England: a Study in International Trade and Development* (Cambridge, 2002), p. 223.

[49] In the 1680s around half the slaves delivered to Jamaica were re-exported to Spanish colonial markets, and a number were transhipped from Barbados: Zahedieh, 'Merchants of Port Royal', 570–93.

[50] Davies, *African Company*, pp. 109–10. Company to Agents at Antigua, 23 August 1687, PRO T 70/57, fo. 9b. For example, the *Daniel and Thomas*, part owned by the merchant

Table 6.2 Royal African Company exports to Africa, 1674–88 (£ sterling)

	1674	1675	1680	1681	1682	1683	1684	1685	1688
Metal and metalwares	7,322	9,380	12,653	13,774	12,482	9,731	7,337	15,928	7,942
British woollens	10,845	9,985	7,971	22,357	18,475	14,530	12,084	9,744	13,713
East India textiles	7,476	8,817	4,394	9,626	17,917	13,683	7,545	9,291	11,105
Misc. textiles	8,622	4,415	4,939	9,732	10,321	12,744	8,594	11,036	9,100
Gunpowder, firearms, knives	1,498	883	4,285	2,770	4,037	3,692	4,051	6,109	3,185
Miscellaneous	1,460	1,277	1,681	6,680	9,693	11,024	6,096	12,658	4,537
Total	37,223	34,757	35,923	64,939	72,925	65,404	45,707	64,766	49,582

Source: Davies, African Company, pp. 351–7.

The risks of breaching the company's monopoly were low. The privileges were based on a Crown charter, which was widely held to be illegal, and was difficult to enforce in the colonies where the governors were usually aligned with local planters and where naval support was weak.[51] Planter views were well represented in Governor Lynch's self-serving arguments that any attempt to starve Jamaica of labour merely deprived the Crown of the customs revenues arising from colonial production. '[Interlopers] may choke the charter or hurt the Royal Company, but not the king's customs or nation's trade, for every negro's labour that produces cotton, sugar, or indigo is worth £20 per annum to the customs.' Furthermore, claimed Lynch, he did not have the resources necessary to hinder illegal importation into the large island with its long, indented coastline and, if slaves were seized, it was almost impossible to secure a conviction in a colonial court, for 'slaves are as needful to a plantation as money to a courtier and as much courted'.[52]

A number of interloping ships were fitted out in both the northern and island colonies for bilateral trade with Africa, where they exchanged rum and other American commodities for slaves. However, the scale of their activity was limited by the difficulties in obtaining appropriate cargoes. Most interlopers took the greater risk of sailing out of European ports, like the New York-owned *Margaret* which took in a cargo at Amsterdam.[53] The 'loose traders' that sailed out of London loaded cargoes similar to those of the African Company, and usually recorded departures for the Canaries, Cadiz, the Straits, or the West Indies.[54] In fact, they sailed for Africa and stood some miles off the coast, where they were supplied with slaves by small boats, without needing to enter the company's forts.[55] Contemporary comments suggest that they increased the supply of slaves by at least a half and perhaps more and, with low risks, and low overhead costs, the private traders could undersell the company and

---

and planter, Rainsford Waterhouse, traded at Madagascar: *James Neale et al* v. *Rainsford Waterhouse*, 20 September 1689, PRO HCA 13/132. Richard Browne captured a Dutch slave ship in 1674, and sold the cargo in Jamaica: BL Egerton MS 2,395, fo. 571.

[51] 'Memo upon Petition of the Royal African Company of illegal importing of negroes from Statia to Nevis', 18 July 1684, PRO CO 153/3, fo. 270; Letter from Council to Johnson, 30 July, *ibid.*, fo. 271; *Considerations Concerning the African Companies Petition* London, 1698).

[52] Lynch to Lords of Trade, 29 August 1682, PRO, CO 138/4, fo. 91.

[53] 'Deposition of William Baker', 8 June 1686, CLRO, MCD, box 40.

[54] 'Petition of Royal African Company', 1676, PRO CO 268/1, fo. 66. A memorial of 1691 notes departure of six interlopers; three entered for the West Indies, one for each of Cadiz, Canaries, the Straits: PRO T 70/169, fos. 88d, 89.

[55] A description of the interloping trade in Africa is provided in William Greene's answers to allegations of Alice Potts and others, 22 October 1683, PRO HCA 13/132.

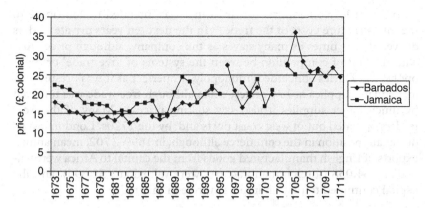

Figure 6.1 Slave prices in Barbados and Jamaica, 1673–1711.

prevent it exploiting its supposed monopoly position.[56] As a result slave prices fell in the decades of supposed monopoly and in 1686, the nominal slave price touched its lowest point in the period of England's domination of the slave trade (at £14 in Barbados), although Eltis, Lewis, and Richardson have recently argued that, in terms of the sugar price, it fell still further in the 1690s (see Figure 6.1).[57]

In 1686 the African Company decided to accept the inevitability of competition in the commerce and took steps to control it by selling licences to private traders. After the Glorious Revolution, and the downfall of James II, it retreated further.[58] The Bill of Rights did not mention monopolies based on royal grants, but they became politically impossible to enforce and the company abandoned attempts to pursue legal action against interlopers and was sued by those who had suffered earlier seizure.[59] After it had failed to obtain a parliamentary charter, an Act of 1698 ended the Royal African Company's monopoly, and opened the slave trade to all on payment of a

[56] In 1680 the planters of Jamaica petitioned for imported supplies from the company at £16 or £17 per head 'which rates the company cannot in reason find fault with' as others would supply them at £14 per head:. 'Planters of Jamaica', 29 November 1680, PRO CO 138/4, fo. 478. Between 1679 and 1682 company agents mentioned thirty-two interlopers in the West Indies. No doubt there were more. In the same period seventy Company ships arrived: Davies, *African Company*, pp. 112–4; Inikori, *Africans and the Industrial Revolution*, p. 227; David Eltis, 'The British transatlantic slave trade before 1714: annual estimates of volume and direction', in Robert L. Paquette and Stanley L. Engerman (eds.), *The Lesser Antilles in the Age of European Expansion* (Gainesville, Fla., 1996), pp. 182–205.

[57] David Eltis, Frank D. Lewis, and David Richardson, 'Slave prices, the African slave trade, and productivity in the Caribbean, 1674–1807', *EcHR*, 58 (2005), 673–700.

[58] PRO T 70/81, fos. 46b, 73, 77, 89, 89b; T 70/82, fos. 19, 25; T 70/61, fos. 69b, 70.

[59] PRO T 70/82, fos. 63, 80b, 83; T 70/83, fos. 113b, 32, 36b, 46.

10 per cent levy on exports to Africa that was intended to contribute to the infrastructure costs of the trade.[60] In the next ten years private traders delivered four times as many slaves as the company, although prices rose with the end of competition between the systems of 'free trade' or monopoly.[61] As Davies concluded, monopoly, 'imperfect as it was', resulted in inadequate supplies at low prices, while although free trade was followed by much larger supplies it also saw soaring prices.[62] Many of the free-traders operated out of west coast ports and, by the 1720s, London lost its dominant position in the commerce although, in 1699–1702, mean annual exports of English manufactured goods from the capital to Africa were valued at £64,038 (foreign manufactures were valued at £52,895), and the capital continued to play an important role in the trade.[63]

Food and beverages

Having furnished themselves with labour the colonists needed to ensure that they had adequate food and drink to sustain the workers. Again London merchants took advantage of the market opportunities.[64] By the Restoration, the mainland colonies were producing sufficient supplies to feed themselves and leave a surplus for trade.[65] However, as sugar production became established in the West Indies, the opportunity cost of using

[60] BL Add. MS 14,034, fo. 93; Tim Keirn, 'Monopoly, economic thought, and the Royal African Company', in John Brewer and Susan Staves (eds.), *Early Modern Conceptions of Property* (London, 1996), pp. 427–66; William A. Pettigrew, 'Free to enslave: politics and the escalation of Britain's Transatlantic slave trade, 1688–1714', *WMQ*, 64 (2007) 3–38.

[61] On the steep rise in slave prices between 1698 and 1700 see William Beeston to Lords of Trade, 5 January 1700, PRO CO 138/10, fos. 32–3. On 15 April 1708 a circular letter was addressed to all colonial governors requesting information about imports and prices of slaves since 1698, distinguishing the company's from the private traders. It is clear that private traders had delivered more slaves than the company but at higher prices: *CSPC, 1708–9*, nos. 94, 109, 142, 192, 197, 215.

[62] Davies, *African Company*, p. 143.

[63] *Ibid.*, pp. 122–51. Total exports to Africa averaged £116,933 in these years: PRO CUST. 3/1–6; Nick Draper, 'The City of London and slavery: evidence from the first dock companies, 1795–1800', *EcHR*, 61 (2008), 432–66.

[64] '[The colonial councillors] and that group of minor traders who got in early on the commerce … made a killing in the provisioning trade from London … The core members of what was to emerge as the colonial entrepreneurial leadership made their initial profits from the provisioning and fur trades': Brenner, *Merchants and Revolution*, p. 118; Ligon, *History of Barbadoes*, p. 110.

[65] Accounts of Robert Cole's plantation between 1662 and 1673 reveal the self-provisioning capacity of small planters in the mid-seventeenth century: Lois Green Carr, Russell R. Menard, and Lorena S. Walsh, *Robert Cole's World: Agriculture and Society in Early Maryland* (Chapel Hill, N.C., 1991), pp. 95–8; Carole Shammas, *The Pre-Industrial Consumer in England and America* (Oxford, 1990), pp. 52–75; Sarah F. McMahon, 'A comfortable subsistence: the changing composition of diet in rural New England, 1620–1840', *WMQ*, 42 (1985), 42–3.

land and labour to grow provisions rose, and there was heavy demand for outside supplies to feed the domestic population and victual ships.

Levels of dependence in the West Indies are often exaggerated.[66] Even the tiny island of Barbados, which was the most densely populated part of the English Atlantic world (with around a third of an acre per head compared with Petty's estimated six acres in England), continued to produce cassava, maize, plantains, potatoes, tobacco, yams, and various fruits and vegetables, alongside local supplies of meat, fish, and turtle.[67] None the less, even in the good years there was a serious shortfall in internal food production and heavy reliance on imports.

Slave provisions were purchased from mainland America and the Atlantic fisheries, but white West Indians relied on Europe for a range of foodstuffs, including beef, pork, olive oil, butter, and cheese.[68] Richard Ligon advised merchants to allow around a quarter of any funds invested in an export adventure to Barbados to be used to purchase goods 'for the belly'.[69] However, the trade statistics reveal that very small quantities were despatched direct from the capital: food exports for 1663/9 were valued at an average of £973 (less than 1 per cent of total export value) and, in 1686, they amounted to £8,496 (4 per cent), largely destined for the Caribbean.[70] The London portbooks of the 1680s combine with the Naval Officers' returns to show that each

[66] Bean concluded after examining the Naval Officers' returns that 'in the earlier years, 1680–1816, it is clear that more food was produced in Jamaica and Barbados than was imported': Richard N. Bean, 'Food imports into the British West Indies: 1680–1845', in Vera Rubin and Arthur Tuden (eds.), *Comparative Perspectives of Slavery in New World Plantation Societies* (New York, 1977), pp. 581–96. By 1672 Whaley had 50 acres planted in Jamaica with 30 acres in canes and 20 acres in provisions including plantains, yams, red beans, bonivie, and cassava: William Whaley to William Helyar, 20 June 1672, SRO, Walker Heneage MSS DD WHh, Addenda papers 12.

[67] Barbados is 21 miles long and 14 miles wide, making 166 square miles (106,240 acres). On Petty's calculations of population densities see Adam Fox, 'Sir William Petty, Ireland and the making of a political economist, 1653–87', *EcHR*, 62 (2009), 388–404. On provisions see Ligon, *History of Barbadoes*, pp. 19–39', 79–84, 99–100; Alexander Gunkel and Jerome S. Handler, 'A Swiss Medical Doctor's Description of Barbados in 1661: the account of Felix Christian Spoeri', *JBMHS*, 33 (1969), 8–10. On potatoes and other provisions see BLO, MS Rawl. A 348, fos. 4–5; Taylor provided a detailed description of provision production in Jamaica in the late 1680s: 'Taylor's history of his life and travels in America', 1688, NLJ, MS 105; Nuala Zahedieh, 'The wickedest city in the world: Port Royal, commercial hub of the seventeenth century Caribbean', in Verene Sheperd (ed.), *Working Out Slavery, Pricing Freedom: Essays in Honour of Barry W. Higman* (Kingston, Jamaica, and Oxford, 2002), pp. 3–20.

[68] Eltis shows that, in 1688–99, over 43 per cent of the value of Barbados's sugar products were exported to North America: David Eltis, 'New estimates of exports from Barbados and Jamaica, 1655–1701', *WMQ*, 52 (1995), 644.

[69] Ligon, *History of Barbadoes*, p. 110.

[70] In 1686 provisions made up 6.6 per cent of total value of exports to the West Indies and 1 per cent of those to North America: BL Add. MS 36,785; portbook database, 1686. The provisioning trade did have an impact on provincial producers as shown in discussion between Thomas Wright of Yorkshire and Charles Marescoe about the wholesale

year a dozen or so ships left London almost empty and loaded provisions in Ireland which exported them to the annual value of about £45,000 in the mid-1680s, and provided over half the food imports into the English West Indies (exceeding those from North America until the 1690s).[71] Nash has calculated that, in 1686–8, around 25 per cent of the Irish provision trade to Jamaica was in London ships and, in 1698–9, around 36 per cent of the same trade to Barbados.[72] The trade was well organized. In the late 1670s, William Freeman engaged in extended negotiations with a number of competing Galway and Waterford merchants who supplied pickled beef. In 1678 he tried to reduce his risks by agreeing to advance contracts for 1,200 barrels of beef at 19 shillings per barrel (after a 5 per cent discount for immediate payment), and settlement was made by bills of exchange on Dublin. 'We thought fit to contract in regard three former years we have paid very dear and by what we understand is likely to be dearer this year than formerly.'[73]

Profits were precarious and it was important to time arrivals with care as the small West Indian markets were easily glutted. In 1688 the Halls of Jamaica reported that, with the arrival of one small ship, the price of beef had halved overnight from a scarcity level of 40 shillings, to 20 shillings, which was scarcely above the Irish wholesale price, and they viewed the trade as 'a lottery sometimes up and sometimes not worth a wish'.[74] The stakes rose in wartime as French privateers intercepted large numbers of supply ships and Caribbean markets were often starved of provisions. Prices rose sky high and those who managed a successful voyage could make a killing.[75] The situation was exacerbated by a few 'moneyed men' in the ports who possessed sufficient capital to 'engross' supplies and further force up prices.[76] In 1696 the governor of Barbados reported that, with shortages and profiteering, the price of imported food had trebled during the war with salt beef rising from its modal peacetime

butter price in May 1668: Henry Roseveare (ed.), *Markets and Merchandise of the Late Seventeenth Century: the Marescoe–David letters, 1668–1680* (Oxford, 1987), p. 229.

[71] Naval Officers' returns, Jamaica, PRO CO 142/13; portbook database, 1686; 'Figures for Irish exports to the English plantations in America', 24 December 1682–25 December 1686, BL Add. MS 4,759.

[72] R. C. Nash, 'Irish Atlantic trade in the seventeenth and eighteenth centuries', *WMQ*, 42 (1985), 329–56. Also see Thomas M. Truxes, *Irish American Trade, 1660–1783* (Cambridge, 1988), pp. 7–45.

[73] Freeman to Thomas Lynch, 24 August 1678; Freeman to Robert Helmes, September 1678; Freeman to Thomas Lynch, September 1678, 'Letterbook of William Freeman', NLJ, MS 134, fos. 22–5.

[74] Halls to John Aylward, 21 November 1688, Brailsford Papers, PRO C 110/152.

[75] Very high prices in French islands tempted many mainlanders to trade with the enemy. In 1693 the price of beef in Martinique was ten times the usual peacetime level: Kendall to Lords of Trade, 18 September 1693, *CSPC, 1693–5*, no. 568.

[76] Beeston complained that 'moneyed men' forced prices up by 50 per cent, Beeston to Lords of Trade, 7 August 1696, PRO CO 138/9, fos. 47–8.

level of 25 shillings per barrel to 75 or 80 shillings.[77] London merchants
who obtained contracts to supply the army and navy at these inflated
prices, but took none of the risks of the voyage, were able to amass great
fortunes.[78]

A West Indian planter remarked that 'drunkeness is the vice the whites
are much addicted to' and Ligon suggested that, in Barbados, the market
for alcoholic beverages was equal in value to that for food. Demand was
also strong on the mainland and, even in Puritan New England, visitors
complained about disorderly conduct associated with heavy drinking.[79]
By the mid-seventeenth century colonists were producing plentiful supplies of beer, cider, rum, and a range of other distilled spirits including whisky, mobby (from sweet potatoes), and perino (from cassava).[80]
However, all regions – above all the richer West Indies – also imported
large quantities of wine, brandy, and English spirits (such as aquavitae).
The ships that cleared London for the plantations in 1663 carried 5,619
gallons of aquavitae, valued at £1,685, and almost double that quantity in
1686.[81] Meanwhile, prominent merchants such as William Freeman were
also involved in supplying brandy which was collected illegally in France
or the French islands.[82] However, wine which, despite all efforts, could
not be produced in the English colonies was in the greatest demand and,
according to Hancock, almost all (over 80 per cent) was supplied by the
Atlantic islands – above all Madeira. They had become important stop-
ping places for ships to water and revictual on the voyage out to America
and it was common sense to also load wine, which was in high demand

[77] 'Representation of the Council and Assembly of Barbados', July 1696, *CSPC, 1696–7*, no. 125.
[78] Commissioners of Transport to Lords of Trade, 29 November 1694, *CSPC, 1693–6*, no. 1,563; 'Articles of Agreement made between Commissioners of Transportation and Christopher Lyell', 5 September 1694, *ibid.*, no. 1,287.
[79] Ligon, *History of Barbadoes*, p. 110. Labat remarked that, in Barbados, it was on account of their extreme drunkenness and the resulting dangers of accident at night that the roads were kept in a very good state of repair: Neville Connell, 'Father Labat's visit to Barbados in 1700', *JBMHS*, 20 (1957), 173; 'Instructions to Harwood', *c.* 1682, BLO, MS Rawl. A 348, fo. 7; David Hancock, 'Markets, merchants and the wider world of Boston wine, 1700–1775', in Conrad E. Wright and Katheryn P. Viens (eds.), *Entrepreneurs: the Boston Business Community, 1700–1850* (Boston, Mass., 1997), pp. 65–6.
[80] Blake wrote that he needed a servant girl to help his wife with 'washing, starching, making of drink and keeping the house in good order is no small task to undertake here': Blake to brother, 1 November 1675, in Oliver (ed.), *Caribbeana*, vol. I, pp. 55–6.
[81] According to Freeman much so-called aquavitae was, in fact, brandy: David Hancock (ed.), *The Letters of William Freeman, London Merchant, 1678–1685* (London, 2002), pp. 111, 168.
[82] Freeman provides detailed accounts of this illegal trade in which he organized the collection of brandy at Nantes for direct despatch to the Leewards: Hancock (ed.), *Letters of William Freeman*, pp. 29, 30, 32, 44, 85, 90, 103, 107, 111–13, 149, 157, 168–73, 183, 213, 214.

in their colonial destinations.[83] The Portuguese island of Madeira bene-fited, not only from a convenient location, but also a clause in the Staple Act of 1663 – not shared by the Spanish Canaries – which exempted its wine from the requirement that goods should be exported via England and allowed its wine to be taken direct to English colonial markets so as to encourage its consumption at the expense of French competitors.[84] In 1686 at least forty ships called at Madeira on their way to the plantations and loaded wines to the value of almost £20,000.[85] As with provisions, gluts of beverages were common, and prices fluctuated, but the trade was well regarded among merchants.[86] According to Freeman the beverage trade was 'the least troublesome' branch of his business and 'will turn best to account taking one time with another' and, on these grounds, he advised his agent to do all he could to retain the taverners' custom, even if it meant losses in time of plenty.[87]

[83] For a merchant on the strong preference for Madeira wine in the West Indies see Tho. Sandes to Charles Knight, 23 January 1701, 'Letterbook of John Browne and Thomas Sandes', BEA, M 7/19. Madeira wine was the premier beverage imported into colo-nial America in the late seventeenth and eighteenth centuries and accounted for 64 per cent of the wine imported into the thirteen colonies between 1700 and 1775, along-side 10 per cent from the Canaries, 7 per cent from the Azores, and 19 per cent from Europe: David Hancock, 'A revolution in the trade: wine distribution and the develop-ment of the Atlantic market economy, 1703–1807' in McCusker and Morgan (eds.), *The Early Modern Atlantic Economy*, pp. 105–53; David Hancock; 'Boston wine, 1700–1775'; David Hancock, 'Commerce and conversation in the eighteenth-century Atlantic: the invention of Madeira wine', *JIH*, 29 (1998), 197–219.

[84] In 1663, the Staple Act forbade direct trade between Europe and English colonial ports while specifically exempting the traffic from the Portuguese wine islands. There is some evidence of contraband trade from Tenerife. But while Fayal wine appears regularly in the Boston shipping records of the 1680s, references to canary wine are rare. The wine merchants could not convince the English Attorney Generals that Canaries were African not European even though they persisted in their lobbying efforts until 1737: G. F. Steckley, 'The wine trade of Tenerife in the seventeenth century', *EcHR*, 33 (1980), 335–50; Lawrence A. Harper, *The English Navigation Laws: a Seventeenth Century Experiment in Social Engineering* (New York, 1939), pp. 59–60.

[85] PRO CO 33/14; CO 142/13. Evidence in William Bolton's letterbook suggests that, in 1702–13, more than two-thirds of shipments from Madeira left for British America: 48 per cent of departures were for the West Indies, 20 per cent for British North America (all New England) and 6 per cent for other parts of America: Hancock, 'Revolution in trade', p. 111.

[86] 'Captain Dobbins, Laycock and ye *Sea Horse* arrived here … they bought about 850 pipes of wine which has fallen the price of them from £20 to £14 and £15': Halls to Brailsford, 1 February 1690, Brailsford Papers, PRO C 110/152. For a detailed insight into the business of a London wine merchant of the mid seventeenth century see George F. Steckley (ed.), *The Letters of John Paige, London Merchant, 1648–58* (London, 1984).

[87] Freeman to Robert Helmes, July 1678, 'Letterbook of William Freeman', NLJ, MS 134, fo.11. Christopher Jeaffreson made similar remarks. Wine bought in Madeira and the Canaries was 'so generally and plentifully drank' that it was 'the best commoditie', in Caribbean trade: Jeaffreson (ed.), *Young Squire*, vol. I, pp. 183, 190.

Manufactures

After satisfying the demand for labour, and provisions, and paying for freight and other commercial services, colonial consumers were left with around half their export earnings to buy a wide range of manufactured goods and, throughout the Restoration period, these commodities accounted for around 90 per cent of the value of London's direct exports to the plantations and, as in the African trade, a growing proportion of the goods was home produced. The value of domestically produced exports to the colonies almost doubled between 1663 and 1686 and, by 1700, they accounted for 71 per cent of goods shipped from London to North America, and 54 per cent of those shipped to the West Indies (Table 6.3).[88] Furthermore, a high proportion of the goods were produced in London which – with its abundance of liquid finance, commercial expertise, good supplies of fuel and raw materials, and skilled labour – was the country's dominant manufacturing centre and was well-placed to take advantage of the promising new export opportunities in protected colonial markets.[89] However, the new colonial markets had more than quantitative significance being qualitatively different from traditional export markets and encouraging the development of new industries, and changes in organization and techniques which underpinned a broadening, as well as a deepening, of England's industrial base.

Rising colonial demand for manufactured goods was driven by the even faster increase in colonial population from around 140,000 in 1660 to over 400,000 in 1700 (Table 2.1). Growth was faster on the mainland than in the islands and, by 1700, almost two-thirds of the colonial population lived in the north but the value of exports to the two regions remained broadly similar: Child was able to claim with some justice that, whereas one Englishman in the West Indies, 'with the ten blacks that work for him', made employment for four men in England, ten men in New England did not employ one man at home (Table 6.4).[90]

[88] 'An accompt of the several goods and merchandises of the growth and manufacture of England exported out of the City of London from Michaelmas 1662 to Michaelmas 1663': BL Add. MS 36,785 and PRO CUST. 2/6; Davies, *African Company*, p. 350.
[89] On the externalities of agglomeration see P. Bairoch, *Cities and Economic Development* (Chicago, 1990), pp. 39–86; H. W. Richardson, *The Economics of Urban Size* (Farnborough, 1973). On London as an industrial city see A. L. Beier, 'Engine of manufacture: the trades of London', in A. L. Beier and Roger Finlay (eds.), *London, 1500–1700: the Making of the Metropolis* (London, 1986), pp. 141–67; Peter Earle, 'The economy of London, 1660–1730', in Patrick O'Brien (ed.), *Urban Achievements in Early Modern Europe: Golden Ages in Antwerp, Amsterdam, and London* (Cambridge, 2001), pp. 81–96.
[90] Child, *New Discourse of Trade*, pp. 207–8.

Table 6.3 *Export of manufactures to English plantations, 1698–1700* (*£ sterling (%)*)

		English	Foreign	Total
1698	West Indies	130,969.5 (54)	110,646 (46)	241,615.5 (100)
	North America	226,161.5 (70)	98,075.0 (30)	324,236.5 (100)
1699	West Indies	137,551.0 (52)	129,445.5 (48)	266,996.5 (100)
	North America	222,623.5 (74)	80,154.5 (26)	302,778.0 (100)
1700	West Indies	134,735.5 (54)	114,519 (46)	249,254.5 (100)
	North America	185,189.0 (71)	75,209.0 (29)	260,398.0 (100)

Source: PRO CUST. 2/2–8.

The West Indians' heavy reliance on imported goods largely reflected the profitability of the region's staple production.[91] While agriculture, and trade, generated high profits they absorbed the bulk of capital, and entrepreneurial attention, and there was little interest in promoting manufacturing industries. There was, of course, some processing of locally abundant raw materials to produce goods in high demand. Every sugar plantation needed hundreds of earthenware pots and, where clay was available, islanders set up local production units which also turned out bricks and household crocks.[92] Locally produced cotton was spun, and woven, to make simple textiles and hammocks in the native tradition, although home officials spoke out against any expansion of this kind of activity.[93] Molasses were distilled to produce rum, although the production of white sugar was discouraged by the tax preference given to semi-processed muscovadoes. Probate inventories show that the larger towns supported the craftsmen needed to make and repair basic necessities such as houses, ships, barrels, and clothing – Thomas Tryon (one

[91] Eltis calculated that, around 1700, white per capita exports from Barbados were worth three times as much as those from Virginia: Eltis, 'New estimates', 647.

[92] 'A brief survey of Jamaica', BL Egerton MS 2,395, fo. 512. 'At the pott work' of Daniel Hicks there were listed 3,050 dripps, 2,000 pots, 1,000 refining pots and dripps, 9 stone jugs, bricks and tiles in: JA, 'Inventory of Daniel Hicks', 1688, Inv. IB/11/3, vol. III, fos. 251–2b. It was usual for large plantations in Barbados to have their own pot work: 'Indenture between Codrington and Browning', 23 March 1685, BA, Deeds, RB 3/14, fos. 460–4.

[93] 'A brief survey of Jamaica', BL Egerton MS 2,395, fo. 512. Spoeri described hammocks used in Barbados instead of beds: 'These are rough coverlets woven out of cotton and are 4 yards long and 4 yards wide. They are pulled tight at both ends like a fish net. Hammocks are suspended at both ends in a room': Gunkel and Handler, 'Account of Spoeri', p. 6. Labat described well-organized production in Barbados, Connell: 'Father Labat's visit', 163. In the 1680s Molesworth proposed to set up a cotton manufactury in Jamaica but was refused permission by the commissioners of the customs who viewed this as a breach of state policy: Molesworth to Lords of Trade, 17 January 1686, PRO CO 138/5 fo. 72; 'Report from Commissioners of Customs', May 1686, PRO CO 138/5, fo. 142.

Table 6.4 *White per capita consumption of exports from London*

Colony	White population in 1680	Value of exports of English goods from London, 1686 (£ sterling)	White per capita exports (£ sterling)
Barbados	20,000	69,359	3.47
Jamaica	c.15,000	30,974	2.06
New England	68,000	40,107	0.59
Chesapeake	55,600	35,107	0.63

Sources: Dunn, *Sugar and Slaves*, pp. 87–8; Zahedieh, 'Trade, plunder, and economic development', 212; McCusker and Menard, *Economy of British America*, pp. 103, 136.

of the fifty-nine big colonial merchants of 1686) started his career as a hat-maker in Barbados. The islands also housed a number of highly skilled craftsmen who made luxury goods such as fine furniture, silverware, and tortoiseshell goods which are now on display in the world's great museums. However, while staple production was profitable, and skilled labour was scarce, most islanders depended on imports for much of their material existence.

High per capita consumption of imports also reflected the wealth of the West Indies following the introduction of sugar – although the rise of slavery allowed whites to engross the wealth. Caribbean slaves consumed little above their subsistence needs, while white planters were reported to live 'like little princes'.[94] The handsome brick houses with glazed windows and magnificent furnishings; the opulent dress in the latest mode; the slaves in livery; the sumptuous feasting and generous entertainment seen in the islands, all drew a mixture of admiration and contempt for the vulgar display of the 'nouveau riche' (Illustration 7).[95] In fact, only the largest planters and merchants were seriously wealthy, and they were few in number. A census of 1680 shows that Barbados, the richest island, had only 175 planters with more than sixty slaves, and as John Bawden was advised, the market for luxury goods was much smaller in the other

[94] Hans Sloane described slave housing in Jamaica in the 1680s: 'small oblong huts in which they have all their moveables and goods which is generally a mat to lie on, a pot of earth to boil their victuals in ... a calabash or two for cups or spoons': Hans Sloane, *A Voyage to the Islands Madeira, Barbados, Nieves, St Christopher's and Jamaica*, 2 vols. (London 1707–1725), vol. I, p. xvii; J. S. Handler, 'Father Antoine Biet's visit to Barbados in 1664', *JBMHS*, 32 (1967), 66; on annual allowances for slaves in the 1680s see 'Instructions which I have observed in management of my plantation', c. 1682, BLO, MS Rawl. A 378, fos. 5–6.
[95] Connell, 'Father Labat's Visit', 163.

islands.[96] None the less, the 'middle and common planters', engaged in smaller-scale production, secured a very comfortable living in the Caribbean which they combined with notorious extravagance. Life was usually short in the unhealthy Caribbean and, in an effort to ensure that it was at least enjoyable, there was frantic consumption of goods: 'people are not very sparing, neither in their clothing, diet, or way of using [great quantities of goods]'.[97] Surviving probate inventories certainly provide ample evidence of comfort and convenience.[98] Shops were stocked with a vast array of merchandise, houses were well furnished with books, clocks, and tapestries, and the frequency with which expensive consumer items are listed in probate inventories suggests that the townspeople of Port Royal were much more affluent than their northern counterparts, and well-off even by London standards.[99]

Finally, the high level of manufactured goods despatched to the West Indies reflected a rising tendency for English merchants to use the islands – above all Jamaica – as bases for direct trade with Spanish America rather than using the traditional route via Cadiz.[100] It is impossible to quantify the trade as it is ignored in official records, but merchant correspondence – such as that of the Halls – provides evidence of healthy activity and, in 1679, Jamaica's Naval Officer reported that the island's sloops had done about £20,000 worth of trade with the Spaniards in the previous sixteen months and had absorbed a substantial proportion of manufactured imports.[101]

Lower per capita consumption of imported goods in the mainland colonies reflects both their greater poverty and their more serious attempts at import substitution. These efforts began early in New England, which lacked a valuable staple crop for export to England, and came later in the Chesapeake when depression in the tobacco trade encouraged a

---

[96] Dunn, *Sugar and Slaves*, pp. 87–106. Henry Blake to John Bawden, 24 July 1674, 4 November 1674, PRO HCA 15/10; Jeaffreson (ed.), *Young Squire*.

[97] Beeston to Lords of Trade, 20 May 1700, PRO CO 138/10 fo. 152.

[98] JA, Inventories, 1678–94, IB/11/3, vols. I–III; 'Taylor's history of his life and travels in America',1688, NLJ, MS 105.

[99] Nuala Zahedieh, 'London and the colonial consumer in the late seventeenth century', *EcHR*, 47 (1994), 239–61.

[100] The French consul in Cadiz estimated that foreign goods to the value of 13.4 million pesos passed through Andalucia in 1670 (11 per cent from England). Of this only 11.5 per cent remained in Spain: H. Kamen, *Spain in the Later Seventeenth Century, 1665–1700* (London, 1980), pp. 116–19. A detailed contemporary account of the organization of non-Spanish involvement in imperial trade can be seen in PRO C 24/859/100. On the importance of Spanish American trade and the advantages of Jamaica as a base see 'An essay on the nature and method of carrying on a trade to the South Sea', BL Add. MS 28,140, fos. 20–8.

[101] Brailsford Papers, PRO C 110/152; 'An account of what passengers, servants and slaves have been brought into this island with account of what goods have been exported from 25 June 1671 to 25 March 1679 being 7 years 9 months': PRO CO 1/43, fo. 59.

diversification that gathered strength during the wartime interruptions to trade in the 1690s.[102] As Sir Thomas Lawrence warned 'if store of shipping comes in the people will mind nothing but planting tobacco; but if otherwise necessity will enforce them to go upon manufactures and handicrafts.'[103]

Leather shoes were seen as a basic necessity but wore out fast – Ligon suggested white servants should be allowed twelve pairs a year – and, by the mid-seventeenth century, New England's own shoemakers were supplying the bulk of the region's needs.[104] Hides were locally available, as well as bark for tanning, and the capital and skill requirements of shoemaking were modest.[105] The success of the industry is reflected in the London portbooks of 1686 which show a mere 2,000 lb of shoes being exported to provide for a population of about 80,000 in New England, whereas 30,000 lb were despatched to the West Indies with half as many whites (slaves were not given shoes).[106] By 1697 the Chesapeake also had a well-established shoemaking trade.[107]

North Americans also established widespread production of rough textiles using wool, flax, and cotton (importing the raw material from the West Indies).[108] By the 1690s the counties of Virginia where the Scots

[102] 'An account of New England', 1675, BL Egerton MS 2,395, fo. 522; 'Province of Massachusetts Bay', CUL CH(H) Papers 84/11; Victor. S. Clark, *History of Manufactures in the United States*, 3 vols. (Washington, DC, 1929); Bernard Bailyn, *The New England Merchants in the Seventeenth Century* (Cambridge, Mass., 1955), pp. 60–74; Lois Green Carr and Lorena S. Walsh, 'Economic diversification and labour organisation in the Chesapeake, 1650–1820', in Stephen Innes (ed.), *Work and Labour in Early America* (Chapel Hill, N.C., 1988), pp. 144–88; C. P. Nettels, 'The menace of colonial manufacturing', *New England Quarterly*, 4 (1931), 230–69; S. D. Smith, 'The market for manufactures in the thirteen continental colonies, 1698–1776', *EcHR*, 51 (1998), 676–708.
[103] 'Memorial of Sir Thomas Lawrence', 1695, *CSPC, 1693–5*, no. 1,916.
[104] 'Account of Massachusetts Bay', 1721, CUL CH(H) Papers 89/11; Clark, *History of Manufactures*, vol. I, p. 66; C. Bridenbaugh, *The Colonial Craftsmen* (New York, 1950), pp. 1–7, 33–64; B. E. Hazard, *The Organisation of the Boot and Shoe Industry in Massachusetts before 1875* (Cambridge, Mass., 1921), pp. 3–24; Ligon, *History of Barbadoes*, p. 115.
[105] J. R. Commons, 'American shoemakers, 1648–1875: a sketch of industrial evolution', *Quarterly Journal of Economics* 24 (1910), 39–84; J. B. Russo, *Free Workers in a Plantation Economy: Talbot County, Maryland, 1690–1759* (New England, 1989); Hazard, *Boot and Shoe Industry*, pp. 3–24.
[106] Ligon, *History of Barbadoes*, pp. 109, 115.
[107] 'Very good leather is also made and shipped to England. An ordinary labouring man's shoes made out of this cost half a crown to three shillings and are much better than those imported from England': Major Wilson to Lords of Trade, 1 September 1697, *CSPC, 1696–7*, no. 1,295.
[108] 'No cloth made there (in New England) above 4s per yard nor linen worth 2s 6d' and half-cotton cloths were common: BL Egerton MS 2,395, fo. 522b. The Barbados shipping returns suggest that around 40 per cent of the island's raw cotton exports were sent to the mainland: Naval Officers' returns, Jamaica, Barbados, PRO CO 142/13; 33/14; Eltis, 'New estimates of exports', 631–48; Richard Beale Davis (ed.), *Fitzhugh and his Chesapeake World, 1676–1701* (Chapel Hill, N.C., 1963) pp. 80, 82, 101, 103.

Irish were numerous were reported to be able to clothe themselves, and in Carolina settlers produced not only woollens and linens, but also some stuffs containing silk and cotton.[109] Iron ore and charcoal were available in all the northern regions and, by the end of the century, colonists were making simple iron goods, such as nails and pots, for local consumption.[110] Given the extensive forests, wooden wares were widely produced, and some fuel-intensive industries such as glass-making, soap-boiling, sugar-refining, rum-distilling, and potteries were started.[111] However, although manufacturing made more progress than mercantilists would have liked (especially in New England), the colonists remained heavily dependent on the mother country for more complex capital goods and higher-quality consumer items, as well as a vast range of miscellaneous manufactures.[112] As contemporaries well understood, the limited size of the market, the 'intolerably dear labour' and the shortage of skills combined to do more than mercantilist regulations to restrict American manufacturing to the processing of local raw materials (wood, wheat, tobacco, and sugar) to fulfil some simple everyday needs, and maintained heavy reliance on the mother country for most of the remainder.[113]

The surge in American demand in the late seventeenth century had a radical impact not only on the volume but also the character of the English export trade. The most striking aspect of this change was the new diversity in the product range (Tables 6.5 and 6.6). England's export trade had been heavily dominated by raw wool and woollen cloths since the middle ages: woollens accounted for 90 per cent of the value of London's exports in 1640, and continued to make up 75 per cent of its exports to Europe in 1675.[114] However, although clothing

[109] 'Memorial of Sir Thomas Lawrence', 25 June 1695, *CSPC, 1693–5*, no. 1,916.

[110] E. N. Hartley, *Ironworks on the Saugus: the Lynn and Braintree Ventures of the Company of Undertakers of the Ironworks in New England* (Norman, Okla., 1957); Arthur Cecil Binning, *British Regulation of the Colonial Iron Industry* (Oxford, 1933), pp. 6–30.

[111] Clark, *History of Manufactures*, vol. I, pp. 73–5.

[112] Lidgett, 28 August 1696, *CSPC, 1696–7*, no. 172; Smith, 'Market for manufactures'.

[113] On the high price of labour in the colonies see Agents of Jamaica to Lords of Trade, 8 March 1697, PRO CO 138/9, to 79; Hartwell and others to Popple, 20 October 1697, PRO CO 5/1309, fo. 88. Contemporary understanding that America's factor endowment favoured raw material production, rather than manufacturing, was frequently expressed. For example, a group that was lobbying for the right to set up a company to provide naval stores proclaimed that,

   if this trade with New England be not promoted the people there will be obliged to manufacture their own cloth (as has been lately done in Ireland) whereas in the time in which they would make so much cloth as they could purchase of the company for 30 shillings they might get timber enough in the woods to sell to the company for £4 –£5.

   Proposals for supplying England with naval stores from New England, 31 July 1696, *CSPC, 1696–7*, no. 121.

[114] Fisher 'London's export trade'; Davis, 'English foreign trade, 1660–1700'.

Table 6.5 *Exports of English goods from London to the West Indies, 1686 (£ sterling)*

Textiles	Silk stuffs	6,851	**Miscel-laneous**	Apothecary	680
	Thrown	1,569		Barrel hoops	1,370
	Wrought	17,176		Books	316
	With gold/silver	160		Candles	1,236
	Ribbon (at value)	41		Chairs	274
	Woollen bays	1,100		Clockwork	30
	Cloths	2,239		Coals	200
	Crepe	22		Cordage	1,164
	Flannel	2,560		Corks	63
	Kerseys	287		Earthenware	144
	Perpetts	475		Glass,window	77
	Serges	1,229		Glasses	2,947
	Stuffs (at value)	3,847		Gunpowder	1,287
	Bone lace	883		Harness/bridles	204
	Cottons	434		Leather tanned	313
	Haberdashery	744		Paper (at value)	119
	Linen (English)	178		Pipes, tobacco	138
		39,795 (36%)		Saddles	1,116
				Skinsss	938
Clothing	Caps	181		Soap	417
	Fans	8		Starch	175
	Gloves	1,249		Turnery ware	95
	Hats	6,405		Uholstery	201
	Hose	1,586		Wax	53
	Leather wrought	1,337		Whips	37
	Shoes	4,251			13,594 (12%)
	Wigs	303			
		15,320 (14%)	**Food**	Bacon	413
				Beer	3,294
Metals	Brass/Copper	2,790		Biscuit	3,700
	Iron	6,209		Butter	793
	Lead	794		Cheese	939
	Nails	2,219		Flour	1,172
	Pewter	1,415		Hops	113
	Tinware (at value)	93		Oats/meal	104
		13,520 (12%)			10,528 (10%)
Bullion	Pieces of eight	750 (1%)	**Goods at value**		11,528 (10%)
			Other		6,337 (5%)
		Total	**111,392**		

Source: Portbook database, 1686.

Table 6.6 *Exports of English goods from London to North America, 1686 (£ sterling)*

Textiles	Silk stuffs	8,222	Miscellaneous	Apothecary	162
	Thrown	1,651		Books	822
	Wrought	12,571		Candles	81
	Ribbon (at value)	8		Chairs (at value)	236
	Woollen bays	11,767		Clockwork	13
	Cloths	47		Coals	209
	Crepe	10		Cordage	3,293
	Flannel	1,641		Corks	2
	Linsey woolsey	160		Earthenware	91
	Perpetts	253		Glass/window	89
	Serges	6,104		Glasses	888
	Stuffs	4,601		Gunpowder	1,677
	Cotton	4,783		Harness/bridles	192
	Haberdashery	1,014		Pipes, tobacco	137
	Lace (at value)	215		Saddles	996
	Linen (English)	267		Skins	2
		53,314 (53%)		Soap	85
				Starch	149
Clothing	Caps	3		Turnery ware	70
	Gloves	909		Upholstery	458
	Hats	5,938		Whips	3
	Hose	10			9,655 (10%)
	Leather (wrought)	873			
	Shoes	5,158	Food	Bacon	1
	Wigs	37		Beer	320
		12,928 (13%)		Biscuit	631
				Butter	71
Metals	Brass/copper	1,229		Cheese	441
	Iron	3,157		Flour	6
	Nails	4,812		Hops	18
	Pewter	1,026		Oats/meal	5
	Tinware (at value)	34		Peas	1
		10,258 (10%)		Wheat/meal	6
					1,500 (1%)
Bullion	Pieces of eight	975 (1%)	Goods at value		4,792 (12%)
			Other		7,119
			Total	**100,541**	

Source: Portbook database, 1686.

and textiles did dominate London's exports to the plantations throughout the Restoration period, the recorded figures suggest that their share
declined from around 70 per cent in the 1660s, to around 50 per cent
in the 1680s, and within the textile sector itself, there was further diversification away from wool.[115] In 1663 woollen cloths accounted for 27
per cent of the value of English goods exported from London to the
plantations but, by 1686, the proportion had fallen below 20 per cent, as
it did in the African trade. Demand held up better in the colder mainland colonies, especially New England, but was very weak in the warmer
West Indies where woollen cloths accounted for as little as 10 per cent
of demand, in line with Ligon's discussion of the structure of trade in
the 1650s.[116] In 1688 the Halls of Jamaica scolded their London correspondent for ignoring their advice when assembling a cargo and stressed
that 'no woollen cloths will do'.[117] The struggling woollen industry had
relatively little success in what was England's fastest growing market in
the late seventeenth century.

Woollen manufacturers, sensible of their long-standing importance to
the national economy, exhorted the state to provide some remedy for
their ailing industry. They sought ways to limit colonial competition and
obtained a clause in the Wool Act of 1699 which ordered that 'no wool,
woollen yarn or cloth produced in the colonies should be shipped to
any other plantation or any other place whatsoever under heavy penalties' but there is no evidence that this legislation was ever enforced.
Merchants also sought help in forcing colonists to substitute woollen
cloths for other textiles and, in the 1690s, there were efforts to form
a 'joint-stock company, established by Act of Parliament, which would
furnish all the American plantations with sufficient quantities of linsey
woolsey (being of the manufacture of England) at as cheap or cheaper
rates than they can now have linen'. Planters would be obliged to clothe
their workers in wool, which it was believed would benefit planters, as
well as merchants, for linsey woolsey was claimed to be a more durable
and healthier option than linen, as it did 'fence them from the land and
sea-breezes, suck up the sweat and supple their bodies whereas foreign
linen shuts up the pores, chills the body and brings on ... distempers'.[118]
The petition failed.

---

[115] BL Add. MS 36,785; Tables 6.5 and 6.6.
[116] Ligon, *History of Barbadoes*, pp. 109–10.
[117] Halls to Brailsford, 13 March 1689, Brailsford Papers, PRO C 110/152.
[118] 'Proposals humbly offered for the yearly consumption of wool, encouragement of the
sowing of great quantities of hempe, improvement of the woollen manufacture, and
benefits of the English plantation in America': BL Sl. MS 2,717, fo. 66. The belief in
the virtues of woollen cloth in warm climates was well established: see, Ligon, *History of
Barbadoes*, pp. 44–5.

Whereas attempts at coercion had little success, some merchants managed a more creative response to the needs of consumers living in warm climates and promoted production of new lightweight cloths that mixed wool with other fibres. In August 1677 the Royal African Company's court instructed its committee of goods to organize the production of annabasses: cheap blue and white striped cloths, with a woollen warp and a cotton weft, developed in Holland in imitation of a type of Indian loincloth which was much in demand in Africa and America.[119] However, mercantilist aspiration 'that this company may be supplied with our own manufactory' was not to be allowed to prevail over profitability. The company insisted that the cloths should not be used 'unless they be as good as those from Holland'.[120] The experiment was, in fact, a great success: between 1680 and 1688 the company shipped nearly 20,000 English annabasses to Africa each year, and others were sent to American markets. Most were produced in Spitalfields, where there was a cluster of highly skilled immigrant textile workers who produced fancy goods of every description.[121] In 1707, it was claimed that in London at least 700 people were employed in the manufacture of 'nicconnees, tapsseils, and brawls', which were shipped to distant markets at the expense of foreign, above all Dutch, industry. However, it is clear that English manufacturers could not, as yet, compete with their Indian rivals on either price or quality and, in 1706, an African agent warned that 'East Indian goods only and not those imitated are saleable'.[122]

Ligon's discussion of the Caribbean market in the 1650s suggests that demand for linens equalled, or exceeded, that for woollens and a wide range was also consumed on the mainland: heavy canvas sailcloth; packing material for sacks and bags; fine linen for the better off; and large quantities of coarse hammels for servants and slaves.[123] In the 1670s Lynch's plantation required an annual supply of one linen jacket, and one pair of drawers, for each male slave, and one frock for each woman, and according to Ligon, servants received a more generous provision of six shirts, and six pairs of drawers.[124] In 1700 Beeston claimed that Jamaica's 40,000 or so

---

[119] Florence M. Montgomery, *Textiles in America, 1650–1870* (New York, 1984), p. 145; Wadsworth and Mann, *Cotton Trade*, pp. 126, 151.

[120] 'Minute book of Court of Assistants', 21 August 1677, PRO T 70/77, fo. 46.

[121] Davies, *African Company*, p. 175; Wadsworth and Mann, *Cotton Trade*, pp. 151–2; 'Evidence of members of the Royal African Company before the Board of Trade', 14 December 1710, *Journal of Board of Trade, 1709–14*.

[122] 'Minute book of Court of Assistants', 18 October 1677, PRO T 70/77, fo. 54; PRO CO 388/10, H. 113; PRO T 70/22.

[123] Ligon, *History of Barbadoes*, p. 109.

[124] 'An account of necessaries to be sent once a year by Mr Tho. Duck to Sir Thomas Lynch for his plantation at Port Morant': BL Egerton MS 2,395, fo. 599; Ligon, *History of Barbadoes*, p. 115.

slaves consumed 200,000 yards of ozenbrigs or canvas a year (five yards per head).[125] However, most linens were produced in France or Gemany.[126] England's own linen industry (using mainly imported yarn) made some progress, but the London portbooks of 1686 suggest that exports of English linen remained small (Tables 6.4 and 6.5). Meanwhile, as in the woollen sector, new products were developed in response to export demand, including mixtures made with cotton in imitation of Indian textiles.[127] As with woollen mixtures, some were made in Spitalfields, but London merchants were also involved in financing production in Lancashire which had a tradition of linen manufacture.[128] In the 1680s Richard Holt maintained an agent and a warehouse in Manchester and contracted to supply local linen drapers with Jamaican raw cotton at a price fixed in advance. The raw material was put out to fustian makers, and Holt received payment in finished cloths for export to American markets.[129]

Although home-produced linens made limited inroads into colonial markets, the infant silk industry had greater success (Table 6.7). After the Restoration English silk production became concentrated in London (having earlier been largely based in Canterbury), and by 1686 the city's silk production employed around 40,000 people.[130] The industry was heavily geared to export. By 1655 the London framework knitters claimed that they sold most of their stockings abroad – above all, in Spanish and English colonial markets. In 1663/9 half the silks exported from London were going to Spain and Portugal (from where a high proportion of imports were transhipped to America) and about a fifth were sent to the English plantations.[131] In 1663/9 silks accounted for around 7 per cent of London's exports to the plantations but, by 1686, they accounted for over

[125] Beeston to Lords of Trade, 14 March 1700, *CSPC, 1700*, no. 251.
[126] Roseveare, *Markets and Merchandise*, p. 291, Marion Balderston (ed.), *James Claypoole's Letterbook, London and Philadelphia, 1681–84* (San Marino, Calif., 1967), p. 104. In 1689, Byrd ordered that 'if French linens continue so dear I would not have any, there is other linens must serve': Tinling (ed.), *Correspondence of William Byrd*, vol. I, p.107.
[127] N. B. Harte, 'The rise of protection and the English linen trade, 1690–1790', in N. B. Harte and K. G. Ponting (eds.), *Textile History and Economic History* (Manchester, 1973).
[128] Wadsworth and Mann, *Cotton Trade*, pp. 127, 151–2.
[129] 'Case of Joshua Browne and Nathaniel Walker against Richard Holt and Thomas Heyrick', PRO E 134/2 Jas. 2/Mich. 30. The case is discussed in Wadsworth and Mann, *Cotton Trade*, pp. 76–8.
[130] On increasing concentration in London in this period see N. K. Rothstein, 'Canterbury and London: the silk industry in the late seventeenth century', *Textile History*, 20 (1989), 33–47; Wadsworth and Mann, *Cotton Trade*, pp. 97–108.
[131] BL Thomason Tract E 864 (3); BL, Add. MS 36,785. On the stocking industry see Pauline Croft, 'The rise of the English stocking export trade', *Textile History*, 18 (1987), 3–16; Joan Thirsk, 'The fantastical folly of fashion: the English stocking knitting industry, 1500–1700', in Harte and Ponting (eds.), *Textile History and Economic History*; BL Add. MS 36,785.

Table 6.7 *London exports to English plantations, 1697 (£ sterling)*

	Woollens (English)	Wrought silk (English)	English manufactures	English and foreign manufactures
West Indies				
Antigua	288	476	4,404	6,250
Barbados	5,072	9,635	39,167	68,842
Jamaica	2,805	6,706	24,654	48,232
Nevis	452	32	1,399	2,548
	8,617	16,849	69,624	125,872
	(12%)	(24%)	(100%)	
North America				
Bermuda	14	—	347	425
Carolina	2,776	1,633	6,761	8,995
Hudson's Bay	81	—	1,169	1,292
New England	15,966	5,170	43,164	63,006
New Providence	10	—	1,078	1,423
New York	939	274	2,930	4,240
Chesapeake	4,506	3,090	19,645	28,368
	24,292	10,167	75,094	107,749
	(32%)	(13%)	(100%)	
West Indies and North America				
	32,909	27,016	144,718	233,621
	(23%)	(19%)	(100%)	

Source: PRO CUST. 2/2.

20 per cent.[132] As shown in the figures for 1697 (Table 6.7), they were in especially high demand in the warm, wealthy, and fashion conscious West Indies where 'they would economize on nothing to dress well' and from where they could also be re-exported to the Spanish colonies.[133] Merchants such as Thomas Brailsford who, in the 1670s, exported silks to America via Cadiz, despatched an agent to Jamaica in the 1680s and became heavily involved in the island's contraband commerce.[134]

Colonial demand encouraged not only product diversification in textile manufacturing, but also process developments which deepened England's industrial base. In the early seventeenth century a high proportion of English cloths were exported undressed and undyed, allowing foreigners to reap the rewards of the very large value added in finishing (30 per cent or more).[135]American and African customers required

[132] BL Add. MS 36,785; portbook database.
[133] Handler, 'Father Biet's visit to Barbados', 67.
[134] Brailsford Papers, PRO C 110/152.
[135] Committee of Goods, 19 May 1691, PRO T 70/127 fo.127; CLRO, 'Inventory of James Brailsford'.

finished products and merchants responded well to the challenge, providing much of the capital needed to develop a competitive finishing industry in London, at the same time as the rise of long-distance trade ensured an improved supply of necessary raw materials. There were also experiments with novel processes such as printing in imitation of the popular Indian cloths. In 1675 Thomas Toogood took out a patent for printing woollens, and in the following year William Sherwin took out another patent for printing both Indian calicoes and Scottish linen. In 1678 the Royal African Company agent at Cape Coast Castle asked for 'cuttannees, a sort stamped in England with flowers' as well as 'printed linen like to Bird's Eye'.[136]

The colonial market also provided a new civilian market for bulk-produced ready-to-wear clothing alongside growing military and naval demand.[137] Planters required annual supplies of hundreds of pairs of drawers, jackets, and petticoats to clothe their workers.[138] Some undertook garment production on their own estates or hired local tradesmen but, as Byrd remarked, the high cost of labour in the colonies made it more cost effective to purchase ready-made clothing.[139] In fact Whaley reckoned that he could halve his costs if he was supplied with everything from home including 'frocks for negroes'.[140] As early as the 1650s, Ligon advised that merchants could buy French linen in London and then 'hire poor journeymen tailors, here in the city, that will for very small wages, make the canvas into drawers and petticoats for men and women negroes'.[141] Attention focused on production to a standard pattern, at highest possible speed, and lowest possible cost – a very different trade from the skill-intensive, quality-conscious, customized fashion business serving the London elites.

Alongside novel textile products, plantation-bound cargoes contained a wide range of other new exports 'which we cannot with any profit carry into other countries'.[142] Manufacturers of clothing accessories such as felt hats, gloves, haberdashery, and shoes found it difficult to sell their goods in continental markets, which were well supplied by their own industries. However, American and African markets offered tempting prospects and, in the 1650s, these items accounted for 15 per cent of Ligon's export budget

[136] Wadsworth and Mann, *Cotton Trade*, pp. 130–1.
[137] Beverly Lemire, *Fashion's Favourite: the Cotton Trade and the Consumer in Britain, 1660–1800* (Manchester, 1991), pp. 176–97.
[138] 'An account of necessaries to be sent once a year by Mr Tho. Duck to Sir Thomas Lynch for his plantation at Port Morant', BL Egerton MS 2,395, fo. 599.
[139] Tinling (ed.), *Correspondence of William Byrd*, vol. I, p .62.
[140] William Whaley to William Helyar, 20 May 1671, SRO, Walker Heneage MSS DD WHh Addenda Papers 12.
[141] Ligon, *History of Barbadoes*, p. 109.
[142] 'The advantages of trading with our plantations', BLO, MS Rawl. A 478, fo. 65.

Table 6.8 *Exports of hats from London to English plantations, 1686*

	value (£ sterling)	West Indies No.	total value, (£ sterling)	North America No.	total value, (£ sterling)
Beaver	0.88	220	194	49	43
Caster	0.47	10,936	5,140	6,353	2,986
Felt	0.17	6,318	1,159	17,113	2,909

Source: PRO portbook database, 1686.

and a similar proportion of London's English exports to the plantations in 1686. Like the silk industry, the infant felt-hat industry was heavily concentrated in London (in Southwark), and geared to export from the start, with half its output going overseas in the 1690s and London accounting for 76 per cent of England's hat exports in 1698.[143] The number of hats exported from London to the plantations increased almost sixfold from about 7,400 in 1663, to 41,800 in 1686, with over 40 per cent being shipped to supply the West Indies, reflecting both the need for all classes to wear a hat for working in the sun, and the much greater reliance on imported manufactures than in the more populous, but poorer, north (Table 6.8).[144]

According to Ligon, metalwares accounted for around 14 per cent of the value of West Indian demand in the 1650s and, in 1686, they made up a similar proportion of London's exports of English goods to the colonies.[145] There was also a substantial demand in the linked African trade (Table 6.2).[146] Ironwares and nails accounted for around 60 per cent of the metal cargoes sent to the West Indies and over 75 per cent of those sent to North America, but there was also a very substantial demand for copper and lead in the West Indies where they were used for boiling equipment, pipework, and cisterns on the sugar plantations (Illustration

[143] Hats and hat-making are described in Randolph Holme, *The Academy of Armory or a Storehouse of Armory and Blazon* (Chester, 1688), pp. 129, 291. Also see David Corner, 'The tyranny of fashion: the case of the felt-hatting industry in the late seventeenth and eighteenth centuries', *Textile History*, 22 (1991), 153–78. 'A proposal for raising the sume of £200,000 or more... by a duty being laid upon all sorts of hats' (*c.* 1692). In 1695, members of the hatting trade claimed that 40 per cent of their annual production was for the export market: *An Answer to a Proposal for Laying a Duty upon Hats* 116 (1695). In 1698 London exported hats to the value of £24,926 and the outports to the value of £7,975: PRO CUST. 2/4. For evidence of merchant involvement in financing London's hat industry see entry of 30 August 1699, 'Journal of Thomas Sandes', 1698–1703, BEA, M 7/4.
[144] In 1675 Whaley requested twenty hats for his workers for 'men cannot work in the sun without them', Whaley to Helyar, 9 December 1675, SRO, WHh 1090/Pt. 2; BL Add. MS 36,785; portbook database, 1686.
[145] Ligon, *History of Barbadoes*, p. 110.
[146] Inikori, *Africans and the Industrial Revolution*, pp. 467–8.

28).[147] The new expanding export markets stimulated growth and investment in England's mining industries and, above all, those extracting non-
ferrous metals which had until the seventeenth century been small and
backward alongside their continental counterparts; in fact copper mining
was not really established as an industry until the 1680s when overseas
demand (above all colonial and African demand) took off (Table 6.9).[148]
In all mining sectors the rise of strong export demand stimulated change
as well as growth with increases in the size of production units, changes
in ownership arrangements, and use of merchant capital as in the case
of the London Lead Company.[149] Productivity improved with increased
division of labour, and technological breakthroughs such as better winding and draining gear, and the reverberatory furnace developed in the
late seventeenth century to provide a way to use coal to reduce certain
ores with less risk of product contamination.

Expanding Atlantic markets also stimulated the growth of the second-
ary metal industries with buoyant demand for large quantities of iron
pots, nails, and a range of – often novel – capital goods.[150] A wide range
of traditional hand tools, as listed by Ligon, were supplied by provincial
producers in Sussex and the Midlands. In addition, the abundance of raw
materials in America, the shortage of skills, and the high cost of labour
combined to encourage greater use of machinery in the plantations than
at home.[151] Whereas in seventeenth-century England timber was sawn by
hand it was, from the first days of settlement, usual to rely on sawmills in
America.[152] In the early days the colonists depended on foreign craftsmen
but, by the late seventeenth century, the metal parts were supplied from

---

[147] For a detailed description of the equipment needed on a sugar plantation see Ligon, *History
of Barbadoes*, pp. 89–91. A planter with 250 working slaves in 1685 had two boiling houses
with twenty-nine coppers suggesting that a copper was needed for every eight or nine slaves.
A copper weighed between 1 and 4 cwt; 'Indenture between Codrington and Browning',
23 March 1685, BA, Deeds RB 3/14, fos. 460–4 'Invoice of iron, brass and copperwork for
a sugar mill', 9 November 1671, SRO, Walker Heneage MSS DD/WHh 1089.

[148] Roger Burt, 'The transformation of the non-ferrous metals industries in the seventeenth and eighteenth centuries', *EcHR*, 48 (1995), 23–45.

[149] A. Raistrick, 'The London Lead Company, 1692–1905', *Trans. Newcomen Society*, 14
(1933–4), 122–5.

[150] On the importance of export markets to the Midlands metal industries see W. H. B.
Court, *The Rise of the Midland Industries, 1600–1838* (Oxford, 1938).

[151] Ligon suggested that a mixed cargo for the West Indies should include

whip sawes, two-handed saws, hand sawes, files of several sizes and shapes; axes for fell-
ing and for hewing; hatchets, that will fit carpenters, joiners, and coopers; chisels, but
no mallets, for the wood is harder there to make them: adzes of several sizes, pick-axes,
and matt-hooks; hoes of all sizes, but chiefly small ones, to be used with one hand, for
with them the small negroes weed the ground: plains, gouges and augurs of all kinds;
hand bills, for the negroes to cut the canes; drawing knives for joiners. (Ligon, *History
of Barbadoes*, p. 110)

[152] Committee of Goods of Royal African Company, 19 May 1691, PRO T 70/127, fo. 127;
Inventory of James Brailsford, 1678 and 1679, CLRO, CSB vol. IV, fos. 22, 56.

Illustration 28 Interior of a sugar-boiling house. The cane juice is boiled into sugar in five open copper cauldrons each smaller than the last. The juice is run into the first copper where slaked lime is added. As the temperature rises a green scum forms and is skimmed off by the sugar-boiler. As it thickens it is transferred to the next copper. Finally the syrup is thick enough for striking or granulation. It is ladled into coolers where it crystallizes. Denis Diderot, *Encyclopaedia* (1751–71).

Table 6.9 *Exports of metal goods from London to Africa and the colonies, 1701*

	Africa	North America	West Indies	Total
Wrought brass (cwt (%))	455 (26)	490 (28)	330 (19)	1,742 (100)
Wrought copper (cwt (%))	597 (36)	29 (2)	822 (50)	1,636 (100)
Nails (cwt (%))	24 (0.22)	4,806 (44)	3,349 (31)	10,839 (100)
Wrought iron (cwt (%))	3,570 (16)	4,903 (23)	6,826 (31)	21,693 (100)
Lead and shot (fodder (%))	646 (6)	84 (1)	134 (1)	11,609 (100)
Tin (cwt (%))	13	23	—	27,042

Source: PRO CUST. 2/9.

England. In the 1680s, William Byrd ordered a crank for his Virginian sawmill and despatched a pattern which was to be made 'exact' so that 'the rack and nut must fit'.[153] He later sent a pattern for a saw and ordered a dozen to be made 'only would have them six inches longer'.[154]

[153] Tinling (ed.), *Correspondence of William Byrd*, vol. I, p. 29.
[154] *Ibid.*, p. 42.

Illustration 29 Juice is pressed out of the sugar cane by feeding it between three vertical rollers. Sugar-mills were powered by animals, wind and water power. Denis Diderot, *Encyclopaedia* (1751–71).

The sugar-mills built in the Caribbean in the late seventeenth century were among the most advanced technical installations of the time and required cogged rollers on brass or steel rods, copper cauldrons, lead pipes and cisterns, millwrights work, and stoves which were all purchased from England (Illustration 29).[155] The letters of George Sitwell, a Sheffield iron-master, show that, by the 1660s the London metalwares industry was geared to supply sugar-making equipment and the skills were being disseminated to the provinces. Sitwell was confident that his men could make sugar-boiling stoves but, as yet, they were of an unfamiliar pattern and he asked for details of the designs wanted, or a model. Alternatively, he proposed sending a potter to London to make a cast. A few months later he solicited patterns for sugar-cane rollers 'or else two pack-threads to indicate their length and diameter'.[156] The needs of distant colonial markets encouraged innovation in the metalwares industry and placed a premium on product standardization, in ways that pointed towards the introduction of interchangeable parts in the late eighteenth century.[157]

Other exports shipped out of London reflected the diversity of colonial needs, and the heavy reliance on the mother country, to supply both consumer and producer goods (Tables 6.5 and 6.6). Cargoes included large quantities of books needed for information and instruction as well as entertainment.[158] Paper was needed in vast quantities to seal connections in this complex commercial world – for letters in duplicate, bills of exchange, bonds, legal documents, printed forms for bills of lading, insurance certificates, and so on.[159] Although a printer set up in business

[155] John Helyar, of Somerset, ordered sugar making equipment for his brother from London, 'Invoice of iron, brass and copper work for a sugar plantation', 9 November 1671, SRO, Walker Heneage MSS DD/WHh 1089.

[156] Philip Riden (ed.), George Sitwell's Letterbook, 1662–66 (Chesterfield, 1985), pp. xx–xxi, 242–3, 261.

[157] D. Hounshell, From the American System to Mass Production, 1800–1932: the Development of Manufacturing Technology in the United States (Baltimore, Md., 1984).

[158] In 1683 John Ive dealt with an order from John Usher (one of the twenty or so booksellers in Boston) for 767 books including many in large multiples: 100 psalm books, 40 copies of Strong's Spelling Book, 20 copies of Fox's End of Time, 18 Greek grammars, 16 copies of Culpepper's English Physician, as well as two copies of Rochester's poems, and a long list of individual items: MHS, Jeffries Family Papers, vol. IV, fos. 89, 91. On the book trade in seventeenth-century New England see Hugh Amory and David Hall (eds.), A History of the Book in America (Cambridge, 2000), vol. I, pp. 83–116. On the book trade in England, M. Plant, The English Book Trade (London, 1974), p. 64.

[159] English per caput consumption of paper increased from 0.25 lb in 1600 to 1.5 lb in 1715: D. C. Coleman, The British Paper Industry, 1495–1960 (Oxford, 1958), pp. 15, 105. On response to the expanding market see Pierre Claude Reynard, 'Manufacturing quality in the pre-industrial age: finding value in diversity', EcHR, 53 (2000), 493–516. Bradford established the first paper mill in British America in 1690 in partnership with two rich Quaker merchants and a recently arrived Dutch papermaker: James N. Green, The Rittenhouse Mill and the Beginnings of Papermaking in America (Phil., 1990).

in New England in the 1630s, and others followed, the presses they used were not made in America until the late eighteenth century.[160] Colonists required spectacles and looking glasses; window and drinking glass; soap and starch; furniture and upholstery; carpets and curtains; carriages and bridles; billiard tables and playing cards; parrot cages and even tombstones. In her will Rachel Benin Louzada of Barbados directed that her son should give her a 'decent funeral' and obtain from London 'a good stone for my grave'.[161]

The growth in colonial demand stimulated changes in both the organization of industry and the techniques of production. The high transaction costs in Atlantic commerce encouraged efforts to trade in bulk and reap economies of scale. Merchants could not entirely ignore taste, and probate inventories show that goods regarded as 'out of fashion' had no value.[162] None the less, the relatively homogeneous character of colonial communities – with both white and black populations less differentiated by class and income than in Europe – favoured provision of a narrow quality range at low unit cost.[163] As seen in the case of hats, the supply of expensive beavers was limited, even in the richer West Indies, and most consumers were provided with low-price casters, or very cheap felts, especially in the poorer mainland colonies (Table 6.8).[164] A cask of 344 hats shipped to Boston by John Reynolds in 1680 reflects the relatively undifferentiated nature of New England demand with large batches, a narrow range of styles and sizes, and a focus on low prices.[165] The stocks

---

[160] A printing press was set up in New England in 1638, Virginia in 1682, Maryland in 1685 and, by 1699, there were presses in New York and Philadelphia: Amory and Hall (eds.), *The Book in America*, p. 199.

[161] E. M. Shilstone, *Monumental Inscriptions in the Jewish Synagogue at Bridgetown, Barbados* (Bridgetown, Barbados, 1988), p. 81.

[162] William Byrd's letters indicate that, even in the Indian trade, consumers displayed preferences for particular colours and styles: Tinling (ed.), *Correspondence of William Byrd*, vol. I, pp. 29–30.

[163] Lois Green Carr and Lorena S. Walsh, 'Changing life-styles and consumer behaviour in the colonial Chesapeake', in Cary Carson, Ronald Hoffman, and Peter J. Albert (eds.), *Of Consuming Interests: the Style of Life in the Eighteenth Century* (Charlottesville, Va., 1994) pp. 59–166; James Horn, *Adapting to a New World: English Society in the Seventeenth Century Chesapeake* (Chapel Hill, N.C., 1994), pp. 325–6.

[164] Tailors, hat-makers, wig-makers, and other tradesmen were in short supply in the colonies and there was less chance of a face-to-face relationship than in the metropolis. William Byrd sent his wig back to London for alteration, and ordered customized hats, and shoes, but few could afford such luxuries: Tinling (ed.), *Correspondence of William Byrd*, vol. I, pp. 107, 41, 60.

[165] The cask contained 243 felts divided between men's and boy's sizes: a large batch of 54 men's felts at 30d and three small batches of about a dozen each at 36–40d. The 101 casters were similarly distributed: 'Invoice of one caske of hats shipped on board the *Samuel and Thomas*', 9 October 1680, MHS, Jeffries Family Papers, vol. VII, fo. 18.

of goods held by Port Royal merchants inventoried in the 1680s suggest a slightly more segmented market in the richer West Indies, with small numbers of better quality foreign-made hats valued at 60d or more, but even here the bulk of supplies were mid-price casters and cheap 'ordinary' felts at 24d, which were needed by both blacks and whites for work in the sun.[166]

Like military and naval contracts, catering for colonial markets encouraged moves towards bulk output of standard quality goods at lowest possible unit cost and focused entrepreneurial attention on different problems from those facing the high-fashion, high-cost, craft industries catering for the London elites.[167] The 1686 portbooks suggest that leading export sectors were becoming increasingly concentrated in relatively few hands – fifteen merchants (including five Jews) accounted for almost 40 per cent of London's silk exports to America, seventeen merchants accounted for 45 per cent of hat exports, and other industries revealed a similar pattern of concentration.[168] Merchant records suggest that these dominant players responded actively to market imperatives by using their capital to increase output and reduce unit costs by expanding the number of production units and organizing an intense division of labour, with merchants providing materials on credit or 'in barter' for the final product.[169]

The Brailsford brothers, who traded with Spanish America and Jamaica, had over £2,000 of capital tied up in the silk industry on the death of James in 1675.[170] The brothers' warehouse contained raw silk

---

[166] For examples of stocks see Inventory of Richard May, February. 1691, JA, Inv. 1B/II/3 vol. III, fo. 394–5; Inventory of Joshua Bright, September. 1690, *ibid.*, fo. 363.

[167] Surviving invoices suggest that it was usual for gentlemen in England to pay 60 shillings and more for a custom-made hat although according to King, the average cost of all hats in 1688 was 27d: 'Deposition of William Thornburgh', May 1686, CLRO, MCD, box 40. 'Annual consumption of apparel' in Laslett (ed.), *Early Classics*. For discussion of the impact of military demand see L. Mumford, *Technics and Civilization* (1934), pp. 93–4. For discussion of a range of 'focusing devices' – such as imbalances in the development of complementary technologies, or labour conflict, or resource limitations, which encouraged engineers to address and overcome key bottlenecks – see N. Rosenberg, 'The direction of technological change: inducement mechanisms and focussing devices', in N. Rosenberg, *Perspectives on Technology* (Cambridge, 1976), pp. 108–25.

[168] Halls to Brailsford, 11 March 1689, 20 January 1690, Brailsford Papers, PRO C 110/152.

[169] Thomas Sandes provided Henry Smith, felt-maker, with beaver wombs and took hats 'in barter'. See entry for 30 August 1699 in 'Journal of Thomas Sandes', 1698–1783, BEA, M 7/4. Corner, 'Tyranny of fashion'; David Mitchell, ' "Good hot pressing is the life of all cloth": dyeing, clothfinishing, and related textile trades in London, 1650–1700', in Herman Diederiks and Marjan Balkestein (eds.), *Occupational Titles and their Classification: the Case of the Textile Trade in Past Times* (Gottingen, 1995), pp. 153–75.

[170] The silk market was volatile. A bale of fine sherbasse or belladine silk, weighing 150 lb, fetched around £150 in England (i.e. £3 per pound) but ardasse silk made half that price and medium quality silk averaged 13 shillings per lb. The potential margin of gross

valued at £195, dyed silk valued at £153, and cochineal valued at £146 which would be put out to independent craftsmen. Small quantities of dyed silk valued at £441 8s 7d were out with forty-two separate weavers. At the same time a large parcel of raw silk, worth £483, was out on credit with Thomas Colborne, a thrower, who organized all the stages of production and oversaw an intense division of labour in throwing, reeling, weaving, trimming, and finishing stockings and ribbons. In return, the Brailsfords received stockings for export to Spanish and English American markets: in 1675, their warehouse contained five parcels of stockings containing 2,339 pairs valued at £820.[171] London merchants also played an important role in provincial industry. Merchants such as Richard Holt hired a factor and rented a warehouse in Manchester from which he supplied local linen-drapers with raw cotton for extending fustian production; others invested in the silk industry; metal mining; the Staffordshire nail industry; Birmingham metal wares; the glass industry and others.[172]

The extension of putting-out arrangements and the speeding up of production to meet export demand at low unit cost did tend to increase the quality range as no two production units made identical goods and greater speed led to more mistakes.[173] Although quality variance might have advantages in small, heavily segmented local markets (as a range of products was available to suit people with very different purchasing power), it caused problems in long-distance trade where large batches of goods were sold unseen and it was important to establish a reputation for predictable quality.[174] Shoddy goods damaged reputations, were sold

profit ranged from 20 to 100 per cent: Richard Grassby, *The English Gentleman in Trade: The Life and Works of Sir Dudley North, 1641–1691* (Oxford, 1994), p. 104.

[171] 'Inventory of James Brailsford', 1675, *CSB*, vol. IV, fos. 22, 56. In the 1680s Thomas began to direct a major part of his hose trade to William and Francis Hall in Jamaica from where much was re-exported to Spanish colonies: Brailsford Papers, PRO C 110/152.

[172] Case of Joshua Browne and Nathaniel Walker against Richard Holt and Thomas Heyrick, PRO E 134/2 Jas 2/Mich. 30; Wadsworth and Mann, *Cotton Trade*, pp. 127, 151–2; Court, *Midlands Industries*.

[173] For full discussion of these problems see Reynard, 'Manufacturing quality in the pre-industrial age'.

[174] Joan Thirsk, *Economic Policy and Projects: The Development of a Consumer Society in Early Modern England* (Oxford, 1978), pp. 106–32. Szostak points to a similar effect in the late eighteenth century when Britain's domestic market became more integrated with falling transport costs and consumers wished to purchase goods of standard quality: Rick Szostak, *The Role of Transportation in the Industrial Revolution* (Montreal, 1991). On the nature of batch production see P. Scranton ' "Have a heart for the manufactures!": production, distribution, and the decline of American textile manufacturing', in C. F. Sabel and J. Zeitlin (eds.), *World of Possibilities: Flexibility and Mass Production in Western Industrialization* (Cambridge, 1997), pp. 310–43.

at a big discount, or worst of all, were returned home.[175] As the Halls complained on returning 150 pairs of silk stockings to Brailsford after the colour ran, 'one never gets nothing by letting the rubbish lie on his hand'.[176] However, heavy sorting expenses and waste all raised costs and low product variance became, as much as low unit cost, a prime quality attribute.

As merchants financed the expansion of output through increased specialization some, such as the iron exporter, Ambrose Crowley, took steps to counter adverse effects on the quality range by financing centralized production units which allowed both division of labour and close supervision of the workforce.[177] Merchants also financed the acquisition of new machinery which could ensure a more even quality than handwork such as 'a great screw press for silk stockings' provided by the Brailsfords.[178] Many of the technological solutions adopted in this period had been invented long before – such as the knitting frame of 1589, the ribbon (or Dutch) loom which was introduced into England in 1616, and various processes in mining and metallurgy – but did not become common until the late seventeenth century, when – in addition to rising real wages and a weakening of the guilds – the rise of new export markets placed a premium on both low unit costs and low variance.[179] However, merchants also encouraged and financed efforts at new innovation such as the development of multi-spindle mills for throwing raw silk and, with the opening of Thomas Lombe's throwing mill in Derby in 1718, silk has been described as the first modern industry in England.[180] As manufacturers moved towards the technological frontier, they began to push

---

[175] In 1685 Byrd complained that 'if I have not as good goods as others I must not expect to sell to any advantage': Tinling (ed.), *Correspondence of William Byrd*, vol. I, p. 30.

[176] Halls to Brailsford, 20 September 1689, Brailsford Papers, PRO C 110/152.

[177] Crowley, who had been involved in iron production in London set up an ironworks at Stourbridge in 1682 (which employed 800 at its peak): Michael W. Flinn, *Men of Iron: the Crowleys in the Early Iron Industry* (Edinburgh, 1962), p. 262.

[178] CLRO, Mayor's Court Original Bills, box 196, no. 42.

[179] On the evolution of Lee's knitting frame between 1589 and 1750, and the particular importance of developments in the late seventeenth century see Peta Lewis, 'William Lee's stocking frame: technical evolution and economic viability 1589–1750', *Textile History*, 17 (1986), 129–14; Thirsk, 'The fantastical folly of fashion'; Wadsworth and Mann, *Cotton Trade*, pp. 98–105. The widespread adoption of new equipment that raised labour productivity twenty–fold and 'must of necessity ruin many families' caused much unrest in late seventeenth century London: Margaret H. Verney (ed.), *Memoirs of the Verney Family from the Restoration to the Revolution, 1660–1696*, 4 vols. (London, 1894), vol. IV, p. 268.

[180] Cary remarked on the fall in price of manufactured goods 'which proceeds from the ingenuity of the manufacturer and the improvements he makes in his ways of working new projects are every day set on foot to render the making of our manufactures easy, which are made cheap by the heads of our manufactures, not by falling the price of poor people's labour': Cary, *Essay on Trade*, pp. 147–8. In the 1690s John Berkstead obtained

forward with new, home-produced innovations such as pumping engines to deal with drainage problems in the deepening mines.[181]

In 1700 the value of London's commodity trade with the colonies and Africa accounted for a mere 14.5 per cent of the city's outward commerce, but the demand for English-made goods was more than twice the estimated value of the important inland hawking trade that 'reclothed rural England'. The new trades created widespread industrial employment, first in London, with the advantages of agglomeration, and later in the provinces, which offered lower wages and rents.[182] Furthermore, colonial (and linked) demand had strategic significance beyond its quantity. The high profits that could be earned in the export trade provided an incentive to diversify England's industrial base and focus entrepreneurial attention on different priorities from those facing producers for smaller, more segmented domestic markets, and focused, above all, on low unit costs, and low product variance. England was diverted away from high-quality, craft production towards an industrial revolution based on cheap export goods manufactured by an army of low-skilled workers who were increasingly dependent on machinery. Colonial demand was not a sufficient condition for industrial development, as demonstrated in Spain and Portugal, but it was certainly important in shaping the incentives facing producers. The scale, and quality, of colonial demand focused entrepreneurial energies on seeking solutions to certain problems, and influenced the economic development of late-seventeenth-century London, and the country beyond, in ways that were important for future growth.

letters patent giving him rights for 'sole making, winding and enjoying a new engine or invention for the making and throwing of silk and sole benefit, profit and advantage thereof'. He divided his patent into 500 shares for sale and called on shareholders to provide a fund of £1,500 necessary for proceeding with experiments with the as yet unproven engine: *Thomas Pilkington v. Francis Clarke and Isaac Loader*, 1693, PRO C 24/1168, no. 40. On Lombe's 'large engines of curious and difficult structure' see 'A brief state of the new manufactory of organzine silk, brought into England by Tho. Lombe', CUL, CH (H), Papers 89/19; Joel Mokyr, *The Gifts of Athena: Historical Origins of the Knowledge Economy* (Princeton, 2002), p. 125.

[181] As demand for coal and metal ores increased, and mines became deeper, there was a large effort to develop engines to drain the mines. The crucial breakthroughs involved early-seventeenth-century scientific analysis of the atmosphere demonstrating the phenomenon of air pressure and the distinction between steam and air which opened the way to exploiting the latent energy of a vacuum created by condensing steam in a closed vessel: John Farey, *A Treatise on the Steam Engine, Historical, Practical and Descriptive* (London, 1827); Alessandro Nuvolari, *The Making of Steam Power Technology: a Study of Technical Change during the British Industrial Revolution* (Eindhoven, 2004).

[182] PRO CUST 3/1; Margaret Spufford, *The Great Reclothing of Rural England: Petty Chapmen and their Wares in the Seventeenth Century* (London, 1984), p. 145.

7   Conclusion

By 1700 London was the capital and commercial hub of a thriving Atlantic empire. In the decades after the Restoration the city had used its political and commercial strength to convert the promising but dispersed, and mainly private, efforts of the pioneer settlers into a coherent Atlantic system which largely conformed with the Navigation legislation which had been re-enacted in 1660. The investment in empire paid dividends through the rapid growth in the volume and value of plantation trade; the dramatic rise in the re-export trade in which colonial commerce played a prominent part; a doubling in the shipping tonnage employed in Atlantic trade between the 1660s and the 1680s; a strengthening and diversification of the city's industrial base; and the emergence of London as a leading financial centre in Europe. At a time of national population decline, weak prices and rents in agriculture, and stagnant export markets in Europe, the expanding colonial trades made a major contribution to the continued growth of London and a commercial revolution.[1] Mercantilism was made to work and this commercial success had long-run consequences for growth.[2]

The Navigation Acts are often given credit for the successes of the commercial revolution. However, as has been emphasized in this book, while the legislation may have provided a nudge in the right direction, it was not alone responsible for the commercial advances of the period. The seventeenth-century state was too weak to enforce legislation which

---

[1] Editor's introduction in W. E. Minchinton (ed.), *The Growth of English Overseas Trade in the Seventeenth and Eighteeenth Cenuries* (London, 1969), pp. 1–63; Ralph Davis, 'English foreign trade, 1660–1700', *EcHR*, 7 (1954), 150–66.

[2] Adam Smith, *An Inquiry into the Nature and Causes of the Wealth of Nations* (1776), 1812 edn, pp. 465–524; Patrick K. O'Brien, 'The reconstruction, rehabilitation and reconfiguration of the British Industrial Revolution as a conjuncture in global history', *Itinerario*, 24 (2000), 126; Robert C. Allen, 'Progress and poverty in early modern Europe', *EcHR*, 56 (2003), 403–43; Kenneth Pomeranz, *The Great Divergence: China, Europe, and the Making of the Modern World Economy* (Princeton, 2000), p. 113; Eric Williams, *Capitalism and Slavery* (Chapel Hill, N.C., 1944); Joseph E. Inikori, *Africans and the Industrial Revolution in England: a Study in International Trade and Development* (Cambridge, 2002).

imposed a heavy cost on those in the commercial front line. As shown by the fate of other ambitious legislation, aspirations would have remained little more than wishful thinking without the accumulation of capital, skills, and enterprise needed to make the Navigation system work at competitive cost. This book takes the evidence of high levels of peacetime compliance with the legislation not as a cause, but as a consequence, and even a crude measure, of improved commercial capabilities. If contemporaries were anywhere near correct in asserting that, at the Restoration, the Dutch could undercut English transactions charges by 20 or 30 per cent, it can be assumed that growing compliance with the legislation reflects English success in improving efficiency to catch up with its rivals and close the cost gap.[3]

England's commercial success in the Atlantic owed much to its relatively large investment in overseas settlements. At the Restoration, Englishmen had established colonies in three regions – New England, the Chesapeake Bay area, and the West Indies – with a combined population of 140,000. By the end of the century they had managed to fill gaps and extend territories and population to form a narrow strip of settlement along the Atlantic seaboard from Maine to Carolina which could be increasingly well sealed against foreign incursions.[4] The territories in North America and the Caribbean gave their 400,000 or so inhabitants a number of strategic economic advantages: they provided good staging posts for plunder or illegal trade – while denying the same to their rivals – and relatively secure access to cheap coastal transport which promoted intra-colonial exchange and a tripartite division of labour within the empire. The northern colonies provided food, fuel, and shipping services which allowed the plantation south (including islands in

[3] Lawrence A. Harper, *The English Navigation Laws: a Seventeenth Century Experiment in Social Engineering* (New York, 1939), p. 243; G. L. Beer, *The Origins of the British Colonial System, 1578–1660*, 2 vols. (New York, 1908), vol. I, pp. 209, 389, 392; Charles Whitworth (ed.), *The Political and Commercial Works of the Celebrated Writer Charles d'Avenant*, 5 vols. (London, 1771), vol. I, p. 427; Ralph Davis, *The Rise of the English Shipping Industry in the Seventeenth and Eighteenth Centuries* (Newton Abbot, 1962), pp. 53–4.

[4] Nicholas Canny, 'English migration into and across the Atlantic during the seventeenth and eighteenth centuries', in Nicholas Canny (ed.), *Europeans on the Move: Studies of European Migration, 1500–1800* (Oxford, 1994), pp. 39–75; K. G. Davies, *The North Atlantic World in the Seventeenth Century* (Oxford, 1974), p. 85. England's success in peopling its colonies was largely attributable to the fuller use of the device of indentured labour: The Dutch were hampered not only by a small domestic population but, more importantly, by the eschewal of the use of white indentured labour: Ernst van den Boogaart, 'The servant migration to New Netherland, 1624–64', in P. C. Emmer (ed.), *Colonialism and Migration: Indentured Labour Before and After Slavery* (Dordrecht, 1986), pp. 55–81; Jan de Vries, 'The Dutch Atlantic Economies', in Peter A. Coclanis (ed.), *The Atlantic Economy during the Seventeenth and Eighteenth Centuries* (Columbia, S.C., 2005), pp. 1–29.

the Caribbean) to specialize in producing high-value cash crops, and the mother country to focus on providing labour, services, and manufactured goods. The specialization enhanced total output within the system and was endorsed by the Navigation Acts, which allowed equal access to all citizens of empire.[5]

As England's Atlantic system grew, and developed, it involved an ever denser, and more complex, web of multilateral exchanges between regions and across imperial boundaries. London provided the strong hub, or clearing house, which was needed to ensure the smooth operation of the system and it was uniquely well equipped to fulfil this need. The city, located near the mouth of a major river and well able to take ocean-going vessels, dominated the nation's overseas trade, and was also centre of court, Parliament, law, finance, and industry. London could offer a range of external economies which gave it a strong commercial edge: abundant capital, labour, skills, information, and good transport links with both the provinces and the continent.[6] Neither the Dutch or French commercial systems had a control-tower to match London in advantages.[7]

The geographic strengths of England's late seventeenth-century empire were compounded by a relatively open and flexible institutional framework which encouraged growth and development. England did, like other European nations, build high protective walls around her empire but, in conscious imitation of the open Dutch Republic, within the walls of the Navigation system, foreign migrants were welcome to settle in English territories and most of the colonies allowed freedom of religion.[8] Groups of Jews, Quakers, and Huguenots were scattered throughout the empire bringing valuable capital, skills, and commercial networks and, as shown by the material in this book, they were prominent among the merchants and craftsmen who exploited the opportunities of empire.

[5] John Cary, *An Essay on the State of England in Relation to its Trade* (Bristol, 1695), pp. 69–70.
[6] Peter Earle, 'The economy of London, 1660–1730', in Patrick O'Brien (ed.), *Urban Achievement in Early Modern Europe: Golden Ages in Antwerp, Amsterdam, and London* (Cambridge, 2001), pp. 81–96.
[7] In the Dutch Republic, economic activity and advantage was more evenly dispersed. Amsterdam did not have the same national weight as London and the harbour was suffering from silting which raised costs for ocean traders. Meanwhile, in France, economic activity was dispersed between thirteen Atlantic ports, all under the shadow of central control in Paris: Jan de Vries and Ad van der Woude, *The First Modern Economy: Success, Failure, and Perseverance of the Dutch Economy, 1500–1815* (Cambridge, 1997), p. 44; K. G. Davies, *The North Atlantic World*, pp. 50–1, 222–39; Josiah Child, *A New Discourse of Trade* (London 1692), p. 188; Stewart L. Mims, *Colbert's West India Policy* (New Haven, Conn., 1912); Nellis M. Crouse, *French Pioneers in the West Indies* (New York, 1940).
[8] Harper, *The English Navigation Laws*; Child, *New Discourse*, pp. 122, 81–2, 154.

Furthermore, although merchants did seek corporate privileges which would allow them to limit competition in the Atlantic sphere, joint-stock organization proved unsuited to the work of colonial expansion and most sectors of the commerce were unregulated, or 'free'.[9] Although the number of traders increased less rapidly than the volume of London's colonial trade, low barriers to entry allowed it to attract very large numbers until after the Glorious Revolution and the portbook database of 1686 lists over 1,500 participants (at a time when a London directory listed 1,829 full-time merchants). The open structure resulted in strong competition, and low persistence rates among the traders in the 1686 portbook database. Not surprisingly, merchants sought privileges which would allow them to reduce risk but the failure of the Restoration settlement to resolve a number of constitutional issues surrounding the prerogative rights and royal finances undermined the power of either the king or the opposition to capture regulation and although, as shown by the story of the Royal African Company, this did not entirely eliminate rent-seeking activity it did restrict its scale and scope.[10] In addition the distrust between Crown and Parliament precluded an expensive foreign policy and, although England suffered from two short wars with the Dutch between 1665 and 1675, it then enjoyed a long period of peace until 1689. In this important formative period England's Atlantic system remained substantially open to all denizens of the empire and (until the Glorious Revolution served to more closely align the interests of Crown, Parliament, and the commercial elites) colonial traders operated in a political and institutional context which provided unusually competitive and peaceful conditions. Ingenuity and enterprise were rewarded, and England improved efficiency to catch up with its rivals.

As promised by Elizabethan projectors, the success of the imperial project and the appropriation of New World lands provided a resource bonanza which was already making a strategic addition to supplies in 1700, although this was not fully reflected in overseas trade statistics.[11] Although Englishmen were disappointed that they did not stumble on gold and silver deposits in the style of the Iberian powers they were able to use their New World bases to establish better access to Spanish or Portuguese treasure and, in the 1680s, direct imports of bullion from

---

[9] Robert Brenner, *Merchants and Revolution: Commercial Change, Political Conflict and London's Overseas Traders, 1550–1653* (Cambridge, 1993).

[10] K. G. Davies, *The Royal African Company* (London, 1957); Nuala Zahedieh, 'Regulation, rent-seeking and the Glorious Revolution in the English Atlantic economy' *EcHR* (2009).

[11] Pomeranz, *Great Divergence*, ch. 6.

Jamaica were estimated to exceed £100,000 a year and almost equal the value of tobacco imports from the Chesapeake, although they were not recorded by port officials. The large volumes of fish which were shipped from Newfoundland to southern markets on London accounts, and the ships and barrels produced with American timber were also overlooked.[12]

Even without this natural bounty, the volume of London's colonial import trade more than trebled between the 1660s and 1700 when it accounted for a fifth of all recorded imports.[13] English settlers – infused with the contemporary spirit of experiment and improvement – had succeeded in harnessing white and black labour to their extensive New World lands and raised various cash crops, with tobacco and sugar accounting for over three-quarters of the value of recorded colonial imports into England. As planters and merchants gained experience in the business, they were able to reduce costs and prices, and former luxuries were converted into everyday staples. More and more people were able to substitute a pipe of tobacco, or a sweetened hot drink, for bread and beer, and as new consumption patterns were established, they helped to relieve the pressure on domestic grain supplies when population resumed its rise.[14] Increased availability of sugar as a preservative also greatly extended the country's effective supplies of fruit, vegetables, and meat. Furthermore, the volume of the tobacco and sugar trades underpinned investment in transport and distribution networks, which also supported a much smaller commerce in minor staples which could not be produced in England and provided a strategic addition to the nation's resource base: raw cotton, dye-stuffs, hardwoods, various drugs, and other raw materials. Further important raw materials were obtained from foreigners in exchange for colonial commodities which accounted for a third of the value of re-exports by 1700.[15]

---

[12] Nuala Zahedieh, 'The merchants of Port Royal, Jamaica and Spanish contraband trade, 1655–1692', *WMQ*, 43 (1986), 570–93; Robert Greenhalgh Albion, *Forests and Sea Power: the Timber Problem and the Royal Navy, 1652–1862* (Cambridge, Mass., 1926); Peter E. Pope, *Fish into Wine: the Newfoundland Plantation in the Seventeenth Century* (Chapel Hill, N.C., 2004).

[13] Gregory King's figures suggest that in 1688 the nation's overseas trade was worth around 20 per cent of national income (he valued overseas trade at £9 million and national income at £43.5 million). Colonial commerce, concentrated on London, was worth 15–20 per cent of the total: 'Seventeenth century manuscript book of Gregory King', in P. Laslett, (ed.), *The Earliest Classics: Graunt and King* (Farnborough, 1973), p. 207.

[14] Per capita beer consumption halved in the eighteenth century: Peter Mathias, *The Brewing Industry in England, 1700–1830* (Cambridge, 1959), p. 375.

[15] Patrick O' Brien, 'European industrialization; from the voyages of discovery to the Industrial Revolution', in Hans Pohl (ed.), *The European Discovery of the World and its Economic Effects on Pre-Industrial Society, 1500–1800* (Stuttgart, 1990), pp. 167–9.

However, the ghost acres which provided England with additional resources did not offer a 'free lunch'. Massive ingenuity and enterprise was required to tame a wilderness located on the other side of the ocean, to create viable communities, to establish production for export, and to organize the necessary networks of supply and distribution. The need to solve multiple organizational and technical problems before reaping the full rewards of overseas expansion provided Englishmen, and above all, Londoners, with a focusing device which encouraged the take-up of neglected best practices, and efforts to further improve efficiency. It also set in motion a cycle of mutually reinforcing feedback effects which allowed more intensive use of domestic resources – both human and natural – with important implications for England's long-run growth. Drawing together material presented in this book, it can be seen that endogenous responses to the market opportunities created by imperial expansion stimulated adaptive innovations on four main fronts: the accumulation and improvement of capabilities which made London the leading commercial centre in Europe; the expansion, diversification, and technological improvement of manufacturing capacity in the capital and beyond; the extension and enhancement of transport networks to create an increasingly integrated and commercialized national economy; and a major investment in the mathematical and mechanical skills which raised England to technological leadership in Europe.

Although London merchants made a limited direct investment in colonial cash-crop production, they did play a crucial role in the creation of the commercial networks needed to supply the colonies and bring their goods to market, adapting and refining best practice to improve efficiency and reduce costs by 20 or 30 per cent to match their Dutch rivals. Largely eschewing company regulation, colonial merchants set about refining alternative mechanisms for minimizing the risks of loss through opportunism and inadequate market information. Robust trust networks were essential and most turned to the familiar strategies of dealing with kin (at least thirty-two of the fifty-nine big colonial merchants of 1686 had kin links in the colonies), co-religionists, or others who shared social capital. Over two-thirds of the big colonial merchants of 1686 spent some time in the colonies (often immediately after completion of their apprenticeship) which allowed them to develop local knowledge and stronger business relationships. Efforts were made to limit agent opportunism with carrots (in the from of high commission rates) and sticks (in the form of hefty bonds for good behaviour) but neither could eliminate cheating in a world where information travelled slowly and was hard to verify.[16] However, the most successful merchants do seem to have reduced the problem through developing very high levels of specialization by place – with forty-six of the fifty-nine big colonial merchants of 1686 concentrating over 80 per cent of their plantation trade on one colonial destination – and very high levels of mutual dependence and shared risks. By the 1680s London merchants were withdrawing from direct investment in the increasingly precarious import trade with more than half the sugar entered on colonial account and the London merchant taking a small, but secure, commission. By the 1690s the Chesapeake tobacco traders were moving in the same direction. The capacity of small, close-knit minority groups – above all the Jews – to limit agent opportunism through better information and more punishment power was reflected in the more dispersed and balanced nature of their business. Other merchants sought to replicate the advantages of these small groups with more efficient collection and dissemination of commercial news, clubbability, and coffee-house culture.

As London merchants refined and improved their network-building skills they could diversify around their core commodity trade and pursue less risky lines of business. As has been highlighted in this book, transaction costs were exceptionally high in colonial trade – freight costs, insurance rates, commission rates, and other charges were three or four times as much as was usual in nearby trades – and invisible earnings not only filled the gap between the value of plantation imports and exports, but could substantially raise merchant incomes.[17] While London merchants who concentrated on trading in a narrow product range, in a small handful of nearby markets, faced lower transaction costs and had less incentive to adopt the most up-to-date techniques, those transacting over long distances, and engaging in complex multilateral trades in competitive conditions, were more anxious to emulate and improve upon continental practices and reduce costs. Instruments of credit were refined to accommodate the needs of Atlantic trade with longer issuance dates on bills of exchange than was usual in trade with Europe and steps were taken to make bills and other paper legally assignable and so reduce the length of time a trader was 'out of his money', and speed up the velocity of circulation. Specialists emerged to handle particular types of business with

---

[16] Ian K. Steele, *The English Atlantic, 1675–1740: an Exploration of Communication and Community* (New York, 1986).

[17] Commission rates were five times as high as in nearby trade, see above pp. 91, 99–101; freight rates were five times as high: see Davis, *Shipping Industry*, pp. 210, 222, 233–9, 262, 282–3; port charges were even greater, see above, p. 169.

savings in costs.[18] Commodity brokerage and insurance also became increasingly specialized and sophisticated. England had entered the seventeenth century as a commercial laggard, but the rapid expansion of long-distance, and above all colonial trade, played an important role in encouraging the accumulation of skills, information, and liquid capital (reflected in falling private interest rates) which by 1700 had allowed London to establish itself as a financial centre to rival, and soon overtake, Amsterdam.[19]

Alongside expanding the City's financial capabilities, London's colonial merchants cooperated to ensure that England was able to service the heavy shipping needs of the plantation trades at competitive cost. On account of the long distances involved, the shipping tonnage needed for any unit volume of goods was much higher than in nearby trades and, by 1686, plantation shipping accounted for 40 per cent of London's total overseas trading capacity. Most of the additional tonnage was English-built – using and improving traditional skills in producing ocean going vessels – and the expansion required a massive capital investment of around £70,000 a year which was largely drawn from within London's commercial community itself as ownership of a vessel was an important way for merchants to exploit their agent networks and diversify business.

As colonial commodity production was established, and volumes of exchange rose, merchants reaped the advantages of 'learning-by-doing', and economies of scale, and made efficiency gains in the carrying trade.[20] Packers learned to fit more in a standard container and stow more on board the vessels. As ships settled into regular trade patterns, and the volume of goods increased, turnaround times were shortened and there was less risk of underlading. Multilateral voyages were developed to make fuller use of vessels and cut back on idle periods in the seasonal trades. Those engaged in the victualling and refitting trades benefited from greater experience, economies of scale, and opportunities

[18] Child, New Discourse of Trade, pp. 7–8; Josiah Child, Trade and Interest of Money Considered (London, 1692), p. 106; Cary, Essay on Trade, pp. 32, 40.

[19] In the 1660s Dutch interest rates were reported to stand at 4 per cent, English at 6 per cent and Spanish and Portuguese at 10–12 per cent. By 1688 English rates had almost converged with the Dutch: Child, New Discourse of Trade, pp. 14–15; Gregory Clark, 'The political foundations of modern economic growth: England, 1540–1800', JIH, 47 (1996), 563–88; P. J. Cain and A. G. Hopkins, British Imperialism: Innovation and Expansion, 1688–1914 (London, 1993).

[20] Russell R. Menard, 'Transport costs and long-distance trade, 1300–1800: was there a European transport revolution in the early modern era?', in James D. Tracy (ed.), The Political Economy of Merchant Empires: State Power and World Trade, 1350–1750 (Cambridge, 1991), pp. 254–6.

for specialization although the success of the lessees of the Legal Quays
in defending and exploiting their monopoly privileges did hamper investment in the Port of London which might have further reduced servicing
costs.[21] Although the detailed evidence on freight rates is limited, it is
clear that, in peacetime, London's commercial community was able to
supply sufficient shipping to service the Atlantic trades and was also able
to do so at declining charge, and so helped provide English consumers
with New World commodities at falling prices.

While making a major contribution to the development of London as
the leading commercial centre in Europe, the expansion of colonial commerce also provided strong incentives to extend, diversify, and improve
the manufacturing capabilities in the capital and the country beyond.
Reference has been made to the large demand for carrying capacity which
underpinned a revival in the important ship-building industry and there
was a linked expansion in the demand for ships' instruments (clocks,
telescopes, and navigation tools) which were not always used in nearby
voyages but were essential for ocean navigation and did, in fact, provide
the main market for instruments as producer goods rather than luxury
consumption goods. With the expansion of demand for navigation tools
in England, and the damage inflicted on the competing French industry
by the large-scale emigration of Protestant craftsmen after 1685, London
had, by 1700, become established as the leading European instrument
making centre in Europe.[22]

Many New World products needed to be processed before consumption and the state used punitive fiscal policies to ensure that the mother
country, and not the colonies, obtained the lion's share of the benefits of
adding value. London was long established as England's largest manufacturing centre and the massive influx of colonial imports, combined
with ready access to capital, skilled labour (swelled by successive waves
of immigration in the late seventeenth century), and cheap coal supplies,
encouraged merchants to invest in processing industries which strengthened and diversified the city's industrial base partly at the expense of
continental centres.[23] Merchants also played an active part in establishing

[21] Henry Roseveare, ' "The Damned Combination": the port of London and the wharfingers' cartel of 1695', *London Journal*, 21 (1996), 97–111.
[22] Karel Davids, 'Shifts in technological leadership in early modern Europe', in Karel
Davids and Jan Lucassen (eds.), *A Miracle Mirrored: the Dutch Republic in European
Perspective* (Cambridge, 1995), pp. 338–66; Joel Mokyr, *The Lever of Riches: Technological
Creativity and Economic Progress* (Oxford, 1990), pp. 111–12, 240–1.
[23] The Dutch Republic faced dwindling supplies of peat by the end of the seventeenth
century, and although it imported coal it paid higher transport costs than in London
and high tax: J. W. de Zeeuw, 'Peat and the Dutch Golden Age: the historical meaning
of energy attainability', *AAG Bijdragen*, 21 (1978), 3–31; R. W. Unger, 'Energy sources

new industries to produce the utensils associated with consumption of colonial goods such as clay tobacco pipes and earthenware vessels for hot drinks, which encouraged the use of novel materials and processes with important consequences for pottery manufacture.[24]

Historians of early English expansion have neglected the export trade but colonies were valued as markets as much as they were valued as sources of raw materials. While it was difficult to break even on the colonial import trade in the late seventeenth century, the export trade continued to offer tempting returns and ensured continued interest in the commerce. Despite the usual emphasis on 'import-led' growth, in the period between 1660 and 1700, London's colonial exports grew faster than imports and an increasing proportion was home-produced. The breadth of colonial demand, and the favoured position of English producers, offered an attractive opportunity to diversify export production beyond traditional woollen cloths, which accounted for less than a quarter of the value of London's home-produced exports to the colonies in the late seventeenth century (Tables 6.5, 6.6 and 6.7).[25] The balance was made up with cottons and silks; clothing accessories such as shoes and hats; iron wares and nails; non-ferrous metals and above all copper; earthenware and glass; and a variety of miscellaneous manufactures (Tables 6.5 and 6.6).

The 170 big colonial merchants of 1686 are seen to have responded with relish to the opportunities offered by colonial markets and made substantial direct investments in industry in London and the provinces. Studies of individual industries including cotton textiles, the Midlands metal industries, non-ferrous metals, and the potteries suggest a common response to increased export demand and the availability of merchant capital.[26] In each case strong growth and improved productivity are seen from the 1680s, with efforts to reap economies of scale and reduce unit costs with larger units of production; more specialization within and between production units and regions; changes in the organization

---

for the Dutch Golden Age: peat, wind and coal', *Research in Economic History*, 9 (1984), 221–53.

[24] Lorna Weatherill, *The Pottery Trade and North Staffordshire, 1660–1760* (Manchester, 1971).

[25] Davis, 'English foreign trade, 1660–1700', p. 83.

[26] 'For discussion of the impact of the American market on European industry see Adam Smith, *An Inquiry into the Nature and Causes of the Wealth of Nations* (London, 1776), 1812 edn, pp. 465–7. A. P. Wadsworth and J. de la. Mann, *The Cotton Trade and Industrial Lancashire, 1600–1780* (Manchester, 1931); W. H. B. Court, *The Rise of the Midland Industries, 1600–1838* (Oxford, 1938); Roger Burt, 'The transformation of the non-ferrous metals industries in the seventeenth and eighteenth centuries', *EcHR*, 48 (1995), 23–45; Weatherill, *The Pottery Trade and North Staffordshire*.

of ownership and the structure of firms; more take-up of best practice techniques and more use of machines; and more interest in finding new solutions to pressing problems such as the coal-fuelled reverberatory furnace and improved drainage equipment in mines. With new market incentives and capital, available knowledge – was pulled into use and improved; Englishmen caught up with the late medieval technical frontier and pushed it forward a substantial distance.[27]

A third, and overlapping way, in which the expansion of London's colonial commerce led to improvements in the nation's adaptive efficiency was through its direct and indirect role in encouraging investment in the country's transport networks. Although around 70 per cent of colonial groceries entered the country through London, only around 15 per cent of retained supplies were consumed in London, and the remainder was carried out to provincial markets. The increased demand for transport out of the capital was met by extensions in the road and waterway networks which, according to Willan, exceeded both the rate of growth of London's population and its total overseas trade but matched the rate of growth in colonial commerce.[28] Better access to the buoyant London market for food, fuel, and manufactured goods, in turn encouraged increased specialization in the domestic economy and more use of best practice in agriculture, mining, and manufacturing with an increase in total output.[29] As shown by mean levels of output in agriculture or industry, England was not operating at a Malthusian frontier in the late seventeenth century, and as farmers, miners, and manufacturers were exposed to more attractive market opportunities, they made better use of latent resources.[30]

A final way in which colonial expansion led to greater adaptive efficiency was through its impact on training and the accumulation of useful knowledge. As reflected in Richard Ligon's description of early sugar

[27] It is well known that the cotton industry was 'brought to maturity in the context of oceanic trade,' but the pull of American markets also encouraged a shift from craft, to bulk production, in a wide range of other industries which had little prospect of success in continental markets: O'Brien, 'European industrialization', 167–69.

[28] T. S. Willan, *The Inland Trade: Studies in English Trade in the Sixteenth and Seventeenth Centuries* (Manchester, 1976).

[29] E. A. Wrigley, 'A simple model of London's importance in changing English society and economy', *Past and Present*, 37 (1967), 44–70.

[30] Karakacili has suggested levels of labour productivity on a group of Ramsay manors before the Black Death which compare with those on the most productive farms of 1800: E. Karakacili, 'English agrarian labour productivity before the Black Death', *JEH*, 64 (2004), 24–55; Hoffman, looking at the Paris basin, concluded that the 'bulk of the evidence points to urbanization being the cause of agricultural productivity gains, not a result; Philip Hoffman, *Growth in a Traditional Society: the French Countryside, 1450–1789* (Princeton, 1996), p. 171; Allen, 'Progress and poverty', 418.

planting, the imperial project rested on a faith in the capacity of men to tame and improve nature through careful observation, experiment, and accumulation of expertise which was reinforced by colonial successes with novel crops, processes, and labour systems.[31] Custom and tradition were valued and respected but increasingly seen as suitable objects for improvement, and the spirit of enquiry and experiment gained purchase as reflected in the formation of the Royal Society with its many colonial correspondents.

Furthermore, while participants in a traditional economy might survive, and even flourish, with poor levels of literacy and numeracy this would not do in the complex world of Atlantic commerce. Overseas merchants were usually required to master arithmetic 'to the rule of three' (which was not covered in the traditional classical curriculum of the grammar schools) before entering an apprenticeship and this was especially necessary in the multilateral long-distance trades. Ocean navigators, using charts and instruments, and ship-builders needed still greater mathematical competency as reflected in the curriculum of the king's scholars at Christ's hospital or Bushnell's handbook on shipbuilding.[32] So too did the surveyors who were employed to chart England's New World lands. Finally, the craftsmen who produced the necessary tools needed mathematical capabilities to calculate the forces and angles and produce very small, high-precision parts. The needs and opportunities of the imperial project nurtured and rewarded mathematical and mechanical skills in a variety of ways and played a major part in creating a cluster of craftsmen, entrepreneurs, inventors, and men of learning who interacted to promote the continuous cross-fertilization of ideas which, by 1700, took London to Europe's technological frontier and made Britain a likely site for the emergence of the new industrial technology which underpinned the Industrial Revolution.[33]

England's extensive growth across the Atlantic, in which Londoners played a pivotal role, offered new opportunities for specialization in the English economy and provided a major stimulus to the development of what Smith described as 'properly a commercial society' but was also an increasingly industrial society.[34] By 1700 the New World was already providing an important addition to the nation's supply base alongside a

[31] Richard Ligon, *A True and Exact History of the Island of Barbadoes* (London, 1657), pp. 86–89.
[32] Pearce, *Annals of Christ's Hospital* (London, 1901), pp. 99, 123–6; W. H. Quarrell and Margaret Mate (eds.), *London in 1710 from the Travels of Zacharius Conrad von Uffenbach* (London, 1934), p. 87.
[33] Mokyr, *The Lever of Riches,* pp. 111–12, 240–1.
[34] Smith, *Wealth of Nations,* p. 33.

new market for manufactures and services but it did not provide a 'free lunch'.[35] The creation of a working Atlantic system posed complex problems and raised solutions which rested on large reserves of capital, skill, and ingenuity which London proved able to provide. This study of the capital's colonial commerce has shown that, in the unusually competitive conditions that prevailed in Atlantic trade between the Restoration and the Glorious Revolution, invention was kept alive, and the mind was not suffered to fall into that 'drowsy stupidity' which could be caused by windfall gains and, according to Smith, had served to 'benumb the understanding' of so many other civilized societies.[36] Adaptive innovations were needed, and devised, on four main fronts – commerce, industry, transport, and technical competence – but as seen in the market for coal, or navigational instruments, pressures, problems and solutions overlapped and reinforced each other in multiple ways that stimulated better use of the nation's latent resources and raised efficiency in commerce, agriculture, and industry. The nation advanced to a new level of wealth and skill.

The Glorious Revolution and the consolidation of power in the hands of Parliament did allow vested interests to tighten their grip on the institutions which regulated imperial income streams and diverted much capital and enterprise into rent-seeking activities. Growth slowed, but the mercantile system which had been set in place after the Restoration proved sufficiently robust to survive with its essential features little changed until the American Revolution. As the volumes of trade increased, it was possible to achieve higher levels of specialization within the tripartite division of labour endorsed by the Navigation Acts, and, while Bristol, then Liverpool, took over much of the day-to-day operation of the slave trade, London retained its clearing-house function and its overall dominance of Britain's colonial commodity trade (accounting for 68 per cent of England's colonial imports and 70 per cent of its exports to the colonies as late as 1772/4).[37] Mercantilism continued to work and England's well coordinated and highly centralized system continued to out-perform other sectors of overseas trade and stimulate adaptive innovations which took the country to a new plateau of possibilities from which Industrial Revolution was not only possible but increasingly likely.

---

[35] Pomeranz, *Great Divergence*, ch. 6. Smith provides lengthy discussion of the problems in the section 'Of Colonies', in *An Inquiry into the Nature and Causes of the Wealth of Nations* (1776); Jack P. Greene, 'Social and cultural capital in colonial British America: a case study', *JIH*, 29 (1999), 491–509.

[36] Smith, *Wealth of Nations*, p. 616.

[37] PRO CUST. 3/72–4: Christopher J. French, 'Crowded with traders and a great commerce: London's domination of overseas trade, 1700–1775', *London Journal*, 17 (1992), 27–35.

Bibliography

ARCHIVAL SOURCES

LONDON

Bank of England Archive
'Journal of Thomas Sandes', 1698–1703, M 7/4
'Letterbook of John Browne and Thomas Sandes', 1701–3, M 7/19
'Letterbook of Thomas Sandes and John Browne', 1692–6, M 7/3
'Minutes of Court of Directors of Bank of England', G 4
'Order Book of Court of Directors of Bank of England'

British Library
Add. MS 4,759, 7,421, 11,410, 12,424, 12,430, 14,034, 25,115, 25,120, 28,140, 28,878, 29,000, 29,800, 36,785, 70,421
Egerton MS 2,395, 2,648
Harleian MS 1,238
India Office X538
Lansdowne MS 83
Sl. MS 2,441, 2,717, 2,724, 2,902, 3,662, 3,926, 3,984, 3,986, 4,020, 36,319
Thomason Tracts E 864, 919
Tracts on Trade

Corporation of London Record Office
Common Serjeants' Book, vol. IV
Journal of Common Council, 1682–8
Loan Accounts, MS 40/34, MS 40/35, Misc. MS/133/25
Mayor's Court Depositions, MCD, boxes 38, 39, 40–42
Mayor's Court Interrogatories, MC 6/1–554
Mayor's Court Original Bills, box 196, no. 42
Miscellaneous Inventories, roll 155, box 55
Orphans' Court Inventories, 302, 1,057, 2,124, 2,200, 2,409, 2,754, 2,817, 2,818, 2,200, 2,501

Guildhall Library
'Day book of Charles Peers', 1689–95, MS 10,187
MS 1,196/1, 4,118/1, 6,679
'Case of the traders of London', 1705, MS A8.4, no. 68

Library of the Society of Friends, Friends House
Cases of Suffering, Mic. 16, 1693, 1694
Yearly Meeting Minutes, vol. I (1668–93)

National Maritime Museum, Greenwich
Letters from Lynch, GOS/5–6
Letters from Victualling Board, 1703–4, ADM/D/2
Naval Office Papers CAD/B4
'Present State of Jamaica', 1688, IGR/71

Public Record Office
Admiralty ADM 7/75–6, 106/303
Chancery
C. 7/405/40 7/530/76
C. 8/242/138
C 9 177/128
C 24/859 1129–35, 1139, 1142, 1161, 1162, 1164, 1168, 1181, 1186, 1309,
    1315, 1317
C 104/128
C 105/12 181, 1181
C 110 /152
C 113/14
Colonial Office
CO 1/17–68
CO 5/848, 858, 859, 959, 1309, 1362
CO 29/3, 4
CO 31/2
CO 33/13–14
CO 138/1–10
CO 140/1–4
CO 142/13
CO 153/3
CO 155/1
CO 195/1–2
CO 268/1
CO 388/1, 10
CO 389/2, 389/16
CO 390/14
Customs
CUST. 2/2, 6, 8, 9
CUST. 3/ 1–6, 21, 72–4
Exchequer
E 112/143, 473
E 134/2
E 190/1 56/1, 136/4, 136/6, 137/2, 5, 8, 139/1,
    141/5, 143/1
High Court of Admiralty
HCA 4/14
HCA 13/27, 77–80, 82, 131, 132, 155

HCA 14/55–7
HCA 15/10, 14
HCA 24/122
HCA 26/1
HCA 30/653, 654, 664, 864
Kings Bench KB 9/10, 21, 37, 39
Privy Council PC 2/69, 73
Royal African Company T 70/1, 10, 12, 22, 57, 61, 75, 77, 80–83, 100, 127, 169, 962–72, 1199
SP 29/281, 417, 418
Wills PROB 4, 5, 11
Prerogative Court of Canterbury 45, 122, 150, 261, 1741
Treasury T 48/89

Westminster Abbey Muniments Room and Library
11,348–49, 11,689, 11,938, 11,940

ENGLISH PROVINCES

Bodleian Library, Oxford
Ashurst Letterbook, MS Don. C169
MS Aubrey 4 (SC 252 79)
MS Clarendon 71, 72, 87, 88
MS Locke c30
MS Rawl. A 348, 478, B 250, C 840, D 924

Cambridge University Library
CH (H) Papers 80/74 84/1–27, 89/1–30.

Leeds City Library, Sheepscar Branch
London portbook (Christmas 1718–Christmas 1719), Newby Hall MS (NH) 2,440

Lincolnshire County Archive, Lincoln
Ancaster MS
Pearson Gregory Papers 2P.G. 12/2/5

Somerset Record Office, Taunton
Bybrook Plantation, 1662–1714, Walker Heneage MSS DD/WHh 1089, 1090, 1151, Addenda Papers 12

OVERSEAS RECORD OFFICES AND LIBRARIES

American Philosophical Society Library, Philadelphia
Journal of George Welch, MS 917.29/W455

Archives of Barbados
Deeds RB 3/14
Wills RB 6/10

Archives of Jamaica, Spanish Town
Inventories, 1B/11/3 vols. I–IV
Powers of Attorney 1B/11/24 vols. I, 7, 8, 9

Essex Institute, Salem, Massachusetts
English Papers, box 1

Historical Society of Pennsylvania, Philadelphia
Norris Papers, vol. I

Island Record Office, Spanish Town
Deeds

Massachusetts Historical Society, Boston
'Boston Merchant's Account Book', 1688–94
Higginson Family Papers
Jeffries Family Papers, vols. I–VII
Shrimpton Family Papers

National Library of Jamaica, Kingston
Letter to Nottingham, March 1689, MS 390
'Letterbook of William Freeman', MS 134
'Taylor's history of his life and travels in America', 1688, MS 105

New York Historical Society
Accounts of James and Henry Lloyd
'Letterbook of Jacobus van Cortlandt', 1698–1700

PRINTED PRIMARY SOURCES

OFFICIAL PAPERS

Acts of the Privy Council of England, Colonial Series, 1680–1720.
Boulton, Nathaniel (ed.), *Provincial Papers: Documents and Records relating to the Province of New Hampshire from 1686 to 1722*, vol. II (Manchester, N. H., 1868).
Calendar of State Papers, Colonial, America and the West Indies.
Calendar of Treasury Books.
Kingsbury, Susan M. (ed.), *The Records of the Virginia Company of London*, 5 vols. (Washington, DC, 1906–35).
Journals of the House of Commons.
Journals of the House of Lords.
Manuscripts of the House of Lords.
Rich, E. E. (ed.), *Hudson's Bay Copy Books of Letters, Commissions, Instructions Outward, 1688–96* (London, 1957).
Stock, L. F., *Proceedings and Debates of the British Parliament Respecting North America*, 5 vols. (Washington, DC, 1924–41).

DIARIES AND LETTERS

Balderston, Marion (ed.), *James Claypoole's Letterbook, London and Philadelphia, 1681–84* (San Marino, Calif., 1967).

Connell, Neville, 'Father Labat's visit to Barbados in 1700', *JBMHS*, 20 (1957), 160–74.

Crouch, William, *Posthuma Christiana or a Collection of Some Papers of William Crouch Being a Brief Historical Account under his own Hand* (London, 1712).

Davis, Richard Beale (ed.), *Fitzhugh and his Chesapeake World, 1676–1701* (Chapel Hill, N.C., 1963).

Forster, Ann M. C. (ed.), *Selections from the Disbursements Book (1691–1709) of Sir Thomas Haggerston Bart.*(Gateshead, 1969).

Gunkel, Alexander and Handler, Jerome S., 'A Swiss Medical Doctor's Description of Barbados in 1661: the account of Felix Christian Spoeri', *JBMHS*, 33 (1969), 8–10.

Hancock, David (ed.), *The Letters of William Freeman, London Merchant, 1678–1685* (London, 2002).

Henning, B. D. (ed.), *Sir Edward Dering: the Parliamentary Diary, 1670–73* (New Haven, Conn., 1940).

Horwitz, Henry (ed.), *Minutes of a Whig Club, 1714–17* (London, 1981).

Ingram, B. S. (ed.), 'Diary of Francis Rogers', *Three Sea Journals of Stuart Times* (London, 1936).

Jeaffreson, J. C., (ed.), *A Young Squire of the Seventeenth Century from the Papers of Christopher Jeaffreson*, 2 vols. (London, 1878).

Latham, R. C., and Matthews, W. (eds.), *The Diary of Samuel Pepys*, 11 vols. (London, 1970–83).

Lubbock, Basil (ed.), *Barlow's Journal of his Life at Sea in King's Ships, East and West Indiamen and other Merchantmen from 1659 to 1703* (London, 1934).

Marshall, J. D. (ed.), *The Autobiography of William Stout of Lancaster, 1655–1752* (Manchester, 1957).

Oliver, Vere (ed.), *Caribbeana: Being Miscellaneous Papers Relating to the History, Genealogy, Topography, and Antiquities of the British West Indies*, 6 vols. (London, 1909–19).

Quarrell, W. H. and Mate, Margaret (eds.), *London in 1710 from the Travels of Zacharius Conrad von Uffenbach* (London, 1934).

Riden, Philip (ed.), *George Sitwell's Letterbook, 1662–66* (Chesterfield, 1985).

Roseveare, Henry (ed.), *Markets and Merchants of the Late Seventeenth Century: the Marescoe–David Letters, 1668–1680* (Oxford, 1987).

Steckley, George F. (ed.), *The Letters of John Paige, London Merchant, 1648–1658* (London, 1984).

Story, Thomas, *A Journal of the Life of Thomas Story* (Newcastle, 1747).

Tanner, J. R. (ed.), *Pepys' Memoires of the Royal Navy, 1679–88* (London, 1906).

Tinling, Marion (ed.), *The Correspondence of the Three William Byrds of Westover, Virginia, 1684–1776*, 2 vols. (Charlottesville, Va., 1977).

Verney, Margaret M., *Memoirs of the Verney Family from the Restoration to the Revolution 1660–1696*, 4 vols. (London, 1894).

BOOKS AND PAMPHLETS

An Answer to a Proposal for Laying a Duty upon Hats (London, 1695).
Arbor, Edward (ed.), *Travels and Works of Captain John Smith* (Edinburgh, 1910).
Besse, *A Collection of the Sufferings of the People called Quakers for the Testimony of Good Conscience*, 2 vols. (London, 1753).
Beverley, Robert, *The History and Present State of Virginia* (Chapel Hill, N.C., 1947).
Blith, Walter, *The English Improver Improved or The Survey of Husbandry Surveyed. Discovering the Improveableness of all Lands* (London, 1653).
Blome, Richard, *A Description of the Island of Jamaica* (London, 1672).
Bosman, *A New and Accurate Description of the Coast of Guinea* (1721).
Brewster, Francis, *Essays on Trade and Navigation* (London, 1695).
A Brief Description of the Province of Carolina (London, 1666).
The British Merchant, 22–25 June 1714
Budd, Thomas, *Good Order Established in Pennsylvania and New Jersey in America* (Philadelphia, 1685).
Burton, Richard, *Historical Remarques and Observations of the Ancient and Present State of London and Westminster* (London, 1684).
Bushnell, Edmund, *The Compleat Ship-Wright* (London, 1662).
C. T. *An Advise How to Plant Tobacco in England* (1615).
Cary, John, *An Essay on the State of England in Relation to its Trade* (Bristol, 1695).
Case of the Fair Trader (London, 1686).
The Case of the Traders of London. As it now stands since the copartnership of the wharfingers (London, 1705).
The Case of William Penn Esq. As to the Proprietary Government of Pennsylvania (London, 1701).
Chamberlayne, John, *The Manner of Making of Coffee, Tea and Chocolate as it is used in most parts of Europe, Asia, Africa and America with their Virtues* (London, 1685).
Character and Qualifications of an Honest, Loyal Merchant (London, 1686).
Child, Josiah, *A New Discourse of Trade* (London, 1692).
  Trade and Interest of Money Considered (London, 1692).
Collins, Greenvile, *Great Britain's Coasting Pilot* (1693).
Considerations Concerning the African Companies petition (London, 1680).
Considerations Humbly Offered to the Honourable House of Commons, by the Traders and others Trading to our British Plantations in relation to the African Company's Petition (London, 1709).
Considerations Humbly Offered by the Planters and Others Trading to our British plantations in relation to the African Company's Petition (London, 1698).
Craigie, J. (ed.), *Minor Prose Works of King James VI and I* (Edinburgh, 1982).
Gentleman's Magazine, III (January, 1733).

Davenant, Charles, *Discourses on the Public Revenues and on the Trade of England in Two Parts* (London, 1698).

De Beer, E. S. (ed.), *John Evelyn. London Revived. Considerations for its Rebuilding in 1666 (Londinium Redivivum, or London Restored not to its Pristine, but to far greater Beauty, Commodiousness and Magnificence)* (Oxford, 1938).

Defoe, Daniel, *An Essay Upon Projects* (London, 1697).

A Plan of the English Commerce (London, 1728).

A Description of Plain Dealing, Truth and Death which all Men Ought to Mind whilst they do live on Earth (London, 1686).

Diderot, Denis, *Encyclopaedia, or a Systematic Dictionary of Science, Arts and the Trades*, 28 vols. (Paris, 1751–71).

A Discourse Consisting of Motives for the Enlargement and Freedom of Trade (London, 1645).

A Discourse of Husbandry used in Brabant and Flanders showing the Wonderful Improvement of Land there; and Serving as a Pattern for our Practice in this Commonwealth (London, 1652).

Evelyn, John, *Navigation and Commerce their Original and Progress* (London, 1674).

Farey, John, *A Treatise on the Steam Engine, Historical, Practical and Descriptive* (London, 1827).

Ghirelli, Michael, *A List of Emigrants from England to America, 1682–92* (Baltimore, Md., 1968).

Glover, Thomas, *An Account of Virginia, its Scituation, Productions, Inhabitants and the Mannor of Planting and Ordering Tobacco* (London, 1676).

Gray, Robert, *A Good Speed to Virginia* (London, 1609).

Hakluyt, Richard, 'A particular discourse concerning the great necessitie and manifold comodyties that are like to grow to this realme of England by the western discoveries lately attempted' (1584), reprinted in *Maine Historical Society Collections*, vol. II (1877).

Handler, J. S., 'Father Antoine Biet's visit to Barbados in 1654', *JBMHS*, 32 (1967), 66.

Hanson, Francis, *The Laws of Jamaica, Passed by the Assembly and Confirmed by his Majesty in Council, February 1683. To which is Added, a Short Account of the Island and Government There of* (London, 1683).

Hartlib, Samuel, *The Reformed Virginian Silk-Worm* (London, 1652).

Hellot, J., *The Art of Dyeing Wool and Woollen Cloth* (London, 1789).

N.H. *The Compleat Tradesman* (London, 1684).

The Pleasant Art of Moneycatching (London, 1686).

Holme, Randolph, *The Academy of Armory or a Storehouse of Armory and Blazon* (Chester, 1688).

Hotten, J. C. (ed.), *The Little London Directory of 1677. The Old Printed List of the Merchants and Bankers of London* (London, 1863).

Houghton, John, *A Collection for the Improvement of Husbandry and Trade*, 12 vols. (London, 1692–1703).

R.J., *Nova Brittania. Offering Most Excellent Fruits by Planting in Virginia* (London, 1609).

Johnson, T., *A Discourse Consisting of Motives for the Enlargement and Freedom of Trade* (London, 1645).

Labat, John Baptiste, *Nouveau Voyage aux Isles de L'Amerique*, 8 vols. (Paris, 1743).

Lansdowne, Henry Fitzmaurice (ed.), *The Petty Papers. Some Unpublished Papers of Sir William Petty*, 2 vols. (London, 1927).

de Laune, T., *The Present State of London* (London, 1681).

Laslett, P. (ed.), *The Earliest Classics: John Graunt and Gregory King* (Farnborough, Hants., 1973).

Lee, Samuel, *The Little London Directory of 1677* (London, 1878).

Ligon, Richard, *A True and Exact History of the Island of Barbadoes* (London, 1657).

May, Robert, *The Accomplished Cook* (London, 1671).

Morgan, William, *London &c Actually Survey'd* (1682)

Moseley, Benjamin, *A Treatise on Sugar*, 2nd edn (London, 1800).

Oldmixon, John, *The British Empire in America*, 2 vols. (London, 1708).

Payne, Robert, *A Brief Description of Ireland made in this Year, 1589* (London, 1589).

Penn, William, 'The benefits of plantations and colonies' (1680), in *Select Tracts Relating to Colonies* (London, 1732).

A Perfect Description of Virginia (London, 1649).

Petty, William, *Essays on Political Arithmetic* (London, 1699).

Petyt, William, *Britannia Languens or a Discourse of Trade* (London, 1680).

A Proclamation to Prohibit His Majesty's Subjects to Trade within the Limits Assigned to the Royal African Company of England except those of the Company (London, 1685).

Reasons Humbly Offered to the Consideration of Parliament why Stockfish and Live Eels should be Imported into England (London, 1695).

Reynal, Carew, *The True English Interest* (London, 1674).

'The Randolph Manuscript', *VMHB*, 17 (1909).

Sloane, Hans, *A Voyage to the Islands Madeira, Barbados, Nieves, St Christopher's and Jamaica*, 2 vols. (London, 1707–25).

Smith, Adam, *An Inquiry into the Nature and Causes of the Wealth of Nations* (London, 1776), 1812 edn.

Stallenge, William, *Instructions for the Increasing of Mulberry Trees and the Breeding of Silkworms* (London, 1609).

Steele, Richard, *A Tradesman's Calling* (London, 1686).

Thomas, Dalby, *An Historical Account of the Rise and Growth of the West India Colonies and the Great Advantage they are to England in Respect of Trade* (London, 1690).

  Propositions for a General Land Bank (London, 1695).

Tryon, Thomas, *Health's Grand Preservative or the Women's Best Doctor* (London, 1682).

  The Way to Health, Long Life and Happiness (London, 1691).

  Tryon's Letters, Domestick and Foreign to Several Persons of Quality Occasionally Distributed in Subjects (London, 1700).

  Some Memoires of the Life of Mr. Thomas Tryon (London, 1705).

The Two Associations (London, 1681).

The Virtues and Excellency of the American Tobacco Plant for the Cure of Diseases and Preservation of Health (London, 1712).

Van Keulen, Johannes, *The Great and Newly Enlarged Sea Atlas or Waterworld* (Amsterdam, 1682).

Whitworth, Charles (ed.), *The Political and Commercial Works of the Celebrated Writer Charles D'Avenant*, 5 vols. (London, 1771).

Wilkinson, William, *Systema Africanum or a Treatise Discovering the Intrigues and Arbitrary Proceedings of the Guinea Company* (London, 1690).

Wilson, Samuel, *An Account of the Province of Carolina* (London, 1682).

Worsley, Benjamin, *The Advocate: or, a Narrative of the State and Condition of Things between the English and Dutch Nation in Relation to Trade* (London, 1651).

Wright, Louis B. (ed.), *The History and Present State of Virginia by Robert Beverley* (Chapel Hill, N.C., 1947).

Wycherley, William, *The Country Wife*, in Robert G. Lawrence (ed.), *Restoration Plays* (London, 1976), pp. 85–160.

SECONDARY SOURCES

Albion, Robert Greenhalgh, *Forests and Sea Power: the Timber Problem and the Royal Navy, 1652–1862* (Cambridge, Mass., 1926).

Allen, Robert C., 'Progress and poverty in early modern Europe', *EcHR*, 56 (2003), 403–43.

Ambrosoli, Mauro, *The Wild and the Sown: Botany and Agriculture in Western Europe, 1350–1850* (Oxford, 1997).

Amory, Hugh and Hall, David (eds.), *A History of the Book in America* (Cambridge, 2000).

Anderson, J. R. C. 'Early books on ship-building and rigging', *Mariner's Mirror*, 10 (1924), 53–64.

Andrews, Charles M., *British Committees, Commissions and Councils of Trade and Plantations, 1622–75* (Baltimore, Md., 1908).

The Colonial Period of American History, 4 vols. (New Haven, Conn., 1934–8).

Andrews, K. R., *The Spanish Caribbean: Trade and Plunder, 1530–1630* (New Haven, Conn., 1978).

Trade, Plunder and Settlement: Maritime Enterprise and the Genesis of the British Empire, 1480–1630 (Cambridge, 1984).

Andrews, K. R., Canny, N. P., and Hair, P. E. H. (eds.), *The Westward Enterprise: English Activities in Ireland and America, 1480–1650* (Liverpool, 1978).

Appleby, John C., 'A Guinea venture, c. 1657: a note on the early English slave trade', *Mariner's Mirror*, 79 (1993), 84–7.

' "A business of much difficulty": a London slaving venture, 1651–54', *Mariner's Mirror*, 81 (1995), 3–14.

Appleby, Joyce Oldham, *Economic Thought and Ideology in Seventeenth Century England* (Princeton, 1978).

Archer, Ian W., *The History of the Haberdashers Company* (Chichester, 1991).

Ashton, T. S., Introduction in E. B. Schumpeter (ed.), *English Overseas Trade Statistics, 1697–1818* (Oxford, 1960), pp. 1–14.

Astrom, Sven-Erik, *From Cloth to Iron: the Anglo-Baltic Trade in the Late Seventeenth Century* (Helsingfors, 1963).

Atkinson, D. and Oswald, A., 'London clay tobacco pipes', *The Journal of the British Archaeological Association*, 3rd ser. 32 (1969), 171–227.

Aymard, M. (ed.), *Dutch Capitalism and World Capitalism* (Cambridge, 1982).

Baetens, R., 'The organization and effects of Flemish privateering in the seventeenth century', *Acta Historiae Neerlandicae*, 9 (1976), 561–96.

Bailyn, Bernard, *The New England Merchants in the Seventeenth Century* (Cambridge, Mass., 1955).

'Politics and social structure in Virginia', in James Morton Smith (ed.), *Seventeenth-Century America. Essays in Colonial History* (Chapel Hill, N.C., 1959), pp. 90–115.

Bailyn, Bernard and Bailyn, Lotte, *Massachusetts Shipping, 1697–1714: a Statistical Study* (Cambridge, Mass., 1959).

Bairoch, P., *Cities and Economic Development* (Chicago, 1990), pp. 39–86.

Baker, Emerson W. and Reid, John G., *The New England Knight: Sir William Phips, 1651–1695* (Toronto, 1998).

Baker, William Avery, 'Vessel types of colonial Massachusetts', *PCSM*, 52 (1980), 3–29.

Barbour, Violet, 'Privateers and pirates of the West Indies', *American Historical Review*, 16 (1911), 529–66.

'Marine risks and insurance in the seventeenth century', *Journal of Economic and Business History*, 1 (1928–9), 561–96.

'Dutch and English merchant shipping in the seventeenth century', *EcHR*, 2 (1930), 261–90.

Barnard, T. C., 'Planters and policies in Cromwellian Ireland', *Past and Present*, 61 (1973), 31–69.

'The Hartlib circle and the cult and culture of improvement in Ireland', in Greengrass et al. (eds.), *Samuel Hartlib*, pp. 281–97.

Barnes, Viola F., 'Richard Wharton, a seventeenth century New England colonial', *PCSM*, 26 (1924–6), 258–70.

Barrett, Ward, 'Caribbean sugar-production standards in the seventeenth and eighteenth centuries', in John Parker (ed.), *Merchants and Scholars: Essays in the History of Exploration and Trade* (Minneapolis, 1965), pp. 147–70.

Bean, Richard N., 'Food imports into the British West Indies: 1680–1845', in Vera Rubin and Arthur Tuden (eds.), *Comparative Perspectives of Slavery in New World Plantation Societies* (New York, 1977), pp. 581–96.

Beckles, Hilary McD., *White Servitude and Black Slavery in Barbados, 1627–1715* (Knoxville, Tenn., 1989).

'The "Hub of empire": the Caribbean and Britain in the seventeenth century', in Canny (ed.), *Origins of Empire*, pp. 233–4.

Beckles, Hilary McD. and Downes, A., 'The economics of transition to the black labour system in Barbados, 1630–1680', *JIH*, 18 (1987), 225–47.

Beer, G. L., *The Origins of the British Colonial System, 1578–1660* (New York, 1908).

The Old Colonial System, 1660–1754, 2 vols. (New York, 1912), vol. I.

Beier, A. L., 'Engine of manufacture: the trades of London', in Beier and Finlay (eds.), *London 1500–1700*, pp. 115–40.

Beier, A. L. and Finlay, Roger (eds.), *London 1500–1700: the Making of the Metropolis* (London, 1986).

Bennett, J. H., 'Cary Helyar, merchant and planter of seventeenth century Jamaica', *WMQ*, 21 (1964), 53–76.

Beresford, M. W., 'The beginnings of retail tobacco licenses', *Yorkshire Bulletin of Economic and Social Research*, 7 (1955), 139.

Bieber, R. P., *The Lords of Trade and Plantations, 1675–1696* (Allentown, Penn., 1919).

Billings, Warren M., 'Sir William Berkeley and the Diversification of the Virginia Economy', *Virginia Magazine of History and Biography*, 104 (1996), 443–54.

Binning, Arthur Cecil, *British Regulation of the Colonial Iron Industry* (Oxford, 1933).

Bloom, Herbert I., *The Economic Activities of the Jews in Amsterdam in the Seventeenth and Eighteenth Centuries* (Williamsburg, Va., 1939).

Boogaart, Ernst van den, 'The servant migration to New Netherland, 1624–64', in P. C. Emmer (ed.), *Colonialism and Migration: Indentured Labour Before and After Slavery* (Dordrecht, 1986), pp. 55–81.

Bosher, J. F., 'Huguenot merchants and the Protestant International in the seventeenth century', *WMQ*, 52 (1995), 77–102.

Boulton, Jeremy, 'Wage labour in seventeenth-century London', *EcHR*, 44 (1996), 268–90.

'Food prices and the standard of living in London in the "century of revolution", 1580–1700', *EcHR*, 53 (2000), 455–92.

Brathwaite, William C., *The Beginnings of Quakerism to 1660* (London, 1912). *The Second Period of Quakerism* (London, 1919).

Braudel, Fernand, *The Wheels of Commerce* (London, 1982).

Breen, T. H., *Tobacco Culture: the Mentality of the Great Tidewater Planters on the Eve of Revolution* (Princeton, N.J., 1985).

Brenner, Robert C., *Merchants and Revolution: Commercial Change, Political Conflict, and London's Overseas Traders, 1550–1653* (Cambridge, 1993).

Brewer, John, and Porter, Roy (eds.), *Consumption and the World of Goods* (London, 1993).

Bridenbaugh, Carl, *The Colonial Craftsmen* (New York, 1950).

Bridenbaugh, Carl and Bridenbaugh, Roberta, *No Peace Beyond the Line: the English in the Caribbean, 1624–1690* (New York, 1972).

Bruce, Philip A., *Economic History of Virginia in the Seventeenth Century*, 2 vols. (New York, 1896).

Bruijn, Jaap R., 'Productivity, profitability and costs of private and corporate Dutch ship ownership in the seventeenth and eighteenth centuries', in J. D. Tracy (ed.), *The Rise of Merchant Empires: Long Distance Trade in the Early Modern World, 1350–1750* (Cambridge, 1990), pp. 174–94.

Brooks, Christopher, 'Apprenticeship, social mobility and the middling sort', in J. Barry and Christopher Brooks (eds.), *The Middling Sort of People* (Basingstoke, 1994).

Buchanan, J. M., Tollinson, R. D., and Tullock, G. (eds.), *Toward a Theory of a Rent-Seeking Society* (College Station, Tex., 1980).

Burnard, Trevor, 'A failed settler society: marriage and demographic failure
    in early Jamaica', *Journal of Social History,* 28 (1994), 63–82.
    'European migration to Jamaica, 1655–1780', *WMQ,* 53 (1996), 769–94.
Burt, Roger, 'The transformation of the non-ferrous metals industries in the
    seventeenth and eighteenth centuries', *EcHR,* 48 (1995), 23–45.
Butel, Paul, 'France, and the Antilles and Europe in the seventeenth and
    eighteenth centuries: renewals of foreign trade', in James D. Tracy (ed.),
    *The Rise of Merchant Empires:. Long Distance Trade in the Early Modern
    World, 1350–1750* (Cambridge, 1990), pp. 153–73.
Butler, Jon, *The Huguenots in America: a Refugee People in New World Society*
    (Cambridge, 1983).
Cain, P. J. and Hopkins, A. G., *British Imperialism: Innovation and Expansion,
    1688–1914* (London, 1993).
Callow, John, *The Making of James II: the Formative Years of a Fallen King*
    (Stroud, Gloucs., 2000).
Campbell, M., 'Of people either too few or too many', in W. A. Aitken and
    B. O. Henning, (eds.), *Conflict in Stuart England: Essays in Honour of
    Wallace Notestein* (London, 1960), pp. 169–201.
Canny, Nicholas, 'English migration into and across the Atlantic during
    the seventeenth and eighteenth centuries', in Nicholas Canny (ed.),
    Europeans on the Move: Studies of European Migration, 1500–1800 (Oxford,
    1994), pp. 39–75.
Canny, Nicholas (ed.), *The Oxford History of the British Empire,* 5 vols.
    (Oxford, 1998), vol. I, *The Origins of Empire: British Overseas Enterprise to
    the Close of the Seventeenth Century.*
Carlos, Ann and Nicholas, Stephen, 'Giants of an earlier capitalism: the
    early chartered companies as modern multi-nationals', *BHR* (1988),
    398–419.
    'Joint stock chartered trading companies', *JEH,* 56 (1996), 916–25.
Carr, Lois Green and Walsh, Lorena S., 'Economic diversification and labour
    organization in the Chesapeake, 1650–1820', in Stephen Innes (ed.),
    Work and Labour in Early America (Chapel Hill, N.C., 1988), pp. 144–88.
    'Changing lifestyles and consumer behaviour in the colonial
    Chesapeake', in Cary Carson, Ronald Hoffman, and Peter J. Albert,
    (eds.), *Of Consuming Interests: the Style of Life in the Eighteenth Century*
    (Charlottesville, Va., 1994), pp. 59–166.
Carr, Lois Green, Menard, Russell R. and Walsh, Lorena S., *Robert Cole's
    World: Agriculture and Society in Early Maryland* (Chapel Hill, N.C.,
    1991).
Carruthers, Bruce C., *City of Capital: Politics and Markets in the English
    Financial Revolution* (Princeton, 1999).
Carter, Jennifer, 'Law, Courts and Constitution', in J. R. Jones (ed.), *The
    Restored Monarchy* (London, 1979), pp. 71–93.
Cell, Gillian T., *English Enterprise in Newfoundland, 1577–1660* (Toronto,
    1969).
Chandaman, C. D., *The English Public Revenue, 1660–1688* (Oxford, 1975).
Chartres, John, 'No English calvados? English distillers and the cider indus-
    try in the seventeenth and eighteenth centuries', in John Chartres and

David Hey (eds.), *English Rural Society: Essays in Honour of Joan Thirsk* (Cambridge, 1990), pp. 330–42.

Chaudhuri, K. N., *The English East India Company: a Study of an Early Joint Stock Company, 1600–1640* (London, 1965).

The Trading World of Asia and the English East India Company, 1660–1780 (Cambridge, 1978).

Clark, G. N., *Guide to English Commercial Statistics, 1696–1782* (London, 1938).

Clark, Gregory, 'The political foundations of modern economic growth: England 1540–1800', *JIH*, 47 (1996), 563–88.

Clark, Victor S., *History of Manufactures in the United States*, 3 vols. (Washington, D.C., 1929).

Clemens, P. G. E., 'The rise of Liverpool, 1665–1750', *EcHR*, 29 (1976), 211–25.

Clowse, Converse D., *Economic Beginnings in Colonial South Carolina, 1670–1730* (Columbia, S.C., 1971).

Coclanis, Peter A. (ed.), *The Atlantic Economy during the Seventeenth and Eighteenth Centuries* (Columbia, S.C., 2005), pp. 1–29.

Cohen, Patricia Cline, 'Reckoning with commerce: numeracy in eighteenth century America', in John Brewer and Roy Porter (eds.), *Consumption and the World of Goods* (London, 1993), pp. 320–34.

Cole, Alan, 'The social origins of the early friends', *Journal of the Friends Historical Society*, 48 (1956–8), 99–118.

Coleman, D. C., 'London scriveners and the estate market in the later seventeenth century', *EcHR*, 4 (1952), 221–30.

'Naval dockyards under the later Stuarts', *EcHR*, 6 (1953), 134–55.

The British Paper Industry, 1495–1960 (Oxford, 1958).

Commons, J. R.. 'American shoemakers, 1648–1875: a sketch of industrial evolution', *Quarterly Journal of Economics*, 24 (1910), 39–84.

Corner, David, 'The tyranny of fashion: the case of the felt-hatting trade in the late seventeenth and eighteenth centuries', *Textile History*, 22 (1991), 153–78.

Court, W. H. B., *The Rise of the Midland Industries, 1600–1838* (Oxford, 1938).

Cowan, Brian, *The Social Life of Coffee: the Emergence of the British Coffee House* (New Haven, Conn., 2005).

Craven, Wesley Frank, *Dissolution of the Virginia Company: the Failure of a Colonial Experiment* (New York, 1932).

'An introduction to the history of Bermuda', *WMQ*, 17 (1937), 176–215.

Croft, Pauline, 'The rise of the English stocking export trade', *Textile History*, 18 (1987), 3–16.

Crouse, Nellis M., *French Pioneers in the West Indies* (New York, 1940).

Cruickshanks, Eveline, Handley, Stuart, and Hayton, D. W. (eds.), *The History of Parliament: the House of Commons, 1690–1715* , 5 vols. (Cambridge, 2002).

Crump, H. J., *Colonial Admiralty Jurisdiction in the Seventeenth Century* (London, 1931).

Curtin, Philip D., *The Atlantic Slave Trade: a Census* (Madison, Wis., 1969).

306 Bibliography

Davids, Karel, 'Shifts in technological leadership in early modern Europe', in Karel Davids and Jan Lucassen (eds.), *A Miracle Mirrored: the Dutch Republic in European Perspective* (Cambridge, 1995), pp. 338–66.

Davies, K. G., 'The origins of the commission system in the West India trade', *TRHS* (1951), 89–107.

'Joint-stock investment in the later seventeenth century', *EcHR*, 4 (1952), 283–301.

The Royal African Company (London, 1957).

The North Atlantic World in the Seventeenth Century (Oxford, 1974).

Davis, Ralph, 'English foreign trade, 1660–1700', *EcHR*, 7 (1954), 150–66.

'English foreign trade, 1700–1774', *EcHR*, 15 (1962), 285–303.

The Rise of the English Shipping Industry in the Seventeenth and Eighteenth Centuries (Newton Abbot, 1962).

A Commercial Revolution: English Overseas Trade in the Seventeenth and Eighteenth Centuries (London, 1967).

The Rise of the Atlantic Economies (London, 1973).

Deane, Phyllis and Cole, W. A., *British Economic Growth, 1688–1959*, 2nd edn (Cambridge, 1967).

Deerr, Noel, *History of Sugar*, 2 vols. (London, 1949–50).

De Krey, Gary Stuart, *A Fractured Society: the Politics of London in the First Age of Party, 1688–1715* (Oxford, 1985).

London and the Restoration, 1659–83 (Cambridge, 2005).

Devine, T. M, *Tobacco Lords: a Study of the Tobacco Merchants of Glasgow and their Trading Activities c. 1740–90* (Edinburgh, 1975).

De Zeeuw, J. W., 'Peat, and the Dutch Golden Age: the historical meaning of energy attainability', *AAG Bijdragen*, 21 (1978), 3–31.

Dietz, Brian, 'The engine of manufacture: the trades of London', in Beier and Finlay (eds.), *London*, pp. 141–67.

Dietz, Brian (ed.), *The Port, and Trade of Early Elizabethan London* (London, 1972).

Dickson, P. G. M., *The Financial Revolution in England: a Study in the Development of Public Credit, 1688–1756* (London, 1967).

Dore, Ron, *Taking Japan Seriously* (Stanford, Calif., 1987).

Draper, Nick, 'The City of London and slavery: evidence from the first dock companies, 1795–1800', *EcHR*, 61 (2008), 432–66.

Dunn, Richard S., *Sugar and Slaves: the Rise of the Planter Class in the English West Indies, 1624–1713* (Chapel Hill, N. C., 1972).

'The Glorious Revolution and America' in Canny (ed.), *Origins of Empire*, pp. 445–66.

Earle, Peter, *The World of Defoe* (Newton Abbot, 1976).

Monmouth's Rebels: the Road to Sedgemoor, 1685 (London, 1977).

The Wreck of the Almiranta: Sir William Phips and the Search for the Hispaniola Treasure (London, 1979).

The Making of the English Middle Class: Business, Society, and Family Life in London, 1660–1730 (London, 1989).

'The economy of London, 1660–1730', in Patrick O'Brien (ed.), *Urban Achievements in Early Modern Europe: Golden Ages in Antwerp, Amsterdam, and London* (Cambridge, 2001), pp. 81–96.

Ehrman, John, *The Navy in the War of William III, 1689–1697* (Cambridge, 1953).

Ekulund, R. B. and Tollinson, R. D., *Mercantilism as a Rent-Seeking Society: Economic Regulation in Historical Perspective* (College Station, Tex., 1981).

Politicized Economies: Monarchy, Monopoly, and Mercantilism (College Station, Tex., 1997).

Ellis, Aytoun, *The Penny Universities: a History of the Coffee Houses* (London, 1956).

Eltis, David, 'New estimates of exports from Barbados and Jamaica, 1665–1701', *WMQ*, 52 (1995), 631–48.

'The British transatlantic slave trade before 1714: annual estimates of volume and direction', in Paquette and Engerman (eds.), *The Lesser Antilles in the Age of European Expansion*, pp. 182–205.

The Rise of African Slavery in the Americas (Cambridge, 2000).

Eltis, David, Lewis, Frank D., and Richardson, David, 'Slave prices, the African slave trade, and productivity in the Caribbean, 1674–1807', *EcHR*, 58 (2005), 673–700.

Emmer, P. C., ' "Jesus Christ was good but trade was better": an overview of the transit trade of the Dutch Antilles, 1634–1795', in Paquette and Engerman (eds.), *The Lesser Antilles in the Age of European Expansion*, pp. 206–22.

Emmer, P. C. (ed.), *Colonialism and Migration: Indentured Labour Before and After Slavery* (Dordrecht, 1986).

Engerman, Stanley L. and Gallman, Robert E. (eds.), *The Cambridge History of the United States*, 3 vols. (Cambridge, 1996).

Engerman, Stanley L. and O'Brien, Patrick K., 'The industrial revolution in global perspective', in Floud and Johnson (eds.), *The Cambridge Economic History of Modern Britain*, vol. I.

Epstein, S. R., *Freedom and Growth: the Rise of States and Markets in Europe, 1300–1750* (London, 2000).

Fairlie, Susan, 'Dyestuffs in the eighteenth century', *EcHR*, 17 (1965), 488–510.

Farnell, J. E., 'The Navigation Act of 1651, the first Dutch war, and the London merchant community', *EcHR*, 16 (1961–2), 439–54.

Finlay, Roger and Shearer, Beatrice, 'Population growth, and suburban expansion', in Beier, and Finlay (eds.), *London 1500–1700*, pp. 37–59.

Fisher, F. J., 'The development of London as a centre of conspicuous consumption in the sixteenth and seventeenth centuries', *TRHS*, 30 (1948), 37–50.

Fisher, F.J, 'London's export trade in the early seventeenth century', *EcHR*, 3 (1950), 151–61.

Flinn, Michael W., *Men of Iron: the Crowleys in the Early Iron Industry* (Edinburgh, 1962).

Floud, Roderick and Johnson, Paul (eds.), *The Cambridge Economic History of Modern Britain*, 3 vols. (Cambridge, 2004).

Fox, Adam, 'Sir William Petty, Ireland, and the making of a political economist, 1653–87', *EcHR*, 62 (2009), 388–404.

Fox, Dixon Ryan, *Caleb Heathcote, Gentleman Colonist, 1692–1721* (New York, 1924).

Fudenberg, D. and Tirole, J., *Game Theory* (Cambridge, Mass., 1992).

Frank, Andre Gunder, *World Accumulation, 1492–1789* (New York and London, 1978).

    Dependent Accumulation and Underdevelopment (New York and London, 1979).

    ReOrient: Global Economy in the Asian Age (Berkeley and Los Angeles, 1998).

French, Christopher J., 'Crowded with traders, and a great commerce: London's domination of overseas trade, 1700–1775', *London Journal*, 17 (1992), 27–35.

Fudenberg, D., Levine, D., and Maskin, E., 'The folk theorem and imperfect public information', *Econometrica*, 62 (1994), 997–1039.

Fukuyama, Francis, *Trust: the Social Virtues and the Creation of Prosperity*, (New York, 1995).

Galenson, David W., *White Servitude in Colonial America: an Economic Analysis* (Cambridge, 1981).

    'White servitude and the growth of black slavery in colonial America', *JEH*, 41 (1981), 38–49.

    'The settlement and growth of colonies: population, labour, and economic development', in Engerman and Gallman (eds.), *The Cambridge Economic History of the USA*, vol. I, pp. 135–41.

Gambetta, D. 'Can we trust trust?' in D. Gambetta (ed.), *Trust: Making and Breaking Cooperative Relations* (Oxford, 1988), pp. 213–37.

Games, Alison, *Migration and the Origins of the English Atlantic World* (Cambridge, Mass., 1999).

Gauci, Perry, *The Politics of Trade: the Overseas Merchant in State and Society, 1660–1720* (Oxford, 2001).

Gerhold, Dorian, 'The growth of the London carrying trade, 1681–1838', *EcHR*, 41 (1988), 392–410.

Gill, Anton, *The Devil's Mariner: a Life of William Dampier, Pirate and Explorer, 1651–1715* (London, 1997).

Glaisyer, Natasha, *The Culture of Commerce in England, 1660–1720* (Woodbridge, Suffolk, 2006).

Goodman, Jordan, *Tobacco in History: the Culture of Dependence* (London, 1993).

Goodman, Jordan, Lovejoy, Paul E., and Sherratt, Andrew (eds.), *Consuming Habits: Drugs in History and Anthropology* (London, 1995).

Gragg, Larry, ' "To procure Negroes": the English slave trade in Barbados, 1627–60', *Slavery and Abolition*, 16 (1995), 65–84.

Grassby, Richard, 'The rate of profit in seventeenth century England', *EHR*, 84 (1969), 721–31.

    The English Gentleman in Trade: the Life and Works of Sir Dudley North, 1641–1691 (Oxford, 1994).

    The Business Community in Seventeenth Century England (Cambridge, 1995).

Gray, Lewis Cecil, *A History of Agriculture in the Southern United States to 1860*, 2 vols. (Washington, 1933).

Greaves, J. P. and Hollingsworth, Dorothy F., 'Changes in the pattern of carbohydrate consumption in Britain', *Proceedings of the Nutrition Society,* 23 (1964), 136–43.

Green, James N., *The Rittenhouse Mill and the Beginnings of Papermaking in America* (Phil., 1990).

Greene, Jack P., *Peripheries and Centre: Constitutional Development in the Extended Polities of the British Empire and the United States, 1607–1780* (Athens, Ga., 1986).

Greengrass, Mark, Leslie, Michael, and Raylor, Timothy (eds.), *Samuel Hartlib and Universal Reformation: Studies in Intellectual Communication* (Cambridge, 1994).

Guttridge, G. H., *The Colonial Policy of William III in America and the West Indies* (Cambridge, 1922).

Gwynne, Robin D., *Huguenot Heritage: the History and Contribution of the Huguenots in Britain* (London, 1985).

Haffenden, Philip S., 'The crown and the imperial charters, 1675–1688: Part 1', *WMQ,* 15 (1958), 297–311.

Hair, P. E. H. and Law, Robin 'The English in Western Africa in 1700', in Canny (ed.), *The Origins of Empire,* pp. 241–63.

Hall, M. G., *Edward Randolph and the American Colonies, 1676–1703* (Chapel Hill, N.C., 1960).

Hancock, David, 'Markets, merchants and the wider world of Boston wine, 1700–1775', in Conrad E. Wright and Katheryn P. Viens (eds.), *Entrepreneurs: the Boston Business Community, 1700–1850* (Boston, Mass., 1997), pp. 63–95.

'Commerce and conversation in the eighteenth-century Atlantic: the invention of Madeira wine', *JIH,* 29 (1998), 197–219.

' "A world of business to do": William Freeman and the foundations of England's commercial empire, 1645–1707', *WMQ,* 57 (2000), 3–34.

'A revolution in the trade: wine distribution and the development of the Atlantic market economy, 1703–1807', in McCusker and Morgan (eds.), *The Early Modern Atlantic Economy,* pp. 105–53.

'Markets, merchants and the wider world of Boston wine, 1700–1775', in Conrad E. Wright and Katheryn P. Viens (eds.), *Entrepreneurs: the Boston Business Community, 1700–1850* (Boston, Mass., 1997), pp. 56–76.

Haring, C. H., *Trade and Navigation between Spain and the Indies in the Time of the Habsburgs* (Cambridge, Mass., 1918).

Harley, David, 'The beginnings of the tobacco controversy: Puritanism, James I and the royal physicians', *Bulletin of the History of Medicine,* 67 (1993), 28–50.

Harper, Lawrence A., *The English Navigation Laws: a Seventeenth Century Experiment in Social Engineering.*

'The effects of the Navigation Acts on the thirteen colonies', in Morris, R. B. (ed.), *The Era of the American Revolution* (New York, 1939).

Harris, Tim, *Politics under the Later Stuarts: Party Conflict in a Divided Society,* 1660–1715 (London, 1993).

Harte, N. B., 'The rise of protection and the English linen trade, 1690–1790' in N. B. Harte and K. G. Ponting (eds.), *Textile History and Economic History* (Manchester, 1973), pp. 74–112.

Hartley, E. N., *Ironworks on the Saugus: the Lynn and Braintree Ventures of the Company of Undertakers of the Ironworks in New England* (Norman, Okla., 1957).

Hatch, Charles E., 'Mulberry trees and silkworms: sericulture in early Virginia', *VMHB*, 65 (1957), 3–61.

Hatcher, John, *The History of the British Coal Industry*, 5 vols. (Oxford, 1993), vol. I.

Hatfield, April Lee, 'Dutch and New Netherland merchants in the seventeenth-century English Chesapeake', in Coclanis (ed.), *The Atlantic Economy in the Seventeenth and Eighteenth Centuries*, pp. 205–28.

Hazard, B. E., *The Organisation of the Boot and Shoe Industry in Massachusetts before 1875* (Cambridge, Mass., 1921).

Heathcote, Evelyn D., *An Account of Some of the Families Bearing the Name of Heathcote* (Winchester, 1899).

Henning, Basil D. (ed.), *House of Commons, 1660–90*, 3 vols. (London, 1983).

Hewson, J. B., *A History of the Practice of Navigation*, 2nd edn (Glasgow, 1963).

Higham, Charles S., *The Development of the Leeward Islands under the Restoration, 1660–1688: a Study of the Foundations of the Old Colonial System* (Cambridge, 1921).

Higman, Barry W., 'The sugar revolution', *EcHR*, 53 (2000), 213–36.

Hinton, R. W. K., *The Eastland Trade and the Common Weal in the Seventeenth Century* (Cambridge, 1959).

Hoppit, Julian, *A Land of Liberty? England 1689–1727* (Oxford, 2000).

Horn, James, *Adapting to a New World: English Society in the Seventeenth Century Chesapeake* (Chapel Hill, N.C., 1994).

Horwitz, Henry, 'Testamentary practice, family strategies, and the last phases of the custom of London, 1600–1725', *Law and History Review*, 2 (1984), 223–39.

Hounshell, D., *From the American System to Mass Production, 1800–1932: the Development of Manufacturing Technology in the United States* (Baltimore, Md., 1984).

Hunter, M., *Establishing the New Science: the Experience of the Early Royal Society* (Woodbridge, Suffolk, 1989).

Hutchison, Terence, *Before Adam Smith: the Emergence of Political Economy. 1662–1776* (Cambridge, 1988).

Inikori, Joseph E., *Africans and the Industrial Revolution in England: a Study in International Trade and Development* (Cambridge, 2002).

Innis, Harold A., *The Cod Fisheries: the History of an International Economy*, rev. edn (Toronto, 1954).

  The Fur Trade in Canada: an Introduction to Canadian Economic History (New Haven, Conn., 1930).

Israel, Jonathan I., *European Jewry in the Age of Mercantilism, 1550–1750* (Oxford, 1985).

  Empires and Entrepots: the Dutch, the Spanish Monarchy and the Jews (London, 1990).

Jacob, Margaret, *Living the Enlightenment: Freemasonry and Politics in Eighteenth Century Europe* (Oxford, 1991).

Scientific Culture and the Making of the Industrial West (New York, 1997).

Jacob, Margaret C. and Stewart, Larry, *Practical Matter: Newton's Science in the Service of Industry and Empire, 1687–1851* (Cambridge, Mass., 2004).

Janzen, Olaf U. (ed.), *Merchant Organization and Maritime Trade in the North Atlantic, 1660–1815* (Newfoundland, 1998).

Jarvis, Rupert C., 'Eighteenth century London shipping', in A. E. Hollaender and W. Kellaway (eds.), *Studies in London History* (London, 1969), pp. 403–25.

'The metamorphosis of the port of London', *The London Journal*, 3 (1977), 55–72.

Jones, D. W., *War and Economy in the Age of William III and Marlborough* (Oxford, 1988).

Jones, J. R., *Country and Court: England 1658–1714* (London, 1978).

Jones, S. R. H. and Ville, Simon P., 'Efficient transactors or rent-seeking monopolists? The rationale for early chartered trading companies', *JEH*, 56 (1996), 898–915.

Jones, Theophilus, *A History of the County of Brecknock*, 4 vols. (Brecknock, 1909–30).

Kamen, H., *Spain in the Later Seventeenth Century, 1665–1700* (London, 1980).

Karakacili, E., 'English agrarian labour productivity before the Black Death', *JEH*, 64 (2004), 24–55.

Karraker, C. H., 'Spanish treasure, casual revenue of the crown', *Journal of Modern History*, 5 (1933), 301–18.

Keirn, Tim, 'Monopoly, economic thought, and the Royal African Company', in John Brewer and Susan Staves (eds.), *Early Modern Conceptions of Property* (London, 1996), pp. 427–66.

Kellaway, William, *The New England Company, 1649–1776* (London, 1961).

Klooster, Wim, *Illicit Riches. Dutch Trade in the Caribbean, 1648–1795* (Leiden, 1998).

Kussmaul, Ann, *Servants in Husbandry in Early Modern England* (Cambridge, 1981).

Kuznets, Simon, *Economic Growth and Structure* (New York, 1965).

Labaree, L. W., *Royal Government in America* (New Haven, Conn., 1930).

Landes, David S., *The Unbound Prometheus* (Cambridge, 1969).

Laudan, Rachel, 'Cognitive change in technology and science' in Rachel Laudan (ed.), *The Nature of Knowledge: Are Models of Social Science Relevant?* (Dordrecht, 1984), pp. 83–104.

Lee, R., 'American cochineal in European commerce, 1526–1625', *Journal of Modern History*, 23 (1951), 205–24.

Lemire, Beverly, *Fashion's Favourite: the Cotton Trade and the Consumer in Britain, 1660–1800* (Manchester, 1991).

Leng, Thomas, 'Commercial conflict and regulation in the discourse of trade in seventeenth century England', *HJ*, 48 (2005), 933–54.

Benjamin Worsley (1618–1677): Trade, Interest and the Spirit in Revolutionary England (Woodbridge, Suffolk, 2008).

Lewis, Peta, 'William Lee's stocking frame: technical evolution and economic
   viability 1589–1750', *Textile History*, 17 (1986), 129–14.
Lewis, Theodore B., 'Land speculation and the Dudley Council of 1686',
   WMQ, 31 (1974), 255–72.
Lorimer, Joyce, 'The English contraband trade from Trinidad and
   Guiana, 1590–1617', in Andrews *et al.*, (eds.), *The Westward Enterprise*,
   pp. 124–50.
McCusker, John J., 'The current value of English exports, 1697–1800',
   WMQ, 28 (1971), 607–28.
   'European bills of entry and marine lists: early commercial publications
   and the origins of the business press', *Harvard Library Bulletin, 31* (1984),
   209–55, 316–39.
   'British mercantilist policies and the American colonies', in Engerman and
   Gallman (eds.), *The Cambridge History of the United States*, vol. I.
McCusker, John J. and Menard, Russell R., *The Economy of British America,
   1607–1789* (Chapel Hill, N.C., 1985).
   'The sugar industry in the seventeenth century: a new perspective on the
   "Barbadian Sugar Revolution"', in Schwartz (ed.), *Tropical Babylons*,
   pp. 289–330.
McCusker, John J. and Morgan, Kenneth (eds.), *The Early Modern Atlantic
   Economy* (Cambridge, 2000).
McMahon, Sarah F., 'A comfortable subsistence: the changing composition
   of diet in rural New England, 1620–1840', *WMQ*, 42 (1985), 26–65.
MacLeod, Christine, 'The 1690s patent boom: invention or stock-jobbing?',
   EcHR, 39 (1986), 549–71.
Machlup, Fritz, *Knowledge: its Creation, Distribution, and Economic
   Significance*, 3 vols. (Princeton, 1980–4).
Magnusson, Lars, *Mercantilism: the Shaping of an Economic Language*
   (London, 1994).
Malone, Joseph J., *Pine Trees and Politics: the Naval Stores and Forest Policy in
   Colonial New England, 1691–1775* (Seattle, Wash., 1964).
Mathias, Peter, *The Brewing Industry in England, 1700–1830* (Cambridge,
   1959).
Matson, Cathy, *Merchants and Empire: Trading in Colonial New York*
   (Baltimore, Md., 1998).
Mauro, Frederick, *Le Portugal et l'Atlantique au XVII siècle (1570–1670)* (Paris,
   1960).
Mazumdar, Sucheta, *Sugar and Society in China: Peasants, Technology and the
   World Market* (Cambridge, Mass., 1998).
Meinig, D. W., *The Shaping of America: a Geographical Perspective on 500 years
   of History* (New Haven, Conn., 1986), vol. I.
Menard, Russell R., 'The tobacco industry in the Chesapeake colonies, 1617–
   1730: an interpretation', *Research in Economic History*, 5 (1980), 109–77.
   'Transport costs and long-distance trade, 1300–1800: was there a
   European transport revolution in the early modern era?', in Tracy (ed.),
   The Political Economy of Merchant Empires, pp. 228–75.
   *Sweet Negotiations: Sugar, Slavery, and Plantation Agriculture in Early
   Barbados* (Charlottesville, Va., 2006).

Mims, Steward L., *Colbert's West India Policy* (New Haven, Conn., 1912).

Minchinton, W. E., *The Trade of Bristol in the Eighteenth Century* (Bristol, 1957).

Minchinton, W. E. (ed.), *The Growth of English Overseas Trade in the Seventeenth and Eighteenth Centuries* (London, 1969).

Mintz, Sydney W., *Sweetness and Power: the Place of Sugar in Modern History* (New York, 1985).

Mitchell, David, ' "Good hot pressing is the life of all cloth": dyeing, cloth finishing, and related textile trades in London, 1650–1700', in Herman Diederiks and Marjan Balkestein (eds.), *Occupational Titles and their Classification: the Case of the Textile Trade in Past Times* (Gottingen, 1995), pp. 153–75.

Mokyr, Joel, *The Lever of Riches: Technological Creativity and Economic Progress* (Oxford, 1990).

The Gifts of Athena: Historical Origins of the Knowledge Economy (Princeton, 2002).

Money, John, 'Teaching in the market place, or "Caesar adsum jam torte: Pompey aderat": the retailing of knowledge in provincial England during the eighteenth century', in Brewer and Porter (eds.), *Consumption, and the World of Goods*, pp. 335–77.

Montgomery, Florence M., *Textiles in America, 1650–1870* (New York, 1984), p. 145.

Morgan, Edmund S., *American Slavery, American Freedom: the Ordeal of Colonial Virginia* (New York, 1975).

Morgan, Kenneth, *Bristol and the Atlantic Trade in the Eighteenth Century* (Cambridge, 1993).

Slavery, Atlantic Trade and the British Economy, 1660–1800 (Cambridge, 2000).

Morris, R. B. (ed.), *The Era of the American Revolution* (New York, 1939).

Mumford, L., *Technics and Civilization* (London, 1934).

Nash, Gary B., *Quakers and Politics: Pennsylvania, 1681–1726* (Princeton, N.J., 1968).

Nash, R. C., 'The English and Scottish tobacco trades in the seventeenth and eighteenth centuries: legal and illegal trade', *EcHR*, 35 (1982), 352–72.

'Irish Atlantic trade in the seventeenth and eighteenth centuries', *WMQ*, 42 (1985), 329–56.

'South Carolina and the Atlantic Economy in the late seventeenth and eighteenth centuries', *EcHR*, 45 (1992), 677–702.

'The organization of trade and finance in the British Atlantic economy, 1600–1830', in Coclanis, (ed.), *The Atlantic Economy during the Seventeenth and Eighteenth Centuries*, pp. 95–151.

Neal, Larry, 'The rise of a financial press: London and Amsterdam, 1680–1810', *Business History*, 30 (1988), 163–78.

Nettels, Cortis. P., 'The menace of colonial manufacturing', *New England Quarterly*, 4 (1931), 230–69.

The Money Supply of the American Colonies before 1720 (Madison, Wis., 1934).

Noordegraaf, Leo and van Zanden, Jan Luiten, 'Early modern economic growth and the standard of living: did labour benefit from Holland's Golden Age?', in Karel Davids and Jan Lucassen (eds.), *A Miracle Mirrored: the Dutch Republic in European Perspective* (Cambridge, 1995), pp. 410–37.

North, Douglas C., *Institutions, Institutional Change and Economic Performance* (Cambridge, 1990).

North, Douglas C. and Weingast, Barry R., 'Constitutions and commitment: the evolution of institutions governing public choice in seventeenth century England', *JEH*, 49 (1989), 803–32.

Nuvolari, Allessandro, *The Making of Steam Technology: a Study of Technical Change during the Industrial Revolution* (Eindhoven, 2004).

O'Brien, Patrick, 'European economic development: the contribution of the periphery', *EcHR*, 35 (1982), 1–18.

    'European industrialization: from the voyages of discovery to the Industrial Revolution', in Pohl (ed.), *The European Discovery of the World*, pp. 154–77.

    'The reconstruction, rehabilitation, and reconfiguration of the British Industrial Revolution as a conjuncture in global history', *Itinerario*, 24 (2000), 117–34.

O'Brien, Patrick (ed.), *Urban Achievements in Early Modern Europe: Golden Ages in Antwerp, Amsterdam, and London* (Cambridge, 2001).

Olson, Alison G., *Making the Empire Work: London and American Interest Groups, 1690–1790* (Cambridge, Mass., 1992).

Ormrod, David, 'The Atlantic economy and the "Protestant Capitalist International", 1651–1775', *Historical Research*, 66 (1993), 197–208.

    The Rise of Commercial Empires: England and the Netherlands in the Age of Mercantilism, 1650–1770 (Cambridge, 2003).

Osborne, F. J., 'James Castillo, asiento agent', *JHR*, 8 (1971), 9–18.

Oswald, A., 'The archaeology and economic history of English clay tobacco pipes', *The Journal of the British Archaelogical Association* (1960), 40–102.

Pagan, John R., 'Dutch maritime and commercial activity in mid-seventeenth century Virginia', *VMHB*, 90 (1982), 485–501.

Page, William (ed.), *VCH Rutland*, vol. II (1935).

Pares, Richard, *Yankees and Creoles: the Trade between North America and the West Indies before the American Revolution* (London, 1956).

    Merchants and Planters (Cambridge, 1960).

Parent, Anthony S., *Foul Means: the Formation of a Slave Society in Virginia, 1660–1740* (Chapel Hill, N.C., 2003).

Paquette, Robert L. and Engerman, Stanley L. (eds.), *The Lesser Antilles in the Age of European Expansion* (Gainesville, Fla., 1996).

Parker, John (ed.), *Merchants and Scholars: Essays in the History of Exploration and Trade* (Minneapolis, 1965).

Pearce, E. H., *Annals of Christ's Hospital* (London, 1901).

Pelling, Margaret, 'Appearance and reality: barber surgeons, the body and disease', in Beier and Finlay (eds.), *London 1500–1700*, pp. 82–112.

Penson, Lillian M., *The Colonial Agents of the British West Indies* (London, 1924).

Pettigrew, William A., 'Free to enslave: politics and the escalation of Britain's transatlantic slave trade, 1688–1714', *WMQ*, 64 (2007), 3–38.

Phelps-Brown, E. H. and Hopkins, S. V. 'Seven centuries of the prices of con-
    sumables compared to the builders' wage rates', in E. M. Carus-Wilson
    (ed.), *Essays in Economic History*, 3 vols. (London, 1954–62), pp. 179–96.
Phillips Jr., William D., 'Sugar in Iberia', in Schwartz (ed.), *Tropical Babylons*,
    pp. 27–41.
Pincus, S., 'From butterboxes to wooden boxes: the shift in English popular
    sentiment from anti-Dutch to anti-French in the 1670s', *HJ*, 28 (1995),
    333–61.
Plant, M., *The English Book Trade* (London, 1974).
Plumb, J. H., *The Growth of Political Stability in England, 1675–1725* (London,
    1967).
Pohl, Hans (ed.), *The European Discovery of the World and its Economic Effects
    on Pre-Industrial Society, 1500–1800* (Stuttgart, 1990).
Pomeranz, Kenneth, *The Great Divergence: China, Europe, and the Making of
    the Modern World Economy* (Princeton, 2000).
Pope, Peter E., *Fish into Wine: the Newfoundland Plantation in the Seventeenth
    Century* (Chapel Hill, N.C., 2004).
Porath, Y. Ben, 'The F-Connection: families, friends, and firms and the
    organization of exchange', *Pop. Dev. Review*, 6 (1980), 1–30.
Postma, Johannes M., *The Dutch in the Atlantic Slave Trade, 1600–1815*
    (Cambridge, 1990).
Prak, Maarten, *The Dutch Republic in the Seventeenth Century* (Cambridge,
    2005).
Prak, Maarten (ed.), *Early Modern Capitalism: Economic and Social Change in
    Europe, 1400–1800* (London, 2001).
Price, J. M., 'Notes on some London price currents, 1667–1715', *EcHR*, 7
    (1954), 240–50.
    'Joseph Martin', *Notes and Queries*, 203 (1958), 440–1.
    *The Tobacco Adventure to Russia: Enterprise, Politics, and Diplomacy in the
    Quest for a Northern Market for English Colonial Tobacco, 1676–1722* (*Trans.
    of the American Philosophical Society*, 51, Philadelphia, 1961).
    *France and the Chesapeake: a History of the French Tobacco Monopoly, 1674–
    1794, and its Relationship to the British and American Tobacco Trades*, 2 vols.
    (Ann Arbor, Mich., 1973).
    'A note on the value of colonial exports of shipping', *JEH*, 36 (1976),
    704–24.
    'Colonial trade and British economic development, 1660–1775' in *Lex et
    Scientia: the International Journal of Law and Science*, 14 (1978), 101–26.
    'Sheffeild v. Starke: institutional experimentation in the Maryland trade c.
    1696–1706', *Business History*, 28 (1986), 19–31.
    'What did merchants do? Reflections on British overseas trade, 1660–
    1790', *JEH*, 49 (1989), 267–84.
    'Transaction costs: a note on merchant credit and the organization of pri-
    vate trade', in Tracy (ed.), *The Political Economy of Merchant Empires*,
    pp. 276–97.
    Perry of London: a Family and a Firm on the Seaborne Frontier, 1615–1753
    (Cambridge, Mass., 1993).
    'Tobacco use and tobacco taxation: A battle of interests in early modern
    Europe', in Goodman *et al.* (eds.), *Consuming Habits*, pp. 165–85.

Price, Jacob. M. and Clemens, P. G. E., 'A revolution of scale in overseas
    trade: British firms in the Chesapeake trade, 1675–1775', *JEH*, 47
    (1987), 1–43.
Pulling, Alexander, *A Practical Treatise on the Laws, Customs and Regulations of
    the City and Port of London* (London, 1842).
Putnam, R., *Making Democracy Work: Civic Traditions in Modern Italy*
    (Princeton, 1993).
Rabb, Theodore K., *Enterprise and Empire: Merchant and Gentry Investment in
    the Expansion of England, 1575–1630* (Cambridge, Mass., 1967).
Raistrick, A., 'The London Lead Company, 1692–1905', *Trans. Newcomen
    Society*, 14 (1933–4), 122–5.
Reddaway, T. F., *The Rebuilding of London after the Great Fire* (London, 1940).
    'Livery companies of Tudor London', *History*, 51 (1966), 287–99.
Reynard, Pierre Claude, 'Manufacturing quality in the pre-industrial
    age: finding value in diversity', *EcHR*, 53 (2000), 493–516.
Rich, E. E., 'Russia and the colonial fur trade', *EcHR*, 7 (1955), 307–28.
    The History of the Hudson's Bay Company, 1670–1870 (London, 1958–9).
Richardson, H. W., *The Economics of Urban Size* (Farnborough, 1973).
Riley, J. C., 'The Dutch economy after 1650: decline or growth?', *JEEH*, 13
    (1984), 521–69.
Roessingh, H. K., 'Tobacco growing in Holland in the seventeenth and eight-
    eenth centuries: a case study of the innovative spirit of Dutch peasants',
    The Low Countries History Yearbook, 12 (1978), 18–54.
Rogers, James Stevens, *The Early History of the Law of Bills and Notes: a Study
    of the Origins of Anglo-American Commercial Law* (Cambridge, 1995).
Roper, H. R., *Men and Events: Historical Essays* (New York, 1957).
Rose, J. Holland, Newton, A. P., and Benians, E. P. (eds.), *The Cambridge
    History of the British Empire* (Cambridge, 1929), vol. I.
Rosenberg, N. (ed.) *Perspectives on Technology*, (Cambridge, 1976).
Roseveare, Henry, *The Financial Revolution, 1660–1760* (London, 1991).
    ' "Wiggins' Key" revisited: trade and shipping in the later seventeenth cen-
    tury', *Journal of Transport History* (1995), 1–20.
    ' "The Damned Combination": the port of London and the wharfingers'
    cartel of 1695', *London Journal*, 21 (1996), 97–111.
    'Property versus commerce in the mid eighteenth century port of London',
    in McCusker and Morgan (eds.), *The Early Modern Atlantic Economy*,
    pp. 65–85.
Rothstein, N. K., 'Canterbury and London: the silk industry in the late seven-
    teenth century', *Textile History*, 20 (1989), 33–47.
Russo, J. B., *Free Workers in a Plantation Economy: Talbot County, Maryland,
    1690–1759* (New England, 1989).
Sacks, David Harris, *The Widening Gate: Bristol and the Atlantic Economy,
    1450–1700* (Berkeley, Calif., 1991).
Samuel, Edgar, 'Manuel Levy Duarte (1631–1714): an Amsterdam merchant
    jeweller and his trade with London', *JHSET*, 27 (1982), 11–31.
Samuel, W., 'A review of the Jewish colonists in Barbados in the year 1680',
    JHSET, 13 (1932–5), 1–97.

Saunders, Ann, *The Royal Exchange* (London, 1991).

Scammell, G. V., *The First Imperial Age: European Overseas Expansion, c. 1400–1715* (London, 1989).

Schnurmann, Claudia, 'Atlantic trade and American identities: the correlations of supranational commerce, political opposition, and colonial regionalism', in Coclanis (ed.), *The Atlantic Economy in the Seventeenth and Eighteenth Centuries*, pp. 186–204.

Schwartz, Stuart B., *Sugar Plantations in the Formation of Brazilian Society, Bahia, 1550–1835* (Cambridge, 1985).

Schwartz, Stuart B. (ed.), *Tropical Babylons: Sugar and the Making of the Atlantic World, 1450–1680* (Chapel Hill, N.C., 2004).

Scott, William R., *The Constitution and Finance of English, Scottish and Irish Joint-Stock Companies to 1720*, 3 vols.(Cambridge, 1910–12).

Scranton, P. ' "Have a heart for the manufactuers": production, distribution and the decline of America textile manufacturing', in C. F. Sabel and J. Zeitlin (eds.), *World of Possibilities: Flexibility and Mass Production in Western Industrialization* (Cambridge, 1997), pp. 310–43.

Shammas, Carole, 'English commercial development and American colonization, 1560–1620', in Andrews *et al.* (eds.), *The Westward Enterprise*, pp. 151–74.

The Pre-Industrial Consumer in England and America (Oxford, 1990).

Sharp, W. Darrell, 'An economic consequence of 1688', *Albion*, 6 (1974), 26–55.

Sheridan, Richard B., *Sugar and Slavery: an Economic History of the British West Indies, 1623–1775* (Barbados, 1974).

Shilstone, E. M., *Monumental Inscriptions in the Jewish Synagogue at Bridgetown, Barbados* (Bridgetown, Barbados, 1988).

Shreiber, Harry (ed.), *United States Economic History: Selected Readings* (New York, 1964).

Smith, Abbot E, *Colonists in Bondage: White Servitude and Convict Labour in America, 1607–1776* (Chapel Hill, N.C., 1947).

Smith, S. D., 'Prices and the value of English exports in the eighteenth century: evidence from the North American colonial trade', *EcHR*, 48 (1995), 575–90.

'Accounting for taste: British coffee consumption in historical perspective', *JIH*, 27 (1996), 183–214.

'The market for manufactures in the thirteen continental colonies, 1698–1776', *EcHR*, 51 (1998), 676–708.

Smith, Woodruff D., 'From coffee house to parlour: the consumption of coffee, tea and sugar in north western Europe in the seventeenth and eighteenth centuries' in Goodman *et al.* (eds.), *Consuming Habits*, pp. 148–64.

Solow, Barbara L. and Engerman, Stanley L. (eds.), *British Capitalism and Caribbean Slavery: the Legacy of Eric Williams* (Cambridge, 1987).

Sosin, J. M., *English America and the Restoration Monarchy of Charles II: Transatlantic Politics, Commerce and Kinship* (Lincoln, Neb. 1980).

English America and the Revolution of 1688: Royal Administration and the Structure of Provincial Government (Lincoln, Nebr., 1982).

Spagnola, Giancarlo, 'Social relations and cooperation in organizations', *Journal of Economic Behaviour and Organization*, 38 (1999), 1–25.

Speck, W. A., 'The international and imperial context', in Jack P. Greene and J. R. Pole (eds.), *Colonial British America: Essays in the New History of the Early Modern Era* (Baltimore, Md., 1984), pp. 384–407.

'Some consequences of the Glorious Revolution', in Dale Hoak and Mordechai Feingold (eds.), *The World of William and Mary: Anglo-Dutch Perspectives on the Revolution* (Stanford, Calif., 1996), pp. 33–5.

Spence, Craig, *London in the 1690s: a Social Atlas* (London, 2000).

Sperling, J., 'The international payments mechanism in the seventeenth and eighteenth centuries', *EcHR*, 14 (1962).

Spufford, Margaret, *The Great Reclothing of Rural England: Petty Chapmen and their Wares in the Seventeenth Century* (London, 1984).

Starkey, Otis P., *The Economic Geography of Barbados* (New York, 1939),

Steckley, G. F., 'The wine trade of Tenerife in the seventeenth century', *EcHR*, 33 (1980), 335–50.

Steele, I. K., *Politics of Colonial Policy: the Board of Trade in Colonial Administration, 1696–1720* (Oxford, 1968).

'The empire and the provincial elites: an interpretation of some writings on the English Atlantic, 1675–1740', in Peter Marshall and Glyn Williams (eds.), *The British Atlantic Empire before the American Revolution* (London, 1980), pp. 2–32.

The English Atlantic, 1675–1740: an Exploration of Communication and Community (Oxford, 1986).

Steensgaard, Neils, 'The growth and composition of the long distance trade of England and the Dutch Republic in the early modern world', in Tracy (ed.), *The Rise of Merchant Empires*, pp. 102–52.

Stein, Robert Louis, *The French Sugar Business in the Eighteenth Century* (Baton Rouge, La., 1988), pp. 1–10.

Stewart, Larry, *The Rise of Public Science* (Cambridge, 1992).

Stols, Eddy, 'The expansion of the sugar market in western Europe', in Schwartz (ed.), *Tropical Babylons*, pp. 237–88.

Stone, Lawrence and Stone, Jeanne C. Fawtier, *Open Elite: England, 1540– 1880* (Oxford, 1984).

Szostak, Rick, *The Role of Transportation in the Industrial Revolution* (Montreal, 1991).

Thirsk, Joan, 'The fantastical folly of fashion: the English stocking knitting industry, 1500–1700', in N. B. Harte and K. G. Ponting (eds.), *Textile History and Economic History* (Manchester, 1973), pp. 30–73.

Economic Policy and Projects: the Development of a Consumer Society in Early Modern England (Oxford, 1978).

'New crops and their diffusion: tobacco growing in seventeenth century England', in Thirsk, *The Rural Economy of England* (London, 1984), pp. 259–85.

Alternative Agriculture: a History (Oxford, 1997).

Thirsk, J. and Cooper, J. P. (eds.), *Seventeenth Century Economic Documents* (Oxford, 1972).

Thomas, Robert P., 'A quantitative approach to the study of the effects of British imperial policy upon colonial welfare: some preliminary findings', *JEH*, 25 (1965), 615–38.

Thornton, A. P., *West India Policy under the Restoration* (Oxford, 1956).

Tolles, Frederick B., *Meeting House and Counting House: the Quaker Merchants of Colonial Philadelphia, 1682–1763* (Chapel Hill, N.C., 1948).

Tracy, James D. (ed.), *The Political Economy of Merchant Empires: State Power and World Trade, 1350–1750* (Cambridge, 1991).

Truxes, Thomas M., *Irish American Trade, 1660–1783* (Cambridge, 1988).

Tullock, G., 'The welfare costs of tariffs, monopolies, and theft', *Western Economic Journal* (1967), 224–32.

Schleifer, Andrei and Vishny, Robert W., 'Corruption', *Quarterly Journal of Economics*, 108 (1993), 599–617.

Unger, Richard W., *Dutch Shipbuilding before 1700* (Assen, 1978).
　'Energy sources for the Dutch Golden Age: peat wind and coal', *Research in Economic History*, 9 (1984), 221–53.
　'The tonnage of Europe's merchant fleets, 1300–1800', *The American Neptune*, 52 (1992), 247–61.

Vann, Richard T. and Eversley, David, *Friends in Life and Death: the British and Irish Quakers in the Demographic Transition, 1650–1900* (Cambridge, 1992).

Vickers, Daniel, *Farmers and Fishermen: Two Centuries of Work in Essex County, Mass., 1630–1850* (Chapel Hill, N.C., 1994).

Vries, Jan de, 'Between purchasing power and the world of goods: understanding the household economy in early modern Europe', in John Brewer and Roy Porter (eds.), *Consumption and the World of Goods* (London, 1993), pp. 177–94.
　'The industrial revolution and the industrious revolution', *JEH*, 54 (1994), 249–70.
　'Economic growth before and after the Industrial Revolution: a modest proposal', in Prak (ed.), *Early Modern Capitalism*, pp. 177–94.
　'The Dutch Atlantic economies', in Coclanis (ed.), *The Atlantic Economy during the Seventeenth and Eighteenth Centuries*, pp. 1–29.

Vries, Jan de and Woude, Ad van der, *The First Modern Economy: Success, Failure, and Perseverance of the Dutch Economy, 1500–1815* (Cambridge, 1997).

Wadsworth, A. P. and de la Mann, J., *The Cotton Trade and Industrial Lancashire, 1660–1780* (Manchester, 1931).

Walker, G. Gould, *The Honourable Artillery Company, 1537–1947*, 2nd edn (Aldershot, 1954).

Wallerstein, Immanuel, *The Modern World System*, 2 vols. (New York, 1974, 1980).

Walton, Gary M., 'Sources of productivity change in American colonial shipping' *EcHR*, 21 (1968), 268–82.
　'The new economic history and the burden of the Navigation Acts', *EcHR*, 24 (1971), 533–42.

Ward, J. R., 'The profitability of sugar planting in the British West Indies, 1650–1834', *EcHR*, 31 (1978), 197–213.

Wareing, John, 'The emigration of indentured servants from London, 1683–86', *Genealogical Magazine*, 19 (1978), 199–202.

Weatherill, Lorna, *The Pottery Trade, and North Staffordshire, 1660–1760* (Manchester, 1971).

  Consumer Behaviour and Material Culture in Britain, 1660–1760 (London, 1988).

Weber, Max, *The Protestant Ethic and the Spirit of Capitalism* (London, 1930).

Webster, C., *The Great Instauration: Science, Medicine, and Reform, 1626–60* (London, 1975).

Whitson, Agnes M., *The Constitutional Development of Jamaica, 1660–1729* (Manchester, 1929).

Whyman, Susan E., *Sociability and Power in Late-Stuart England: the Cultural Worlds of the Verneys, 1660–1720* (Oxford, 1999).

Willan, T. S., *River Navigation in England, 1600–1750* (London, 1936).

  The Inland Trade: Studies in English Trade in the Sixteenth and Seventeenth Centuries (Manchester, 1976).

Williams, Eric, *Capitalism and Slavery* (Chapel Hill, N.C., 1944).

Williams, Neville, 'The London port books', *Transactions of the London and Middlesex Archaeological Society*, 18 (1955), 13–26.

Wilson, Arthur M., 'The logwood trade in the seventeenth and eighteenth centuries', in Douglas McKay (ed.), *Essays in the History of Modern Europe* (New York, 1936), pp. 1–15.

Wilson, Charles, *Profit and Power* (London, 1957).

Woodhead, J. R., *The Rulers of London, 1660–85* (London, 1965).

Woolf, Maurice, 'Foreign trade of London Jews in the seventeenth century', *JHSET*, 24 (1974), 35–58.

Wrigley, E. A., 'A simple model of London's importance in changing English society and economy, 1650–1750', *Past and Present*, 37 (1967), 44–70.

  'Urban growth and agricultural change: England and the continent in the early modern period', *JIH*, 15 (1985), 683–728.

  'The divergence of England: the growth of the English economy in the seventeenth and eighteenth centuries', *TRHS* (2000), 117–41.

  'The transition to an advanced organic economy: half a millennium of English agriculture', *EcHR*, 59 (2006), 435–80.

Wrigley, E. A. and Schofield, R. S., *The Population History of England, 1541–1871: a Reconstruction* (Cambridge, 1981).

Yamey, B. S., Edey, H. C., and Thomson, H. W., *Accounting in England and Scotland: 1543–1800: Double Entry in Exposition and Practice* (London, 1963).

Zahedieh, Nuala, 'Trade, plunder, and economic development in early English Jamaica, 1655–89', *EcHR*, 39 (1986), 205–22.

  'The merchants of Port Royal, Jamaica and Spanish contraband trade, 1655–1692', *WMQ*, 43 (1986), 570–93.

  ' "A frugal, prudential and hopeful trade": privateering in Jamaica, 1655–89', *JICH*, 18 (1990), 145–68.

  'London and the colonial consumer in the late seventeenth century', *EcHR*, 47 (1994), 239–61.

  'The capture of the *Blue Dove*, 1664: policy, profits and protection in early English Jamaica', in R. McDonald (ed.), *West Indies Accounts: Essays on*

the History of the British Caribbean and the Atlantic Economy in Honour of
   Richard Sheridan (Kingston, Jamaica, 1996), pp. 29–47.
'Overseas expansion and trade in the seventeenth century', in Canny (ed.),
   The Oxford History of the British Empire, vol. I, pp. 398–422.
'Credit, risk and reputation in late seventeenth century colonial trade', in
   Olaf W. Janzen (ed.), Merchant Organization and Maritime Trade in the
   North Atlantic, 1660–1815 (Newfoundland, 1998), pp. 53–74.
'Making mercantilism work: London merchants and Atlantic trade in the
   late seventeenth century', TRHS (1999), 143–84.
'The wickedest city in the world: Port Royal, commercial hub of the
   seventeenth century Caribbean', in Verene Sheperd (ed.), Working Out
   Slavery, Pricing Freedom: Essays in Honour of Barry W. Higman (Kingston,
   Jamaica, and Oxford, 2002), pp. 3–20.
'Regulation, rent-seeking and the Glorious Revolution in the English
   Atlantic economy', EcHR (2009).
van Zanden, Jan Luiten, 'The development of agricultural productivity in
   Europe, 1500–1800', in B. J. P. van Bavel and E. Thoen (eds.), Land
   Productivity and Agro-Systems in the North Sea Area (Middle Ages–20th
   Century), CORN publication ser. 2 (Turnhout, 1999), pp. 357–75.
'Early modern economic growth: a survey of the European economy,
   1500–1800', in Prak (ed.), Early Modern Capitalism, pp. 69–87.
Zook, G. F., The Company of Royal Adventurers Trading into Africa (Lancaster,
   Penn., 1919).

UNPUBLISHED THESES

Andrews, K. R. 'The economic aspects of Elizabethan privateering', unpublished doctoral thesis, University of London (1951).
Jones, D. W., 'London overseas merchant groups at the end of the seventeenth century and the moves against the East India Company', unpublished doctoral thesis, University of Oxford (1970).
Matthew, I. R., 'The role of the Royal Navy in the English Atlantic empire,
   1660–1720', unpublished doctoral thesis, University of Oxford (1995).
Nash, Robert C., 'English transatlantic trade, 1660–1730: a quantitative
   study', unpublished doctoral thesis, University of Cambridge (1982).
Price, Jacob M., 'The tobacco trade and the treasury, 1685–1733: British
   mercantilism in its fiscal aspects', unpublished doctoral thesis, Harvard
   University (1954).
Wareing, John, 'The regulation and organisation of the trade in indentured
   servants for the American colonies in London, 1614–1718, and the career
   of William Haveland, emigration agent', unpublished doctoral thesis,
   University of London (2000).

Index